NORTH ATLANTIC TRIANGLE
THE INTERPLAY OF CANADA, THE UNITED STATES AND GREAT BRITAIN

THE RELATIONS OF
CANADA AND THE UNITED STATES

———

A SERIES OF STUDIES
PREPARED UNDER THE DIRECTION OF THE
CARNEGIE ENDOWMENT FOR INTERNATIONAL PEACE
DIVISION OF ECONOMICS AND HISTORY

James T. Shotwell, *Director*

NORTH ATLANTIC TRIANGLE

THE INTERPLAY OF CANADA, THE UNITED STATES AND GREAT BRITAIN

BY

JOHN BARTLET BREBNER

NEW HAVEN : YALE UNIVERSITY PRESS
TORONTO : THE RYERSON PRESS
LONDON:GEOFFREY CUMBERLEGE:OXFORD UNIVERSITY PRESS
FOR THE CARNEGIE ENDOWMENT FOR INTERNATIONAL
PEACE : DIVISION OF ECONOMICS AND HISTORY

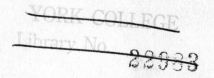

First published, August, 1945
Second printing, February, 1946
Third printing, February, 1947
Fourth printing, August, 1949

TO
ADELE

FOREWORD

THIS book appears at a time when the attention of all thoughtful people is centered upon the United Nations Conference at the Golden Gate. Its theme may seem to some as remote from the planning of a postwar world as the fog-wrapped passing of Drake along the San Francisco coast. But those who look behind the façade of events to their real meaning will find in this history of the relations of the three great branches of the English-speaking peoples, Great Britain, Canada, and the United States, an illuminating and a necessary guide in determining the realities of present and future. For it is a survey, by a master of the subject, of the greatest single chapter in the history of international intercourse anywhere in the world. It covers every phase of political and economic experiment from colonial life, through independent empire and commonwealth, through war and economic struggle, through compromise and peaceful settlement, in the whole changeful stretch of modern history. It weighs the forces of the past against those of the future and presents to the planners of world organization a description of the most successful of all international arrangements, one which is hardly an arrangement at all.

This very fact, however, that the Atlantic Triangle of the United States, Canada, and Great Britain is based upon the strongest of all forces for international peace—the will to have it—must not blind us to the equally solid fact that as late as the closing years of the nineteenth century the threat of war was by no means absent, and that even in the twentieth century there were ominous shadows of disagreement over Anglo-American and Canadian-American relations. We have, therefore, in this narrative, both phases of the international relations with which the general international organization of the United Nations will have to deal, the threatening clash of what are regarded as vital interests and the solution of difficulties by the conference method of diplomacy, backed by public opinion.

It seems proper under present circumstances to stress the pertinence of this history to the larger theme of world affairs which is now taking shape under the impact of the second World War. But Professor Brebner writes as a historian and not as a publicist. There is no stricter discipline than that which holds the historian to the search for truth, and this volume is from first to last informed with the spirit of scientific objectivity. Nothing is extenuated when plain speaking is called for, but the tolerance that springs from an understanding of motives as well as of evidence is never lacking. Thus we have the checkered history of the relations of the United States with the two British nations set forth in the light of contemporary events. The fact that this can now be done without offense or misunderstanding on either side of the Atlantic is both a measure of past successes and an assurance for the future.

It is a strange pattern for civilization which this history presents. One might have expected that in the logic of events the resort to pacific measures for the settlement of disputes by the three English-speaking nations would develop international bodies which could furnish a model to the world. It would have been logical to have erected between these countries something more comprehensive and more permanent than occasional arbitration on the basis of diplomatic agreement or legislative action for each problem as it arose. Yet, except for the International Joint Commission of the United States and Canada, there were more formal provisions for the pacific settlement of disputes between the nations of Europe than between the North Atlantic Triangle. History has now clearly shown that the legal restraints which the European statesmen agreed to in the vast network of treaties of arbitration and conciliation never reached the ultimate of realities. Policy was determined by forces to which they did not give adequate expression, by forces stronger and more readily accepted than the mechanism of peace. The history here set forth presents a complete contrast to the break-down of these provisions between the nations of continental Europe. In this case peace has been preserved as much, if not more, by the tempering solvent of like-mindedness and common sense than by legal precautions of an institutional nature.

In other words, the North Atlantic Triangle presents the supreme example of that which so bewilders the continental mind, Anglo-Saxon polity. No definition can be framed in logical terms which will wholly describe that subtle but unyielding sense of reality within it which dictates conduct according to fundamental rules of equity and fair play. The heritage of freedom is impatient of restraints, but it makes for peace when it recognizes the similar heritage of others. While these ideals have been departed from on many occasions, and bullying and force have by no means been absent from the history of those who share in the great tradition of democracy, nevertheless there has grown up in nations which share the heritage of freedom a sense that resort to violence is an indecent thing and unthinkable between neighbors, and that, while there is and can be no slackening in defense against aggression, the control of international affairs should be attuned to those ethical principles which each country works out in its own domestic affairs.

The real test of an institution is whether it works or not. Applying this test to the North Atlantic Triangle, we see that here is a field where international obligation and domestic policy have been welded toward a common purpose. Even the grievances persisting after unpopular decisions of international tribunals, of which the Canadian-American arbitrations furnish outstanding examples, have not been allowed to stand in the way of subsequent agreements. But if this process is to grow and strengthen so that resort to it will not only be likely but inevitable in the settlement of the problems of the future, it is necessary to understand its history; for no one can study the international settlements of the past without a realization of the narrow chance that lay between success and failure on more than one occasion. It is a sobering history, one which should challenge the interest of thoughtful citizens as well as of statesmen in both countries. Fortunately, it is also one of the few situations left in the world today where constructive international planning need not be misunderstood.

As Professor Brebner himself points out, this is the last of a series of volumes, published under the sponsorship of the Carnegie Endowment for International Peace, designed to cover the whole field of political, economic, and cultural relations between Canada and the United States, and those relations with Great Britain which bear upon this large area of North American history. Work upon this plan enlisted the interest and the generous support of the Carnegie Corporation, a support which made possible the completion and publication of some twenty-five volumes. A list of the series will be found at the end of this volume. Taken together, they fill the largest single gap which had been left almost untouched by the writers of North American history.

It is a source of great satisfaction to the Director of the Division of Economics and History of the Carnegie Endowment, under whose auspices this work began, that the final volume should be written by Professor Brebner, for the whole Series owes much to his mastery of the whole field, and to his scholarly criticism and editorial coöperation.

JAMES T. SHOTWELL

AUTHOR'S PREFACE

SINCE this book represents a novel, and probably only partially successful, experiment in historical writing, it might be useful to explain what I have tried to do.

My primary aim was to get at, and to set forth, the interplay between the United States and Canada—the Siamese Twins of North America who cannot separate and live. By interplay I do not mean merely the manifestations in what are usually called international relations, but the various kinds of things which the peoples of the two countries did in common, or in complementary fashion, or in competition. For an example of common activities, millions of these North Americans moved about, almost ignoring international boundaries for nearly two hundred years, while they settled the continent, harvested its forests and other resources, and mastered unique problems of transportation and agriculture. In complementary fashion, and in spite of economic nationalism, they built up the largest bilateral international exchange of money and commodities on earth. They competed for territory, transportation, raw materials, and markets. They coöperated in creating the unique North American standard and pattern of living. They invented and have operated for one hundred and fifty years an increasingly comprehensive and effective international machinery for the liquidation of some inescapable consequences of their interlocked destinies.

The great obstacle to a simple account of this interplay was that many of these activities could not be explained in merely North American terms. Most notably of all, the United States and Canada could not eliminate Great Britain from their courses of action, whether in the realm of ideas, like democracy, or of institutions, or of economic and political processes. And, since the United States attained nationhood by rebellion against Great Britain, and Canada by gradual growth within the British Empire, not only were their responses to the mother country usually sharply contrasted, but their understandings of each other were habitually warped. A further complication was added by the fact that the original settlers of Canada were French, who, although estranged from their own mother country by her course after 1760 and thrown back upon the Vatican for their principal outside reinforcement, could not be expected to develop an emotional attachment to their conquerors, whether thought of as Britons or as North Americans. In fact the minority position of the French Canadians made them resistant to both, with graver consequences in Canada than in the United States because they formed an almost monolithic bloc amounting to about 30 per cent of the Canadian population, whereas even their great expansion into New England did not substantially alter the patterns of life there, except insofar as they cast their votes in something like unison.

In dealing with all these matters, I have felt forced to give Canada more attention than her importance relative to the United States and Great Britain would ordinarily justify because I could not count upon any large amount of common knowledge concerning her. Americans and Britons know next to nothing about Canada because they have usually been able to take her for granted without serious consequences to themselves. Even Canadians, because harsh circumstances have made them self-obsessed, and sectionally so at that, have only begun to estimate what has happened to them locally in terms of what has happened to Canada as a whole during her uneasy course among the powerful currents of attraction and repulsion which have been set up by the United States and Great Britain.

This book is not a summary of the volumes of the Series in which it appears. During the past ten years its main outlines have been used as a partial framework, or blueprint, for that Series while an international band of scholars and men of affairs has been trying to fill gaps in our knowledge of the Canadian-American relationship. Now that the blueprint has been amplified into a book, perhaps it may serve as a general view of the subject until the remaining unexplored areas, as, for instance, education and law, have been surveyed. Since I have naturally had to depend more upon the research work of others than upon my own, it is unfortunate that for reasons of space it is not practicable to acknowledge in detail my obligations to scores of American, British, and Canadian scholars. Instead, I have added an appendix about the works to which I have been principally indebted and which themselves provide close guidance for those who may want to dig below my attempt at synthesis.

My greatest direct debt is to Professor James T. Shotwell. His mind seized upon the wider implications of a discussion of Canadian and North American history in its bearing upon the fundamental problems of international peace. With the resources of the Carnegie Endowment for International Peace and the Carnegie Corporation to aid him, he thereupon initiated investigations by American and Canadian scholars whose published results (and repercussions in North American thinking) have made it unjustifiable for any serious inquirer into Canadian-American relations to plead ignorance today.[1] In addition, his foresight in sponsoring four biennial conferences on Canadian-American affairs at the St. Lawrence University and Queen's University has meant that in both countries statesmen and men of affairs, as well as publicists and scholars, have entered the present world conflict with a living sense of an interplay which was far too little known a decade ago.[2]

While it has been a great privilege and a broad education to have been associated with these enterprises during the past twelve years, I am under particular obligations for assistance in completing this book. Four friends—Professors D. G. Creighton and H. A. Innis of the University of Toronto, Professor Allan Nevins of Columbia University, and Mr. A. E. McFarlane of the Carnegie Endowment for International Peace—have read its first version with close attention. Their criticisms, and particularly the differences among their criticisms, have been of the greatest value, both in guarding me against errors and in revealing where my achievement had fallen far short of my aims. Largely for reasons of space and proportion, it has not always been possible to include the additional matter, or to enter fully into the alternatives of interpretation, which they suggested, but they all urged that their observations be considered subject to the stringent demands of design and selection which this unconventional historical study involved. I should like also to draw attention to the cartographical skill of Mr. John Philip of the American Geographical Society with whom I have worked on the unusual maps demanded by the volumes in this Series, many of which now serve for a second time. The

1. The volumes of the Series are listed on p. 386, below.
2. The *Proceedings* of the Conferences of 1935, 1937, 1939, and 1941 have been published by Ginn and Company.

construction of an index for this book, largely because it must serve as a guide to forces working to and fro among three and sometimes more sources of energy, proved to be unusually difficult. Thanks to Dr. Shotwell, it was made, patiently and skilfully, by Miss Harriet J. Church.

I have inscribed this book to my wife, who forwarded a protracted and much-interrupted enterprise by her steady encouragement and shrewd commentary.

J. B. B.

Columbia University
    June, 1944

A second printing and the kindness of some skilful critics have permitted me to make a few brief amendments to the original edition. Suggestions as to larger revisions will be welcomed for consideration in case a new edition should prove justified.

J. B. B.

January, 1946

CONTENTS

The Canadian Shield and the American middle west (1); North
American topography (3); avenues to the interior (3); climatic
peculiarities (3); rainfall and vegetation (5); the Canadian-
American Area (6); its Eastern Region and its resources (7); the
Central Region (8); the Plains (10); the Pacific Region (11);
variation in the pace of development (12).

The aborigines and their regional cultures (14); the early migrants from Europe (15); from bullion to fish, fur, settlement,
and penetration of northern North America (16); Champlain vs.
Hudson (18); the Hudson–St. Lawrence competition (20); development of the Hudson Bay gateway to the interior (21); development of the Mississippi gateway (22); international rivalries
for the mid-continental Indian trade (24); competition and conflict between New France and the British colonies (24); the wars
for mastery in North America (27).

Victory and new problems of empire (30); some general North
American characteristics (31); diversities (32); the North American French in contrast with the British colonists (32); disunity
and sectionalism in the British colonies (35); the routes of migration and expansion (37); rivalries in fur trade and fisheries (38);
obstacles to imperial consolidation (39); fiscal policy and mercantilistic control (41); the centers of colonial defiance (41); the regions of acceptance (42); the currency problem (43); the problem
of the trans-Appalachian west (43); the anomalies presented by
French colonists (44); the demand for colonial autonomy (44);
the parliamentary upheaval in Great Britain (44).

Faction in the British Parliament (46); study and statesmanship
in the colonies (46); the Quebec Act (49); the New Englanders
of Nova Scotia (51); Newfoundland (51); cores and margins of
revolution (52); the War of American Independence (52); the

MAPS AND DIAGRAMS

NORTH ATLANTIC TRIANGLE

THE INTERPLAY OF CANADA, THE UNITED STATES AND GREAT BRITAIN

CHAPTER I

THE PATTERNS OF THE CONTINENT

CANADA'S first and greatest contribution to her partner and competitor in the exploitation of North America was the fertile soil of the northern and central United States. Four, possibly five, successive glaciations of northern North America scoured the ancient rock formation which underlies three-quarters of the continent, depositing soils and the constituents of future soils in sprawling aprons beyond their outer margins. When the ice retreated, it had bared the huge area of the Canadian Shield, which forms the northern and eastern two-thirds of Canada—a slight plateau of scarred rock with a few ranges of low mountains, but consisting for the most part of a rough fabric of lakes and rivers, marshes and muskeg, coniferous forest and thinly carpeted tundra.

Herein lay the principal reason why future North Americans would distribute themselves on the continent in the proportion of twelve Americans to one Canadian. Canada did not lose all the valuable glacial off-scourings, but her share was badly broken up into scattered parts—the fertile areas of southern Ontario, Quebec, and the Maritime Provinces; the cold and ill-drained flatlands along the western shores of James and Hudson bays; and a broad strip running between the Shield and the Rockies from North Dakota to the mouth of the Mackenzie River. In the interior of the United States, on the other hand, rich, finely disintegrated soils rewarded the migrant from the Atlantic Coast or Europe almost wherever he wandered, from the southern shores of the Great Lakes to the Gulf of Mexico. Today those who notice the block of inhospitable upland which emerges from the High Plains in Llano and Burnet counties, Texas, or one section of the ribbon-like patterns exposed by the Colorado River in the Grand Canyon, are viewing what the glaciers uncovered in much of Canada, but mantled with the good earth in a large part of the United States.

By and large, the harvests reaped from the central valley of the United States have been the greatest single factor in maintaining her growing population. The Canadian Shield, on the other hand, encouraged activities like the fur trade, lumbering, mining, paper-making, and the production of hydroelectric power, none of which fostered large, adjoining settlements. They did give Canada economic foundations for independent existence, but the Shield itself also constituted a mighty barrier to Canadian development. It deflected expanding population into the United States, it divided east from west, and its limited productivity challenged the road and railroad builders of Canada as Americans never were challenged. The Shield *is* Canada from Hudson Strait to the upper St. Lawrence; its southern margin hugs the Ottawa Valley and the northern shores of Lake Huron and Lake Superior, and then marches northwest toward the mouth of the Mackenzie. As if to underline by a geological whim its fateful role in North America, the lip of it which enters the United States to form northern Minnesota contains rich, easily worked, and cheaply accessible deposits of iron such as have never been equaled in Canada.

Shield and Middle West, while especially emphatic in determining the activities and the distribution of Americans and Canadians, were only two of many factors. Men have traveled over and claimed huge expanses of North America, in the fur trade, for example, scores of years before other men were able or thought fit to settle them. Some human activities, like agriculture and factory industry, have produced thickly settled regions and supported many urban communities, while others, like fishing and forest operations and mining, have barely peppered great regions with meager, often precarious, villages. In the days before steam, population was largely distributed and the exchange of goods determined by the possibilities for water transportation, both on the oceans and on inland lakes and rivers. Wild animals and Indians discovered and beat paths through the passes in the hills and mountains which white men later broadened into roads and then paralleled by railroads, generations before the airplane was able to ignore them. While it is true that mere sustenance was enough to attract some persons to North America and establish them there, yet the growth of population at a rate far beyond natural increase was based upon great natural resources which the rest of the world wanted and for whose exploitation it would provide both men and money. The economic rivalries among North Americans who today base their operations on Hudson Bay, the St. Lawrence River, the Hudson River, and the Mississippi River, or in the North Atlantic fisheries, or along the Pacific Coast, can be traced back to the earliest ambitions of Europeans in those regions. Furthermore, North American climate is so extraordinary in its pattern over the continent that it has played a dominant part in determining where people live and how they carry on their lives from Florida to Alaska and from Labrador to California.

North America is like a V-shaped trough, tapering to the south. During the writhings of the earth's skin, pressure inward from the beds of the Atlantic and the Pacific buckled and folded the margins of the continent but left the huge interior an almost level plain. On the Atlantic side the Appalachian ridges run from Alabama to Newfoundland, seldom very high or violent in contour, and only in the section immediately south of the Gulf of St. Lawrence as much as four hundred miles across. Their slopes toward the interior and the coast are gradual, and a subterranean apron or shelf stretches far out to sea. On the Pacific side the continental Cordillera is a much more forbidding affair. From one end of the Americas to the other it rises abruptly to great heights from the ocean and from the interior plains. Never much less than five hundred miles across, it comes close to being a thousand in the latitudes of California and the Yukon. Its several parallel ranges are tortured and jagged, marked by abundant signs of recent volcanic action, and topped by snow fields and glaciers.

There are only four inviting avenues to the interior of North America —two Canadian and two American. Hudson Strait and Hudson Bay carry the ocean navigator to the center of a basin whose rivers, like spokes of a wheel, drain about a quarter of the continent. The St. Lawrence subsidence and the Great Lakes Basin which it drains stretch from the Atlantic to the geographical center of the land. The Hudson River, a fiord like the St. Lawrence, reaches the low Mohawk gap westward through the Appalachians to the Great Lakes Basin. The Mississippi and its long tributaries drain the southern central plain, an area somewhat larger than the Hudson Bay Basin in the north. The great contrast between the Canadian and the American entries is that ice locks Hudson Bay for all save four months or so of the year and keeps ocean vessels out of the St. Lawrence for about five months, whereas New York and New Orleans are year-round ports from which travel inland is only slightly interrupted by the seasons.

Yet this winter contrast distorts the international picture, for broad belts of roughly equal temperature levels go to and fro all along the Canadian-American boundary. Altitude explains some of these vagaries, but more important are the movements of the upper air in response to the collisions of northern and southern weather-breeding, to the rotation of the earth, and to the influence of the oceans. North America lies between the warm Pacific with its contracted outlet through Bering Strait and the cold North Atlantic with the icecap of Greenland to keep it chilled. Warm moisture-laden winds blowing east from the Pacific rapidly dry out against the mountain wall, but carry some of their heat to the western

A Rocky Mountain Barrier
B Ozark Mountain Barrier
C Appalachian Mountain Barrier
D Hudson Bay Basin
E Mississippi River Basin
F Great Lakes Basin

Relief Map of the United States and Canada

KEY TO NUMBERS

1. Lake of the Woods
2. Rainy River
3. Pigeon River
4. Georgian Bay
5. Trent River
6. St. John River
7. St. Croix River
8. Kennebec River
9. Chaudière River
10. Richelieu River
11. Lake Champlain
12. Connecticut River
13. Mohawk River

14. Erie Canal
15. Hudson River
16. Delaware River
17. Susquehanna River
18. Potomac River
19. Genesee River
20. Allegheny River
21. Monongahela River
22. Cuyahoga River
23. Muskingum River
24. Sandusky River
25. Scioto River
26. Detroit River

27. Lake St. Clair
28. St. Clair River
29. Miami River
30. Maumee River
31. Kalamazoo River
32. Green Bay
33. Fox River
34. St. Marys River
35. Wisconsin River
36. Wabash River
37. Passamaquoddy Bay
38. Bay of Fundy

margin of the central plain. In winter they circle the northwestern quarter of the continent, in summer the southwestern. Icy winds from the Arctic Archipelago of Canada sweep south and east across the continent in winter, but in summer the Gulf of Mexico evens the balance by winds which fan out over the interior almost to Hudson Bay and join a prevailing trend toward Greenland and Iceland. These eastern winds lose their moisture quite gradually. The total effect is that the zones of equal temperatures for the northern half of the United States and Canada assume roughly semicircular form down from the northeast and the northwest in winter, and in summer run a little north of west from the Atlantic across the continent until they swing much farther north to follow the Mackenzie Valley and the eastern face of the Rockies to Alaska and the Arctic. The mid-continent is colder in winter and hotter in summer than the margins, and the northwest is warmer than the northeast.

Another factor which makes the climatic environment almost identical for a majority of both peoples is that most Canadians live well to the south of the forty-ninth parallel, whose arresting international line across the map from the Lake of the Woods to the Pacific takes the eye away from the fact that the Maritime Provinces and nearly all the solid settlements of Quebec and Ontario lie below it. Continue the forty-ninth parallel east from the Lake of the Woods and notice that it skirts the north shore of Lake Superior and the mouth of the St. Lawrence, while south of it the international boundary, following the river and the lower Great Lakes, drives a wedge down to the forty-second parallel, that is, almost to the center of population of the United States. Average annual temperatures do not vary much, whether you live in Halifax (Nova Scotia), Boston (Massachusetts), Toronto (Ontario), Detroit (Michigan), Des Moines (Iowa), or Victoria (British Columbia).

Add rainfall to the other ruling elements and the continent breaks up into patterns of vegetation which conform only partially to the international division. The cold, wet tundra, or barrens, of the Canadian north and northeast, with its dwarfed plants and mosses and lichens, counterbalances the hot, dry deserts of the American west and southwest. The so-called northern forest of conifers, a belt which circles the Canadian northeast from Labrador to the mouth of the Mackenzie and clothes the eastern face of the northern Cordillera, is exclusively Canadian except where it sticks out a finger into Idaho and western Montana. The mixed forests and meadows which reach from the mouth of the St. Lawrence to New York on the Atlantic Coast, narrowing as they swing northwest to Lake Winnipeg and thence down the left bank of the Mackenzie, vary in their proportion of arable soils according to the presence of the Appalachian Highlands and the Canadian Shield. The great spring wheat area is about evenly divided between the two countries in the plains west of the Mississippi and Lake Winnipeg, but is more unevenly shared in the high inner plateaus of the Rockies in British Columbia and Washington. The wet, mild forest area, along the ocean side of the Cordillera, with its mammoth trees, rich meadows, and pastures, extends from California to Alaska without much variation. In the final balance, however, Canada's deficiencies, compared to the plant productivity of the United States, stand out in her lack of equivalents for the market-gardening strip along the Atlantic tidewater area from Cape Cod to Georgia; the almost tropical regions of humid Florida and the irrigated southwest; and the succession of Corn Belt, Winter Wheat Belt, and Cotton Belt which stretches across the Mississippi Valley (and the southern Atlantic piedmont) between Iowa and the Gulf of Mexico.

In our own day of extensive industrialization and rapid transportation, the whole of the United States and Canada is integrated to a remarkably high degree, but this is a comparatively recent development. Vigorous interaction among the European migrants to northern North America began in the sixteenth century along the Atlantic Coast between Newfoundland and Chesapeake Bay. Gradually the Hudson Bay Basin, the Great Lakes Basin, and the Mississippi Valley were added, and lastly the far west and the Pacific Coast. The final outcome was that the region of continuous Canadian-American interplay amounted roughly to a zone across North America between the thirty-eighth and fifty-second parallels, with a variety of activities reaching farther north into Canada and Alaska and farther south into the United States. The story of how this solid Canadian-American Area, peopled as it came to be by men and women of precisely the same stocks, closely intermingled by marriage and migration, happened to produce two self-conscious nations instead of one is long and complicated. It must be sufficient here to suggest that at least three forces were effective in separating the two peoples during the opening-up of North America—the natural dividing line of the St. Lawrence and Great Lakes with the Canadian Shield to the north of them, the slight but perceptible height of land between the Missouri Valley and the valleys of the Assiniboine and the Saskatchewan, and men's inclinations to find comfort in the fact that they and their regional groups are not as other men are.

Yet as the Atlantic migrants and their North American descendants made their way westward across the Canadian-American Area, they could not help but be deeply affected by natural divisions of the continent which ran more nearly north and south than east and west. Today

there are perhaps a score of distinct regions straddling the long international boundary, where local influences have pushed men and their
apparatus of living to and fro for generations. Some of them are as
small and half forgotten as the St. Croix Valley between Maine and New
Brunswick, others are as large and urgent as the industrialized communities on both sides of the Niagara and Detroit rivers or of the boundary
between British Columbia and Washington. These local dramas took
form successively during the development of the Canadian-American
relationship, but some of the great forces underlying them can be detected by examining the four principal subdivisions of the Canadian-
American Area.

To begin where the Europeans began, there is the Eastern Region.
From Alabama to Newfoundland, approximately the same Appalachian
heights separate the central plain from the Atlantic, but because the
direction of the formation is northeastward, the men of New England,
the Maritime Provinces, and Newfoundland are farther removed from
the inviting interior than the men of the Middle States. This Eastern
Region shared prominently in the westward exploitation of the continent,
but it was also subject to influences which nourished persistent local activity and which kept a good many of its inhabitants looking outward to
the north and east and south.

Chief of these is the Continental Shelf, which, from New Jersey northward, creates vast ocean shallows or banks which are actually broader
in extent than the good lands between the Appalachians and the shore.
These shallows, from the revealingly named Cape Cod to the Grand Banks
east of Newfoundland and round both sides of that huge island to the
Labrador coast, are probably the greatest nursery for edible fish in the
world. In particular, a happy combination of warm and cold currents,
of varying depths, and of abundant food supply has made the waters
around Nova Scotia, in the southern Gulf of St. Lawrence, and off the
Atlantic shores of Newfoundland and Labrador an ever-filled reservoir
of food for the Americas and southern Europe.

When the North American of the Eastern Region sought the inland
boundaries of his empire, he found them in the mountain uplands, whether
he turned inward from the St. Lawrence or from the Atlantic Coast. The
long valleys of the Hudson and the Richelieu, carrying the Great Valley
of the Appalachians to its final corridor in the St. Lawrence, formed a
natural western line, but, particularly when combined with the westering
valley of the Mohawk, the Hudson also gave him his best entry to the
interior. By the Hudson-Mohawk approach he could reach the Great
Lakes and the Ohio more easily and cheaply than from Delaware or

Chesapeake Bay, and the advantages of this route over working up the natural outlet of the Great Lakes were great because it was much shorter, ice blocked the St. Lawrence entry from December to May, and long stretches of impassable rapids made the transit from Montreal to Lake Ontario very difficult.

There was plenty to engage the attention of the Easterner at home, however. The Appalachians and the Canadian Shield nourished immense forests of white pine, other evergreens which were almost as desirable, and useful hardwoods in great variety. Everywhere there were long rivers whose spring freshets would float the soft woods to the settled regions and the ocean ports. White pine was the prize, for mankind has found no other wood to equal its combination of beauty, strength, workability, and broad usefulness. The eastern forests proffered expanses, which only Scandinavia and Russia could rival, of the towering, straight trees that were taller than any mast mariners had ever envisaged and from which clean, knotless timbers could be hewn or planks be sawn of the largest dimensions which men could handle. The supplies seemed inexhaustible until the local and world markets of the nineteenth century cleaned out the accumulation of past years and forced the lumberman to calculate his production by rate of natural growth.

Northeastward from Chesapeake Bay the coastal plain, the valley lands, the fertile dyked marshes of Nova Scotia, and the lower slopes of the uplands invited an agriculture which was insufficient for self-support in some localities, but which in its total produced surpluses for regional distribution or for export. In addition, the very rocks of the Eastern Region rewarded its occupiers. Other parts of North America subsequently eclipsed its deposits of gold, silver, copper, lead, and so on, but it possessed the sure warranty of success in an industrial civilization in the coal, iron, gypsum, building-stone, and clays which were distributed from Pennsylvania to Newfoundland. Here again, however, geology seemed to handicap the Canada-to-be, for its coal and iron were "down east" at the outer limit of the continent, whereas Pennsylvania's riches were in a "Middle" State.

The second great Region, which might deserve the name of Central, included the basin of the upper St. Lawrence and the Great Lakes and the upper central valley of the United States, for the height of land between them was almost negligible. It was approximately half Canadian Shield and half the gently rolling areas of rich soils which had been smoothly deposited on the shores or at the bottoms of the ancient inland seas. But since the upper St. Lawrence and Ottawa valleys and the north shores of Lakes Huron and Superior formed the dividing line between the two areas, the westering North American seekers for farm lands were rewarded on both sides of Lake Ontario, and, after being deflected to the north of Lake Erie by the rough Appalachian plateau of Pennsylvania and the swamps of northern Ohio, were in turn deflected southward round Lakes Huron and Michigan because the Shield blocked the way west by the north of the Lakes. That is why what is now southern Ontario was full of "Americans" between 1783 and 1850, why the northern Middle West was full of "Canadians" between 1840 and 1900, and why the Canadian plains attracted hundreds of thousands of "Americans" after 1895.

The firstcomers to the Central Region had been fur traders, whose thinly held, but hotly contested arena it was for about two hundred years. Just before the opening of the nineteenth century, its natural conquerors, the farmers, poured into it in an irresistible, tumbling flood. They made much of it Agriculture's own forever, but they were preceded or accompanied by a smaller, but no less avid, horde who were drunk with the vision of the mightiest pine forests that North Americans had yet seen. Across northern and western New York, northern Pennsylvania and Ohio, Michigan, southern Ontario, the Ottawa Valley, and the upper St. Lawrence stretched ranks of huge trees, with abundant waterways for their carriage, and no man knew how much farther westward they extended around Lake Superior and northward within the Canadian Shield. In a little over a century the reasonably accessible forests of the Central Region were swept so clean that a North American lumber yard today either does not attempt to pay the high price of that nineteenth-century staple, "Number One Northern Pine," or stacks a little in a dry shelter for the few buyers who must have it and can pay for the privilege. The firstcomers had wastefully floated out the trees as square timber, the really devastating horde had sawn them into boards, and today the paper companies grind up meager tree trunks, which their predecessors would have scorned, in order to make cardboard to replace the wooden containers used by earlier generations.

In our own time the Central Region has provided more generously than during the earlier years of its occupation other rewards for human enterprise. Its waters, which used to float vessels and timber rafts, and run mills, have been harnessed to make electricity, which has both created new industrial regions, as around Niagara, and has been carried, little diminished, across hundreds of miles to older centers. In the second place, immense deposits of anthracite and bituminous coal situated close to the Great Lakes waterway which led to the very margins of the Lake Superior iron mines, forcibly drew the industrial center of North America westward from the Atlantic. Again, the world of petroleum products, which began in western Pennsylvania, was first nurtured by the draining of the reservoirs which lay beneath southern Ontario and the States south of the Great Lakes. Moreover, the much-abused Canadian Shield has revealed and been forced to yield up a quite unexpected wealth of minerals. Lake Superior copper, silver, and iron, which were the first rewards, gave a promise which was far more than fulfilled when the railroad builders uncovered in northern Ontario deposits of nickel, cobalt, silver, platinum, and copper which metallurgists learned to master and to which huge areas of gold-bearing rock have since been added.

The third Canadian-American Region, consisting of the Great Plains and the High Plains, which extends from southern Texas to the arctic shores of Alaska, except for one broad interruption in the Yukon, enjoys the distinction of having required a new set of tools and techniques—indeed, a new culture pattern—for its conquest. Elsewhere men had found the transition from European to North American ways of living to be a gradual, fairly obvious adaptation. Furs and fish were more abundant, but were acquired in much the old ways. There were new farm products, like maize, tobacco, or pumpkins, but agriculture did not alter much. A new food, like the hominy (coarsely ground maize) which almost alone made possible the journeys by canoe or horse to and from the mid-continent, could be quickly taken into everyday use. The canoe or the dugout pirogue was not unlike the European boat, indeed it was being supplanted by a number of compromises between American and European craftsmanship before the nineteenth century began. But the Great Plains formed the Great American Desert until North Americans had painfully learned the secrets of its mastery.

The dry steppes of the Plains presented immeasurable acres of grass and herds of bison to the white man, they soon sheltered wild or half-tamed bands of the horses which he had introduced, and the combination of grass, bison, and mounted Indians forced him to pause or perish. Gradually, however, and in spite of many fatalities, the conquest was made. New clothing was necessary, new horse management had to be learned, water supply became the very basis of life and movement, the bison were exterminated, and cattle and sheep took their place. Timber had to be sought in the rare river bottoms or brought either from the east or from the mountains to the west. The repeating rifle and the revolver were invented to reënforce the white man's advantage over the Indian. Justice reverted to the Old Testament patterns laid down by the herdsmen of Syria, Palestine, and Arabia. Barbed wire was devised when the cowboy with lasso and branding iron proved unable to prevent costly clashes among the cattlemen and between them and settlers. For finally even the cultivator succeeded in entering the region, when in the south he taught himself dry-farming, and in the north he gradually bred wheat which would ripen during the short summers, even under the margin of the Arctic Circle. Windmills pumped water from deep wells, and steel ploughs "busted" the tough sod. In arid regions where there happened to be mountain-fed streams, some of the farmers of the Great Plains developed the difficult techniques of irrigation.

The invaders from the east did not think of the Plains as providing minerals except where intrusions from the Canadian Shield yielded lead, silver, or graphite, or where that odd eastern outcropping of the Rockies, the Black Hills, furnished gold. Only in relatively recent years did the seekers for petroleum find that it and its companions—coal, asphalt, and natural gas—lay below or beside the Great Plains at intervals from Texas to the valley of the Mackenzie.

The white man reached the Pacific Coast by sea before he was able to discover and make regular use of routes across the mid-continent. Long before Alexander Mackenzie made the first of such transcontinental journeys, in 1793, Spain had investigated the Coast to a point beyond the fortieth parallel and the Russians had reached across from Asia and explored the Alaskan coast and islands. Also before Mackenzie, Captain Cook had done a thorough job of mapping the north Pacific, leaving only the details to later men.

The exploitation and occupation of the Pacific Region have always been thoroughly international affairs and promise to continue to be so. The Russians and Cook's men revealed a treasure house, not only of such staple furs as beaver, but of the more valuable sea otter and Alaska seal. For a century and a half the ransacking of this wealth occupied Russian, British, American, and Canadian adventurers until the extinction of the animals was barely averted and the human controversies were liquidated in a multilateral international convention.

Even more spectacular was the mineral exploitation, which began in Central America during the active career of Columbus, leaped to Mexico with Cortes, and had spread into New Mexico and Arizona by the middle of the eighteenth century. A lull followed until 1848, when placer gold in California provided a magnet to draw adventurers from all over the world to the most intense, sustained, and successful quest for minerals in history. The Cordillera seemed to contain almost every ore desired by man. The placer miners raced north through British Columbia and the Yukon to Alaska in fifty years, skimming the cream which a man with small capital could collect. After them came the mining industries extracting from the rocks themselves gold, silver, mercury, copper, lead, zinc, and coal. Oil rewarded its seekers, first in the lowlands, then even beneath the sea, and, finally, at the bottom of holes drilled thousands of feet into mountain slopes and plateaus. Today, a flier traveling above the Cordillera from Panama to the Arctic could seldom look down on it without seeing some outward evidence of man's assault on its mineral hoards.

The salmon, a mass-migrant between ocean depths and the coastal rivers, does much to compensate the Pacific Region for its narrower Continental Shelf and relatively smaller supply of sea fish than are enjoyed by the Eastern Region. Most of the culture of the Pacific Coast Indians was built around this fish, which entered the rivers in silver floods which almost filled them. The white man improved upon the opportunity, first by using the smoked fish as a food supply for journeys into the interior, and finally by preserving it in cans for the markets of the world. The lowly Londoner who today can have salmon on his table as well as the nobleman who is enjoying one of the few British survivors of this "royal" fish is thereby supporting an industry which has been born and developed in the Pacific Region as a whole, with little regard to international boundaries.

When the same Londoner's eye is caught by apples rosier and more perfect in contour than any Britain boasts, he is likely to have been tempted by another product of this Canadian-American Region, and it would be impossible for him to tell by the apples themselves whether they came from the agriculture of Oregon or of Washington or of British Columbia. Similarly, should he build a new house or inspect one of his country's new housing developments, it would be a toss-up whether the wooden timbers and boards which he saw came from the Canadian or the American forests. In them the most gigantic trees of North America are being felled to furnish a substitute for the eastern North American softwoods which an earlier generation was fortunate enough to command.

History usually forces the geographic or economic determinist to qualify his bold outlines. This has been notably true of the history of the white man in North America, and yet some natural forces have persisted in determining the regions of settlement, the lines of communication and transport, the kinds of economic enterprise, and the political divisions or subdivisions. It has seemed imperative, therefore, to survey the Canadian-American stage and to sketch its setting and stage machinery before attempting to explain the actions of the North Americans who played their pre-determined, chance-determined, and self-determined parts upon it. The stage once set, however, it must be remembered that the action does not unfold at a conveniently uniform pace. In the early

days, before steam, electricity, and internal combustion engines contracted measures of continental distances from months to hours, Time
helped to make trains of events more understandable to the observer. In
later days the action becomes confused, for the accelerating *rate* of
change is more important than any static calendar scale, until finally
techniques vault from Colorado to the Arctic or from British Columbia
to northern Quebec at the speed of a multimotored plane.

CHAPTER II

THE PEOPLES AND THEIR RIVALRIES
(1492–1763)

THE first North Americans came from Asia, crossing the steppingstones of the narrow gap at the northern end of the Pacific in repeated waves during tens of thousands of years. Whatever they may have been like in Asia, North America gradually molded them to its varied environments. Along the northern coasts, on the islands of the Arctic Archipelago, and for varying distances into the tundra, the Eskimos built their lives and ways around fish and sea mammals, the herds of caribou, the skin boat, and the latticed sled. Along the Pacific Coast, the Indians split the straight cedars for the timbers and boards of enormous houses which they built beside the salmon rivers, and burned or hewed out huge logs to make the seagoing canoes in which they sought other food during the off-seasons of the salmon. In the forest and park areas of the north and northeast, the Indians were nomadic hunters and fishermen, moving in bark canoes or on snowshoes over ranges of country which they had made their own and whose resources of game and fish were the fundamental facts of their lives. As the forest gave way to meadows, the cultivation of maize, beans, sunflowers, squash, and tobacco diminished the importance of the hunt and encouraged the building of semipermanent villages and the development of handicrafts like weaving and pottery-making. As the meadows changed to the plains, life centered more and more in the buffalo (bison), whose meat, wool, skin, and dried dung provided food, shelter, and heat for the tribes who followed the wandering herds across the grasslands or built their villages of domed sod houses near river crossings or other places to which the buffalo resorted. In the arid southwest the Indians chose irrigable river bottoms among the mountains for their plantings, but protected their large town settlements by building them in the faces of soft rock cliffs, on the tops of defensible tablelands, or in compact agglomerations of multistoried adobe buildings whose high, windowless, outer walls turned a fortress front to marauders.

In Mexico, Central America, and Peru, the first North Americans reared civilizations which challenged comparison with whatever mankind had achieved elsewhere on the earth. They knew neither iron nor the use of the wheel, yet drawing upon the abundant and variegated productivity of these regions, they created great empires whose buildings, arts, learning, and political and economic arrangements remain in many senses admirable today. They cherished and accumulated gold and silver and pearls and jewels, and their upper classes enjoyed amenities of life which excited the envy of outsiders, whether of the original North American stock or of the newcomers who made their ways from Europe and Africa across the Atlantic.

The westward migration to the Americas was a much more difficult affair than the eastward had been and came much later in human history. Not only was the North Atlantic broad and open toward the icebound Arctic, but the prevailing winds and currents blew adversely from north and west to east. The first Europeans to reach North America were Scandinavian sea rovers who had learned how to hunt along the margins of the ice pack and how to maintain themselves in regions where the summers were as short as in the Faeroes and Iceland. Yet even they proved unable to hold on when they pushed still farther westward from warmer seas to colder at the end of the tenth century. Their grip on Greenland was broken after two centuries of effort and nowhere on the North American mainland do they seem to have maintained their settlements for more than a few years. They failed to find and to exploit the resources which would have made their colonies strong in themselves and profitable enough to sustain ties of interest with the European homeland. It took six hundred years for Europeans to learn how to make northern North America support them.

Effective European migration and settlement awaited the more assured mastery of ocean navigation which was built up when the Italians ventured through the Straits of Gibraltar carrying eastern and southern goods to exchange for northern, and when Italian navigators blended their skills with those of the Portuguese who were bringing the Atlantic islands and the west coast of Africa under their economic sway. By the second half of the fifteenth century, the time was ripe for Europeans to plan how they might eliminate middlemen's charges and the high expenses of land carriage from the costs of eastern goods by sailing their own ships to the Indies, China, and Japan, either round Africa or westward across the broad ocean which might now be a highway instead of a barrier to their designs. They did not know that the Norsemen had found that North America lay between them and the Far East.

It was Spain's good luck that when Christopher Columbus sailed west in 1492 on the latitude of Japan, he found then or later, in the West Indies and on the coasts of South and Central America, far greater riches than his Norse predecessors had discovered in the north. His four voyages led progressively to the pearls and gold and the imposing civilizations of the mainland. Those who followed him looted Mexico, Central America, and Peru of their accumulated hoards of bullion and then set the first North Americans to work extracting more. Christopher Marlowe spoke for many non-Spaniards when he coveted "from America the golden fleece that yearly stuffs old Philip's treasury."

England seemed to have run into the blind alley which had defeated the Scandinavians when John Cabot ("another Genoese like Columbus") found Newfoundland and Nova Scotia in her behalf in 1497. This discovery was built upon the Anglo-Portuguese dealings which had for many years profitably bound together Lisbon, the Azores, Bristol, and Iceland, and it was followed by over a hundred years of English, Portuguese, and French efforts to break through or round the barrier to Asia which northern North America represented. Spain could be, and was, scornful of these enterprises, except when they threatened to encroach upon her own preserves near the Caribbean. "What need have we of what is found everywhere in Europe?" wrote Peter Martyr. "It is towards the south, not towards the frozen north, that those who seek fortune should bend their way; for everything at the equator is rich."

Yet, by a high irony, the monopoly of good fortune in the Americas which Spain guarded so jealously worked out in such a way as not only to enrich other European countries more enduringly than Spain, but also to enable them to found colonies whose varied productivity rapidly eclipsed the output of precious metals from Spanish America. To begin with, Spain, having expelled her Jewish and Moorish craftsmen, had more money to spend than goods to buy, so that much of the American bullion merely paused for a while in the Iberian Peninsula on its way into the hands of more industrious peoples elsewhere in Europe. In the second place, the immense influx of American gold and silver into the European economy produced a prolonged and unprecedentedly rapid rise in prices; that is, it created a marvelous opportunity for enrichment to men who were learning the fascinating operations of commercial capitalism. Spaniards disdained trade and remained relatively loyal to the medieval Catholic prohibition of usury, but ambitious businessmen of France, the Low Countries, and England were less orthodox, indeed many of them joyfully embraced the new Protestant ethic laid down by Jean Calvin, which approved of capitalist accumulation through the operation of interest. All in all, the economy of the Iberian Peninsula got so out of line from that of the rest of western Europe that Spain and her conquest, Portugal, began to succumb to the degeneration which comes when a mere purse pits itself against productive energies.

One of the commodities which Spain and the rest of Catholic Europe needed was fish, and fish in unparalleled abundance was about the only useful product which John Cabot and his successors had discovered along the northern reaches of the Americas. For a while, Portuguese and Spaniards formed a part of the extraordinary annual fishing assembly off Newfoundland and the North Atlantic shores, but gradually the incentive died out in them and it was English and French fishermen who made fortunes from that bold enterprise during the sixteenth century. There had been a brief flurry of excitement between 1534 and 1543 when Jacques Cartier of St. Malo and Francis I of France had persuaded themselves that a passage to China or empires like Mexico and Peru were to be found up the St. Lawrence, but reality had pricked those bubbles. For a hundred years after Cabot, therefore, most men thought that Spain had preëmpted the only valuable parts of the Americas. French and English fishermen knew otherwise, but few of them realized that by crossing the Atlantic every year they were building up an enterprise secondary to the fisheries which would not only yield added profits but would also lead to settlement of the despised north.

This was the fur trade which slowly developed as Frenchmen and Englishmen found it advantageous to establish temporary shore stations at which they might dry fish for the European market during the summer months. Prolonged contacts with the first North Americans were the natural consequence. These Indians were suddenly confronted by men whose casual possessions—woolen goods, nails, knives, axes, iron or copper kettles, and alcoholic liquors—could eliminate at a stroke much of the endless travail of Indian life.

But these boons could not be had for nothing. The eager Indians discovered that in furs they had a staple for which the sailors would always barter; but this very success sold the natives into a permanent servitude, for what were originally merely their desires imperceptibly became needs. They first despised and then forgot their old skills in making their living. Moreover, they committed themselves to levies on the fur-bearing animals which natural increase could not support, and the axes which they earned gave them such an advantage over the beaver in their easily locatable lodges that in region after region they exterminated the animal whose fur was most in demand. During the last quarter of the sixteenth century, therefore, the fur trade gave birth to settlement in, and penetration of, the northern half of the continent, because fur traders yearned for unexploited regions and unsophisticated Indians, and settlement was the only means by which local trade monopoly could be established.

It would be a mistake to claim that the fur trade was alone responsible for the successful and practically simultaneous efforts of the French, the English, the Dutch, and the Swedes to found colonies in northern North America at the beginning of the seventeenth century, but it is obvious that the combination of fisheries and fur trade prevented a general repetition of the disastrous failures which had attended similar efforts during the sixteenth century. From Virginia to Acadia the story was the same. "Fish and Furres was then our refuge," wrote Captain John Smith in 1614, and his testimony as to the critical first years could be corroborated for any of the successful settlements. In some of them, fish and fur continued to be the principal supports for continued existence; in others, they provided life insurance while old incentives, like the search for the Pacific or for the wealth of the mines, or while new ones, like the relief of European unemployment by the exploitation of American forests and fields, could be experimented with. Nowhere, from the Caribbean northward, did the fur and Indian trades disappear, but as time went on their relative importance varied in inverse proportion to the breadth of the fertile slope between the Appalachians and the Atlantic. Climate also played its part, for northern furs were better than southern.

The distribution of the various Europeans along the Atlantic Coast was the result of chance, mixed motives, and action based on slim and often inaccurate information. But mere survival bred success and, whereas most of the first settlers had been the social, economic, religious, and political casualties in Europe whose misfortunes had laid them open to compulsion or cheap inducement to risk everything in an unknown land in behalf of callous promoters, the succeeding waves contained a substantial proportion of men and women who could have made their way in Europe, but who preferred the greater freedom and economic opportunity across the Atlantic. These people had some choice as to where they would settle, but the bases for that choice had been laid for them by others. Indeed, the almost compulsory directions for the expansive energies of the two dominant peoples of the Canadian-American Region were forecast by the strangely contrasted careers of Champlain and Hudson.

Samuel de Champlain was the great pioneer geographer of the northern region. For over thirty years he maintained himself in North America by earning dividends from the fur trade for his European backers, but meanwhile he and his assistants were engaged in collecting whatever geographical information they could. To it Champlain applied his remarkable geographical sense so successfully that his Dutch and English competitors soon learned to appropriate, if not to acknowledge, his maps and his general conclusions. On the basis of what he had found out during a two-year visit to the Spanish colonies and during a summer's investigation of the Gulf and River St. Lawrence in 1603, he formed a remarkably accurate picture of the Americas. Seven years before Hudson discovered that Hudson Bay existed, Champlain had decided that it must be there, and it seemed to him that the most important problem to be solved was the relation of that bay with the "sea" in the interior (Lakes Huron, Michigan, and Superior), about which the natives had told him, and with the Pacific.

His greatest inspiration, however, and one which ran counter to the obvious possibilities of the St. Lawrence River entry as the center for the most profitable North American fur monopoly, was his belief that somewhere down the southwestward trend of the Atlantic Coast there must be a river which would provide a much shorter and a less winter-bound approach to the interior waters. He succeeded in transferring his activities to the mouth of the Bay of Fundy in 1604 and during the next three years he examined and mapped the coast and its rivers down as far as Cape Cod. But before his progress could carry him to the Connecticut or to the Hudson, business considerations snatched him back to the St. Lawrence, where, from his base at Quebec, he quickly created the fur monopoly which that region invited and which the New England coast had discouraged. He and his associates prospered by focusing the offerings of the Algonquins, Hurons, and Montagnais which were drawn from the St. Lawrence and Ottawa valleys, the basin of the lower Great Lakes, and even from the James Bay region. The greatest of his prospectors, Étienne Brulé, slipped across the Niagara River in the autumn of 1615, and, working southward, found the Susquehanna, which he followed to Chesapeake Bay that winter; but the discovery of this short cut from the Atlantic to the Great Lakes came too late.

The reason that it did so was to be found in the brief public career of the enigmatic Henry Hudson. This man had flashed into world view only during the last five years of his life. He was a good navigator and ready to gamble his life on the chance of making great discoveries, but he was vacillating almost to helplessness at times and he was a fatally bad leader of men. On his first three recorded voyages he succeeded in nothing which he had been sent out to do. On his fourth (1610) he obeyed orders exactly and courageously, but managed his men so badly that they mutinied and abandoned him, and the world would not have learned of Hudson's Bay had not an Irish fishing boat sighted the *Discovery* just as the eight survivors were about to expire.

His discovery on an earlier voyage of the great river which has so fundamentally influenced Canadian-American development had been the result of an afterthought. His men had mutinied in the Arctic north of

Russia against further attempts to pass eastward of Novaya Zemblya. They consented to continue the voyage in warmer climes while Hudson looked for a sea leading to the Pacific which the somewhat irresponsible Captain John Smith had told him could be found on the Atlantic coast of North America about 40° N. They found the Hudson River within what they calculated was half a degree of that spot, and before the autumn of 1609 closed in, they had explored it about as far as the mouth of the Mohawk. The Dutch, by whom Hudson had been employed, immediately set about exploiting the rich fur resources of the valley.

Thus ineptitude, error, and chance were better rewarded than intelligence, knowledge, and geographical imagination. But Canadians who sometimes feel that their country was condemned to be weaker than the United States because the Hudson was not made tributary to their economy, are thereby suppressing in their memories the complex patterns of what happened in North America between 1609 and 1783. It was not the Hudson alone, but the Hudson in relation to the Englishmen settled to the east and west of it along the northern Atlantic Coast, which was to give the United States a mighty advantage over Canada.

The implications of Hudson–St. Lawrence competition were made obvious as early as 1615, when Champlain was visiting the Huron Indians south of Georgian Bay. He learned that Dutch traders had reached the upper Susquehanna Valley the year before, thus creating the threat that the Iroquois Indians of that region would send their furs to the Hudson instead of to the Hurons or Algonquins for transmission to Montreal. Indeed the Dutch had unconsciously given the great Iroquois confederacy its chance for revenge on the northern Indians whose contact with Europeans at the mouth of the St. Lawrence during the sixteenth century had equipped them to expel the Iroquois from the fertile upper valley of that river.

The contest began at once, for the Iroquois, extending as they did from Lake Champlain to Lake Erie, were in a better position to drain the Great Lakes Basin of its furs than the Hurons and Algonquins, who occupied the region bounded by the lower Great Lakes and the Ottawa Valley. Armed by the Dutch, the Iroquois embarked upon what was probably the greatest military achievement of an Indian people in recorded North American history. By 1665 they had exterminated or dispersed the native allies and trading associates of the French from Lake Michigan to Montreal and from the lower Great Lakes to the valley of the Rupert leading into James Bay. Cut off from its economic lifeblood, New France languished and was about to expire when France acted to save it. A European army was sent out and in smashing panoply it marched through rough country to the Iroquois settlements and farms. By destroying these, the French forced their enemies into temporary quiescence. Having spent a full generation in wars, the Iroquois were now so reduced in number that they were doing their best to recruit their strength by adoptions from other tribes. After the great defeat they turned their attention to the possibilities in the Ohio Valley.

This would have been the moment for an attempt to redress Champlain's failure to find the Hudson. The more astute leaders of New France had already been urging their mother country to encircle New England and to reduce the Iroquois to dependence by capturing Dutch New Amsterdam and Fort Orange. But at the court of Charles II in England there was a group of enterprising men, half courtiers and half speculators, who saw immense possibilities for profit from the King's favor if they could use it in the exploitation of North America. They knew a great deal about North American potentialities because they had taken the trouble to digest the knowledge acquired during the past fifty years and to get hold of the colonial experts of Cromwell's day. While France hesitated, they struck, and the Dutch and Swedish settlements fell into English hands. Now the French, established in Acadia (Nova Scotia) and the St. Lawrence Valley, were more than counterbalanced by the English, settled with but short interruptions from Virginia to Massachusetts Bay.

The foundation of "New" York and "New" Jersey was the starting gun for a sort of wild competition among Spain, France, and England for the mastery of North America. Very quickly North Americans themselves entered into a contest in which their knowledge and interest were gradually to give them determinant roles. Unknown portions of the continent were added to the known. Indeed so interlocked were the white man's activities between the humbling of the Iroquois in 1666 and the end of New France a hundred years later, that occurrences as far south as the Spanish borderlands contributed directly to the location of settlements and the choice of enterprises in what was to become the Canadian-American Region.

Between 1650 and 1675, for instance, the necessities of the fur trade focused attention on the unused gateways to the mid-continent—Hudson Bay and the Mississippi River. The former had been zealously explored for twenty-five years after Hudson's death by English and Danish sea captains who wanted to believe that it opened somewhere into a navigable Northwest Passage. The Mississippi had been discovered and explored for several hundred miles above its mouth during the first half of the sixteenth century by Spaniards in search of American empires. Yet these corridors had not been used or occupied by the invading Europeans because neither the appetites nor the abilities of the settlers could reach out to regions so distant.

Two able and imaginative fur traders of Three Rivers in New France, Radisson and Groseilliers who are usually jointly (and misleadingly) represented by Radisson because he was the more articulate, deserve the credit for seeing (about 1660) that Hudson Bay and the Mississippi must be brought into use. They had daringly pursued the Indians dispersed by the Iroquois to their refuges in almost unexploited country between Lake Michigan and Lake Superior, and in doing so had learned that trade with the center of the continent required new and expensive organization. Canoemen could not carry with them the food necessary for a two-way journey from Montreal, and even if depots could be established in the interior for the collection of maize and animal fat against the return journey, transportation costs would be greatly increased.

Radisson, who knew the interior of the Dutch territory quite well, would have been delighted if the French could have captured New Netherland and thus both settled the Iroquois problem and simplified transportation, but the English got there first. In default of this possibility, he and his associate thought they saw two other ways of reviving the fur trade and yet keeping down costs. They had secured from the Indians confirmations of the old reports that there was a "great river" to the southward of Lake Superior which led to the sea, and they had also learned that north of Lake Superior there were easily traveled water routes to long-deserted Hudson Bay. Of these two corridors into the continent, they chose the northern, partly because of the still redoubtable Iroquois south of the Lakes and partly because, as has been noted, furs were better in the colder regions. But since the French administrations in Canada and Europe could not be persuaded to add to their already substantial burden of defense by trying Hudson Bay as a means of carrying goods in and furs out, and since the New Englanders with whom Radisson and Groseilliers then negotiated in Acadia were daunted by the ice floes which they met at Hudson Strait, the two explorers turned over their idea and their services to the English. Once again the speculators at the court of Charles II were swift to recognize an opportunity. "The Governor and Company of Adventurers of England trading into Hudson's Bay" began their remarkable commercial career in 1668 and received a royal charter in 1670. Radisson became a servant of the Hudson's Bay Company, but Groseilliers ultimately went back to work among his own countrymen in New France.

This English preëmption of the fur trade of the immense Hudson Bay

Basin almost instantly stimulated French and Canadian determination to balance it by control of the Mississippi Basin, not only for the sake of its Indian trade, but also as a possible avenue to the riches of New Spain. Ever since the mid-sixteenth century both the French and the English had been excited by the hope that they might penetrate inland from the North Atlantic Coast far enough either to make contact with the Spanish mining regions of the southwest or at least to get into areas near them where they too might harvest gold and silver. The trouble was that no one knew how broad North America was and the portable chronometers of the day were too faulty to permit accurate calculation of longitude. Moreover, the knowledge of southern North America and of the Pacific Coast which individual Spaniards had acquired during the sixteenth century had not yet been consolidated or communicated to the outside world. Englishmen and Frenchmen, therefore, had to find out for themselves during the next century how far the Spanish mines and the regions promising similar fortune were from the Atlantic Coast, and how difficult it must be to discover and maintain any kind of a back entrance to them. In the process they could hardly overlook the Mississippi Valley.

To the French in the north, the "great river" so frequently spoken of by the Lakes Indians might lead to the Gulf of Mexico and thereby open a new fur region with a transportation system of its own, or it might lead to the Gulf of California and expose New Spain to French competition. Either eventuality was much to be desired. La Salle, the great explorer and premature reorganizer of the fur trade, was to have been the investigator, but when his self-interest and grandiose designs impaired his usefulness to the Quebec authorities, they sent out Jolliet to find the river. He and Father Marquette did so, by way of Green Bay, in 1673. By traveling down to the mouth of the Arkansas River they satisfied themselves that the Mississippi led to the Gulf of Mexico and by returning up the Illinois River they discovered the easy Chicago portage.

It took twenty-five years to realize upon these discoveries, however, largely because La Salle and the court at Versailles wasted their energies in an effort to make up for not having reached the Gulf of California by reaching out westward along the Gulf of Mexico before the Mississippi itself was occupied. Only after La Salle had been murdered by his men in 1687 during a miserable effort to establish a base in Texas for the conquest of the Spanish mines, did the abiding consequences of French enterprise emerge. A new fur trade, with what were to be permanent French settlements, grew up in "The Illinois," that is, the region embracing the junctions of the Missouri, Mississippi, Illinois, and Ohio rivers. This region was at first tributary to Montreal, but just at the end of the seventeenth century the basis for its future affiliation was laid when France and New France succeeded in founding Louisiana at the mouth of the Mississippi.

Meanwhile the English had not been standing idly by, handicapped though they were by the Appalachian barrier. Their Indian traders, especially from Virginia, had been probing here and there for the passes and game trails through the mountains. On the whole, however, the tapering off of the Appalachians tempted them to round the barrier by the south, so that the most attractive way to the great river lay along the southeastern (Spanish) frontier. Again it was the court and business group around Charles II who encouraged Virginian exploration and who founded at Spain's expense the new colony of the Carolinas. It is easy to overlook the fact that it was from this colony, famed for its tobacco, rice, and indigo, that many English traders exploited the Mississippi region, both south of the Appalachians and, thanks to guidance from French deserters, through the mountains to the Tennessee and Ohio river routes to the Mississippi. Virginians broke through to the Kanawha River and by it to the same regions.

Farther north, the fur traders of Maryland, of the region that became Pennsylvania in 1681, and of New York also found their ways to the Mississippi Valley before the end of the seventeenth century. Like the Carolinians, they were assisted by renegade French *coureurs des bois*, whose desertion to the English was ominous for the future. Already, it would appear, France was paying for the European wars of Louis XIV by an inability to compete successfully with England in producing the staples for the Indian trade. The Shawnees of the Ohio Valley sought out the English from Chesapeake Bay to the Hudson and guided them through the Appalachians, greatly to the annoyance of the French in The Illinois, who had been the first to reach them.

By 1700, Spain, France, and England had surveyed eastern and southern North America and had indicated pretty clearly what they hoped to make of it for themselves. In each case, although reach greatly exceeded grasp, there were regions and pursuits in which active international friction had developed. So far as the future Canadian-American Region was concerned, Spain could be eliminated from calculations, but the conflicting ambitions of France and England from Newfoundland to Hudson Bay in one direction, and as far as the mouth of the Mississippi in another, were certain to be fateful. In fact, two long battle lines were drawn and there was no one in Europe or North America to cry "Peace."

The most widespread source of friction was in the trade with the Indians. The Indian market for European goods had become so vast and insistent that the white traders had stimulated in response much more than a trade in furs. The Indians now conducted special deer hunts to secure the thousands of buckskins which they tanned and sent to make European soldiers' breeches. Others collected bison hides and wool. Still others collected and dried sassafras and ginseng for European pharmacies and, through them, even for unknown China. The interior of North America had become a curious, but large, and as yet unlimited, arena for commerce, and its natives had proved apt in learning how to play off the Spaniards, the English, and the French against one another. Yet, while the Indians were not guiltless in fomenting the so-called Indian wars, behind them lurked the European traders who were chiefly responsible.

Behind the European trader, in turn, lay the productive apparatus of his home country. France and England, the principal contestants in the north, had been not unevenly matched until Louis XIV began to spend his country's resources on the wars by which he planned to supplant the Habsburgs in the hegemony of Europe. Spain was an easy victim for him, but by his designs on the Low Countries he created an Anglo-Dutch alliance which almost destroyed him. These maritime countries responded to the demands of overseas commerce and European wars by building up industrial and commercial equipment superior in some ways to that of France. Moreover, England in particular revealed a new genius in the production of solid staple goods. The result in North America was that English and colonial rum, and English-manufactured tobacco, woolen goods, and hardware enjoyed a decisive advantage over French cognac and trade goods. So much so, that in the Hudson Bay Basin, the St. Lawrence Valley, Acadia, and the Newfoundland fisheries, the French themselves offered cash or barter in exchange for English staple goods.

The situation emerged sharply and portentously in the northeast. There England gradually increased her advantage in the Newfoundland fisheries, while France tried and failed to link her very successful Gaspé and Cape Breton fisheries with Canada and the French West Indies so as to create a great circular commercial exchange with the mother country in which profits could be made all along the line. The ice in the St. Lawrence and the autumn storms in the Caribbean which fatally handicapped France in this effort presented commercial New England and New York with an opportunity which they began to grasp at the beginning of the eighteenth century.

New England had compensated herself for the rapid exhaustion of her furs and the relatively meager possibilities of her agriculture by developing from fisheries and forests the greatest commerce in North America.

She built ships, hewed, sawed, and split timber, and cured fish. With these, foodstuffs, and English manufactured goods to offer, Boston became "the Mart Town" for the West Indies. Its warehouses frequently had a codfish for a weather vane, but also housed sugar, rum, and slaves. As the local schooner gradually evolved in conformity with the needs of the Atlantic fishery, New Englanders reached out across their Gulf of Maine to Nova Scotian shores and set up at Canso a sedentary fishery almost as successful as that of their French rivals on Cape Breton. Purveyors of masts and spars and other naval stores worked northeastward along the coast from river mouth to river mouth.

Around the Bay of Fundy the enterprising New Englanders came upon the Acadian people who had been planted by Champlain and his successors. These men and women had conquered the great fertile marshes which the high tides of the Bay of Fundy had created at the river mouths and along the sea basins, by reproducing the dykes of their French homeland. They supplemented their easy, bounteous agriculture with the fur trade and fisheries, but they lived in a region which could be much more easily reached from Boston than from Quebec. Indeed New Englanders could sell farm products to the Cape Breton fisheries more cheaply than the Fundy Acadians could. France and New France found it convenient, often necessary, to neglect the region, whereas from its earliest days New Englanders had been almost compelled to involve themselves in its destinies. They had warehouses at Port Royal and their small vessels fished, collected furs and grain, and peddled all sorts of commodities among the Fundy settlements.

Meanwhile New York aimed to launch its commerce from the Hudson by way of Lake Champlain to Montreal, by way of the Mohawk to the lower Great Lakes, and by way of the Ohio to the Mississippi Valley. It had learned that the staples it had to offer were so attractive in quality and price that the Montrealers would buy them with furs or cash in order to use them in their own trade. The New Yorkers were not particularly anxious to make war and they found that the Iroquois alliance was both costly and unreliable, but they were unable to arrange any permanent peace or neutrality along their border. Just at the beginning of the eighteenth century, Samuel Vetch, a Scotsman who had married into a group of aggressive Scottish-American traders at Albany, conceived the idea of reaching round to Acadia and New France by sea. By transferring his operations to Boston he, as it were, married the commercial ambitions of Boston and New York which looked toward Acadia and New France. It was a natural next step for him to draw up the first practicable scheme for the investment and conquest of the French by sea from the northern colonies and overland from the Hudson.

Southwestward from New York, the Indian traders carried on their complicated maneuvers in competition with the French and Spaniards, and they were somewhat unexpectedly reënforced to the westward of the plantation colonies by the new note of explicit territorial ambition. About the middle of the eighteenth century it was becoming apparent that southern plantation agriculture was exhausting the soils of tidewater and that the piedmont was being preëmpted by small farmers. The south was characteristically a region, not of moderate-sized farms, but of large slave-worked estates. Its overlords became urgently aware that the time had come to see whether the trans-Appalachian park lands which were being ranged by the rival Indian traders were suitable for grazing and agriculture and, if so, to preëmpt them for the territorial expansion of their colonies.

It has been the American fashion to call the first three of the large-scale North American wars King William's, Queen Anne's, and King George's, and only the fourth by the North American title of the French and Indian War. It was true that these wars, coinciding as they did with European conflicts, were apparently declared, financed, and concluded in Europe. Yet in actuality North Americans were so definitely at war among themselves that through the Indians they kept up almost continuous conflicts and at the last started their own direct warfare two years before it was declared in Europe. It would be fairer, on the whole, to say that North Americans from 1688 to 1763 used the occasions of formal wars among the European powers as opportunities for violent attempts to attain their own local objectives and to thwart their rivals.

The more formal wars were conducted by European leaders, with substantial European military and naval aid. White North Americans took their parts within the European forces or in units of their own, which for the most part were armed and paid by Europe. Quite possibly, however, it was the older North Americans, the Indian tribes, who should be credited with having borne the major burden of the long contest. Since their white masters almost never allowed or encouraged them to be at peace, they were the principal sufferers both by direct violence and by recurrent disruptions of their economic life. The white man traditionally recalls the massacres of his own kind in the St. Lawrence Valley, on the Hudson, along the frontiers of New England, and in the Acadian settlements because he knows the names and numbers of those who were lost. Yet these lives were the price paid for a much larger loss of life among the Indians which was caused by the white men's rivalries and by their shameless exploitation of Indian inability to resist an overpowering new civilization.

In the North American wars, France and her colonies enjoyed the advantage of central authority, good strategy and tactics, and very remarkable local enterprise. Yet the French colonies were thinly peopled, far-flung across the continent, and barely self-sufficient, even counting the profits of the fisheries and fur trade, whereas the British colonies were solidly occupied, contiguous along the highway of the Atlantic, and daily growing in superabundant strength from a great variety of profitable economic enterprises. The British effort was badly coördinated because the colonists of one region regarded others as foreigners and competitors, and the mother country did not know how to weld them together. In spite of Marlborough, the English were not a military people in the French sense. Indeed it was during the eighteenth century that Great Britain began to win her victories by blundering but overpowering expenditures of money and of latent economic strength. During the same period she learned that land campaigns could be won at sea. Without her superior navy Great Britain could not have captured and successfully retained the citadels of Canada—Louisbourg, Quebec, and Montreal.

The first war, between 1689 and 1697, resulted on the whole in stalemate and no change. The second, between 1702 and 1713, was marked by French victory in Hudson Bay and defeat in Acadia, but, owing largely to Marlborough's startling successes in Europe, France had to give up all the outposts of her northern empire—Acadia, Newfoundland, and Hudson Bay. The third war, between 1744 and 1748, signalized North American potentialities when an amateur expedition of psalm-singing Protestants from New England aimed a blow at Rome as well as at France by capturing the Gibraltar of the St. Lawrence at Louisbourg with the aid of the British navy. This American success was counterbalanced by British failure in India, and a precarious truce restored things as they had been.

In 1754 North Americans clashed again—this time without any formal declaration of war—and a North American war spread like wildfire from the Caribbean to Hudson Bay. The New Englanders, who now dominated Nova Scotia, promptly expelled its Acadian French inhabitants because they would not promise to act as British colonists. When Pitt at last succeeded in giving British and colonial potentialities something like effective expression, he won most of the known continent for his country. Defeated France retreated to two small islands (St. Pierre and Miquelon) south of Newfoundland, yielding to Great Britain mastery over eastern North America from the Arctic to the Gulf of Mexico.

Spain, driven from Florida and relinquishing some of her Caribbean islands, nevertheless emerged as mistress of the southwestern quarter of the continent.

The French and English of the future Canadian-American Region were now all British subjects, unless they chose to return to Europe or to cross the Mississippi to become subjects of Spain. The Indians, bewildered by the sweeping political changes and rendered desperate by an abrupt decline in the market value of their services and their commodities, excelled themselves for a few months under the military genius of Pontiac by trying to drive in the whole white frontier from Louisiana to the Great Lakes. When that effort failed, the white settlers of northern North America, in various regions, began to direct their attention westward to what their successors were pleased to call fulfillment of Manifest Destiny. To their disgust, they discovered that a commercially-minded Great Britain was determined to save the Indian hunting grounds and the Indian market by keeping settlers east of the Appalachians. A Royal Proclamation of October, 1763, prescribed a line along the watershed of the mountain barrier beyond which only licensed traders might go. This seemed to be but one of many symptoms that the time had come for North Americans to assert their coming-of-age, to find out where they stood, to search for the strands of unity which had been developing among their separate communities, and to hammer out in North America itself the readjustments and compromises which must precede their taking their future into their own hands.

CHAPTER III

DIVERSITIES UNDER ONE FLAG
(1763)

WHEN the princes and plenipotentiaries had completed their treaty-making at Paris in 1763, the British people and their North American colonists naturally let themselves go as they rolled the sweets of victory under their tongues. For the moment no one chose to think much about the problems of reconstruction or of how the new parts of the empire could be fitted to the old. When the Duc de Choiseul, sore with defeat, suggested that the older American colonies might prove to be a handful now that they were relieved of the menace of the French, the natural reply was, "Sour grapes." It would have been impossible to convince any substantial group in Europe or America that within twelve years thirteen of the colonies would be in revolt and that the twentieth anniversary of Britain's triumph of 1763 would be marked by the humiliation of parting with the central core of her American possessions. Few men wanted to worry about the disturbing rivalries and other fissures that were inherent in the situation or about what would happen when the British Government attempted to bind together a host of disjointed elements into a single imperial structure. Yet any dispassionate survey of North American affairs or of the imperial problems as they existed in 1763 would have shown that not only was it impossible equitably to unite Great Britain and her new empire, but even to weld her North American possessions and peoples into one.

To begin with, the colonists had ceased to be Europeans. There was some recognition of this in North America, even though no one had produced an acceptable definition of what made up an American. But in Europe a smug assumption that the emigrants must be a lesser breed took the place of thinking seriously about what they were like and about what their legitimate aspirations might be. In reality, of course, the various kinds of North Americans of the eighteenth century were well entitled to be proud of themselves and of their achievement. They had planted themselves in a new land so firmly that they could not be rooted out; they had made it evident that their expansive energies must in time deliver the whole continent into their hands; and they had even reached the point of devoting some of their wealth and leisure to the founding of colleges and libraries so that their young men and spiritual leaders might be learned and their elders might indulge in humane thought and letters.

The most conspicuous qualities of these peoples seemed to be their great energy and vitality. Five or six generations of North American living, particularly in the northern regions, had purged colonial societies of their weaker members and it was a tough stock which had survived. The very tempo of life was more urgent than in Europe, and the scale of enterprise was larger. The staccato beat of canoe paddles in French Canadian hands, the quickness on the trigger of Tennessee hunters' fingers, and the lavish, wasteful methods of agriculture, lumbering, and fisheries never failed to startle European observers.

Quantity already had a way of eclipsing quality. The horizons were invitingly empty, the waters teemed with fish, the forests seemed endless, the soils inexhaustible, and the subsoils a treasure house of valuable minerals. Here and there in all sections ambitious men constantly pushed higher and higher the totals of what one man might wrest from the continent in a lifetime. There seemed to be no natural limits to the size of enterprises, whether they were the great plantations of the south, the ever-expanding merchant fleets of the north, or such a limitless fur empire as the one which a handful of white men had induced to pour its tribute down to Hudson Bay. North Americans could disregard or even scorn the penny-pinching ways of the European craftsmen and farmers, for they could be lavish with materials, their estates could be as large as European townships, and their flocks and herds were so numerous that a pound or two one way or the other of beef, mutton, or wool per animal did not greatly matter.

Naturally enough, the exuberance of North American life attracted a constant stream of immigrants. While they did not find the streets paved with gold and they did find earlier comers very strongly entrenched, yet they could win clear title to lands and dwellings more easily than at home. Within Protestantism, at least, they could find broad religious toleration in Rhode Island and Pennsylvania. Connecticut could be called politically democratic as compared to the oligarchies existing in England and the other colonies, and the immigrant who made his way to the frontiers found there an equalitarianism which embraced men and opportunity in ways long forgotten by settled Europe. There was a feeling in the air that a free man need not stay in any one place longer than he wanted to and this bred a notorious impatience of restraints. Americans already made many laws, but they had little assurance that the whole of any colonial society would observe them.

All in all, there were enough kinds of fluidity and resilience about the North American communities to give any man's individuality a chance. Not that there were not strong forces operating for uniformity. The

upper classes and the older colonial families maintained, at least region-
ally, strong standards of social and religious decorum and they had
fallen into deeply engrained habits of living. The newcomers, with an
insatiable longing to be initiated and to be superior to still later immigrants, fairly tumbled over themselves in trying to learn the tricks and
guises which should make them indistinguishable from other Americans.

Generalizations about North Americans in 1763 can go little farther,
however, for almost any colonist would have vigorously denied that there
was, or could be, a common North Americanism. Southern planters
thought that Pennsylvania and the Middle Colonies contained a hopeless
social mixture, that pacifistic Quakers were dangerous fools, and that
the merchants were a crass lot. New Englanders and other colonial Protestants believed that the Acadians and the French of Canada and the
Mississippi Valley were the subhuman, misguided tools of that archcon-
spirator, the Pope at Rome. The French responded by despising "les
Bastonnais" (New Englanders) as barbarous heretics and destroyers of
all that was to be cherished in the European tradition. Communication
between the North American settlements was slight and unfriendly. Intercolonial roads were almost negligible and only a few men and a few colonial newspapers fostered acquaintanceship by sea. North America was
almost like medieval Europe in the days when a man was a foreigner if he
lived two days' journey away.

The most nearly impassable chasm between one group of North Americans and another, aside from that between white and negro, lay between
the French and the British colonists. Here geography played a substantial role, for nowhere were they in close contact except to a limited degree
in Newfoundland, in the Champlain-Richelieu Valley, and near the lower
Great Lakes. In Nova Scotia only a meager remnant of the Acadian
people lived in uneasy sufferance among the New England settlers, while
rough uplands divided the frontier settlements of New England and New
York from the seigneuries along the St. Lawrence. The French fur traders' villages of the Great Lakes and the Illinois country were far from
the settlements along the Atlantic Coast, and Louisiana lay to the west
of newly acquired East and West Florida, neither of which contained any
substantial group of British colonists.

Moreover, the geographical gap was accentuated by cultural and institutional differences. The French Canadians had formed a remarkably
solid and homogeneous bloc even before the conquest of 1760, and had
alarmed recent French administrations by their independent spirit. Their
desertion, as they thought, by the King of France in the treaty of 1763,
marked as it was by the departure of the official class and the officers of

the armed services, embittered them, even though they did not know that Voltaire had dismissed their colony as "a few acres of snow" and had written to the King's Minister that he liked peace much more than the possession of Canada. As a conquered and abandoned people they were thenceforth to pour a passionate, powerful, and successful devotion into the maintenance—indeed, the intensification—of their particularism among the communities of North America. Five generations of stern contest with an exacting environment had endowed them with wonderful capacities for survival and growth. These North Americans were destined to endure and to maintain the values which they had learned to cherish.

It is easy to exaggerate the significance of the contrast between French and British political institutions in the colonies. The French had been governed, in theory at least, by the hierarchy of Governor, Intendant, and Bishop, with the small, nominated Sovereign Council as the only forum of discussion. Over 80 per cent of them lived on the land as tenants of about 230 lay and ecclesiastical seigneurs whose rights over them were supposed to run the whole range of ancient feudal privilege from court rights to *cens et rentes* and *banalités*.[1] Actually they were fairly characteristic North American pioneer farmers—sturdy, gay, independent freemen who might be led but could not be driven. The most daring young men among them had been defiantly taking to the woods in the fur trade since the earliest days of the colony, while those who stayed on the farms had either reduced their lay seigneurs to the modified equalitarianism of pioneer society or had matched their wits successfully with the estate managers of the church communities whose tenants they were.

When it came to the real crux of government, that is, to local government, the seigneur and the priest had to make compromises between the habitants' wishes and the orders of the central administration, largely by acting through the outstanding habitant who had been chosen captain of the local militia detachment in much the same way as the New Englanders went about it farther south. Indeed it was such a far cry, politically and in other ways, from the habitant of North America to the agricultural serf of France itself that after the war, when a group of especially favored Acadian exiles was placed by the French King under the wing of an enlightened, "improving" physiocrat in France, they soon

1. Modest annual dues and obligations to the seigneur. Quebec, with about eight thousand inhabitants, many fine buildings, and a learned and cultivated society, had seemed to a European visitor like Peter Kalm to be the most attractive center in North America, but its character changed sharply with the conquest. Fur-trading Montreal, half its size, provided much the same mixture of shrewd mercantile enterprise and uproarious frontier behavior as Albany. Three Rivers, the only other urban community, had less than a thousand inhabitants.

begged—successfully—to be allowed to emigrate to Spanish Louisiana and British Nova Scotia.

Although the British and French colonists were basically not very different as political beings, they were far apart in culture. The British Americans were the heirs of a thoroughgoing Protestant Reformation and of the unquestioned secular fame and influence of Newton and Locke. They lived in an atmosphere of free inquiry which was continuously freshened by the printed works which crossed the Atlantic, hot from the press, to be noted in colonial newspapers and discussed by many inquisitive minds. In addition, North America was an almost perfect environment for the acquisitive Puritan ethic which had rooted itself firmly in seventeenth-century England.

The French, on the other hand, were children of, and actors in, the Catholic Counter-Reformation. Their very colony was almost as much a product of the missionary spirit of the seventeenth century as it was of commercial or political enterprise.[2] Their core of culture was the Catholic classicism upon whose broad foundations the more worldly cultivation of Louis XIV's Court at Versailles had been raised. The corrosive ideas of the eighteenth-century philosophers which were steadily undermining the *ancien régime* in France had reached only a few private libraries in New France, and had been kept from the populace because the colony had no printing press and the Church saw to it that, except for a few technical accomplishments for boys and girls, education should be almost exclusively *ad majorem Dei gloriam*. What skepticism and worldliness there were amounted to little more than the natural individualism of self-reliant, if slightly cultivated, men.

Finally, while the French official and mercantile communities were as covetous and acquisitive as any corresponding band of British Protestants, the mass of the population retained a great deal of medieval Catholicism's disapproval of trade and of the taking of interest. They had the traditional countryman's tendency to disapprove of mortgaging the future and of the rapid exploitation of natural resources. They believed instead in the gradual development and *inheritance* of North America by themselves and their descendants at a rate roughly proportionate to their capacity to use and consume its fruits. Their land was a hard land compared to the coastal slope farther south and it did not hold out the same allurements to speculation. They were comparatively few in number—about 65,000 in all, of whom 1,000 were far off near Detroit and about 1,200 in the Illinois country—and their population grew only

2. The Huguenot pioneers were excluded from the French colonies after 1628.

by their remarkable rate of natural increase instead of by the aid of the continuous immigration which poured into the British colonies.[3]

If the French North Americans displayed a solidarity which was firmly based upon their unified political institutions and the cherished homogeneity of their religion and culture, the British colonists were almost equally unanimous in clinging to those heritages of the seventeenth-century contest with the Stuarts which they described as "the rights of Englishmen." These were the common law, representative government, habeas corpus, and trial by jury. To be sure, these institutions were often enough so warped and twisted by local circumstance that they meant one thing in one part of the colonies and another in another, but they had in common a strong antiauthoritarian strain. The French Canadians might frighten the home and colonial administrations by their independence as they did in the middle of the eighteenth century, but they did not have at hand the same long-respected instruments for the expression of their will as the British colonists had, and their homeland had reared a despotism during the fateful seventeenth century while the English had created a quasi-republican oligarchy of property. Time was to show that French Canadian aspirations to self-government were as strong and as apt as British North American, but for the moment they had inadequate channels of expression.

The differences among the older British colonies were less striking than those between British and French colonies. Some of them were the results of geography and of varied ways of making a living, some were internal class and economic divisions, and more were varieties of racial, linguistic, and religious tradition, but they had had the common effect of preventing internal and intercolonial solidarity and of postponing any embracing sense of unity. Home and colonial authorities had tried and failed to combine the colonies from Pennsylvania eastward for Vetch's grand enterprise against Acadia and Canada at the beginning of the eighteenth century. When Benjamin Franklin put his ingenious plan for a quasi-federation before representatives of seven colonies at Albany in 1754, he found that he was ahead of his time because the colonial assemblies "thought there was too much *prerogative* in it" and "in England it was judged to have too much of the *democratic*." Perhaps most strikingly of all, in the most recent North American war only Massachusetts, Connecticut, and New York had raised their full quotas of troops, and during Pontiac's savage onslaught on the frontiers in 1763 and 1764 the seaboard rulers of Pennsylvania and other colonies were to fail to arrange for proper protection of their own obscurer citizens in the interior.

3. From Virginia northward there were about 1,200,000 white British settlers.

In 1763 British North America was the scene of sectionalisms of many sorts. Deepest and most abiding were the cleavages and rivalries between north and south, east and west. The north had built a huge semi-industrial and mercantile superstructure above its fur trade, its fisheries, its agriculture, its lumbering, and its ship-building. The south, although a great producer of raw materials, was, by comparison, but little concerned with their manufacture and marketing. The great estates of the New York patroons and the New England township-mongers, when in use, were divided up among tenants, so that, along with the characteristic individually owned farms they gave the north a social and economic aspect quite different from the plantations of slave-importing, slave-breeding Virginia, or from the Maryland that was absorbing nearly all the victims of the British criminal transportation system. The south was willing enough to accept both goods and workers from British suppliers. The north wanted to make its own goods or buy them in the cheapest market and it contained few slaves and relatively few bond servants in town or country.

In north and south alike, the east, between the Atlantic and the head of navigation (fall line) on its rivers, was pretty much the preserve of the firstcomers and the controllers of capital. They owned its urban property, its tidewater plantations, its town and country mansions, its warehouses, shipyards, and merchant fleets. Owning also the principal available public offices and rigging the governmental structures for the benefit of their class, their oligarchy imitated its prototype in Great Britain and stifled the aspirations of town labor and frontier farmers. The west, "the old west," was the interior upland which lay between the fall line of the rivers and the meandering crests of the Appalachians. The frontier of settlement in the future Canadian-American Region now ran from the Great Valley of Virginia across upland Pennsylvania and by the Mohawk Valley to the upper Housatonic and Connecticut, and thence south of the White Mountains across the face of the white-pine forests to tidewater again in Maine and Nova Scotia. Here dwelt industrious Germans, turbulent Ulstermen, and the marginal tenant farmers of England, Scotland, and Ireland whom rising rents had driven across the Atlantic. Here were fur traders, lumbermen, cutters of masts and spars, and burners of potash. Here were stubborn squatters, graziers, and the rural pioneers whose clearing and soil-breaking created land values for eastern speculators as well as livings for themselves. The north-south cleavage split the colonies as a group. The east-west fissure divided colony after colony within itself.

Everywhere the Have Nots were restive beneath the stern control of the Haves, for there was not a single colony which later generations would consider democratic, politically, economically, or socially. High property and other qualifications for the vote and for office and barefaced manipulation of the constituencies made the colonies quite safe for oligarchy. Only in Quebec was this conflict between rulers and ruled deeply accentuated by difference in race, but German and Ulster populations added more than a tincture of that kind of unrest in Pennsylvania, Maryland, and Virginia.

In the towns mercantile and industrial capital dictated stiff terms to borrowers and workers. Country merchants and frontier debtors paid and, if possible, passed on to others the usurious rates for credit which the seaboard demanded. The tidewater oligarchy of office and capital also controlled the distribution of that bountiful commodity, land. Governors and their friends could get the deeds for whole counties and with them the right to expel or to exploit the pioneer squatters and other settlers whose labors could build value into the grants. The same masters decided what defenses and roads and public services might be vouchsafed to these conquerors of the continent. The land-hungry artisan or farm laborer who could not afford to buy or rent the close-held lands of the coastal slope had to carry himself and his goods toward the Appalachians or toward the northeast, there to make what terms he could with the great grantees or with the speculative land companies and town proprietors.

Heavy immigration and rapid natural increase kept North Americans on the march, anyway, not as yet into the central valley of the continent, because Pontiac had made that unhealthy, and King George's proclamation of October 7, 1763, had temporarily succeeded in reserving the trans-Appalachian lands to be a hunting ground for the Indians. Obviously, however, these barriers could not long restrain the restless peoples, for, as Governor Dunmore reported to London in 1772, the Americans "acquire no attachment to Place: But wandering about Seems engrafted in their Nature; and it is a weakness incident to it, that they Should for ever imagine the Lands further off, are Still better than those upon which they are already Settled."

Between the fall of Montreal in 1760 and the conclusion in 1768 of the long negotiations for an "Indian Line" sufficiently west of the Appalachians to give the colonists a chance at the upper Ohio Valley, there were three conspicuous streams of North American migration, two outward from the centers of population and one toward them. From the Hudson westward, the migrants who were thwarted by the landed proprietors of New York and the Jerseys, or daunted by the available arable remnants of upland Pennsylvania, launched a slow-moving flood which gathered more members as it rolled across upper Maryland into the Valley of Virginia and even beyond, either across the piedmont of the Carolinas and Georgia into the newly conquered East and West Florida, or, greatly daring, across the Appalachians into the valleys of the Kanawha and Monongahela.

From the Hudson eastward, New Yorkers and New Englanders who could not break through the privileged proprietorship of the older settled regions migrated north and east. The Hudson–Lake Champlain–Richelieu River route drew some toward the fertile upper St. Lawrence Valley and reared others to be the angry malcontents known later as the Green Mountain Boys. Still others worked up the Housatonic and Connecticut or the New Hampshire rivers, or took ship to Nova Scotia to people the emptied Acadian townships which were so eagerly promoted by their seaboard townsmen. At the mouths of the rivers of Maine, the Bay of Fundy, and the south shore of Nova Scotia there rose still other townships of fishermen and lumbermen who supplemented their incomes from the fur trade.

Finally, the main inward stream of North American migration should not be forgotten, although it might fairly properly be merged in the great migration from Europe. Newfoundland was a halfway house between Great Britain and the continental colonies. To it came every year as many "servants" of the fisheries as there were settlers on the island, about fifteen thousand. Some of them fulfilled their engagements by returning home on the vessels which had brought them, but countless others either escaped to join some Newfoundland community, thereby probably dislodging Newfoundlanders toward the continent, or negotiated a passage to Quebec, Nova Scotia, or New England. Canada and the United States had their little colonies of Newfoundlanders long before it occurred to them to mention the fact.

A cluster of half-old and half-new divisive forces was revealed when, to the surprise of many North Americans, it was discovered that the victory of 1760 had by no means ended the regional rivalries in the Indian trade. Some of the shrewdest Albany traders promptly migrated to Montreal after Amherst's triumph there, but the competition between the Hudson and the St. Lawrence was bound to persist. Both before and after Pontiac's exploits, the interior beckoned irresistibly to the Indian traders, *boschlopers*, and *voyageurs* and to their backers. Alone or in little groups, the daring experts of the fur trade asked only for the chance to go back among mid-continental Indians who could not get along without the white man's goods.

Once more the New Yorkers hoped to exploit the advantage given them by their understanding with the Iroquois and their relatively level water route from tidewater through the Appalachians. But now they and the Montrealers were looking beyond the semiexhausted Great Lakes regions to fabulous treasuries of furs farther west; for twenty years before the fall of Montreal, La Vérendrye and his family had solved the riddle of the rivers at the crossroads of the continent and had established the relationship of the Missouri with the water highways that gathered in the Manitoba Basin before tumbling down to Hudson Bay. The rub was that the furs of the mid-continent could be taken out most profitably by the Mississippi or by Hudson Bay. At Prairie du Chien on the Mississippi and below the Mandans on the Missouri, therefore, and at Lake Winnipeg and along its tributaries, the fur traders from the Atlantic slope had to compete with Franco-Spanish companies launched from Louisiana and with field agents of the Hudson's Bay Company.

The other great focus of regional rivalry was along the shores of, and on the waters surrounding, the northeastern cornice of the continent. There Newfoundland lay like a mother ship moored by the Banks, with fishing and trading vessels hovering around her. Between the Labrador and Massachusetts, men from half a dozen regions competed madly for whales, fish, walrus hides, oil, and ivory; for masts, spars, and lumber; and for the profits of contraband trade. Newfoundland itself was the century-old battleground between the *livyeres* (settled inhabitants) and the annual visitors from the English West Country. Nearby, St. Pierre and Miquelon served as bases for the still-active French fishery and for illicit trade. At Cape Breton, the Gaspé, and around the Gulf of St. Lawrence, able Channel Islanders more than held their own with adventurers who operated from Quebec, Nova Scotia, and New England. Nova Scotia itself, now rapidly filling up with New Englanders in the places of the Acadians, was the rather passive victim of an intermittent competition between New England and Old. Southwest of it to the borders of Massachusetts, men were seeking fortunes and dodging the wardens of the King's forests while they stripped the river banks of the most accessible trees for masts and spars and other timber.

Presumably these North American communities, had they been left alone, could have fought out their differences, domestic and external, and have slowly achieved a unity, or unities, of a sort, in spite of the forces which divided them. But Great Britain was the sovereign of some twenty-five or thirty mainland and island colonies in North America and convention demanded that the mother country rule them and hammer them into a single imperial and mercantilistic structure. In England, the political and economic oligarchies, somewhat blinded by victory, airily and ignorantly set about the task, only to demonstrate promptly in a dozen ways that not only were they unable to articulate the North American empire in itself or with Great Britain, but that many of the North American colonies were coming of age and were prepared to reject such parental disciplines as seemed to conflict with interests of their own.

The truth was that Great Britain had not yet produced within her ruling class the skill and wisdom necessary to formulate tolerable working arrangements for coöperation between herself and her variegated North American colonies. H. A. Innis has boldly summarized the situation as follows:

The complexity of an empire including the West Indies and Newfoundland with strong influential groups [of lobbyists] in England, the colonies including Nova Scotia in possession of a powerful tradition of assemblies, a conquered territory in Quebec, and a charter company in Hudson Bay, imposed too severe a strain on the constitutional resources of Great Britain, taxed by the addition of Scotland in 1707 and the corruption of parliament under Walpole and George III.

In this whole matter it is useful to recall that the seventeen continental colonies, Newfoundland, and Hudson Bay, were fractions of a much larger empire and were not considered the most important fractions at that. Even in North America alone, the West Indies seemed more desirable because of the sugar industry and the opportunities for trade in slaves and goods with Spanish America. The exhaustion of the soils in the British islands had made their costs of production much higher than in the more recently cultivated French islands, but the vested interest was so enormous that during the past generation an elaborate system of bounties and controls had been established in order to ensure home and colonial consumption of British sugar products. Any serious dislocation of this structure would have endless perturbing ramifications. At the peace negotiations of 1761–1763 one of the most serious problems had been whether Great Britain would take the little island of Guadeloupe instead of the vast area of Canada. The relative importance of the West Indian market for British goods was vividly demonstrated by the single island of Jamaica, which during the decade before 1760 bought about as much as Virginia and Maryland, more than Pennsylvania and New York, and more than all New England.

All in all, the contradictory and centrifugal forces which were at work were appalling. In the interior of North America, the Hudson's Bay Company faced competition from the northern coastal colonies, which were in turn competing among themselves. The North Atlantic and Gulf of St. Lawrence fisheries presented vigorous contests among West Country Englishmen, Channel Islanders, Newfoundlanders, Nova Scotians, *Québecois*, and New Englanders. The West Indies, which were the best market for the lower grades of fish, offered three powerful inducements for defiance of British mercantilistic controls—the dependence of the French islands upon many North American products, the relative cheapness of French sugar products, and the ease of securing commodities from France herself to be smuggled into the American mainland or to be used in the extensive trade which accompanied the keen competition in the northern fisheries. Any British government in quest of an over-all North American policy was bound to be thwarted as it was pulled this way and that by the experts and lobbyists who represented special domestic or colonial interests.

As the political managers of Britain's enormous mercantile and colonial enterprise contemplated the job of consolidating it, their most insistent concern was financial. The national debt had been doubled by the Seven Years' War and the annual cost of the American establishment had quintupled. The benefits of victory, home and colonial, were obviously great, but now the beneficiaries must be maneuvered into paying the bills. At the same time, the new empire seemed to invite careful organization along traditional mercantilistic lines, with colonial raw or semimanufactured products assured of a market in England by tariffs, bounties, and navigation acts, and British manufactured goods equally and similarly provided with markets in the colonies. No great leap of imagination was required to hit upon the idea of using customs duties to enforce mercantilism and spending the proceeds to maintain the colonial establishments.

The trouble was that many of the North American colonists had for two generations blandly ignored British regulations whenever they seriously interfered with their profitable pursuits. British customs appointees, conceding the situation, drew good salaries at home and did not worry greatly about the activities of their deputies in America, who in turn excused their laxity by pointing out the difficulty of getting convictions for smuggling in the colonial courts and by reminding their critics of how widespread smuggling was in Great Britain itself. The Molasses Act of 1733 was a beautiful monument of mercantilistic orthodoxy on the British statute books, but hundreds of thousands of gallons of Rhode Island rum were distilled from French molasses as if it had never existed. Providence men and other colonists indignantly fired upon intrusive British customs vessels. Any attempt to initiate strict enforcement of British mercantilism would mean an earthquake whose tremors would agitate Americans of all sorts and conditions.

Little disturbed by regulation or by qualms of conscience, the colonists had been building mercantilistic structures of their own. From Newfoundland to Charleston, but chiefly in New England and the Middle Colonies, colonial seamen and merchants assembled native products which were in demand in the West Indies, notably food, horses, and lumber, and took them to the French islands where sugar and molasses were cheaper than in the British islands. Other trading skippers took American products, particularly the fish of finer grades than were judged appropriate for negro slaves and plantation workers, directly to foreign markets in Europe and Africa, there to exchange them for money or foreign goods without passing through the wicket gates of British controls and without giving British goods their chance. Many a New England family fortune grew out of a triangular maritime commerce which some of its Abolitionist inheritors in later generations tried to forget—rum and trade goods to Africa, slaves to the West Indies or the southern plantations, and molasses for more rum back to Medford or Boston. In addition, while it was all very orthodox in mercantilistic theory for the British Government to forbid colonial manufacturing which competed with her own, yet with furs for hatters, pulp and rags for paper, ore and fuel for iron, and other domestic products inviting the ingenious artisan, acceptance of the ban was too much to expect of human nature.

In these matters there were important differences between the colonies south of the mouth of the Bay of Fundy and those north of it, that is, between the regions which were to become the United States and Canada. Nova Scotia, although remarkably like New England and peopled largely by New Englanders, was a marginal or debatable land where New England and Old competed for economic mastery and between them retarded the maturing of the region to economic independence. Newfoundland, dependent on a single staple export, was just beginning to shake herself free from English West Country control and, for lack of capital and capital equipment, was as yet unable to pursue a self-directed course. Quebec, cut off from France and no longer able to trade with the French West Indies through contacts around the Gulf of St. Lawrence, found that she needed the British connection in order to secure attention to her interests in the stern competition of the Gulf fisheries and of the fur trade in the interior. The Hudson's Bay Company was a living extension of the British industrial and commercial organism, and severance from it was unthinkable to the directors and shareholders. In fact, the District of Maine (then part of Massachusetts) might have been taken as a sort of boundary between British colonies which were able and inclined to resent British mercantile control and those which looked to it for nourishment and aid. Significantly also, past events had demonstrated that the latter group could be both controlled and defended by the exercise of naval power.

One common obstacle to transatlantic understanding was that Britons never could be made to see what an intolerable strain orthodox mercantilist control must be on economies that were expanding and crying for capital at the rate of the American colonies. None of them could manage to keep enough hard cash in circulation to make business reasonably simple. Southern planters found an apparently easy way out by converting their debts to London supply houses into mortgages, with the result that the Londoners sent out efficient young men to tell the planters what they could and could not do with their property. The Middle Colonies and the northeast tried, on the whole vainly, to get British approval for paper currencies and banking institutions. When they embarked independently on such experiments, they either crippled an expanding trade as Rhode Island did after 1715, or went through the grim ordeal which Boston had to suffer in order to substitute "hard" money for "soft." It seemed almost impossible to shake free of the expensive tyranny of "bills on London." Small wonder that many colonial exporters wanted to trade directly with foreigners or that the colonial merchant's strongbox usually held more Spanish coinage than British and more paper promises than either.

On still another count, Virginia and Maryland could not see eye to eye with their British masters. Each year their tobacco planters mined from the soils of tidewater and piedmont a greater treasure than the gold and silver which the Spaniards wrested from Mexico and Peru, but the soils of tidewater were so light that the fertile humus was exhausted by three or four years' tillage, and required at least twenty years for rehabilitation; and although clay made the soils of the piedmont more stable, that region had been settled in large part by individual white farmers who raised general crops. The park lands of trans-Appalachia beckoned irresistibly to large-scale operators, therefore, and during the twenty years before the peace, Virginia, whose charter claims to westward expansion could only be bounded by a foreign frontier, granted away over three million acres of as yet unoccupiable western lands. Expansionists and speculators from Maryland to New England had similar ambitions, if less knowledge and less urgent need. Yet these were the lands which the Royal Proclamation of 1763 reserved as an Indian hunting ground, with white entry confined to a few licensed traders.

Little as London relished it, or the British colonists paused to consider it, the question of what was to be done with the new French subjects in Quebec also formed a serious imperial problem. How could foreign Roman Catholics, unused to British institutions and ways of living and thinking, be fitted into a North American entity in which even once-Catholic Maryland had gradually become the severest persecutor of the church without which Acadians and French Canadians could not exist? How could Albany fur traders and Boston merchants face commercial risks in a Quebec or a Montreal which knew not the English law of contract or bankruptcy? Great Britain had little to her credit from her forty-five years' government of the Acadians, but shame over their tragic expulsion, coupled with dictates of expediency, at least determined that there should be no question of expelling the Canadians. Yet the omens for their successful accommodation to the rest of the colonies, or for their exercise of Catholicism under existing English law, were not good. In Nova Scotia, for instance, the British authorities were already struggling with the apparently hopeless task of persuading the new arrivals from New England that the small remnants of the Acadians were not only harmless, but useful, and ought to be allowed to occupy some of the empty and least desirable parts of the province.

Most of this long catalogue of clashes and rivalries involving Great Britain and her American colonies was certain to be the subject of hot debate in colonial legislatures, and these quite naturally would reflect colonial interests and ambitions distinctly more than British. London could not command and expect to be obeyed merely because a political apparatus called "royal government" existed on the statute books as an instrument for the control of the majority of the colonies. American legislators and their predecessors had been struggling fairly successfully with their domestic problems for generations, and after 1763 they were not only aware that they could keep it up, but were now determined to do so. "The people of the colonies say," wrote Governor Thomas Pownal of Massachusetts in 1765, "that the inhabitants of the colonies are entitled to all the privileges of English men . . . that no commands of the crown . . . are binding upon them, further than they please to acquiesce . . . and that therefore they must have all the rights, privileges, and full and free exercise of their own will and liberty in making laws . . . uncontrolled by any power of the crown."

It is barely possible that Great Britain might have found a formula to solve the North American problems which she faced in 1763 had her rulers been unconventional enough to ponder the novel constitutional ideas of a few Americans like Benjamin Franklin; but if only one circumstance had been needed to destroy that possibility, it was present in the domestic political ambitions of George III. After his accession in 1760, his disturbing maneuvers very largely monopolized the attention and the energies of British politicians, for they were even more prone than Americans to think that home affairs transcended everything else.

The new King had inherited a corrupt parliamentary structure through which the propertied classes in Great Britain had been exercising almost uninhibited political power for two generations, for the sovereigns could achieve very little of a positive sort unless they could secure the coöperation of an organized majority in Parliament. The creation and maintenance of parliamentary majorities were arts which had been slowly elaborated by certain parliamentary managers since the Glorious Revolution of 1688, and the principal binding material was bribery or patronage. Two Whig politicians, Sir Robert Walpole and the Duke of Newcastle, had been such consummate artists in this business that their party had enjoyed power for forty years. Power bred some arrogance, so that during the last years of George II's reign the heir to the throne and his stupid friend, the Earl of Bute, decided that the time was ripe to capitalize and unify the hostility to the Whigs in order to reëstablish a larger monarchical influence in the government of Great Britain.

The instruments to George III's hand were his favor and his powers of patronage. The Earl of Bute quickly proved to be a broken reed, but the King's quest for a new parliamentary manager, combined with inner stresses among the ruling oligarchy, produced a kind of factional chaos in Parliament. George III tried seven different administrations between his accession in 1760 and his discovery in 1770 that Lord North not only could build and maintain a majority, but would use it to carry out the King's wishes. Thus British politics went through a confusing and, as it proved, disastrous experiment in domestic reaction just at the time that sheer genius was needed in order to cope with unprecedented imperial problems.

While British politicians were to be obsessed by a most complicated domestic struggle for power, and were painfully to learn that their correct constitutional course lay forward toward self-government and not backward toward royal rule, loyal British colonists, only half conscious of their maturity, first became critics of British colonial policy, then objectors to it, and finally, when force entered as a factor, gave birth to active minorities which provoked overt resistance. Thereupon the disruptive forces in the British Empire were given free play.

CHAPTER IV

THE GRAND PARTITION
(1763–1791)

GREAT BRITAIN'S attempts from 1763 to 1774 to regulate her North American empire have come to be regarded as a classic example of political inefficiency and ineptitude, but the circumstances were hardly conducive to anything else. The divisions among the governing class at home were at least as bad as the divisions in the colonies abroad. The King's political ambitions were creating anarchy among the politicians, the financiers were clamoring for some balance in the national accounts, and a few farsighted statesmen were adjusting their old patterns of thought to the novel free-trade ideas which Adam Smith was formulating, but which were a mystery to the landed aristocracy, and heresy to most merchants and manufacturers. It would have been appropriate, on the whole, if the Pennsylvanians who honored Wilkes and Barré by naming a town after those critics of the King's party in England had carried on the good work by prefixing "Adam" to the name of one of their Smithvilles or Smith's Corners.

For eleven years, one British government after another imposed one set of controls after another on the American colonies, only to withdraw or alter them in the face of increasingly stubborn and united resistance. Yet since the King and his satellites could never bring themselves to the point of admitting that colonies could be allowed to govern themselves, the whole complicated, contradictory process could have only one outcome—the flat assertion of British sovereignty, an equally blunt colonial rejection of it except as it concerned external relations, and appeals to force on both sides.

Indeed, during the first twenty years of George III's reign, it seemed as if the political genius of the English-speaking peoples had migrated westward across the Atlantic. Most of the members of Parliament and of the governing class neglected the responsibilities of imperial statesmanship while they gave themselves up to the exciting pettiness of making and breaking the short-lived coalitions of parliamentary factions upon which depended the execution of "the King's business." Among the Whigs, the elder Pitt gradually withdrew into an impenetrable labyrinth of personal pride and incipient insanity; Burke was a man of letters who was establishing himself politically and materially by placing his magnificent natural gifts at the disposal of a factional leader, the Marquess

of Rockingham; and Charles James Fox was a young rake whose elo-
quence and independence hardly made up for his dissolute personal life.
In 1770 the King at last found his parliamentary manager in Lord
North, who felt obliged to carry out the King's wishes even when he be-
lieved that they would lead to disaster. While faction held sway, the
American problem was treated as a quite secondary matter until the
Revolution began, in fact it was not until after the Revolution had suc-
ceeded that a new Tory party was created by the younger Pitt and
Britain reverted to government by contest between two political parties,
neither of which could be called the King's.

Meanwhile a number of colonial leaders, despairing of ever getting
serious consideration of their grievances from Parliament, were earnestly
studying the political theories which had accompanied and followed the
English Revolution of the seventeenth century. The outcome was anomalous. In Britain politicians still paid lip service to the principles of the
Glorious Revolution; in America they actually applied them to their own
condition. The British high priests of the political gospel according to
John Locke had so utterly submerged the realities of their faith in the
pursuit of mere liturgy (witness their treatment of John Wilkes) that
they could not admit its validity when it became the working credo of
able, fervent disciples across the Atlantic.

The American leaders were scattered and because of their provincialism they were at first discordant, but men of the stature of Benjamin
Franklin, Thomas Jefferson, James Wilson, John Adams, and John
Dickinson slowly began to loom larger as statesmen than their counter-
parts in London, and, as their convictions hardened, they found common
ground. Great agitators like Samuel Adams and Patrick Henry translated political theory into direct action. Unity in resistance emerged
clearly when the Stamp Act of 1765 imposed revenue duties on all manner of papers and documents. When representatives of nine colonies
gathered in order to discuss this measure at New York in October, Christopher Gadsden of South Carolina both echoed Locke and signalized the
future: "We should stand upon the broad common ground of natural
rights. . . . There ought to be no New England man, no New-Yorker,
known on the continent, but all of us Americans."

Nine years later, at Philadelphia, the situation had ripened. Now
representatives of twelve colonies brought with them a collection of
grievances fit to rival the Bill of Rights which had been entered on the
English statute books as justification for the rebellion against James II
a century before—taxation without representation; governmental enforcement of the East India Company's tea monopoly; the stern meas-

ures recently employed in order to dragoon Massachusetts, Virginia, and New York; and the sweeping assertions of overriding British sovereignty which had been made even by "friends of America" like the elder Pitt, as well as by the King and his supporters. Moreover, these Americans demanded liberty, and their leaders—radical, moderate, and conservative—had reached substantial agreement that basically liberty meant that the colonies should be regarded as states which had a common sovereign person in the King and which must coöperate in common foreign policy, but which in all else should govern themselves. Only in its federal implications was this new doctrine, but there was hardly a member of the governing class in Great Britain who could see, let alone admit, that the American creed was the logical expression of British political theory and practice.

By a piece of wishful thinking, the Philadelphia gathering called itself the Continental Congress, although Nova Scotia, Georgia, and Quebec had sent no special delegates, and Maine and Vermont were represented by proxy. These communities occupied marginal, debatable lands in the conflict; indeed the existence and recent expansion of Quebec were partly responsible for the anxious convention. No one had lost sight of the fact that Quebec in the hands of the British could be as potent a threat to its neighbors as it had been in the hands of the French. As early as the autumn of 1759, General James Murray, although still bottled up in Quebec by the French army from Montreal, had written home about Quebec's usefulness in keeping the coastal colonies on their best behavior, and the idea had taken some hold in civil as well as in military circles. It was kept alive in North America and Great Britain because of its apparent or real harmony with the governmental ideas of Murray and his successor Guy Carleton during the succeeding fifteen years when these soldiers, acting as civil governors of Quebec, were under orders to try the hopeless experiment of imposing British law and institutions on sixty to seventy-five thousand French North Americans.

The whole Quebec situation was perplexing. It had been hoped in Great Britain that the provisions of the Royal Proclamation of October, 1763, would divert some North American migration from the forbidden Indian hunting reserve west of the Appalachians to the newly acquired French province. Land had been offered on easy terms, and the establishment of English law and institutions had been promised as an added bait. Quebec City, which had been occupied by British troops and their sutlers and had become the capital, contained a small English-speaking community of a semiofficial character. Montreal, on the other hand, had been the objective of regiments raised in America and was the coveted base

for an expanding Indian trade. Its English-speaking population, therefore, was strongly representative of New York and Boston as well as of
the Scottish merchant adventurers whose kind had been profiting from
England's empire ever since Scotland's seventeenth-century effort to
found a commercial empire had crashed at Darien on the Isthmus of
Panama. Altogether, George III's civilian "old subjects" (as contrasted
to the French) in the province of Quebec numbered perhaps five hundred,
and their interest was predominantly mercantile. Their charter was the
Proclamation, whose promise of British law and institutions they clung
to stubbornly in spite of their forming such a meager minority relative
to the French.

By 1770, however, it had become evident that the French Canadians
could not be Anglicized unless some catastrophic event should break
down the monolithic character of their society, institutions, and culture,
and submerge the fragments beneath some alien flood. They had proved
to be almost impervious to British influences during the years since the
fall of Quebec. It had been found impracticable as well as unjust to impose upon them the English language, English law, English Protestantism, or English representative government. Except for a perceptible
increase in their resistance to the economic privileges of their seigneurs
and ecclesiastics, and except for the improvement in their sense of well-
being which flowed from the substitution of peace and even-handed British business methods for war and the corruption of the last French administration, the habitants continued to carry on their lives in the traditional patterns which had been adapted from European models by four
or five generations of their ancestors.

When Governor Carleton became convinced that Quebec was not amenable to any substantial change in character, he began urging the British
Government to abandon the policies of 1763 so far as Quebec was concerned and to set up a new scheme which should regularize the existing
state of things. Since a series of test cases in the Quebec and the British
courts seemed about to establish the fact that almost all the actions of
the Quebec administrations since the Proclamation of 1763 were *ultra
vires*, the British Government felt impelled to accede in 1773. Having
brought to bear upon the problem the great mass of general and technical
information which had been accumulated since the Conquest, and with
Carleton on hand to advise them, they drafted a bill which made its way
through Parliament in May and June, 1774.

Viewed in terms of Anglo-American relations, the exact provisions of
the Quebec Act of 1774 were much less important than the interpretations which embittered Americans placed upon them. In the first place,

the Act, although the end product of almost ten years of systematic endeavors to work out an appropriate government for a large body of colonists of alien character, was passed in the pestilent company of the so-called Intolerable Acts, whose evident aim was to bring the older American colonies to heel. Tainted by this association, its statutory establishment of the civil law, the nonrepresentative government, the seigneurial system, and the tithe-supported Roman Catholicism to which the Canadians had been accustomed, was naturally, if uncritically, regarded as the systematic re-creation of the old northern threat to the coastal colonies, this time for British ends. In spite of the fact that the Act contained a clause which expressly provided "that nothing herein contained relative to the boundary of the province of Quebec shall in any wise affect the boundaries of any other colony," irritated "old Americans" ignored this and pointed to the new boundaries of Quebec, which had been extended to include most of the trans-Appalachian territory north of the Ohio and westward to the Mississippi and the Lake of the Woods. This was a quite defensible arrangement for the attachment of the unsettled mid-continental fur area to its natural outlet and seat of governmental regulation, but it was only too easy to argue that its real intention was to write finis to the ambitions and claims of the older colonies to expand westward beyond the mountains.

To the delegates at Philadelphia, the Quebec situation presented a harsh dilemma. For generations their peoples had been damning the French for their submissive acceptance of authority in church and state, and for the barrier which they had presumed to set up along the Appalachian ridge. The Act of 1774 seemed to indicate that in these matters the victory of 1760 had brought about no change. On the other hand, however, the French had been so recently conquered that presumably they would have less love than hate for Great Britain and might the more easily be won over to the side of the Congress. It was known, too, that while the Quebec Act was highly congenial to Canadian churchmen because it restored ecclesiastical authority and legalized tithes, and to Canadian landlords because it reëstablished the obligations of the feudal system, it was resented by a large number of the habitants who had for fifteen years been taking some advantage of the fact that there was no law to compel them to pay dues either to priest or to seigneur. The problem, then, was how to pump up among the rebellious British colonies a convincing display of friendly fervor toward the Canadians while at the very same time the Quebec Act was being denounced as the Machiavellian work of the tyrant George III and his subservient Parliament.

The behavior of Georgia falls outside the Canadian-American relationship, but Nova Scotia provides an interesting example of how a region which was on the outskirts of the revolution was so torn by conflicting forces that it was reduced almost to passivity. By 1775 the province contained seventeen to eighteen thousand settlers, of whom at least three-quarters were New Englanders. Yet during the period of their migration and settlement since 1749, New England had been so concerned with what seemed more important matters that her long-established economic grasp on the province had gradually weakened. In Halifax, the capital, therefore, the usual colonial oligarchy of officialdom, finance, and business had fallen under the sway of a London mercantile group which had the advantage of enjoying the confidence of the colonial authorities in England. In Nova Scotia they were able to exercise a remarkably free hand because the representative system was heavily weighted to favor the propertied classes of Halifax, both locally and in terms of the whole province, and because distance and expense made it nearly impossible for the elected representatives of the impoverished out-settlements to attend the sessions of the legislature.

As the revolutionary tensions heightened, the Nova Scotians found that the sea cut off most of them from direct contact with their former homelands in New England and that roadless Nova Scotian wildernesses separated their settlements from each other. Sporadic outbursts of many sorts all over the province made it obvious where the sympathies of a majority of the people naturally lay; but it was impossible for them to get together, to maintain close relations with New England, to bend the provincial administration to their will, or to break down the private and public controls which were exercised from London. Loyalism not only had a natural appeal in pensionary Halifax, but it also promised to confer many material benefits, and Halifax was determined to keep the lid on the out-settlements in order to reap them. By a beautiful irony, the very people who had conquered Acadia, expelled the Acadians, and occupied their lands now had forced upon them the curse which had once lain upon their victims, that is, of being caught between the millstones of a persistent North American conflict.

Newfoundland, at the outer end of the great northeastward arc of the Atlantic Coast, was so far from the center of active hostilities that there were no compulsions stringent enough to draw her into decisive positive action. The seas and shores within the great Labrador–Gaspé–Grand Banks triangle were still an international region where Newfoundlanders, English West Countrymen, Frenchmen, Iberians, Channel Islanders, Canadians, Nova Scotians, and New Englanders followed pursuits which were competitive in the main, but often complementary enough to blur the outlines of any single rending division. The fact that the New Englanders were traders in fish rather more than fishermen, for instance, meant that their rivalry with Great Britain was more one part of the great mercantile struggle between them than an urgent competition for territory.

Thus, taking British North America as a whole in 1774, the fires of imminent revolution may have been glowing fiercely in a number of places near the geographical center, but the heat grew less as it radiated outward to the margins. Generally speaking, in the region from South Carolina to southern New Hampshire the hot cores of anti-British agitation were near enough the melting point to form some kind of an amalgam, but outside that area various influences, added to distance from the center, made a larger agglomeration either very difficult or impossible. In some cases it was definitely repugnant. Georgia, Vermont, Maine, and Nova Scotia hung in the balance; East and West Florida, the West Indies, Bermuda, Newfoundland, and Hudson Bay barely felt the compulsions of the hot passions emanating from Philadelphia; and Quebec was too alien to it all to be able to respond either way with any assurance. No single formula, of course, can embrace the variegated responses of Britain's colonies in North America to attempted central control, but, if an approximation would serve, it would be found in the maturity of ten or eleven of the central continental colonies. In terms of substantial, well-rooted populations, political aptitude in libertarian English institutions, and economic resources and resourcefulness, they were grown-up enough to resent oppressive parental authority to the point of defying it.

The open revolution, which began in 1775 and turned loose such a host of clashing forces, was a curious affair in many ways. Great Britain started out with the hope that a resolute show of force would settle things without enough fighting to create abiding hatreds. In the more independent colonies an angry minority refused thus to be impressed, and by resolute, skilful attacks on officials, soldiers, and sailors, gradually goaded the shaky federal Congress and the hesitant British leviathan into a fight to a finish. Then it became clear, on the one hand, that Great Britain lacked the ability to create and maintain a force sufficient to conquer her colonists and their vast domains, while on the other, the Congress could not win enough support in the colonies to do more than wage a fairly useful brand of guerrilla warfare.

In this revolution, therefore, a conclusion had either to await exhaustion or be hastened by the stimulus and response of outside intervention. Great Britain bought German troops outright. The United Colonies were more fortunate because France and Spain were thirsting for revenge and saw a chance to fish profitably in troubled waters by allying themselves with the rebels. Holland also formally ranged herself on the American side and much of the rest of Europe showed similar sympathies. Meanwhile, at Westminster and throughout England, resentment against the effects of George III's interference in politics made his critics think of him somewhat as the Americans did and persuaded many of them to applaud and help the revolutionary cause at home and abroad. Elsewhere in Europe the intellectual distinction of the rebel leaders and the artistry of their propaganda made a deep appeal to those liberals who despaired of ever rousing European societies to redemption from conservatism and decay. Not only soldiers of fortune, but idealists from the British Isles, France, Germany, and central Europe crossed the Atlantic to provide material and moral support for the American War of Independence.

The war itself was largely fought along classic, predictable lines. Before it broke out in earnest Ethan Allen and his Vermonters made a quick dash at Ticonderoga and the Champlain–Richelieu Valley, and New England privateers tried to brush aside the British barriers to the Bay of Fundy and Nova Scotia. After these preliminary skirmishes, Washington and the Congress settled down to the modification of the traditional plan of campaign for North America which was forced upon them by their lack of a navy. Without one, Nova Scotia could not be conquered unless Nova Scotians did the job, and even then they could not consolidate their province with New England. A few Nova Scotians made the effort in spite of Washington's warnings, and failed as he saw they would fail. The mass of the population, most of them only fifteen years or less away from New England, could only fall back upon neutrality—the very device which the Acadians had clung to during the Anglo-French wars. The "neutral French," as the Acadians had been called by the British colonials, were thus succeeded by the "neutral Yankees" in Nova Scotia.

The same lack of a navy made an attack on Quebec by sea impossible and its retention, if captured by land, unlikely. Nevertheless, Benedict Arnold was willing to chance it by leading a small army overland through the empty wilderness by the Kennebec River to the height of land and thence down the Chaudière River to face the grim old fortress across the St. Lawrence. This astonishing gamble had its justification only if two other gambles succeeded. Preliminary missions from the Congress to the American element in Montreal had on the whole been discouragingly received, but a minority there, angry over Carleton's attitude toward them and the apparent termination by the recent Quebec Act of their hopes for "the rights of Englishmen," showed some willingness to coöperate. In addition, the Congress had addressed an ingenious, if naïve, letter of appeal to the French Canadians to throw off the British yoke, and this was creating some disturbing ferments among the independent habitants as it worked upon their uneasiness over the authoritarian implications of the Quebec Act. These favoring circumstances could presumably be enlarged by prompt use of American military force against the western part of Quebec in order to create a base in the interior, north of New York and New England. Then an American army which had followed the Lake Champlain route to Montreal from the Hudson could advance down the St. Lawrence to join Arnold for the capture of Quebec, and the combined forces, if they could buy or otherwise win some popular support, might make it even harder for Great Britain to reconquer the province of Quebec from the sea than it would be, for instance, to conquer Pennsylvania.

This daring plan failed. Early in November, Montreal fell easily to an

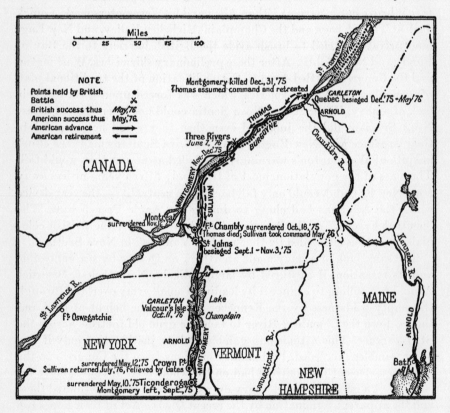

The American Invasion of Canada, 1775–1776

overwhelming Hudson army under Montgomery because there were less than eight hundred British troops in the whole province and the Canadians would not defend the region, but Governor Carleton managed to escape down river to Quebec. Here he was suddenly confronted by Arnold and the tattered seven hundred who had struggled across the wilderness and arrived with little more equipment than what they could carry on their backs. Montgomery, hearing of their arrival, left his snug winter quarters and went down the river to support Arnold. Most of his troops had gone home, so that after he had manned garrisons he had only about three hundred Americans and the moderate amount of support in services of supply and transport which his cause and his hard cash obtained from the Canadian people. On New Year's Eve, 1775, he and Arnold daringly risked an attack on Carleton's improvised garrison and attenuated defenses. But Montgomery was killed, Arnold was wounded, siege artillery was lacking, and Quebec's walls were more stable than Jericho's. More than half of the American force was killed or captured. In May the British fleet arrived at Quebec with a large expeditionary force, whereas the Congress had been reduced to sending to its reinforced, but smallpox-ridden and ill-equipped armies mere paper promises instead of bullion with which to pay the Canadians for supplies and services. The Americans, their hazard thrown and lost, retreated up the St. Lawrence and Richelieu to Ticonderoga again, taking with them a few French Canadians and some Montreal merchants whose assistance to the invaders had made Quebec too hot to hold them.

Now it was Great Britain's turn to learn that if the Thirteen Colonies could not conquer North America neither could she. It was relatively easy to keep Washington on the run, even with forces whose base was across the Atlantic, but the attempt to use Montreal as the entrance for a corridor to New York and Philadelphia which would separate New England from Virginia failed spectacularly at Saratoga in 1777. Burgoyne surrendered there, defeated by Carleton's politic refusal to act decisively in 1776, by brisk blows from Benedict Arnold's freshwater navy on Lake Champlain and from the angry Green Mountain Boys in Vermont, and by inability to adapt European systems of military transport and communication to the North American wilderness.

Thereafter, the American front could be pushed in as it was in northern New England and around New York and Philadelphia. The American armies, without a naval shield, could not prevent the British armies from occupying ports they wanted or from marching all over the countryside. The four years that passed in this sort of thing, however, got no one anywhere. Then, suddenly, France seized a chance to break through the British naval cordon, Washington tossed mere personal ambitions aside when he saw the chance of an irresistible coördinated blow, and, in the autumn of 1781, with the French navy on guard at the mouth of Chesapeake Bay, a Franco-American army dictated the surrender of the outnumbered main British army at Yorktown. George III then had to allow his ministers to enter upon informal negotiations for peace.

Open war had had the usual effect of brutally settling some conflicts and of smothering or postponing others while armies fought out the crucial issues. Peacemaking opened Pandora's box. Within the victorious States the conservative ruling classes faced the awkward job of purging their politics of loyalist elements of the Right and democratic elements of the Left. Benjamin Franklin's Tory son and the backcountry farmers who rose under Daniel Shays against the authorities of Massachusetts in 1786 neatly typify both aspects of the problem. Most of the loyalists could be counted on to swallow their defeat without causing trouble, while the conspicuously objectionable and the really stubborn elements could be expelled. The democrats, on the other hand, had helped to win independence, but had at the same time seized upon the opportunity to encroach on their local oligarchies. In Pennsylvania they had obtained a substantial revision of the constitution even before the Declaration of Independence, and they had been clamoring for similar concessions everywhere else. These were *their* States and they refused to be denied a voice in their direction. The best that the oligarchs could do by their utmost skill and ingenuity was to postpone a complete democratic triumph for a generation. Meanwhile an only slightly diluted aristocracy would represent the great body of independent Americans at the Paris peace conference of 1782.

There the victors fell out. France and Spain looked very different to the Americans when they ceased to be allies on sea and land and became instead competitors for the spoils. If France secured territory near the North Atlantic Coast she would become once more a potential menace to the fisheries. On the St. Lawrence she would be an even worse territorial threat. With Spain likely to get back the Floridas to add to Louisiana, not only would the southern frontier be limited and probably menaced by hostile Indians, but the Mississippi, the only effective outlet for the bulky products of trans-Appalachia, would be in foreign hands. The Spain which had revived so startlingly under Charles III seemed destined to be mistress of most of the continent, thereby denying the interior to the swelling populations of the Atlantic slope, and, in addition, the American commissioners knew that Vergennes, the director of French policy, hoped at least temporarily to strike a balance between the United

States and Spanish power and at the same time to hem in the Americans by conceding the upper end of the Mississippi Valley to Great Britain.

With a mature realism which surprised European statesmen, the American commissioners broke their obligation not to negotiate peace apart from their allies, and set about extracting a congenial bargain from "the friends of America" to whom George III had been forced to entrust the peacemaking.

The casual way in which Lord Shelburne and his agent Richard Oswald seemed prepared, during the spring of 1782, to throw in all Canada as a gratuitous addition to an independent United States can be explained by the first steps which these men had taken along the road leading from orthodox mercantilism toward the New Jerusalem of Free Trade. Roughly their idea was that Great Britain possessed such a commanding lead over the United States in industry and commerce that the formerly British North America must continue to be a rich and expanding market, whether independent or not. The real objective was to exclude France as thoroughly as possible. Franklin was shrewd enough to sense this in a general way, but various intrigues and delays prevented him from concluding a peace on these terms early in 1782, and allowed the British time to win a great naval victory over the French in the West Indies, and to demonstrate in Europe that France and Spain could not take Gibraltar. The preliminary treaty made at the end of November, 1782, therefore, while a remarkable surrender on the part of the power which again commanded the sea, held the principal ports of the United States, and faced only Washington's shrunken army, did at least retain Canada for the British Crown.

The boundary which the definitive Treaty of 1783 established between the United States and British North America was an odd mixture of tradition, ignorance, and surrender to expediency in finding a compromise for the division of the interior between St. Lawrence commerce and the expansive energies of the American States. At its Atlantic end, to Nova Scotia's distress at the time and to the still greater distress of the later Dominion of Canada, the British conquest of Maine was set aside and the dividing line was made to begin at the mouth of the St. Croix River, the eastern frontier which Massachusetts had skilfully won for herself in 1763. Also, although no one knew the course of the St. Croix, and indeed there was still ignorance of what stream was the true St. Croix, the line was to run north from the river's source to meet a line which was to run southwestward along the height of land between the St. Lawrence and the waters flowing into the Atlantic until it crossed the forty-fifth parallel of latitude. From that point it was to follow the parallel west-

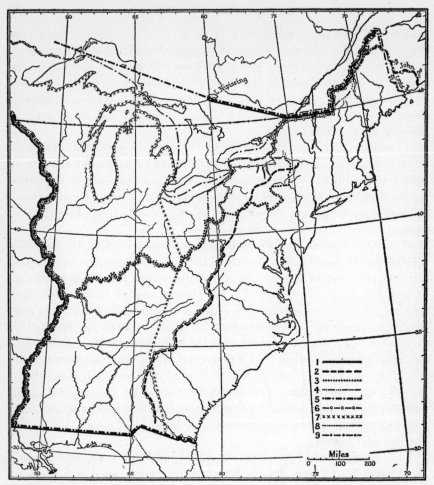

The Evolution of the Boundary in the Negotiations for Peace, 1782

1. The southern boundary of the old Province of Quebec as defined by the Proclamation of October 7, 1763.

2. The "Proclamation Line" limiting white settlement, October 7, 1763.

3. The "Fort Stanwix Line" defined by the Treaty of Fort Stanwix, November 5, 1768.

4. The southern and western boundary of the old Province of Quebec as defined by the Quebec Act, 1774.

5. Line prescribed by the Continental Congress in the Instructions of August 14, 1779. (From Lake Nipissing it was to run straight to the source of the Mississippi, then unknown but supposed to lie much farther north than it is.)

6. Possible boundary according to Gouverneur Morris, 1781(?).

7. Western line proposed by Aranda, August 3, 1782.

8. Western line proposed by Rayneval, September 6, 1782.

9. The northern boundary of the United States, with alternatives between the St. Lawrence and the Mississippi, as defined in the preliminaries of November 5, 1782. (With the elimination of the alternative along the forty-fifth parallel, it became the line of the preliminaries of November 30, 1782, and of the definitive peace treaty, September 3, 1783.)

ward to the St. Lawrence between Montreal and Lake Ontario. The portion of the line which thus extended south and west from a point not far from Chaleur Bay to the St. Lawrence at 45° was approximately the same line which had been set up by the Proclamation of 1763 and reaffirmed in the Quebec Act of 1774 in order to preëmpt the whole Atlantic slope for English-speaking settlers against French expansion from Quebec. Now, ironically enough, it was combined with the undetermined St. Croix boundary to separate loyal British colonists from those who had achieved independence.

The line west from the St. Lawrence at 45° presented most complicated problems which reached far back into the Anglo-French contest, and came down through the Proclamation of 1763, Pontiac's War, the new Indian line established at Fort Stanwix in 1768, and the boundary set up by the Quebec Act of 1774. It was this puzzling medley which, combined with Shelburne's commercial ideas, almost propelled all Canada into Franklin's eager hands early in 1782, but, following Britain's decision to keep Canada, some division of the interior had to be worked out in order to compromise American, British, and Franco-Spanish aspirations. The Americans finally offered to the Britons a choice between continuing along the forty-fifth parallel until it reached Spanish Louisiana at the Mississippi, or a line up the middle of the St. Lawrence and the Great Lakes to the northwest corner of the Lake of the Woods and thence west to the Mississippi which, it was thought, lay that far north.

British acceptance of the second alternative because of its clear-cut geographical character appeared to sever the fur trade of the southern half of the Great Lakes Basin from its long-established base at Montreal, but it was mutually understood at the time that a supplementary agreement would arrange for commercial reciprocity in the region, a plan which fell through because of later British objections. Had the first alternative for the boundary been chosen, the future Canada would have been a queerly truncated structure, deprived of the rich and fertile southern part of Ontario, and condemned to the effort to incorporate the northern four degrees of latitude of the future United States, from Michigan westward, by means of a line of communication and transportation up the Ottawa Valley and across the Lake Nipissing portage route to Georgian Bay and Lake Superior.

Shelburne's complacence about cutting in two Montreal's fur empire in the Great Lakes Basin was based upon good Smithian economic nationalism. Why should Great Britain maintain very costly garrisons in the interior for the sake of a trade, most of which the Indians would direct toward Montreal anyway, and the remainder of which, through

American channels, would ultimately find both its principal fur market and its source of trade goods in London? For some time, at least, Britain must maintain certain posts in the territory surrendered to the United States in order that the merchants there might liquidate their trade.[1] During the interval before their surrender, trade would shake down into new channels, Great Britain's commerce would adjust itself to them, and the Montrealers might make the best practicable arrangements for the future with the Indians. Britain's Iroquois allies from the Mohawk Valley were settling in new homes on the north shore of Lake Ontario and in the valley of the Grand River north of Lake Erie. At no distant date the British Treasury would be relieved of the huge costs of garrisons and "presents," in part of the Indian country, at least.

This situation proceeded to breed most unfortunate results in Anglo-American relations. The Indians of the area bounded by the Great Lakes, the Ohio, and the Illinois, could not believe that their recent ally, Great Britain, had carelessly handed over their lands to the United States without considering the native rights which she had so expressly guarded against settlers' encroachments during the past twenty years. They made it abundantly clear to the Governor of Quebec, General Haldimand, that they expected Great Britain to retain the Western Posts as their support against the waves of Americans who could so speedily transform hunting grounds into farms. In fact, they pointedly conjured up memories of Pontiac's three years of terrible assaults on the frontiers after 1763, and convinced Haldimand that if he did not keep up the forts a repetition of that sanguinary war would certainly be waged against Americans and Britons alike. Montreal merchants, fearful that their property would be swept away in war, fire, and massacre, underlined the Indians' threats; and Haldimand persuaded a new and economically more orthodox government in London that he must be allowed to violate Article VII of the Treaty by retaining the Posts.

Great Britain had an apt excuse for agreeing, since the United States was also violating the Treaty. Thus peace began with each party excusing its flagrant fault by the equally flagrant fault of the other. The American sins concerned the treatment of the loyalists in the Revolution. Great Britain had demanded, and the Americans had conceded, special treaty provisions for the restoration of their property, twelve months' residence in order to realize upon it, and the opening of the States' courts

1. In addition to two forts at the head of Lake Champlain, the so-called "Western Posts" were: Oswegatchie (Ogdensburg, N. Y.), controlling the upper St. Lawrence; Oswego, controlling the route from Lake Ontario to the Mohawk; Niagara; Presqu'isle (Erie, Pa.) and Sandusky, controlling the routes from Lake Erie to the Ohio; Detroit; and Michilimackinac, at the mouth of Lake Michigan.

to British actions for the recovery of the enormous volume of prewar debts. The American signatories of the Treaty had made it clear to the British that the Congress lacked authority to enforce the execution of these provisions on the States, but they and like-minded Americans did their utmost to make other Americans carry out their explicit and precise treaty obligations. Over a period of years a good deal was achieved, but it fell far short of what was just. American laws were changed and some British and loyalist debts and property were recovered, but there were States which simply ignored their duty, and some took positive steps which made it practically impossible to honor the Treaty. Little was done to curb mob action and other persecution. Since many of the loyalists migrated to the British North American provinces, their memories of the manhandling and violence which they so often suffered and of the gross violation of property rights which they experienced were ill omens for future relations.

The British mixture of new and old imperial ideas emerged quite clearly in Shelburne's closely related formulas for dealing with the North Atlantic and West Indian rivalries. In spite of Sam Adams' reiterated, strident demands in behalf of the New England fishermen, Nova Scotia had not been surrendered, but the Americans did receive the "liberty" (though not the "right") to take fish even in the territorial waters of the British regions, and also to dry and cure fish on any unsettled part of their shores. Because of the distance, however, these "liberties" promised to add relatively little to the products of their own fisheries in the Atlantic and the Gulf of St. Lawrence except larger quantities of the inferior "Jamaica" or "Tal Qual" cured fish which found its normal market in the West Indies. The New England trading fisherman could and would defy regulation, but he was at least formally excluded from the British ports where he could barter for the superior "merchantable" fish which could be sold in the exacting European markets.

In the West Indies, of course, Britain could no longer prevent the Americans from trading with the French sugar islands, but she could and did plan to reserve the market in her own tropical colonies for northern products from more friendly sources. This scheme went back to 1774, when Lord Dartmouth had planned with the enthusiastic support of his kinsman, Governor Francis Legge of Nova Scotia, to use that province to supplant New England in supplying fish and other commodities to the British sugar islands. Quebec, too, was brought into the design, in fact, the British colonial authorities drew up something like a replica of the old French project of binding Canada, the North Atlantic fishing region, and the West Indies to the mother country in a circular trade.

The British scheme was to fail only a little less completely than the French one had, because ice in the St. Lawrence and adverse winds on the Atlantic held up the movement of surplus Canadian wheat and flour at just the wrong seasons, and Nova Scotia either could not produce a surplus of breadstuffs or could not concentrate it at Halifax in the years when she did. Anglo-American relations in the West Indies and the North Atlantic fisheries, therefore, were to continue to be sore spots because of the contradictions between British mercantilistic policies and American natural advantages.

Later generations found it convenient to forget the highly equivocal behavior at this time of another marginal region—the present State of Vermont. The sanctimonious Ethan Allen and his scheming brothers, Ira and Levi, are usually thought of as the star-spangled patriots who stirred up the wasplike clans in the Green Mountains to seize Ticonderoga and Crown Point in 1775 and to turn back one of Burgoyne's pillaging parties two years later. The truth is that the Allens were land speculators whose hope of profit lay in getting control of the rich lands between the northern Connecticut and Hudson valleys which were in dispute between New Hampshire and New York. It was for this purpose that they roused the backwoods squatters with an appropriate mixture of evangelistic, patriotic, and libertarian catchwords. By June, 1777, they felt strong enough to defy a mandate of the Privy Council, the commands of the Congress, and the courts of the State of New York, by setting up an independent commonwealth.

Contributing to the Allens' self-interested defiance of old and newly constituted authorities was the handicap to their schemes which arose from the fact that Lake Champlain and the Richelieu River must be their corridor of transportation to the outside world until someone found the skill and money to build a canal over the height of land to the Hudson. Perhaps, then, their destiny, like Nova Scotia's, lay within the British Empire? At any rate, the possibility must be explored. Even while the Revolutionary War was going on, therefore, the Allens started bargaining with the Canadian governor for neutrality and recognition of Vermont's independence. These negotiations reached their culmination in 1789, when Levi went to London, offering George III a Vermont regiment as the price of a commercial treaty. By this time, however, the Allens' relations with the people of Vermont, whom they had used but had failed to admit to their confidence, had become too ticklish to last, and the bickering American States had finally created a federal government with some power. The Allens had to get off the international fence. Fortunately for the United States, New York relinquished her land claims in 1790, so that the new Congress was able to pull Vermont down on the United States' side early in 1791.

Thus between 1775 and 1791 the first grand partition of the British empire in North America had been made, and the most urgent issues between independent and colonial Americans had been ironed out. Plenty of only slightly less urgent issues remained, and many others were to arise in the future, but before moving on to examine these it will be useful to take into consideration the new governmental arrangements which were made for the communities on both sides of the international boundary. In the United States, leading citizens had had to turn from using English political theories in a negative way, as justification for their independence, to the positive task of fabricating from them some kind of harness by which the energies of a dozen sturdy particularisms could be directed toward national ends without limiting local independence so strictly that an individual state might "kick over the traces." In the British North American provinces the task had appeared to the home authorities to be that of cultivating Britoness among North Americans in order to avoid the contagion of independence. None of the provinces was mature or self-assured enough to lay its new course alone; geography prevented them from getting together and pretty well separated them from the United States; and Mr. Pitt and his associates calculated that a nice adjustment of the political balance of power in favor of executive authority in the colonial constitutions would bring about the compound of local autonomy and imperial subordination which they were at the same time prescribing for a restive Ireland.

Between 1774 and 1787, the independent Americans, by their unexpected genius in state-making, amply justified the acclaim with which British and other European lovers of liberty had hailed their bid for independence. "This people," wrote Turgot in 1778, "is the hope of the human race," and to liberal Europeans, bound down by all sorts of corrupt and reactionary controls, they verily seemed to be so as the States won their war, hammered out governmental compromises for themselves, and then had the vision and courage to surrender enough of their local sovereignties to create the first great federation the world had seen. The Constitution of 1787, and the amendments in the form of a Bill of Rights which were the great price paid for its acceptance by the States, were unique in human experience at the time of their creation and have since proved to constitute the most remarkable single compound of statesmanship of which we have record, but originally they seemed more than a little precarious. Few outsiders thought that such efforts could be maintained for long or that a coherent United States would be able to survive in the North American cockpit with Great Britain, France, and Spain. Yet the very attempt gave birth to new and cheering hopes for mankind. Time was to show that men would remember what the Americans had done when France and England and their emulators found ways to break down old systems of government and turned to making new.

While submissive loyalists within the United States were gradually promoted from probation at home or recalled from abroad to rejoin the groups where their interests lay—probably twice as many stayed as left, and such things happened as the election of Henry Cruger to the New York Senate while he was still a member of the British Parliament—and while the democrats of the towns and of the frontier were either deftly dehorned or sternly repressed, the established leaders of the American societies laid down the blueprints for new commonwealths. Since they were well aware that for all their recent vigorous assaults on British government they could not shed their own ingrained reliance on English institutions, they turned for an acceptable differentiating principle to the Frenchman Montesquieu, that shrewd eighteenth-century analyst and critic of the system which he saw and admired across the Channel. This is not the place for discussion of how the central and local state makers worked out varied blends of the English Bill of Rights of 1689, the political philosophy of John Locke, the eighteenth century's passion for fixed constitutions and natural law, and Montesquieu's theory of the separation of powers. It must be sufficient to note that the States did manufacture their own written constitutions based upon the idea of sovereignty derived from the people, and that, after fourteen years' testing of a shaky and often impotent form of association, in 1788 nine of them ratified the new federal constitution and thereby brought into existence a strong United States which the four others of the "old thirteen" found it wise to join before 1790 was out. It was not surprising that all of these constitutions were remarkably solicitous regarding property and entrusted to its owners more than their numerically proportionate weight in controlling government; for the victory over their kings won by the English men of property in the seventeenth century still formed the core of political philosophy in the English-speaking world. It was John Locke who remarked that it might sometimes be justifiable to kill a man, but never to rob him of his purse.

While Americans were treading the thorny path toward unity, British North Americans were being systematically divided. In 1791 there was returned to Newfoundland the Coast of Labrador which had been attached to Quebec since 1774, and thenceforth the great island pretty consistently faced outward to Europe. For the most part outsiders carried on both her European trade and her intercourse with the American mainland and the West Indies. Meanwhile her nearest continental neighbor, Nova Scotia, had been undergoing the throes caused by the dumping of thirty thousand exceedingly self-righteous loyalists on top of two-thirds as many neutrals in the Revolution. These loyalists were drawn to a considerable degree from the aristocratically-minded officials, naval and military officers, and propertied classes of the tidewater section of the revolted colonies. Reintroduction to frontier conditions, even when cushioned by generous assistance from Great Britain, was to prove too hard for many of them, and, as Patrick Campbell, a Scottish investigator, observed in 1791 and 1792, a goodly number accepted land grants and other aid, enjoyed a brief period of too-pretentious state, and then fled from their creditors by returning to their former homes on the gamble that time would have tempered the hostility which had driven them forth. The majority, who had the spiritual or material resources with which to build new lives, had little use for the older Nova Scotians. Moreover, as was natural, they were distributed over the more thinly occupied regions of the huge old province and, in accordance with London's policies, were expected to form useful soldier settlements near the frontiers. Some of them asked, and a British government which believed in *divide et impera* was pleased to grant, that Nova Scotia be broken up. In 1784 the region north of the Bay of Fundy became New Brunswick, and Cape Breton Island temporarily also became a separate colony, to form with peninsular Nova Scotia and park-like Prince Edward Island in the Gulf of St. Lawrence four maritime provinces of British North America. The seas and the wilderness which separated these sturdy communities of "old" North Americans confirmed the wisdom of the partition until such time as steam could be called upon to conquer the barriers.

Up the St. Lawrence a second migration of men and women who could not stomach the United States or be stomached by them, but who were determined to remain on the continent which their forefathers had conquered, transformed the Province of Quebec into Upper and Lower Canada. While a number of Governor Carleton's loyalist entourage quite naturally followed him when he left his military post in New York to resume his civil duties in Canada, and while Quebec had attracted a few loyalists who had found Nova Scotian prospects forbidding, the majority of the seven thousand inland migrants differed in social background from the loyalists in the Maritimes. The social standing of some of them might be masked by the commissioned ranks which they had held in the British forces, but they were at bottom chiefly frontier folk from the back country of New England, New York, and Pennsylvania.

The truth is, that underlying the attraction and repulsion that dislodged perhaps forty thousand North Americans to seek new homes on their continent, there were older forces at work. The migration of coast dwellers to the Maritimes followed lines laid down by an expansion of New England which had been under way since the seventeenth century. The parallel migrations of loyalists from the inland regions also followed old lines of expansion: the Hudson–Champlain–Richelieu corridor to the fertile acres of the upper St. Lawrence, and the avenue which the Mohawk made, either to Oswego and the shores of Lake Ontario, or still farther west, to the Niagara River and the tempting free lands beyond. No one will ever be able to determine how many of the new British North Americans were loyalists and how many were North Americans on the march to Promised Lands. In Kingston on Lake Ontario, for instance, when lands and supplies were being distributed to the loyalists, the executioner of the British spy André received a loyalist grant before he was discovered and whipped out of town.

The hapless English-speaking minority of Quebec, made semirespectable again by the departure or submission of revolutionary sympathizers, had welcomed the loyalists because their numbers and their institutional heritage seemed to be irresistible arguments for the establishment of "the rights of Englishmen" in the French-Canadian colony. Unfortunately for them, their Governor did not like representative government and, in spite of the failure of the French Canadians to help him in 1775 and 1776, believed that the majority of the population should retain their old institutions. The loyalists who had been sent to Gaspé or who had settled south and east of Montreal must, like the town dwellers, take their chances as a minority. Only those who were settling down to the west on the good lands south of the Ottawa might receive a separate organization by which to regulate their societies in their accustomed way.

After long and intricate negotiations, by the Constitutional Act of 1791 the British Government authorized the division of the old Province of Quebec along a line just west of Montreal Island and thence westward up the Ottawa. This act did not, as some persons might have expected, show any signs that the American Revolution had changed, in the direction of greater self-government, British ideas about how North American colonies should be ruled. The Quebec Governor's principal adviser, William Smith, late Chief Justice of New York and now Chief Justice of Quebec, had neatly summarized what seemed to men like him in Britain and America the cause of the Revolution. "All America," he said, "was abandoned to democracy." The mistake must not be repeated. In 1791 all of the North American colonies had governments of the most authoritarian prerevolutionary type, with executives as independent as possible of the representative assemblies, and appointed legislative councils to balance the assemblies in legislation. In the Canadas there was even provision for a hereditary colonial nobility and generous endowment for the Church of England. The provisions for a governor-in-chief over British North America were nullified only by the obstacles to intercolonial travel.

Thus, while the British Empire may have been a new empire in several senses after 1783, it was just about as old as ever in terms of political and economic controls. In part this was owing to the belief that the Thirteen Colonies had rebelled because Britain's grasp on the reins had been too lax, and in part it was because British statesmen were obsessed by a more important matter—the necessity of restoring stability and assurance in the relations between King and Parliament which had been so unstable and undependable since the accession of George III. Immediately after the peace, therefore, it was a simple matter to impose upon the Maritime Provinces constitutions of the authoritarian Nova Scotian model which had seemed to work so satisfactorily during the Revolution. The problem of a French-Canadian majority and an Anglo-American minority in Quebec meant that the handling of that province called for greater deliberation. But meanwhile the victimized Irish, by their formidable Volunteer Movement and by their shrewd constitutional arguments and political maneuvers, had deposited the problem of colonial self-government like a foundling on the very doorstep of the British Government.

In this matter, as in many others, the younger Pitt was actuated by liberal motives at the time of his accession to power in the mid-eighties, but the Irish problem was much too complicated to be solved quickly. Negotiations for freer trade and for the concession of political autonomy met obstacle after obstacle, whether threatened British commercial interests or the King's compunctions about granting full political rights to Roman Catholics. And then, suddenly, the French Revolution frightened the governing class of Great Britain into black reaction. The "New" Empire of the end of the eighteenth century, with its calculated subdivision, its authoritarian controls in the colonies and in London, its soldier settlements, and its naval and military bases, evidenced much the same panic-stricken conservatism as that which dragooned an unwilling Ireland into the United Kingdom in 1800. Three revolutions—American, French, and Irish—produced reaction instead of reform in the British Empire. Fundamental change for the better must await the vaguely foreseen consequences of another kind of revolution—the industrialization of Great Britain.

CHAPTER V
OCEANIC AND CONTINENTAL CONFLICTS
(1783–1814)

THE mere fact of American independence could not immediately revolutionize the balance of forces which embraced Great Britain, the United States, and British North America. While the mother country had lost immensely in territory, population, resources, and mercantile marine, she was nonetheless still the greatest power in the world and was equipped with the full apparatus needed for resumption of her imperial course. The new United States was substantial, particularly after the adoption of the constitution of 1787, but it could not safely sever the stout economic ties with Great Britain which had existed for so long. It would take many years of trial and error before the Americans could discover and exploit their natural and acquired advantages sufficiently to bargain on anything like equal terms. Meanwhile the British North American colonies were very far from being able to chart their own courses, in fact, they were almost at the beginning of their long struggles to diminish the overpowering effects of British and American policies upon their chosen ways of life. Finally, as the wars of the French Revolution and Napoleon were soon to demonstrate, Great Britain would normally subordinate her relations with the United States and British North America to her more vital interest in the European balance of power.

It almost goes without saying that the prime aim of British policy after 1783 was the increase of national power, and that power to Britons meant sea power. Except for India, Great Britain showed no consuming interest in territorial acquisition for about a century after the American Revolution, but she did reach out for small footholds all over the world which would serve as naval bases and as outlets for her expanding commerce. Until about 1820, when confidence had been restored by the victory over Napoleon, old orthodoxies dictated that commercial and colonial policies must take second place after considerations of naval strength. The fisheries must be kept up as the nursery for seamen, and the mercantile marine must be nurtured so that the press gangs could lay their hands on trained men for armed vessels in time of war. Adam Smith uttered the creed of these times when he wrote:

The defence of Great Britain . . . depends very much upon the number of its sailors and shipping. The Act of Navigation therefore very properly endeavors to give the sailors and shipping of Great Britain the monopoly of the trade of their own country. . . . The Act of Navigation is perhaps the wisest of all the commercial regulations in England.

Contributing to this aim, if subject to it, conservative, post-Revolutionary, British colonial policy was designed to reconstruct the economic pattern of the Old Empire, that is, Britain wanted her own colonies to supply subtropical and warm temperate products, but not other foodstuffs or wool. She needed naval stores—masts and spars, flax and hemp, tar, pitch, and turpentine—and would stimulate their production where possible by bounties and customs preferences.[1] She did not intend to permit colonial manufactures to compete with her own unless these products could be meshed into some pattern of continuous ocean-borne commerce which would increase the British carrying trade. In any conflict of British and colonial shipping, the colonial must take second place. Two statements by William Knox, the British under-secretary who laid down the regulations for post-Revolutionary colonial policy, neatly summarize it: "It was better to have no colonies at all, than not to have them subservient to the maritime strength and commercial interest of Great Britain"; and "There can be no better test devised to discover whether it be the wish of a colony to continue an appendage of Great Britain or separate from her, than the *satisfaction* or *impatience* the inhabitants express under our *navigation laws.*"

None of the policy makers lost sight of the importance of the United States as a market; indeed, leading British statesmen were most anxious not to allow France to develop the recent American alliance into any kind of exclusive trade relationship. Yet Shelburne's willingness in 1782 to include commercial reciprocity in the peace settlement had been blocked in London, precisely because more cautious minds felt that it would contradict traditional policy. Great Britain had decided to try to exclude the United States, like any other foreign country, from her commercial and navigational system. If her own colonies could not at once provide the immense flow of commodities which the Thirteen Colonies had once poured into the channels of Britain's world-wide trade, then British ships would go to the United States to get them rather than let American vessels deliver them just as if the Revolution had never occurred. The British merchant marine, with colonial additions, would grow; the colonies would build up their capital and productive apparatus; and the United States would be kept outside the imperial Garden of Eden.

1. Her remaining colonies tried and failed to respond so far as flax, hemp, tar, pitch, and turpentine were concerned.

It was perhaps natural that British statesmen seriously underestimated the United States in these calculations. The facts were that the new nation was appreciably increasing her already very effective productivity. She had the commodities which Great Britain and her colonies needed and produced them both cheaply and well. She had a huge accumulated capital of skilled labor and management, of commercial knowledge, and of the ships and crews which could find their ways (and make them pay) anywhere in the world. In brief, the tidewater region of the United States had a substantial and expanding mercantilistic apparatus of its own which had been evading British controls for a century or more and was now more capable than ever of doing so.

Against British and American strengths, the British North American colonies had little to offer. In every field of production and sale, except the fur trade, they were seriously inferior to the Americans, largely for want of equal resources and capital of their own, but partly because of their subordination to British imperial policies. The New England trading fisherman had better equipment than Nova Scotians and Newfoundlanders, and in effect he frequently induced them to work for him by exchanging cheap contraband goods for their finished fish.[2] The New Englander's forest industries were better organized and better served by transportation. The British maritime colonies (except Prince Edward Island) usually had to import foodstuffs, and winter ice in the St. Lawrence limited the competitive position of agricultural production in the St. Lawrence Valley and the Great Lakes Basin beyond. Generally speaking, British North American flour, meat, lumber, and other commodities were both inferior to, and more expensive than, American. The British colonies might and did obtain some minor economic concessions on the grounds of the imperial connection, but apparently they were condemned to a rather lowly position during the long, hard pull toward greater productive efficiency.

The first round in the Anglo-American contest may be said to have lasted from the peace of 1783 until about 1803. Down to 1793 it was a fairly straightforward affair, but the outbreak of war with revolutionary France in that year opened a much more complicated period during which Britain's interest in the United States and in British North Amer-

2. The fisheries provisions of the Treaty of 1783, by permitting Americans to land on unsettled coasts, or in settled regions by permission of the inhabitants, invited smuggling. The Americans flooded the Maritimes with tea, sugar, rum, molasses, wine, fruit, cotton goods, iron, and leather goods. "You can scarce enter a House, but you see an American package," complained a Nova Scotian merchant in 1787. This traffic swelled to enormous proportions among the islands of Passamaquoddy Bay whose sovereignty was in question and which served as points for transshipment of cargoes of the Maritime Province gypsum which was extensively used as fertilizer on American tidewater farms.

ica progressively fell into the background. During these twenty years, however, there emerged quite clearly the dual aspects of British policy toward North America which were to persist for at least another twenty years, that is to say, the oceanic and the continental. Any matter which affected tidewater, the great semicircle from Newfoundland to the West Indies, or world markets, was bound to receive closer attention and more deliberate regulation than what happened in the interior of the North American continent. Maritimers were pretty well told what to do. American and British sea traders fought out compromises. Canadians were allowed to do almost whatever they could.

During this period, the British West Indies occupied the key position. They were accustomed to a continuous provision trade with American tidewater and they could not get along without it. They first had to explode the myth that the northern colonies could take the place of the Americans as suppliers. Edward Long disposed of this scornfully in 1784:

Whatever your North American has predicted of the eventual grandeur, population and ability of Canada and N.S., he must certainly be aware that the inhabitants of our West India Islands . . . will not bear to be kept upon rations of refuse, cod-fish and a short allowance of musty bread for years to come. . . . A hundred years is an inconsiderable time to wait for a Bellyful.

The next stage was the British effort, either to have American goods brought to New Brunswick or Nova Scotia, whence British ships would carry them to the West Indies, or to send British ships directly to American ports where they might replace the British manufactures which they carried with produce or supplies for the islands. By 1790, both of these designs had failed, for the Americans managed to evade British controls and trade directly with their eager Caribbean customers by frequent visits of small ships, whereas the British ships were too big and too inelastic in their sailing schedules to build up a triangular trade.

During the wars with France, which began in 1793 and drew British eyes to Europe, both the British and the French West Indies had frequently to fend for themselves. It was at this time that the United States adopted her characteristic attitude toward foreign wars, that is, the strict, even costly, maintenance of neutrality as long as possible "because war is full of chances, which may relieve us from the necessity of interfering; and if necessary, still the later we interfere, the better we shall be prepared," as Jefferson put it in 1790. President Washington sent John Jay, the first Chief Justice, as special envoy to London in 1794 in order to clear up Anglo-American conflicts which threatened war. On the maritime and commercial side ("neutral rights"), he was much less successful than in the arrangements for the interior which we shall notice later. He got a trade agreement whose West Indian provisions were so unsatisfactory that the Senate struck them out, and Britain refused to make concessions in the vexed matters of impressment of American seamen, search of American vessels for contraband, and the effects upon American commerce of the British blockades of France and French possessions. Jay's Treaty probably averted war, and the Americans went on supplying the West Indies, but one great category of clashes between British power politics and American ambitions was left to fester until its poisons (among others) found vent in the War of 1812. Europe was more important to Great Britain than America.[3]

Yet it was during the uneasy interlude between Jay's Treaty and the War of 1812 that Great Britain and the United States invented the lend-lease technique which they were to employ on such an immense scale a century and a half later. It had happened by 1798 that the relations between the French and the American republics had reached the verge of war, a war for which the United States was manifestly unprepared. Timothy Pickering, the American Secretary of State, thereupon asked the authorities in London and Halifax whether they would sell, lend, or give back to South Carolina for the defense of Charleston "a parcel of iron 24-pounders taken in the French ship Foudroyant" which George II had once given to the former colony, but which the British had retaken and carried off to Halifax during the Revolution.

Within a few days of receiving the requests, George III and his government in London, and the Duke of Kent and Sir John Wentworth in Halifax, sent word of their willingness to lend the armaments "on condition of their being returned . . . into the King's Stores at Halifax whenever the Occasions of public Service may induce the British Government to make a requisition to that effect." Naturally, President Adams was quick to instruct his Secretary of War to forward an agreement to this stipulation and to order the Secretary of the Navy to send ships and convoy to Halifax for the guns and shot. Meanwhile, Pickering confided to Rufus King, American Minister in London, that "altho' the guns and shot are only loaned . . . I presume they will never be redemanded,"

---

3. During these years, the Maritimes shipped fish and lumber to American ports, and American merchant shippers carried them in mixed cargoes to the West Indies. One highly significant, but little noticed, development of this period was that, following Eli Whitney's invention of the cotton gin about 1792, the United States rapidly and completely supplanted the West Indies as cotton-grower for the expanding British industry. In such ways the young republic overshadowed the colonies as economic adjuncts to Great Britain.

and indicated that he had suggested as much to the British Minister at Washington. That gentleman told him that he hoped and trusted so, although "neither the Commanders at Halifax nor myself could talk of them otherwise than as a Loan." It was George III who made the final gesture of good will by sending back the American engagement to return the munitions, "thus terminating," wrote the British Minister, "a transaction which, while it discovers on the part of my Sovereign a perfect confidence in the sentiments of the American Government, cannot but tend to consolidate the connection so happily subsisting between the two Countries."

Before turning to the degeneration of these happy relations in the sensitive area of naval power and national prestige which culminated in the War of 1812, we must notice the second aspect of British policies toward North America, that is, their relative indifference to what happened beyond the reach of ocean navigation in the interior of the continent. For, while Great Britain and the United States were struggling toward some compromise of their competition in the oceanic carrying trade, substantial layers of the North American population from Georgia to the Canadas were paying very little heed. These people were being squeezed out of the old settlements by restlessness, inability to get on at home, and a population pressure which was increased by heavy immigration from Europe. The confiscated crown lands and loyalists' estates in the United States failed to slow up the movement perceptibly. In spite of the Revolution, there was little or none of the modern sense of nationality among these loose-footed Americans. They remembered their European home in a clannish way if they were recent immigrants, or the colony or state which they or their parents had sprung from if they were older North Americans, but the quality, accessibility, and price of new lands were more important to them than the flag that waved over them. Their willingness to become Spanish or British subjects is somewhat surprising to those who learn of it today.

The situation in the Canadian-American Region was well illustrated by the observations of Patrick Campbell, a Scottish land-seeker who made a tour of investigation in 1791 and 1792 through New Brunswick and the Canadas as far west as the Grand River, north of Lake Erie, then back across New York State to Albany, and down the Hudson to New York City and New Jersey. Much as he admired the farm lands of New Brunswick, he felt that Upper Canada and western New York were still more promising and, quite aside from his British leanings, he believed that the pioneer could get on farther and faster in Canada than in New York because the lands were so much more easily obtainable. Land-hungry Americans had been damning the New York landlords for a generation past and passing on to more considerate regions of the tidewater or piedmont. Now the impecunious migrant in the northern United States often cursed the privileged landlords and land companies of northern and western New York again and tried to hold out long enough to reach the Canadas. The Hudson-Champlain depression led into the fertile lands south and east of Montreal, and, if the Mohawk Valley was followed, it led either to Oswego and round the eastern end of Lake Ontario or, after traversing flat western New York and sheering off from the rough country of northern Pennsylvania, across the Niagara River into the gently rolling lands north of Lake Erie. Pious German sectaries from Pennsylvania and New Jersey, whose worldly wisdom was drawn from Holy Scriptures that knew kings and kingdoms but not republics and presidents, loaded up whole trains of Conestoga wagons for the same destination. To all of these people it was an added inducement that the western Indians liked the British and hated the Americans. Some of the emigrants to Canada saw no harm in posing as loyalists in order to secure special land grants, thus giving rise to the ironic title of "late loyalist." By 1812 eight out of ten inhabitants of Upper Canada were of American birth or descent and only a quarter of these were loyalists. Between 1791 and 1812 an influx from New England and New York flooded over the empty southwestern corner of Lower Canada.[4]

This northern flow to the west, while enormously important to the Canadas, of course occupied a smaller place in continental history than the streams of migrants which poured round the south of the Pennsylvanian highlands through Appalachian passes into the Ohio Valley. The reservoir of energies behind the latter groups was larger, the pressures greater, and the glamour of the lands so long withheld by France and Spain and Britain had been exercised for a longer time over larger numbers of people. This thundering movement, the first clear promise of the sweep across the continent, promptly dashed itself against Spanish control of the south and west and British control of the north and west. For a time its frontal waves slopped over the Spanish and British barriers and were lost in the almost empty lands beyond, but as the dammed floods piled up it was clear that they must either bend or break the obstacles.

In spite of the long-established conflict between the coastal populations and the frontiersmen, and the various threats to oligarchical control which it so clearly involved, the rulers of the United States showed statesmanship of the highest order in dealing with their western problems.

4. Compare settlements in 1791 and 1815 on the map opposite this page.

Oddly enough, it had been possible to persuade the individual states to surrender to the central government their paper claims to western empires during the very years that many of the old states' capitals were being moved from tidewater to the fall line of the rivers in response to popular demand and fear of attack from the ocean. This surrender of trans-Appalachian claims meant that whole new states would rise beyond the mountains. Gouverneur Morris put the matter very plainly to the Constitutional Convention of 1787 when he said that "if the Western people get the power into their hands, they will ruin the Atlantic interests," but he and his like could at best wage a skilful delaying campaign against powers which they could not destroy. They could either put up with the western frontiersmen, gradually yielding what they had to, or see them on the brink of placing their lands under the sovereignty of Spain or Great Britain.

During the four years before the Constitutional Convention of 1787, the old Congress, largely under the influence of Jefferson, had begun to formulate the principles for the orderly westward expansion of the United States. In 1784 Jefferson's plan for sixteen weirdly if classically named trans-Appalachian states which should gradually become absolutely equal with the original thirteen was adopted but shelved. In 1785 a land ordinance for the western territories was passed which reflected in part the successful New England township system. Its rectangular divisions, six miles square and divided into 640-acre blocks, were to persist in later land legislation, and were to be impressed like the grids of a waffle iron, not only on American western lands, but on countless acres of Canada as well. In 1787 the famous Northwest Ordinance set up a political apparatus which showed that the offspring of an imperial people could produce imperial statesmanship which was superior to the original brand. For the first time since ancient Greece, a growing nation laid down in detail the formal steps by which its colonies could progress with self-respect and certainty from a generous measure of autonomy to free federal association with it.[5] It is often forgotten in British circles that "dominion status" had a worthy Anglo-Saxon predecessor as early as Vermont's admission to the Union, and that that happened in the same year (1791) which saw the Canadas subjected to antique "royal government." As Charles James Fox said, the British Parliament gave them "something like the shadow of the British Constitution, but denied them the substance."

5. It might be argued that the ineffective British peace proposals of 1778 to the United States, and the equally ineffective proposal of 1782 for settlement of the Irish problem, at least adumbrated the American policy, but British priority did not extend to practice.

The wise American territorial regulations were carried on by the new federal government and served fairly well to hold the new states of Kentucky (1792) and Tennessee (1796) in the lands south of the Ohio against the wooing of the Spaniards. North of that far-famed river, Great Britain's "Indian empire" was retreating slowly before the migrants who came pouring down the Pittsburgh road from the Middle States and New England. The very existence of the mid-western Indians was wrapped up in their economic dependence on Montreal and in their resistance to oncoming Americans who had no perceptible Indian policy except the aphorism that the only good Indian was a dead one. The guns and powder and other supplies which came from Great Britain to support the tribesmen as hunters also supported them as the lurking braves who picked off American pioneers, or the tribal raiders who burned and scattered tiny settlements in 1791. But the flood was not to be denied, and in the autumn of 1793, "Mad Anthony" Wayne, once a land agent in Nova Scotia and lately a hero on the American side in the Revolution, marched a tough little army to build a fort in the heart of the Indian country, and set about training them for a conclusive campaign. Just north of him the British built a new Western Post to command the Miami Valley route to the Wabash. From Washington, the first president dispatched John Jay to bargain in London for the surrender of the Western Posts.

Jay got his treaty and the promise of the surrender of the Posts by June 1, 1796, but it was Wayne's military campaign which determined the final settlement in the middle west. He and his men raided, defended their fort, and finally in the spring of 1794 advanced to build a new fort on the Miami itself. After offering the peace which the Indians knew would be no peace, he utterly defeated the tribesmen in a tangle of fallen timbers almost in sight and hearing of the British fort. The battle took forty minutes, the peace-making at Greenville next year took six weeks, but the end of it all was the surrender of much of the northern Ohio country from the middle of Lake Erie to a point beyond the valley of the Great Miami River in return for annuities to the value of about ten thousand dollars. As the settlers passed in and the Indians retreated, Montreal slowly swung her gaze farther north and farther west. Spain opened the Mississippi (1795), the British surrendered the Posts (1796), Congress consolidated the land policies of the Ordinances of 1785 and 1787 (1796), and the United States opened its land offices at Pittsburgh and Cincinnati. New England and the Middle States sent forth their sons and daughters to build snug little replicas of older American villages in the midst of richer lands. Ohio became a state in 1802.

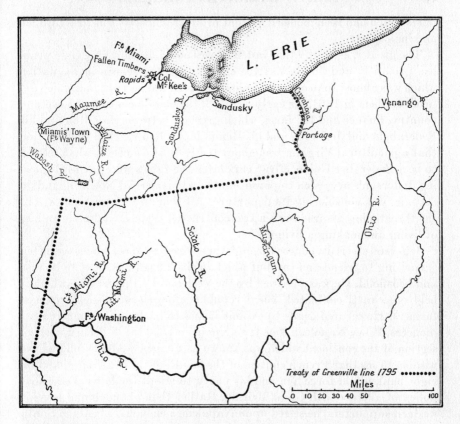

The Campaign on the Maumee, 1794, and the Treaty of Greenville, 1795

That the treaty made by Wayne at Greenville in 1795 did not end the Canadian-American contest for the middle west was, of course, largely owing to the attraction toward Canada and the repulsion from the United States which were the only possible attitudes for the Indians of the region. On the one side, under the reciprocal commerce clauses of Jay's Treaty, Canadian administrations pursued an accustomed policy, but did so with a care for international correctness which was in contrast with that of the days before the Treaty and the Battle of the Fallen Timbers, when they had occasionally come close to inciting the Indians to fight the Americans. On the other side, American Indian policy amounted to little more than averting official eyes while the tribes were extinguished by disease, alcohol, and rifles. Settlers gradually consolidated their holdings. An apparatus of government-operated trading posts which had been modeled on that of Massachusetts was graft ridden and inadequate.

The great reason why the United States could not solve the Ohio problem promptly and finally was the existence of the schism in the nation which was almost to produce secession and civil war in 1812 and which did produce them in 1861. As early as 1798, the classic contest of town and country, finance and the farm, which grew up between Hamilton and his Federalists and Jefferson and his Republicans, had reached such tension that agricultural Virginia was about ready to secede from what seemed to be a Federalist Union. Five years later the tables were turned following Jefferson's accession to power, and now commercial New England, in despair, was considering its departure. All thinking men were aware of the threatening fissure between two contrasted systems and philosophies of living and making a living.

Jefferson steered a course through these circumstances which was often surprising to friend and foe, but which in the large turned out to be wise and beneficial. He was obsessed by the west and by the promise which it held of a vast, contented, rural republic of upright, critical, yeomen farmers. He secured funds to exploit it and to back up its unaccredited pioneers. When Napoleon took from Spain in 1800 the ill-defined western section of the continent which was known as Louisiana, Jefferson had the wisdom to see that French control of the mouth of the Mississippi and its right bank would force him and his party to adopt the hated Federalist policy of alliance with Great Britain. Rather than abandon and lose his western supporters, he seized upon Napoleon's embarrassments in Santo Domingo as an occasion for buying control of the eastern side of the great river mouth. To his surprise and satisfaction, in April, 1803, his emissaries were able to acquire France's poor title to the whole of Louisiana, that is, the outlet and the western half of the Mississippi Valley, for about fifteen million dollars. Now the trans-Appalachian west had abundant water transportation to the sea at New Orleans, and the United States was no longer held between Spanish and British pincers.

Up till then north and south had loyally maintained the tacit bargain as to slavery that lay deep in past circumstance and, while tolerated, allowed the States to continue United. By it the Mason and Dixon Line which ran along the southern boundary of Pennsylvania was continued westward along the Ohio to divide fairly equally the slave states from the free. Yet the Franco-Spanish slavery which had existed for a century in the Mississippi Valley from The Illinois to New Orleans could not lightly be disturbed. The Spanish Floridas at which the United States was already gnawing were also a slave region. It seemed as if the delicate balance was about to be lost and the south either hold the north to ransom in the Union or see it break away. Just-minded men felt that it was imperative to build free states north of the Ohio at once, and greedy ones whispered that for a true balance to the Floridas the Canadas must be incorporated as well.

Meanwhile, what of the Canadas? Because of the accessibility of Quebec and Montreal by sea, Lower Canada had at least some of the desirable character of a maritime colony in British eyes, in spite of the closure of the Gulf by ice in winter, but Upper Canada lay far inland beyond great stretches of rapids on the St. Lawrence and Ottawa rivers. "Examine the map of the globe throughout every Quarter, and there shall not be found a single district of an equal number of acres, which is more perfectly removed from all possibility of benefitting us, by settling it as a colony, than Upper Canada," wrote a choleric and orthodox British pamphleteer. Over against this view, the colony's first lieutenant governor, John Graves Simcoe, asserted that the St. Lawrence must be the great highway and transportation route into and out of the unexploited interior of the continent, and that Upper Canada must become "the secure medium, as Holland is to Germany, of the most profitable Intercourse with all the Inhabitants between the Apalachian Mountains and the Mississippi." The bulky products of the entire Great Lakes Basin, American and Canadian, he argued, would float down to Montreal after having been exchanged for British manufactures in thriving Upper Canadian commercial centers.

Yet Simcoe's dreams could not prevail over British imperial orthodoxy. Upper Canada could contribute little to maritime power; it involved heavy expenses for the garrisons in the Western Posts which covered the Indian trade; and it was practically indefensible against the United States. "Upper Canada," declared Knox in 1804, "can no longer be expected to remain a British colony than the United States continue in Friendship with Great Britain." A great deal of subsequent Canadian history was to be an exemplification of that British belief.

It was in the face of British indifference, therefore, that Montrealers took their fate into their own hands and embarked on the creation of what D. G. Creighton has portrayed as "The Commercial Empire of the St. Lawrence." It was impracticable to enforce British mercantilistic controls upon intercourse between the United States and Canada west of Montreal, possibly even undesirable, either there or on the Richelieu River outlet from Vermont. Herein lies much of the explanation of the contrast between British intransigence on maritime issues and complaisance on continental ones in the Treaty which John Jay concluded in November, 1794. The principle of good neighborhood which the Treaty invoked was already in existence in the case of Vermont, New York, and the Canadas in spite of the Indian problem, and the reciprocally equalized customs duties which it established were already the normal procedure in the form of practically free trade between American and Canadian frontiersmen. To men like Knox, all this would make little or no difference to British sea power.

While Jay's Treaty was something of a freak, a secondary settlement made during a British war with France, and while the regrettable War of 1812 fairly well eclipsed it, it holds a place of special honor in the relations among Great Britain and her offspring in North America. For all of them, and therefore to a considerable degree for the rest of the world, it inaugurated, at Jay's suggestion, the use of arbitration, that is, of the judicial process, in the settlement of international disputes. This principle was resorted to for the settlement of the continuing problem of debts and loyalist claims and for the determination of the boundary in the disputed St. Croix Valley and also to the west of the Lake of the Woods. The Treaty also established for a hundred and thirty-five years the right of American and Canadian citizens and of the Indians of both countries "freely to pass and repass by land or inland navigation" from one country to the other.[6]

During the ten years after Jay's Treaty, settlers continued to pour into the Canadas from the United States, and the Montreal fur traders began, in a sort of clockwise wheeling movement toward the west and north, the withdrawal of their operations in the United States which was dictated by advancing American settlement and cushioned by the trade and travel clauses of the Treaty. They had substituted an inferior portage route from Fort William on Lake Superior to the Lake Winnipeg Basin for the long-traveled Grand Portage which fell to the United States by the Treaty of 1783, and from Fort William they were probing the great river systems between the Rocky Mountains and Hudson Bay.

From 1800 onward, however, Napoleon's capture of authority in France, and his speedy harnessing of French energies to a design of world mastery, began rapidly to dislocate the delicately balanced relationships between Great Britain and North America. The Island Kingdom was engaged in a last titanic struggle with France and this time every other consideration had to be subordinated to survival. From the very beginning of the Napoleonic wars, the Emperor and his Russian and other collaborators aimed to bleed Britain white by destroying her ocean-

6. This right was gradually eliminated when the United States began to restrict immigration after 1918, the final test case being *Karnuth* v. *United States* of 1929.

borne traffic, that is, both her supplies from abroad and the exports upon which she depended for the revenues with which to fight her own campaigns and to subsidize her allies. Blockade and counterblockade, backed by wishful decrees which authorized almost any kind of arbitrary action against men, ships, and cargoes rapidly altered patterns of production and distribution all over the world and played hob with "the rights of neutrals." In particular, the sea-trading United States was brutally gripped between the giant millstones.

The most remarkable early effect of Napoleon's wars on Anglo-American relations was the abrupt elevation of the British North American colonies from obscurity and poverty to prominence and prosperity. Britain discovered that she needed not only all the timber, lumber, and wheat which they could produce, but all that they could attract to their ports from the United States. Colonial wood products had hitherto been most unpopular in Great Britain, partly because they were inferior to Baltic supplies in quality and in processing, but also because the London wood merchants did not want to sacrifice their investments and connections in the Baltic. Now the British Government began systematically to impose ever higher duties on the Baltic products, while the duties on North American were kept negligible.[7] The declining Maritimes sprang to vigorous life; Quebec and Montreal became great timber ports; and everywhere shipbuilding expanded rapidly, for it was often possible to sell even the most crudely put together vessel along with its cargo of timber or lumber. In 1807 an imperial statute permitted the entry to British colonial ports from the United States of a large variety of provisions, wood products, and naval stores, and not only did these flow in abundantly from New England, upper Vermont, and the Lakes states, but American lumbermen and farmers migrated to British regions where their chances were better than at home. Colonial agriculture hardly rivaled colonial forest industries in capacity to provide a surplus, but American acres used the British provinces as a funnel into Great Britain for grain and meat products.

All of these processes were remarkably accelerated after December, 1807, by the willingness of the United States to carry the principles of neutrality to the point of blockading herself by means of embargoes on export and import trade.[8] Here the guiding hand was that of Thomas Jefferson, sustained at first by Congress. He may have saved a substantial part of American merchant shipping from French and English seiz-

7. Because of special, long-established British specifications for sawn and planed lumber (*e.g.*, "deals"), much of the colonial production was exported as hewn timber.
8. Compare the neutrality programs of the 1930's in Chapter XVI, below.

ures, but he plunged his whole country into profound depression. Needless to say, some of his countrymen refused to obey, and the British colonies were quite ready to accept such help in taking over American foreign trade. Their ports hummed with commerce; their revenues rose to unprecedented heights; smugglers ruled Passamaquoddy Bay; and giant rafts and trains of sleighs converged on Montreal. American exporters proved quite ready to fight off their own patrol craft either in the Atlantic or on Lake Champlain and to shoot interfering customs officers along the land frontiers. "I applaud Jefferson very much as an Englishman and especially as a New Brunswick Agent," exulted William Knox. From Philadelphia came the bitter suggestion that the merchants of Halifax and St. John ought to send the President a testimonial in the form of a piece of plate.

Even the War of 1812 between Great Britain and the United States failed to halt this traffic, indeed the availability of the British provinces as entrepôts for American trade with Great Britain contributed greatly to making the war the stalemate which it proved to be. The mercantile communities of American tidewater from Chesapeake Bay to New Brunswick did not want the war, voted against it in Congress, and did their utmost to thwart it when it came. Why, then, was there a war at all?

Of the several contributing causes, one whole group which together provided the dominant cause arose from British behavior toward the United States in the course of countering Napoleon's Continental System. Britons were blinded by the limits to which the United States would go in the maintenance of neutrality and by their own habitual arrogance toward Americans. Goaded on by their desperate plight and refusing to believe that the United States would strike at them during the death grapple with Napoleon, naval officers and other officials treated Americans and American property in ways which no proud people could bear. It was true that Napoleon's France behaved just as badly or worse toward ships and cargoes, but the Emperor had fewer ships on the seas and his naval officers, unlike the British, did not habitually comb the crews of American vessels for their compatriots liable to impressment, often kidnaping good Americans in the process. From 1807 onward, thanks to incident after incident, war and peace hung in a delicate balance. The very obviousness with which Britons relegated American rights of life and property into the background of the duel with Napoleon gradually forced Americans to conclude that in such circumstances maintenance of neutrality was incompatible with national honor.

The course of events after 1807 seems to demonstrate that by 1812 the effects of years of abuse would have overborne the unyielding resistance of American merchant interests to a declaration of war, but even if they had not, the continental side of the Anglo-American conflict would have tipped the balance anyway.[9] As we have seen, the unending stream of westward migrants was continuously confronted by the retreating Indian tribes of the middle west who looked to Montreal and London for the support of their existence. While, from the American point of view, Greenville and the Louisiana Purchase had determined the future, and while embattled Britain had almost lost interest in her old unrealistic idea of an Indian buffer state in the mid-continent, the Indians themselves attempted to halt the steady eating away of their hunting grounds through the nefarious American "treaty" technique. Just as in 1763 and 1784, a core of resistance was formed around two gifted leaders, the one-eyed Shawnee whose religious fervor won him the name of "The Prophet," and his warrior brother, the organizer Tecumseh. They established headquarters in the Wabash Valley of Indiana Territory and set about creating a united defense of their homeland. In November, 1811, the Governor of the Territory, W. H. Harrison, marched against their village during Tecumseh's absence. After a savage skirmish at Tippecanoe Creek, which wiped out a quarter of Harrison's force, the Indians abandoned "Prophet's Town," and Harrison's men were able to withdraw as rather dubious victors.

The west now had a hero to symbolize its cause for war against Great Britain. Tecumseh's organization had collapsed, so that the moment for conclusive action seemed at hand. Why not end the menace once for all, and punish unreachable Britain at the same time, by conquering Canada? The war in Europe left few energies or resources for its defense and anyway Upper Canada was said to be full of good Americans who were longing to be freed from British tyranny. Such sentiments were flamboyantly voiced in Congress because the election of 1810 had recruited a large group of southern and western expansionists who had put Henry Clay in the Speaker's chair and who saw a chance to get even with their commercial and financial overlords in the tidewater regions. "Manifest Destiny," the idea that all North America was fated to be embraced in the United States, was again on the march. If the free north should add to itself the Canadas, the slaveholding south might even the balance by seizing the Floridas.

Matters came to a head in Congress during the spring of 1812 and at

9. This matter is still in debate. A. L. Burt not only rejects the view of J. W. Pratt that there would have been no war without the grievances and ambitions of the west, but he also minimizes them as contributory factors to what seems an extreme degree. See Bibliographical Notes under Chapter V in Appendix.

the end of May President Madison put the question of war or peace up to the nation's representatives. Their decision of June 18 to declare war opened a most paradoxical contest which apparently accomplished nothing except to create an abiding bitterness against the United States on the part of the Canadas which so astonishingly survived the ordeal.

Presumably almost eight million North Americans attacked less than five hundred thousand, of whom only about one hundred thousand lived in Upper Canada, the principal target. Actually, however, New England would have no part of the war, came perilously near to setting up a separate federation, conducted continuous trade with the enemy, and supplied its armed forces. The Governor of Massachusetts even negotiated with the authorities at Halifax for a separate peace and a British alliance. In the Middle States the uplands wanted war, while tidewater wanted trade. The west and the southwest eagerly promoted the war, and were bitter in their attacks on New England for the forces which it raised in its own defense against the United States and for the threat of secession implied in the summoning of representatives in convention at Hartford in 1814. Fortunately the cooler heads in New England smothered this threat of a second American civil war long enough to prevent domestic bloodshed.

Canada was lucky to have on hand at the beginning her one first-rate military leader in Sir Isaac Brock, while the United States did not find hers in Jacob Brown, Winfield Scott, and Andrew Jackson until 1814. When William Hull, Governor of Michigan, marched an army of overconfident troops from Dayton to Detroit in order to roll up the Canadas from the west, Brock daringly moved seven hundred regulars and some artillery to meet six hundred Indians at Detroit, where he frightened Hull into surrender on August 16, 1812. Hull had been badly served by Congress, and the parallel American operations on the Niagara front which he had expected to take pressure off the western flank had been suspended by the commander of the northern armies, General Henry Dearborn. Brock could place little reliance on the western Canadians, for, as he reported, "the magistrates, etc., etc., appear quite confounded and decline acting . . . the officers of militia exert no authority . . . everybody considers the fate of the country as settled and is afraid to appear in the least conspicuous to retard it." He hurried back to the Niagara frontier to meet the revived attack which the American Government had prepared after disavowing the armistice which Dearborn had arranged with the Governor of Canada. There Brock was killed on October 13, 1812, after rallying the retreating British forces at Queenston Heights for a charge and victory. The refusal of the New York militia to leave their own state to join the battle which was going on before their eyes across the river led to the surrender of the whole invading force. The Niagara campaign thereafter degenerated to such a degree that American soldiers were reasonably suspected of firing into their general's tent instead of into Canada.

Thanks to the aged and diffident Dearborn, and to another refusal by American militia to leave the United States, the equally diffident Sir George Prévost had not had to face the thrust which might well have settled everything by the capture of Montreal and severance of the supply line to the west. The Maritimes were unthreatened by New England and, in spite of some bold American naval enterprise early in the war, their share in it speedily became an agreeably exciting and profitable mixture of contraband trade and privateering. In other words, the war against Great Britain in North America resolved itself into a series of efforts, sometimes well conducted, but often badly managed and in general ineffectively coördinated, to conquer Upper Canada by occupying it from the west.

Brock's capture of Detroit and swift, successful British strokes against Michilimackinac, Fort Dearborn (Chicago), and Prairie du Chien (the fur traders' rendezvous on the Mississippi) saved the Indian country for the Montrealers, but in 1813 the United States went to work systematically on the conquest of Upper Canada and on the supposed salvation of the American population there. In these efforts freshwater navies played a prominent role. While Harrison was utterly failing to get an army through Indian and British barriers to recapture Detroit, Oliver Perry was building a little fleet on Lake Erie which outnumbered and defeated the opposing British vessels in September, 1813. Thereupon the British forces felt obliged to evacuate the Detroit River positions and Harrison moved to the attack with unaccustomed swiftness by water. With a force of three to one, he practically wiped out his military opponents in the battle at Moraviantown on the River Thames where the great Tecumseh finally met his death.[10] His victory won, Harrison neglected to exploit it except by devastations, and fell back on Detroit.

He had some excuse for this inertia in the comparative failure that year of the same combination of naval and military enterprise in the vicinity of Lake Ontario. Its feeble beginnings removed Dearborn from the scene, but he was succeeded by James Wilkinson, who was so utterly incompetent, and so unprincipled a person, that he completely estranged his subordinates. Dearborn's ineptitude and Wilkinson's defects, con-

10. The story goes that the Kentuckians divided up his skin for razor strops.

fronted by British and Canadian resolution, brought about American military defeats on both the Niagara and the St. Lawrence frontiers.[11] A superior American naval force, based on Sackets Harbor (which repelled a violent three-day amphibious assault), was not strong enough alone to take Kingston, the Canadian base. This year was marred by disgraceful raids and town-burnings, by the pillaging of York (the capital of Upper Canada) and the burning of Newark at American hands, and by the loosing of the Indians against American civilians by the British.

By early 1814 the United States had replaced its bad commanders with good ones, but Napoleon's defeat allowed Great Britain to pour regular troops into Canada during the summer. In addition, the Kingston navy temporarily got the whip hand over the Sackets Harbor navy by the capture of Oswego and the naval stores assembled there. The result was that Jacob Brown's well-conducted Niagara campaign ended in a bloody drawn battle at Lundy's Lane in July before the Americans could dominate the lake again. By all reasonable calculations, Sir George Prévost was now more than capable of marching his thousands of British veterans past Lake Champlain into New York and the Hudson Valley. But Thomas Macdonough was on the lake and, in a merciless battle off Plattsburg, he destroyed the British vessels upon which Prévost felt he was dependent. Prévost retired, as if to show that British generals could be as bad as American ones.

Meanwhile, the British navy had enlarged its successes of 1813 along the Atlantic Coast into complete domination, for the United States found it impossible to create anything approaching equal strength on salt water. Maine was occupied as far as the Penobscot, Cape Cod served as a naval base, Chesapeake Bay was scoured clean, and the White House was burned in revenge for the American treatment of York. It was somehow in keeping with the whole character of the war that fighting ended at remote New Orleans, a month after peace had been concluded. In January, 1815, Andrew Jackson, an Indian fighter who had just disposed of the Spanish and Indian menace in West Florida, successfully defended the river-mouth city against a too-long delayed and suicidally conducted assault.

Peace was concluded with considerable swiftness during the interlude of Napoleon's exile to Elba, because both sides felt that they had to have it. The Duke of Wellington warned his Government against thinking

11. Loyalty and willingness to fight on the part of the Canadian militia increased in a sort of progression from the Americanized west to the loyalist east of Upper Canada. French Canadians fought valiantly in defense of Lower Canada.

that it could conquer the United States, and if Americans were tired of war, the British people had had over twenty years of it. An uneasy Europe which needed reconstruction after Napoleon seemed much more important than North America. The United States was disillusioned with war, on the brink of outright disruption into two parts, and determined to have an end to the embargoes and the British blockade which had dislocated the whole economic structure of the nation. Thanks to British preoccupation with European affairs, the American negotiators managed to get back northern Maine, in spite of its recognized desirability as a land bridge for winter communications between the Atlantic Coast and Canada, thus obviating the one threatening exception to the restoration of the territorial *status quo ante*. In fact, the Treaty of Ghent did little more than end the war. Following the precedent of Jay's Treaty, the principal matters in dispute were referred to the more leisurely and more temperate action of joint commissions which should be sitting during times of peace.

CHAPTER VI

A NEW ALIGNMENT OF FORCES
(1815–1823)

THE Treaty of Ghent which closed the War of 1812 was a curiously empty document which had to be implemented by several Anglo-American agreements during the next few years. For instance, it made no mention whatever of the dangerous issues in the area of "neutral rights" which had been the principal causes of the war, indeed many of those problems remained still unresolved to plague Anglo-American relations a hundred years later. Yet, as the international adjustments of 1815 to 1823 were to reveal, the war had marked the achievement of a kind of mutual respect between the United States and Great Britain which, combined with certain changes in the directions of their ambitions, was to establish a new alignment of forces and to lay the foundations for almost uninterrupted peace between them. Great Britain now recognized more clearly than ever the intrinsic strength of the United States and the vulnerability of the Canadas, but on the other hand the United States had been awakened both to the awful threat of her own domestic schism and to the overwhelming power of the British navy. Both nations were aware of their mutual dependence in trade.

The relations between the two great nations and the British colonies were of less importance, but they could not be ignored in either American or British calculations. The contraband trade and their own increased productivity had catapulted the Maritimes to dizzy economic heights which they would fight hard to hold. To their own surprise, the Canadas had emerged territorially intact from the war, and their governing classes, at least, were imbued by it with a reënforced hostility to the United States. Henceforth the old loyalist attitude, enhanced by the ordeals and the property losses of the war, would be the taproot of an orthodox anti-American Canadianism which might be contradicted daily in dozens of practical ways, but which would persist because it harmonized perfectly with the natural feelings of a small people toward an overpoweringly large one next door.

The Canadians were to be spared from outright aggression, however, for although the American people remained faithful to the creed of Manifest Destiny which had been so eloquently voiced during the Revolution and so resoundingly reasserted by the south and west during the War of 1812, yet their failure to conquer the Canadas and other recent

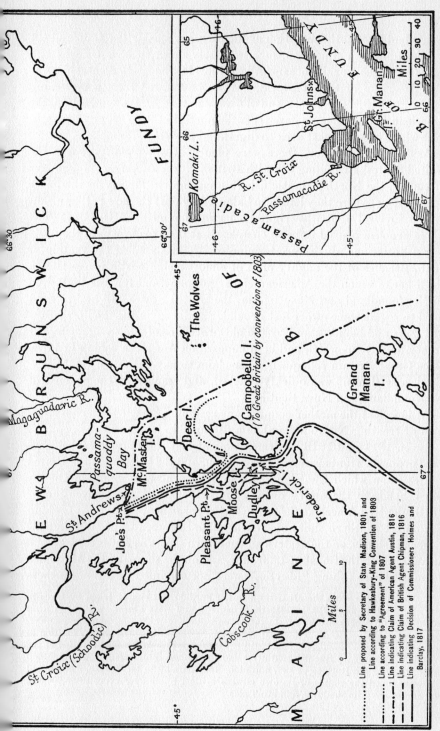

Islands in the Bay of Fundy with Inset from Mitchell's Map Showing His St. Croix and "Passamacadie" Rivers

Redrawn with permission of the American Geographical Society, from Charles O. Paullin and John K. Wright,
Atlas of the Historical Geography of the United States

events had altered the direction of their expansionism. The Ohio and the Mississippi, both American, now led freely down to New Orleans and passage to the world's oceans. West Florida almost to Pensacola was also American and East Florida was to be wrested from a weakening Spain in 1819.[1] The rivers and the very nature of the lands drew the American frontiersman's gaze from the north to the south or the south-west where he had a vast area to digest and new states to make.

Aside from territory, there were plenty of other things worth the United States' struggling for with British North America. As a matter of course, the North Atlantic fisheries had figured largely in the peace negotiations, where they had been balanced against the now rather mean-ingless survival of British rights of navigation on the Mississippi. The whole problem proved to be so complex that it was referred to the post-war negotiations which were terminated by the so-called Convention of 1818. Because of the mighty fillip of almost monopolistic prosperity in the fisheries which the American embargo policy and the war had given to Newfoundland and Nova Scotia, the United States had had to fight hard to regain some of her lost ground. She did so by the familiar means of tariffs and bounties and by the old procedure of simply ignoring the treaty limitations which had been imposed on American fishing in 1783. Once Great Britain relinquished her claim to navigation on the Missis-sippi, a settlement was quickly reached, and reached at the expense of Newfoundland and Nova Scotia.

At long last the mother country was resigning herself to the hopeless-ness of treating Newfoundland as a fishing ship instead of as a colony. Between 1811 and 1818 settlement was at last formally tolerated, pri-vate property rights received recognition, and the trade with the United States upon which the island was so dependent was legalized. On the other hand, to the angry dismay of the colonists, the Convention of 1818 admitted American fishermen to the permanent "liberty" of taking fish on the southern shore of Newfoundland between Cape Ray and the Rameau Islands, on the western and northern shores as far as the Quirpon Islands, along the Coast of Labrador, and on the shores of the Magdalen Islands. These fishing "liberties" were accompanied by certain others

1. West Florida from the Mississippi to the Perdido was simply taken by force in two bites of 1810 and 1813. In 1819 the remainder and East Florida were yielded up in the face of American filibustering, Jackson's punitive raids against the Seminoles, and other pressures, by the Adams-Onís Treaty. Spain, with widespread revolution in the Americas on her hands, surrendered the Floridas in return for the definition of the boundary between the Spanish southwest and the United States along the Sabine and other rivers to the Rockies at 42°, and along that parallel to the Pacific. The United States assumed the claims of its own citizens against Spain amounting to $5,000,000, and surrendered its shadowy claim to Texas.

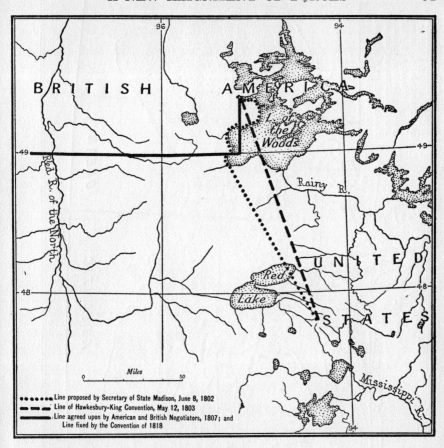

The Northwest Boundary Gap

Redrawn with permission of the American Geographical Society from Charles O.
Paullin and John K. Wright, *Atlas of the Historical Geography
of the United States*

permitting the Americans "for ever" to dry and cure fish on unsettled
portions of the southern coast of Newfoundland and of the Coast of Labrador, and to enter other bays and harbors solely for shelter, repairs,
fuel, and water. While by the Convention Nova Scotia regained the
monopoly of her own shores and coastal waters, yet she now had to face
once more the almost unimpaired competition of New England in the
Atlantic fisheries generally and in the extensive commerce which was so
closely interlocked with them.

For, once the war was over, Great Britain and the United States had

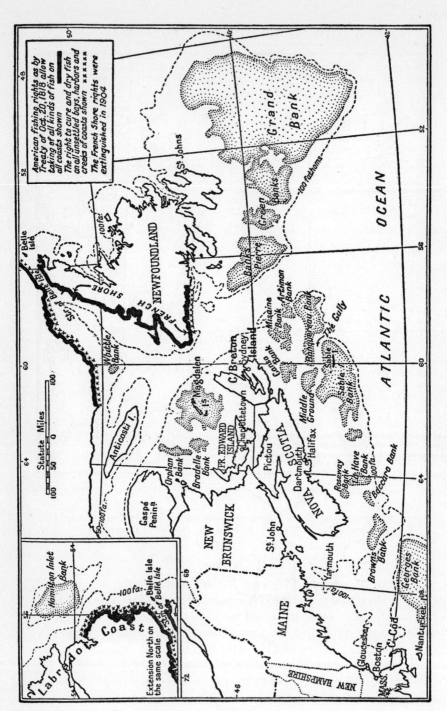

American fishing rights as by
Treaty of Oct. 20, 1818 allow
taking of all kinds of fish on
all coasts shown

The right to cure and dry fish
on all unsettled bays, harbors and
creeks shown ×××××

The French Shore rights were
extinguished in 1904

Belle
Isle

NEWFOUNDLAND

St. Johns

FRENCH SHORE

Whittle
Bank

St.

Grand
Bank

Green
Bank

Banks

St.
Pierre

100 fathoms

ATLANTIC

OCEAN

Anticosti I.

Statute Miles

100   50   0   100

Gaspé
Penin?

Orphan
Bank

Bradelle
Bank

Magdalen
Is.

PR. EDWARD
ISLAND

Charlottetown

C. Breton
Island

Sydney

Misaine
Bank

Artimon
Bank

Banquereau Bank

The Gully

Sable
Bank

NEW

BRUNSWICK

St. John

MAINE

NEW HAMPSHIRE

Gloucester
Boston

MASS.

C. Cod

Nantucket Is.

Pictou

NOVA

SCOTIA

Dartmouth

Halifax

Yarmouth

Roseway
Bank

La Have
Bank

100 fa.

Baccaro Bank

Browns
Bank

Georges
Bank

Middle
Ground

Canso
Bank

50 100 fa.

Hamilton Inlet
Bank

Labrador   Coast

100 fa

Belle Isle
St. of Belle Isle

Extension North on
the same scale

The Fishing Banks from Cape Cod to Labrador

resumed the mercantilistic contest which had been interrupted by the Embargo of 1807, and the Maritimes, although greatly strengthened by eight years of extraordinary good fortune, had to accept the consequences. In this matter the United States enjoyed such immense natural advantages in trade with the West Indies that Britain and her colonies ultimately had to bow to them. By a commercial convention of July, 1815, Great Britain and the United States had agreed upon reciprocity of tariffs between them, but regulation of colonial trade was another matter; indeed it speedily involved an outright contest for triangular freights between the British and the American navigation systems, each using much the same weapons of exclusion and counterexclusion. After a complicated battle of navigation laws, the struggle ended with British surrender in 1822. A statute of that year, by naming certain free ports in the West Indies and British North America to which provisions, timber, and naval stores could be carried in either American or British vessels, brought to an end British and colonial hopes that the American trade with the West Indies could be routed through the Maritimes for the benefit either of the British shipping interests or of the colonial merchants. In effect, the United States had fought her way successfully inside Great Britain's mercantile empire. Henceforth the Maritimes had to stomach the consequences of their disadvantages relative to the United States in the form of smaller returns for equal enterprise.

This blow, to be sure, was somewhat cushioned by the continuance of small colonial preferences in customs duties, but about the same time the Maritimes and the Canadas had to sustain still another shock, this time in the British market. British takings of colonial timber had risen spectacularly from 1803 to 1819, the annual average having climbed from half a million cubic feet to nine and a half million. Naturally, however, after 1815 the Baltic merchants in England tried every legitimate and illegitimate means to rebuild their formerly privileged trade. In the ensuing contest, the colonists were not without powerful British friends who had invested heavily in the new North American trade, and there was also a natural reluctance in governmental circles to have again to run the strategic risk of exclusive dependence on the Baltic. In addition, Britain's industrial revolution and the attendant growth of industrial towns were being reflected in what Malachy Postlethwayt once called "the spirit of house-building," so that immense supplies of cheap timber were in demand. The outcome of the competition between Baltic and North American timber, therefore, was that the European product was resorted to for "the more valuable description of buildings" and other choice uses. New duties which were established in 1821, while they lowered the colonial

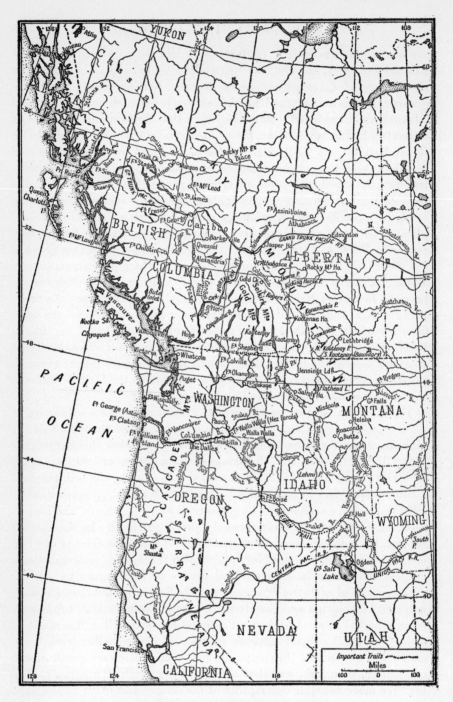

The Exploration of the Pacific Slope

preference perceptibly, still gave British North American timber a very substantial preference. Once the colonies had absorbed the shocks of depressed postwar prices and lowered preferences, they were able to go back to their old game of selling both their forests and the ships which carried the timbers across the Atlantic.

Meanwhile conflicts of every kind were again under way in the fur trade of the North American continent, conflicts which not only extended from New York, Montreal, and Boston to California, Oregon, and Alaska, but embraced London and far-off India and China as well.

It will be recalled that Montreal's monopoly of the fur trade of the interior had given ground south of the Great Lakes before the advance of American settlers, the expedition of Anthony Wayne, and the diplomacy of John Jay, but that during the War of 1812 the Canadian fur traders had made good their hold west of Lake Michigan by the capture of Michilimackinac, Fort Dearborn, and Prairie du Chien. Yet the peace makers of 1814 and the boundary makers of 1818 drew the international frontier from the northwestern point of the Lake of the Woods along the forty-ninth parallel to the Rocky Mountains. Unable to determine the sovereignty over the region from the Rockies to the Pacific between Spanish California at 42° and Russian Alaska at 54° 40′, Great Britain and the United States agreed in 1818 that this huge territory should be free and open to the nationals of both for a term of ten years.[2] What had been going on which could explain the projection of American and British interests from their Atlantic world all the way across the continent to the Pacific?

It had been the Russians who had drawn to the northern Pacific Coast Spaniards from Mexico, Canadians from Montreal and Hudson Bay, Americans from St. Louis, and maritime traders from India, China, New England, and Europe. Russian fur traders had cut a bloody path eastward across Asia until, held off by China, they swung northeast to discover America from the west in 1741. In the Bering Sea and along the coasts of the American continent, they found a rich treasury—the best of the fur seals and the most desirable fur-bearing animal yet found, the sea otter. The coveted products of their raids on this unexploited hoard soon began to excite questionings among British East India Company agents in China who happened on traces of them, and gradually the foreign scientists who had been gathered together at St. Petersburg satis-

2. The northern boundary of Spanish territory was determined by the Adams-Onís Treaty of 1819. The Russian boundary was uncertain until the treaties of 1824 and 1825, with the United States and Great Britain, respectively.

fied the curiosity of the outside world by recounting the discoveries of Bering and his companion, Chirikof.

Spain's fears and ambitions were naturally aroused first. Beginning her determined efforts from Mexico in 1769, she overcame the mountains and the sandy wastes at the head of the Gulf of California, and explored Lower and Upper California by sea and land as far as San Francisco until a network of trails, beaded with missions, claimed that section of the coast for Spain. Great Britain entrusted the satisfaction of her curiosity and interest to that king among navigators, Captain James Cook. On his way by the North Pacific to the Arctic Ocean in 1778, he paused at Nootka Sound on the outside of Vancouver Island, where members of his company picked up for trifles furs which proved of astonishing value when they later visited China. One of Cook's marines, an ebullient, dramatic youngster from Connecticut named John Ledyard, deserted as soon as he got back to American Atlantic shores again, hurriedly turned out a narrative of Cook's voyage, and devoted the brief, spectacular remainder of his life to unsuccessful attempts in the United States and Europe to win backing for what he was convinced must be a very profitable circular trade. Ships carrying manufactured goods from Europe or the United States would exchange them for Pacific Coast furs, and trade these in turn for Chinese and Indian products which they would carry back to their home ports. British or Canadian traders would be seriously hampered in such enterprises unless they could somehow evade the East India and South Sea Companies' monopolies, but Americans could have a free hand.

With extraordinary swiftness the East India Company's agents in India and China found their way across the Pacific. Attentive New England pioneers in the Far Eastern trade followed them, and Spain launched marine expeditions northward in order to establish the territorial claims which might hold back the Russians and keep out British and American interlopers. In 1789 a Spanish force seized some British vessels which it found trading at Nootka and sent the crews to prison in Mexico, but a prompt British threat of war extracted a convention in 1790 by which Spain made full restitution and admitted that California did not extend to the Northwest Coast.

Great Britain thereupon sent out Cook's former midshipman, George Vancouver, to settle property and boundary claims with Spain by a meeting at Nootka itself in 1792. This apt pupil of the great navigator made the first thorough survey of the coast, but he accidentally missed the mouth of the Columbia River on his way north for the first circumnavigation of the island that bears his name. On his return after the

Anglo-Spanish conference, he repaired his oversight and one of his officers explored far up the river, but did so without knowing that the American trader Robert Gray had had the good luck to establish a prior discovery for the United States during the interval. Vancouver carried on his excellent map-building in 1793 and 1794, and in the latter year Great Britain and Spain agreed to maintain free access to Nootka, to build no permanent establishments there, and to prevent any other nation from establishing dominion over the region. Thus, as late as 1794, the Pacific Coast from San Francisco to Alaska was still a debatable ground, where four governments very largely agreed to differ about boundaries, while their maritime merchants became princes or paupers, according to their skill at guessing or creating the tastes of the independent, capricious Indians who had furs to sell.

If Vancouver's men, who were charting the North Bentinck Arm at the mouths of the Dean and Bella Coola rivers in June, 1793, had been there some six weeks later, they would have met the man whose arrival from the interior was to give matters along the Pacific Coast a new direction for over fifty years. On a rock face of the Dean Channel he recorded with a thin paint of grease and vermilion the first successfully sustained attempt to cross the full breadth of the continent from Atlantic to Pacific: "Alexander Mackenzie from Canada, by land, the twenty-second of July, one thousand seven hundred and ninety three. Lat. 52° 20' 48"." The Northwest Passage had been made three centuries after the first European attempts at it and had had to be made by land.

Mackenzie was a Montreal Scot, the fruit of a generation of enterprise based upon old French-Canadian knowledge and skill, but led by the Anglo-Scottish-American adventurers who poured in after Amherst's armies in 1760. These men had fought their way through Pontiac's onslaughts, uncongenial law, credit difficulties, American competition, and savage, unscrupulous contests among themselves, at their base and in the field, to end by forming a succession of trading associations which operated powerfully throughout the middle and the far west. In the process, they were half-consciously drawn into two North American contests which went back a century to the days of Radisson and Groseilliers. Once more Montreal gambled an invincible spirit and highly specialized techniques against the natural advantages enjoyed by the traders who used the Mississippi and the Hudson Bay gateways to and from the mid-continent. If the long river tributaries which fed these outlets could be crossed and cut by superior skill and determination, the best and lightest furs could be carried across inferior transportation routes to pour wealth on the long island at the junction of the St. Lawrence and the Ottawa.

By miracles of a driving will which used to the limit improved Great Lakes shipping and the superior capacities of French-Canadian and half-breed *voyageurs* in canoes and York boats on the rivers, this effort was sustained in whole or in part, for almost two generations. The middle west north of the Ohio and the upper Mississippi Valley sent their best furs down the Lakes until after the War of 1812. In addition, Montrealers were the first white men to retrace La Vérendrye's trails from the Manitoba Basin to the upper Missouri, and from the late 1760's onward they swung northwest from Lake Superior in a successful effort to pick out the furs which they could best afford to handle from the packets which the Indians were carrying down the Saskatchewan and Churchill rivers to the rival posts on Hudson Bay.

Between 1780 and 1785 some of the Montrealers became mightily excited over the crossing, by their misanthropic associate, Peter Pond of Connecticut, from the sources of the Churchill to the headwaters of a vast river system leading north and west; for his reports of its character seemed to hold the promise that its outlet was on the North Pacific Coast, about whose richness in furs they had just been reading in the reports of Ledyard and Cook. In the summer of 1789, therefore, young Mackenzie, who had succeeded Pond as trader at Lake Athabaska, followed the great waterway now named for him to its end, only to be bitterly disappointed by finding himself on the Arctic Ocean. His successful plunge through to the Pacific four years later was achieved by a terrible journey up the Peace River into the Rockies and thence by canoe and by forest trails to salt water. Now Montreal believed that it could tap the wealth of the Pacific, at great costs in transportation overland, or by a risky infringement of old British monopolies when vessels were sent round the Horn. In the latter enterprise they soon found that the only profitable method was to make arrangements to operate through American affiliates.

During the next twenty-five years overland venturers toward the Pacific gradually supplanted the maritime traders who had preceded them. The sea otter was being exterminated, but the sources of wealth afforded by desirable land animals seemed inexhaustible. Simon Fraser built up a fur trade in the heart of the northern Rockies upon Mackenzie's foundations, and in the summer of 1808 he made the perilous descent of the Fraser River to the sea, only to realize sorrowfully that it was not the Columbia. President Jefferson, recalling the bright dreams which Ledyard had so insistently sketched for him in Paris, decided that there might well be more in the Louisiana Purchase than free navigation of the Mississippi. In 1804 he sent out at public expense a substantial expedition under Lewis and Clark in order to see whether a way could not be found to link the vaguely known Missouri with the Columbia. They followed the prevailing fashion by employing French *voyageurs*, and along the lower Missouri they not only fished for information from the Montrealers whom they met, but in one of them, Charbonneau—or, better, in his Shoshone wife—they found their guide to the passage of the mountains. In 1805 Clark, like Mackenzie twelve years before, was able to inscribe on the shores of salt water the record of his successful crossing of the continent. Meanwhile the best geographer of them all, David Thompson, once a Hudson's Bay man, but now employed by the great Montreal consolidation of 1804 which was known as the North West Company, was slowly piecing together his magnificent maps of the capricious waterways and scrambled mountains between the forks of the Saskatchewan and his coveted destination at the mouth of the Columbia. Less famous agents of the aroused Hudson's Bay Company were, at the same time, matching wits and enterprise with the Montrealers in the same regions and collecting, for their own purposes first and for Mr. Arrowsmith's famous maps later, the knowledge which they needed in order to carry on the fight.

It was the world-girdling imagination of John Jacob Astor, a German immigrant to New York, which wove the oceanic and continental elements of the North American fur trade into an imperial design which, if successful, would have made him master both of the world's trade in furs and of the lucrative commerce which could be grafted upon every branch of it. Astor's nose for money had led him into the fur trade within a year or so of his arrival at New York in 1783. By 1787 he was reaching out from a depleted New York State to "the big money" in Montreal, where he built a warehouse and became a substantial buyer.[3] Until Jay's Treaty legalized free trade, he was supposed to import his Canadian furs *via* London, but he was notorious for his corruption of officialdom, and furs had, in fact, been smuggled from the St. Lawrence to the Hudson for a century or more. Astor's Montreal base exemplified both the retreat of the Lower Lakes fur trade before the advance of American settlements and the firm grip in which Montreal held the trade farther west. In 1799 Astor tried to break into the Missouri trade based upon Franco-Spanish St. Louis, but was repulsed by the merchants who dominated it. He did, however, get footholds at Detroit and in the Ohio country and became the principal middleman for the Canadian traders at Michilimackinac about 1807.

Meanwhile his world design was rapidly taking shape. During the last

3 Part of Astor's Montreal establishment still stands there.

decade of the eighteenth century his general merchandising in New York had become large and varied. In April, 1800, he sent his first consignment of furs to the great Canton market in China. By 1805 the Louisiana Purchase and the Lewis and Clark expedition had filled the last great gaps in his projected commercial empire; and in April, 1808, New York State chartered the engine of his ambitions, the American Fur Company.

Astor's plans were breath-taking in their scope and complexity, and yet most of the capital they represented and most of the profits they promised were his own. He even managed to evade the American embargoes after 1807 by means of a mixture of audacity, bribery, and official favoritism. He next proceeded to buy or squeeze out his Montreal associates from control of the Michilimackinac Company, setting up in its place, in January, 1811, the South West Fur Company in which he held a majority interest. He had already, in June, 1810, established the Pacific Fur Company, a subsidiary of his American Fur Company. In the autumn of 1810 he launched a mixed company of Montreal and Illinois *voyageurs* from Michilimackinac across the continent by way of St. Louis, in order to improve upon the Lewis and Clark routes to the mouth of the Columbia; and at the same time, from New York he sent round the Horn in the *Tonquin* a shipload of Canadian experts to the same destination.

In spite of the presence of experienced Nor' Westers, both expeditions were badly handled and were sadly diminished by death and disaster. The *Tonquin* expedition managed with difficulty to found Astoria in the spring of 1811, but not long before their ship captain's ineptitude led to the massacre of two-thirds of them by the Indians of the coast of Vancouver Island. That summer, also, David Thompson of the North West Company arrived at the mouth of the Columbia after his painstaking explorations of its complete course, the forerunner of stern competition from Montreal. Early in 1812, however, Astor's straggling overlanders and the *Beaver*, his supply ship from New York, set Astoria on its feet again. Astor had succeeded in cutting across the headwaters of the flows of furs which his Montreal and St. Louis rivals were hoping to drain. Meanwhile, after two years of negotiation, he had also secured a provisional agreement with the Russians of Alaska by which the North West Company and the Hudson's Bay Company would be excluded and the Pacific Fur Company have the exclusive right to supply the Russian trading community and conduct their provision trade with Spanish California.

The full circle seemed to have been completed. Astor would assemble at New York manufactured goods from Europe, and other trade goods, like tobacco and rum, from the Americas. These, when carried into the interior, would bring furs to his agents at Michilimackinac, Detroit, Montreal, St. Louis, and New Orleans. When sent to the Pacific by sea, they would secure furs from the Indians and the Russians which would be carried by way of the Pacific islands to Canton and there exchanged for eastern goods like tea and silk for distribution in North American or any other markets. This continuous commerce, draining the larger part of the unexhausted fur regions of North America, would endow Astor with the power almost to dictate his own terms to the Hudson's Bay Company, the North West Company, and the stubborn French traders of St. Louis in the fur markets of the world.

Then came the War of 1812 and the incisive thrusts of the Canadian fur traders which shattered the structure which Astor had created at Montreal, on the Great Lakes, in the mid-continent, and on the Pacific. Through his influence at Quebec and Washington, he did manage to get his furs away from Michilimackinac at the expense of forewarning the British authorities, and he continued to share in the profits of the South West Fur Company, but everything else went to smash. News of war reached Astoria in January, 1813, and the Astorians decided to give up if no American aid came.[4] Instead of aid, the rival Nor' Westers arrived in force in April and had persuaded the Astorians to sell out by October. Next month a British naval vessel underlined the decision. In 1814 Astor's Pacific Fur Company wound up its affairs.

After the war, thwarted by superior Canadian competence in the overland trade, Astor drew in his horns, but he wielded great influence in excluding Canadian fur traders from the United States so that he might monopolize the region south of the boundary. Already a favorite of Jefferson, he had also maneuvered Presidents Madison and Monroe and Governor Cass of Michigan into the sort of dependence on him which made them most considerate of his wishes. An American statute of April 29, 1816, forbade the activities of Canadian fur traders within American territory. This meant that Astor could take over the Canadian share of the South West Fur Company. He still had to depend on Canadian field agents, but official complaisance enabled him to circumvent the law. He also succeeded in both smashing the competitive governmental system of trading posts by 1822 and in dominating his American rivals at St. Louis and Green Bay about the same time, thereby assuring his quasi monopoly of the trade of the American west as far as the Rockies. In brief, Astor became almost the monopolist of the fur trade of the United

4. The mission which they sent overland to report to Astor discovered the famous South Pass.

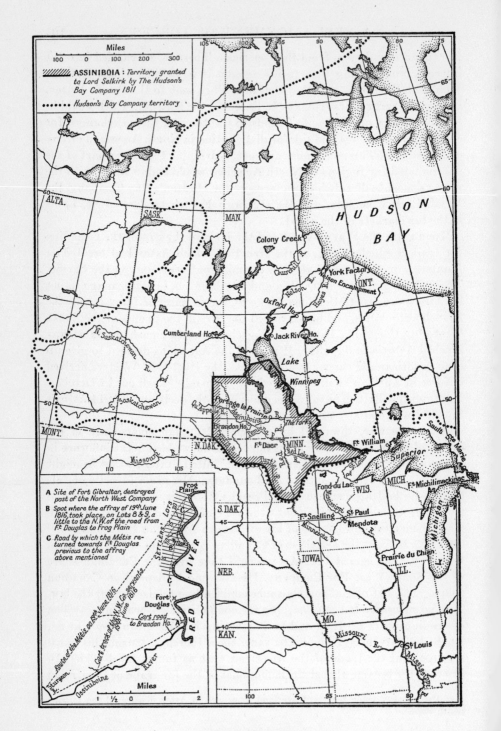

The Selkirk Grant

States and, if the Hudson's Bay Company and the North West Company had escaped his clutches, they had to face his ruthless competition in the world's markets. Far off in Canton, the East India Company's agents and other foreign merchants had to admit that John Jacob Astor almost ruled the roost. By and large, the American seaboard had failed to extend its commercial empire overland to the Pacific, but had succeeded by sea, whereas Canada, unable as yet to combine with Nova Scotia in an efficient sea-borne commerce to such distant regions, did possess the technical skill and experience which were needed for transcontinental trade.

During Astor's postwar rehabilitation, a number of occurrences gave new contours to the contests in the interior and the far west. One of the most interesting and significant of these was the Agreement made in 1817 by Richard Rush, in behalf of the United States, and Charles Bagot, in behalf of Great Britain, for naval disarmament on the Great Lakes. By it the two nations quietly eliminated what might well have been an interminable competition in shipbuilding for quite disproportionate stakes. Strictly speaking, this disarmament never extended completely to land fortifications as well, but the Agreement gradually acquired a symbolic value and the so-called "undefended frontier" between Canada and the United States became an object of pride and satisfaction to both peoples. Another expedient which was arrived at during these years was the agreement of 1818 for the joint occupation of Oregon which was a direct reflection of Astor's failure to make good by occupation Robert Gray's discovery of the Columbia River. The overland traders from Montreal were so obviously the effective occupiers of the great empty region between California and Alaska that some Anglo-American compromise had to be reached.

Meanwhile, within British North America, Montreal had to fight it out with Hudson Bay for the furs of the northern half of the continent, and in this contest the convictions of Radisson and Groseilliers were finally substantiated, for it proved to be more efficient to trade with the deep interior by means of the northern oceanic entry than by the St. Lawrence, the Great Lakes, and the river systems beyond. Thanks to the philanthropy of a Scottish noble, the Earl of Selkirk, the Hudson's Bay Company was able to drive this lesson home from 1811 onward by settling successive groups of Scottish crofters and Swiss mercenaries on the good lands along the Red River south of Lake Winnipeg. These luckless folk, planted at the crossroads of the continent, were to create a base for food supplies and to assert the Company's charter rights over the whole Basin whose waters drained into the Bay.[5] Inevitably there were bloody clashes with the Nor' Westers which culminated in a savage massacre at Seven Oaks in June, 1816; for the Montrealers, bent upon erasing the colony whose continued existence threatened their own operations, egged on the half-breeds of the region.

Yet Selkirk persisted, and before he died in 1820 he had the satisfaction of having firmly planted the Red River settlement. Moreover his and the Hudson's Bay Company's hazardous determination had stimulated the Montrealers to efforts which had exhausted them. In 1821, therefore, the two companies merged as the Hudson's Bay Company just in time for both to escape bankruptcy. Thereafter, while that organizing genius, George Simpson, set about bringing the whole British fur area under single, businesslike control, based upon the Arctic entry, Montreal relinquished her hold. The once boisterous forts along the waterways between the St. Lawrence and the Red River fell strangely silent and their factors wrote pathetic letters to old comrades in the livelier north and west telling of their boredom and of its occasional petty reliefs.

On the whole, the outlook for Montreal and the Canadas was somewhat grim after 1820. Thanks to British puzzlement or indifference concerning inland colonies which could not be fitted into a maritime mercantile empire in orthodox ways, the Canadians could be and were to a large extent the architects of their own fortunes. They adjusted themselves to postwar depression and to the lowered timber preferences in the British market and they worked out ways by which they might share modestly in maritime trading which embraced the fisheries of the Gulf and Atlantic, the entrepôts of the Maritimes, the West Indies, and Great Britain. But after the severance of the far western fur trade, their hopes for the future began to center once more on the possibility that most of the commerce of both sides of the increasingly populous and productive Great Lakes Basin, and perhaps even of the upper Mississippi Valley as well, could be grafted upon the St. Lawrence entry for the benefit of the capitalists and merchants of Montreal.

Herein lies much that explains a most complicated interplay among the commercial policies of Great Britain, the United States, Lower Canada, and Upper Canada which went on from Jay's Treaty to the failure in 1822 of an attempt to unite the Canadas under one political, and therefore economic, control. Disregarding what were, on the whole, the subsidiary actions of the British and American governments, this

5. Their lands were situated in the midst of a much-used hunting ground for the buffalo, whose dried flesh and fat in the pemmican bags alone made possible the immense range of the fur traders in the northwest.

interplay was basically the continuance of the two-hundred-year-old contest between the St. Lawrence and the Hudson. In spite of Montreal's daring, in the last analysis New York held the stronger hand. For a few years after Jay's Treaty, Canada sold large quantities of British and West Indian goods in the Lakes district because transportation costs from Montreal to Kingston were about one-third of those from Albany to Oswego. In 1801, however, Congress yielded to mercantile pressure and set up tariffs and ad valorem regulations on the interior trade which discouraged the indirect entry of such goods. The Canadas made another ingenious bid after the War of 1812 in order to maintain something like the proportions of the flow of American products which had been stimulated in the days of the Embargo and not wholly checked by the war itself. In effect they reciprocated the American rebuff to the import of British and West Indian manufactured or processed goods by way of the Canadas, but they conceded free entry to the American natural products with which they hoped to swell the commerce of the St. Lawrence. After some misgivings the British government acquiesced.

Already, however, the writing on the wall for the future had become legible. Possessed of the ocean fiord which reached into the interior as far as Albany, energetic New Yorkers were almost ready to nourish their metropolis by cutting canals through the low heights of land between the Hudson and the St. Lawrence, Lake Ontario, and Lake Erie. These artificial waterways would be no more hampered by winter ice than the St. Lawrence and, while they could not carry great ships, they could carry many cheap barges; and horse power, if slow, was abundant and could provide continuous, direct passage. Montreal was about to face another challenge to its will and to its capacity to make the most of a perceptibly inferior position.

Speaking generally, the Anglo-American partition of Europe's former empires in the east, center, and west of North America had been practically determined by 1821. Spain in the southwest and Russia in the northwest had still to be ousted, but the outlines of the future United States and Dominion of Canada were in the main forecast. Fishing, fur trading, and forest operations, along with their tributary agriculture and commerce, provided sustenance and some substantial surpluses for small clusters of population in the Maritimes and the Canadas as well as a *raison d'être* for the activities of white men, half-breeds, and Indians in more than half the continent. Territorially, compared with the future Canada, the United States grew more slowly, but the rich and varied natural resources of its lands, in the old regions and in the new, made it grow solidly in thickly populated, contiguous communities instead of sketchily in scattered ones. As time went on, its massive bulk extended menacingly alongside the British provinces, yet did not engulf them.

Some of the reasons for this abstention have already been considered, most notably of all the character of the War of 1812 and the weakness of Spain, and their domestic repercussions by way of schisms in the United States. But in this matter, as in so many others during the ensuing years, probably the underlying reason for Canada's salvation lay in the improved relations between Great Britain and the United States. If British North America was vulnerable to land attack, the American seaboard was vulnerable to the British navy. Gradually purely economic considerations triumphed over the ancient politico-economic orthodoxies which were the support of British sea power. The United States had forced its reëntry into the British mercantile empire on almost equal terms. An industrialized Great Britain was on the brink of an entirely new kind of economic nationalism which should be keyed to commercial reciprocities and free trade. This must be achieved by a gradual process, but it would revolutionize Britain's relations, not only with her colonies, but with the United States.

Perhaps, therefore, the real reasons for the termination of the great trial of strength between Britons and their American offspring, and the foundation of the basic understanding between them which has survived a century and a quarter of exacting strains, are to be found in the Anglo-American collaboration which produced the Monroe Doctrine of 1823. It is true that the Doctrine fell out of sight for many years and that for about a generation after 1815 Americans turned their backs on Europe during an intoxicating obsession with their own sense of nationality and with the expansion of their territory at the expense of Spain. Yet a very real kind of reliance upon the Anglo-American understanding which was reached in the face of the independence movement in Spanish America persisted throughout these years, and during them the United States did little more than occasionally twist the British lion's tail by means of aggressive moves in the direction of British North America.

At bottom, in 1823, Great Britain and the United States found themselves in agreement, both against the Holy Alliance and Metternichian legitimism, and in defense of the Spanish-American colonies which had proclaimed their independence during and after the Napoleonic wars. Their motives may have been mixed and rather highly colored by hopes of commercial advantage for both, of security for British investments, and of territorial advantage for the United States, but the ruling circumstance was their agreement against the reactionary European powers. Great Britain had a navy which could bar the seas, and the United

States was rapidly transmuting her original foreign policy of neutrality into the equally congenial and self-defensive principle of denying the right of European powers to intervene in the affairs of the Americas. George Canning, John Quincy Adams, and President Monroe effected the marriage of the two national interests during the autumn of 1823; but, once sure that the British navy would put real teeth into an otherwise rather empty assertion, Adams and Monroe proceeded to a unilateral declaration on the part of the United States.

In his annual Message to Congress on December 2, 1823, Monroe warned the world that the Americas "are henceforth not to be considered as subjects for future colonization by any European powers"; that the United States "should consider any attempt on their part to extend their system to any portion of this hemisphere as dangerous to our peace and safety"; and that, while the United States would not interfere "with the existing colonies or dependencies of any European power," yet "with the Governments who have declared their independence . . . we could not view any interposition for the purpose of oppressing them, or controlling in any other manner their destiny, by any European power in any other light than as the manifestation of an unfriendly disposition toward the United States."

Actually Canning had, single-handed, compelled France to disclaim any intention of intervention in Spanish America two months before Monroe's enunciation of his Doctrine, a fact which Canning rapidly advertised to the world once the Message to Congress became known. Metternich helplessly denounced Monroe's "indecent declarations," and Russia quickly withdrew her Alaskan boundary claims from 51° to the later-to-be-famous line at 54° 40′. The Latin American republics wasted no gratitude on President Monroe, for they recognized that their real bulwark had been the British fleet, and Great Britain retained her moral, commercial, and financial leadership in Spain's former empire. There was substance in Canning's boast of December 12, 1826: "I resolved that, if France had Spain, it should not be Spain with the Indies. I called the New World into existence to redress the balance of the Old."

While Adams and Monroe had been concerting their policies during the fall of 1823, the President had sought and secured the approval of his predecessors, Jefferson and Madison. From Monticello, on October 14, 1823, the eighty-year-old Jefferson dealt with the proposed Anglo-American policy in a letter to Monroe which aptly revealed the evolution of his own outlook and of the relations between the United States and Great Britain since he had penned the Declaration of Independence almost half a century before. In it he said:

The question presented by the letters you have sent me, is the most momentous which has ever been offered to my contemplation since that of Independence. That made us a nation, this sets our compass and points the course which we are to steer through the ocean of time opening on us. And never could we embark on it under circumstances more auspicious. Our first and fundamental maxim should be, never to entangle ourselves in the broils of Europe. Our second, never to suffer Europe to intermeddle with cis-Atlantic affairs. America, North and South, has a set of interests distinct from those of Europe, and peculiarly her own. . . . One nation, most of all, could disturb us in this pursuit; she now offers to lead, aid and accompany us in it. By acceding to her proposition, we detach her from the bands, bring her mighty weight into the scale of free government, and emancipate a continent at one stroke, which might otherwise linger long in doubt and difficulty. Great Britain is the nation which can do us the most harm of any one, or all on earth; and with her on our side we need not fear the whole world. With her then, we should most sedulously cherish a cordial friendship; and nothing would tend more to knit our affections than to be fighting once more, side by side, in the same cause. Not that I would purchase even her amity at the price of taking part in her wars. But the war in which the present proposition might engage us, should that be its consequence, is not her war, but ours. Its object is to introduce and establish the American system, of keeping out of our land all foreign powers, of never permitting those of Europe to intermeddle with the affairs of our nations. . . . But I am clearly of Mr. Canning's opinion, that it will prevent instead of provoking war . . . all Europe combined would not undertake such a war. For how would they propose to get at either enemy without superior fleets? Nor is the occasion to be slighted which this proposition offers, of declaring our protest against the atrocious violations of the rights of nations, by the interference of any one in the internal affairs of another, so flagitiously begun by Bonaparte, and now continued by the equally lawless Alliance, calling itself Holy.

This wise old man almost seems to have foreseen what was going to happen a century later.

CHAPTER VII

SEA, FORESTS, WATERWAYS
(1815–1850)

IT often seems to be a far cry from high policy to everyday life. Certainly it is a difficult gap to bridge; so much so that historians are almost forced to confine themselves to what they think have been the dominant forces during the periods with which they choose to deal. Between 1815 and 1850 Great Britain and North America were bound together by immense compulsions of many sorts, in politics pure and simple, both external and domestic; in the economic interplay which at the same time served and dictated national ends; and in the to-and-fro movement of people and ideas which has been a continuous process in the English-speaking world.[1] While these great determinants cannot be ignored, yet the homely activities of ordinary men and women also deserve their record. Their names, when known, are easily forgotten, but the work which they did laid the foundations for the societies of their descendants. In this and the succeeding chapter, therefore, we shall diverge from high politics to the broad patterns, the folkways, of North Americans during the first half of the nineteenth century.

During that period much of what happened in Great Britain was almost as important in the lives of North Americans as what happened at home. In particular, as has been seen, the United States found it to her own interest and within her powers to stimulate and accelerate the transition in Great Britain from protectionism to free trade which was being nurtured in any case by the mother country's commanding lead in industrialization. During the same process the less sturdy British North American colonies found themselves somewhat hard put to it to adjust their policies to the fluctuations which ensued. Again, Great Britain and the United States found themselves in a kind of basic, if competitive, agreement over the break-up of the Spanish Empire in the Americas—North, Central, and South. There were also very obvious mutual advantages for Britons and North Americans in the outpouring of British investment funds. The New World soaked up this flow of capital like

1. This is perhaps a convenient occasion to recall some measurements of migration whose widespread significance seems often to be neglected. Between 1815 and 1940 approximately twenty-eight million persons emigrated from the British Isles to join other English-speaking societies. Of these about 58 per cent went to the United States, about 18 per cent to Canada, about 10.5 per cent to Australasia, about 6 per cent to South Africa, and about 7 per cent to all other regions.

blotting paper, for that was its oldest economic habit, but no one could foresee what it might mean in terms of future relationships.

Britain's eighteenth-century inclinations toward freer trade had been merely driven underground during the reactionary period of the French Revolution and the Napoleonic wars. For a few years after 1815 the urgent problem of public revenue seemed to prohibit the abandonment of receipts from the customs duties, but during the 'twenties "nuisance" obstacles to the movement of commodities into the British Isles began to be pruned away. As the national economy gained in strength, one foreign raw or semimanufactured material after another rapidly found its pathway cleared toward its consumers. When once Britons had been persuaded that the war-time device of an income tax could be an acceptable companion to excises in order to provide the fiscal sinews for the peace-time body politic, the completion of free trade was assured. British agriculture put up the sternest battle against competition from the grains of eastern Europe and North America, but finally potato blight in Ireland produced a famine in the face of which corn laws could not be maintained. With their repeal and the "virtual" accomplishment of free trade in 1846, the old navigation laws seemed quite anomalous, and in 1849 British waters were opened to the rest of the world.

Meanwhile Great Britain had been exporting capital both to North America and to the republics which rose in Latin America. Some of this capital accompanied the hundreds of thousands of emigrants who left the British Isles. Some went in the form of British textile and other machinery for which New England in particular ardently connived. Other large sums went to build harbor facilities and warehouses in undeveloped regions, or were lost in such harebrained schemes as the export of dairy machinery (and Scottish dairymaids) to the South American pampas in order to salvage the milk of the great herds of cattle there and to convert the Gauchos to the use of butter.

The largest proportion, however, went into the purchase of securities already floated in the expanding United States. State, municipal, and canal bonds and stocks helped to pay for imported British goods. The repudiation of millions of dollars' worth of these securities by public and private authorities after the American crash of 1837 tempered British receptiveness a little and made investors look with greater favor on more dependable regions, such as British North America. Nevertheless the whole Canadian-American Region had to pay in goods and service for its borrowings just at the time when the British Isles dropped their barriers to such enterprise.

During this period the intricate economic interrelationships among Great Britain, the West Indies, the United States, and the Maritimes gradually settled down after the convulsions through which they went between 1775 and 1822. The Maritimes had become substantial communities which were engaged in export trades which were only a little less remunerative than those of wealthier, more highly organized New England. By 1830, when Great Britain allowed American ships to supply the British Isles as well as the colonies directly, the Maritimes were capable of taking advantage of the privileges which were extended to them at the same time. They were not only permitted to trade directly with foreign countries, but also to warehouse foreign goods in their own "free ports" without paying duties. Thus Nova Scotia, in particular, was equipped and ready to sail the world's oceans at the moment when the British sugar colonies entered upon their most abrupt decline. The islands' soils were becoming exhausted, the institution of slavery was abolished in 1833,[2] and in cotton and sugar culture they were being outdone by the United States, East India, the French West Indies, and Brazil.

All in all, however, Nova Scotia had arrived late on the stage of world trade and was never able to rear a commercial empire like New England's. Her achievement between 1800 and 1850 was substantial, and Bluenose skippers sailed the world's seas by hundreds, making their presence felt in all its harbor marts; but even with some aid from Great Britain, Nova Scotians could not surpass the advantages enjoyed by New England and the other Atlantic States, particularly in their association with the rest of the rapidly expanding American Union. Probably as good a summary as any would be to say that Nova Scotia became to Newfoundland and to some foreign markets what New England had once been, and that for two generations she skilfully conducted a world trade quite remarkable in its dimensions.[3]

Although the Maritime Provinces and New England were economic rivals and belonged to competing political systems, they nevertheless formed, together, an almost homogeneously prosperous area because their peoples, bred from the same stocks, could turn their talents and energies to almost anything. They farmed and cut firewood; they shaped the frames and sawed the lumber for ships and assembled them; they made up cargoes of fish, potatoes, oak staves, and livestock which they had prepared for market; and in off-seasons they sailed away to Boston,

2. The slave trade had been abolished in 1807.

3. In 1850 the combined tonnage of the Maritime Provinces stood fourth in magnitude in the register of the world's ocean shipping.

or the West Indies, or much farther afield, where they readily turned merchant in disposing of one cargo and acquiring another.

Posterity remembers them as masterly shipbuilders. Along the Atlantic Coast from Montreal to New York the most ingenious marine architects that the world had known wrought competitively on all kinds of vessels from homely dories to majestic clipper ships, bent on reaching the pinnacles of perfection for each particular service which man's needs demanded. Never was an enterprise more truly international. The form of small rowboat known as the dory, which could weather Atlantic swells when properly handled, was the end product of the accumulated wisdom and craft of European fishermen from Portugal, Spain, France, and the British Isles, and of shore fishermen from Newfoundland, Gaspé, Cape Breton, and the coasts of Nova Scotia and New England. Massachusetts bred the schooner from the two-masted ketch of the seventeenth century. In its structure the men of New England gradually proved that mastery of the oceans need not depend upon the round, bluff vessels of the type in which Europeans had ventured forth on the oceans in the fifteenth century. Not only did they lengthen out their ships in proportion to their beam, but they showed that the slimmer vessel, with a proper keel, could carry what seemed dangerously large areas of canvas without being unseaworthy, and in this way safely attain ever-increasing speeds.

The process culminated in the brief glory of the Yankee clippers—that period of fifteen or twenty years at the middle of the century when those towering ships raced across the oceans in the tea trade, to and from the Australian and Californian gold fields, and across the Atlantic. Day's runs of over four hundred nautical miles, Boston to Liverpool in less than thirteen days, Liverpool to Melbourne in sixty-three, New York to San Francisco in eighty-nine—these were the records that drew thousands of admiring spectators to the whole world's ports whenever a new clipper came in. They also nurtured in Asiatic, European, and American shipping centers a unique international school of art, that of the marine painters who limned the stately clippers so minutely that their proud skippers could not discover a piece of important gear that was not in its proper place. The ships have passed away, but they are commemorated in thousands of these naïve evidences of their owners' pride.

Yet the clippers were Yankee only by a generous extension of the term, for the lore of every Atlantic port went into their creation. Montreal was building ships for the China trade early in the nineteenth century, and as long as the wooden ship was to the fore Quebec had a school of masterly shipwrights. The great concentration of skill and production, however, began east and south from Gaspé and rose in an intermittent crescendo all along the indented Atlantic Coast to its climaxes at Boston and New York. The attention of the whole maritime world was focused for a few years on a short stretch of the North American Atlantic Coast. Matthew Maury, the great oceanographer of the day, was a Virginian; Simon Newcomb, the mariners' mathematician and astronomer, was a Nova Scotian; and it was somehow fitting that Donald McKay, the genius of clipper-building, the man who outdistanced his competitors and his own past achievements with each new ship, was born and reared in Nova Scotia, learned his craft in New York, practiced it in Maine, and raised it to its pinnacle in those yards at East Boston which were Mecca to the devotees and servants of the wooden ship.

The Atlantic region was also North America's nursery of lumbermen. From the days of its discoverers, Europeans, faced by depleted forests at home and often precariously dependent on the output of the easily closed Baltic, had been unable to contain their enthusiasm over the magnificent straight trees which clothed the eastern slopes of North America. Their keenest appetite was for masts and spars, but the colonists soon learned how to supplement this supply with squared timber and sawn boards. In Maine and New Brunswick, particularly, where long river systems carried the loggers and their harvest to and from the otherwise inaccessible interior, profitable exploitation was developed a stage farther. These regions built special ships for the lumber trade, often ill-seasoned and crudely thrown together, but successfully designed to be sold along with their cargoes at foreign ports.

The forest industries have always been subject at best to violent fluctuations, but the Maine–New Brunswick area during the first half of the nineteenth century exceeded the characteristic ups and downs. The vicissitudes during the Napoleonic wars and the modified preferential system for the colonies in the British market which followed them have already been noticed. During the 'twenties and 'thirties there were alternate boom and depression in New Brunswick. Lumbermen moved to and fro across the ill-defined international boundary in accordance with the degree of profit which colonial timber could earn in the British market, for the more diversified economy of the United States provided a broader shelter during adverse times, whereas recovery in the British market revived New Brunswick before it affected Maine. The more substantial New Brunswick producers, of course, always hung on for better times, but even they received a shocking blow in the 'forties when Great Britain adopted free trade.

During these years one international conflict among the lumbermen of the region was settled in a fashion which was to have very serious conse-

quences for the future Dominion of Canada. Had it occurred within the
United States or within British North America it would have been quickly
forgotten along with scores of other lumbermen's "wars," but the Aroostook "War" of 1839 necessitated the determination of an important international boundary.

The roots of the conflict went far back into the seventeenth century.
The principal determinant of the settlement was the skill of Massachu-

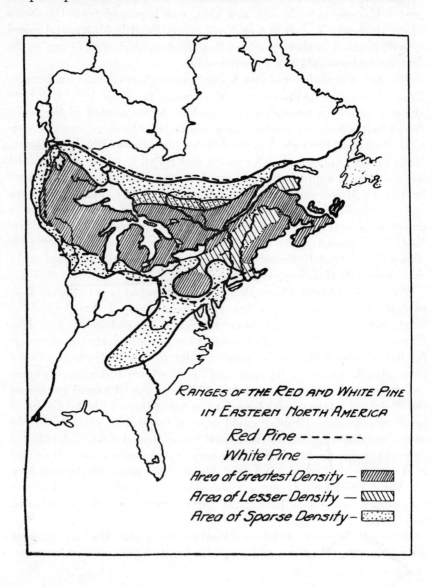

RANGES OF THE RED AND WHITE PINE
IN EASTERN NORTH AMERICA

Red Pine - - - - - -
White Pine ————
Area of Greatest Density — ▨
Area of Lesser Density — ▨
Area of Sparse Density - ▨

setts (of which the "District of Maine" was then a part) in securing the
St. Croix River instead of the Penobscot or the Kennebec as the boundary
between herself and Nova Scotia (of which New Brunswick was then a
part) in 1763. At that time no one knew the interior, and half-a-dozen
attempts to agree on its division had failed by 1839, when the lumbermen
on the forest frontiers of Maine (a State since 1820) and New Brunswick
(a Province since 1784) clashed so violently that troops had to be sent
to the scene. The trouble had arisen in the valleys of the St. John and the
Aroostook, both of which rose in Maine and flowed to the sea through
New Brunswick. Daniel Webster and Lord Ashburton skilfully com-
promised the matter in 1842, evoking choruses of woe from both Maine
and New Brunswick, but it seems highly unlikely that any of the parties
foresaw the principal consequences, for the locomotive whistle had not
yet been heard in the forested interior. A glance at the map, however,
will show that the northward projection of Maine has made an all-Canadian railway from Montreal to the Atlantic Coast a most uneconomically
roundabout affair. At the time, however, Great Britain was well satisfied
by a boundary settlement which created a territorial buffer for the only
practicable overland military road between the St. John Valley and
Quebec.

From the reminiscences of later "lumber barons" of the upper Great
Lakes region, many of whom got their start in New Brunswick or Maine,
it is apparent that exhaustion of the pine forests in the Atlantic region
set in motion some of the most picturesque and persistent of the North
American migrations. The army of loggers, whether "Pay Ays" (Prince
Edward Islanders), "Bluenoses" (Nova Scotians), "State of Mainers,"
began to disperse. Their first jump was to the forests of New York
and Pennsylvania, where they merged quickly with "Yorkers," "Pennsylvania Dutch," and "Canucks." But here, too, they rapidly exhausted
the forests and condemned themselves to further wanderings.

Speak of the lumberman to the average North American and he thinks
of New England or the Great Lakes region. The epic hero of "letting
daylight into the swamp," as the loggers called their harvest of the pine,
was Paul Bunyan, the Rabelaisian giant whom "single men in barracks"
built up around a French-Canadian prototype. Yet these conventional
views overlook the fact that the most important central hives, from
which the swarms of lumberjacks went forth in all directions on the continent, were in the uplands of northern and western New York and Pennsylvania. During the middle decades of the nineteenth century those
states led the whole Union in lumber production. Williamsport, the Saw-
dust City, on the west branch of the Susquehanna in Pennsylvania, still

shows traces of the miles of sawmills which gave it primacy for almost forty years. The very place names of northern Pennsylvania and New York commemorate the vanished forests—witness Whitepine and Cedar Run in one state and Forestport and Felts Mills in the other.

The loggers who moved north from the New York–Pennsylvania boundaries broke into two new forest empires, the one tributary to the Mohawk or to Lake Ontario, the other the massif of the Adirondacks, from which many streams flowed in all directions into the Mohawk, the Hudson, the Champlain and St. Lawrence valleys, and Lake Ontario. The Adirondack region was so large that it kept some lumbermen busy for many years, but others passed on to Lake Ontario and the St. Lawrence where they merged with their kind who had entered the upper St. Lawrence from northern New England and from the lower river, bent upon supplying overseas, rather than North American, demands. The most tempting immediate objective was the Ottawa Valley, for it was almost 700 miles long and its enormous basin (some 60,000 square miles) was solid with trees and drained by many rivers. In fact the Ottawa and its tributaries have perhaps constituted the most enduring pinery in eastern North America. There French, British, and American North Americans mingled in the shanties and reflected their robust, but pitiable, history "of alternate toil and indolence, hardship and debauch," in a very few, very bad, ballads like "The Jam on Garry's Rocks," or in the endless saga of Paul Bunyan and his blue ox, Babe.

Just above the city of Ottawa the town of Wrightville commemorates Philemon Wright of Massachusetts who spied out a township for himself in the Ottawa empire in 1799 by climbing "to the top of one hundred or more trees to view the situation of the country." When he went home with his news, he said, "I was enabled to obtain and hire as many men as I wanted, in order to commence the new settlement." The men of Massachusetts built a gristmill, a sawmill, a hempmill, and a tannery, for they had the full power of the Champlain Rapids and Chaudière Falls at their disposal, but they set the tune for the whole valley when, some years later, they ran the first raft of squared timber down the river. In its pioneers and in its emigrants who worked in the forests elsewhere, the Ottawa provided a great example of how the lumbermen ignored nationality when the pine forests beckoned them on.

But no single region could at any one time satisfy the demands. The loggers swept over the eastern forest regions like the waters of a flood. Between the Ottawa and the Great Lakes lay the triangle of what is now southern Ontario. Here the stands of pine were not as closely ranked as those which were later found like a deep-piled carpet above the sandy

Michigan Peninsula, but they contained many of the largest recorded white pine cut in North America, some of them measuring 250 feet in height and six feet in diameter. From about 1790 onward, therefore, the double-bladed axes laid down the forests in swathes, as the loggers moved west and south from the junction of the Ottawa and the St. Lawrence.

South of the Lakes the tributary regions of New York, Pennsylvania, and Ohio were far more quickly stripped, so that the American wing of the forest invaders in the Lakes region was biting into the southern margin of the Michigan Peninsula and its lake-shore fringes before the Canadian wing had completed its march to the shores of Lake Huron and Georgian Bay. In effect the decade of 1850–1860 is a convenient date to mark the transit of the white-pine empire from the lower to the upper Great Lakes. It had taken a little over half a century to skim the cream of the white-pine and red-pine forests in a broad crescent from Gaspé and Nova Scotia to Detroit, surely one of the most astounding harvests of nature's bounty in man's history.

Our own generation in North America, which builds with steel and concrete and brick, has pretty well forgotten the social prestige which was conferred by a brick or stone house a century or so ago. While this was not the case in French Lower Canada, where stone had long been characteristic, and while in a considerable part of Upper Canada there was a strong tendency to make the transition from the pioneer's buildings of logs or squared timbers to replacements of brick or stone, yet all North American buildings required a great deal of wood for their inner structures and, except in part of the Canadas, it also furnished the outer shell for most. Like most distinctions, that of the brick or stone building was based on rarity in a world where easily worked lumber could be fabricated into buildings which would last for generations with reasonable care.

The prevalence of wooden houses on farms and in villages was, indeed, often still is, taken for granted, but it would be a mistake to overlook what was involved when dozens of cities, even future metropolises, made a large proportion of their buildings out of wood. To this day an inquisitive searcher can find a few rows of old wooden buildings where they might least have been expected to survive, in the metropolitan areas of Philadelphia, New York, Boston, Montreal, and Toronto. If he goes farther afield, he can find, in spite of fires and clearances, whole sections of lesser cities which obviously were once composed chiefly of frame structures. As recently as 1900 the European visitor to the cities of the Maritimes, New England, New York, western Ontario, Ohio, and Michigan was likely to be more impressed by the blocks of painted wooden houses than by any other single feature of those cities. Imagination boggles at the task of converting those square miles of buildings back into terms of the square miles of forest from which their materials came.

It was the sprouting and growth of wooden cities along the paths of northern and western migration near the Great Lakes region, culminating as they did in the almost explosive emergence of a new metropolis at the southern end of Lake Michigan, which dictated the stripping of the pine from the northeastern forests. The Atlantic seaboard and Europe made their own demands, but inner North America could be greedier still. About 1850 the tempo was speeded up by a host of forces which are best summarized in the human occupation of the relatively treeless middle west. It was at that moment that all past achievements in forest-razing were eclipsed in the vicinity of the upper Great Lakes. One era closed and another began when the population of the newly created city of Chicago increased by over 500 per cent in the single decade of the 'forties.

The immense scale of the lumbermen's enterprise on a rough, sprawling continent devoid of roads, and the bulk and weight of their product, meant that they performed a minor miracle in transportation. The principal key to their success, of course, was that even fresh-cut softwoods, like white and red pine, would float. By felling the enormous trees and sawing them into logs during the winter, the "sticks" of timber could be dragged or carried on heavy sleighs to the water's edge over snow roads which were glazed every night by the sprinkler sled.[4] Thanks to the topography of the forest regions, the distance of haulage was never, in the cream-skimming days, more than five miles or so.

What is difficult to understand today, when one crosses famous old lumbering areas, is how the meager streams which one finds carried their burdens of logs down to the greater rivers and lakes. One part of the explanation is that the destruction of the forests a century ago so bared the drainage basins, and so hastened the run-off of their moisture, that former rivers have shrunk to mere brooks and chains of shallow pools. More important, however, is the fact that today's visitor finds few traces of the river works which the lumbering tribe created. Their materials of rock and wood were always at hand; their axmen could cut the mortises and tenons of timber joints with planelike smoothness; and if the dams had to be blown up to release the flood waters in one spring, they could be rebuilt if necessary before the next. A single stretch of twenty-five miles might be marked by a dozen dams and almost as many immense

4. The Atlantic term "sled" became "sleigh" in the New York woods, and remained so all the way to the Pacific.

"chutes," or timber troughs, built to carry the hurrying logs past obstructions.

While the "drive" was on after the winter break-up, the rivermen worked to the limit of their endurance. They slept little and ate if and when the cook reached them. A "hung-up" drive, with logs stranded for miles along a stream which would not freshen for another year, was a disaster. A "jam," or pile of logs which blocked a river, summoned the most capable and courageous men available to risk (and often lose) their lives in dislodging the key logs. Small wonder that men five months in the depths of the forest and six weeks on the drive blew in their pay resoundingly in Bangor, Maine, and all the other Bangors.

But if logs and even squared timber were thought sturdy enough to survive the buffeting passage down rocky streams, sawn lumber was not. The lumber trade, therefore, added its insistence to a host of other demands which lie at the roots of the great North American canal-building era.

Canals were the response to the rough topography and broad extent of the Canadian-American Region which defied the road-building efforts of all but the most thickly settled communities. A road would begin its career as a trail worn by wild animals or Indians or "blazed" by the white settlers, following a crooked course along the drier, less-tangled ridges of the wooded, hilly country, circling the swamps, and seeking out the safest, narrowest crossings of the numerous creeks and rivers. Wheeled traffic was ordinarily out of the question for many years, during which men and goods moved to and fro on horseback and livestock carried themselves. Where settlement became compact and the terrain was amenable, proper roads, ferries, and a few bridges (originally rafts of logs) were among the first fruits of local government, but the long trunk roads and the painful ascents and descents of the "gaps" and passes had to wait, usually for the peremptory needs of military expeditions to the frontier, but occasionally for the pressure which influential land speculators could bring to bear on central governments so that the land hungry and their chattels could reach untilled areas. Elsewhere, in general, winter was the best season for land transportation.

The natural consequence was that, until the railroad came, most heavy traffic was water-borne. The coastal movements were enormous and full advantage was taken of the many lakes and of the long rivers which reached back into the mountains. Where falls and rapids interrupted water passage, towns flourished on the proceeds from the services which they could provide. They built portage roads, established slides or skidways up and down which the flat-bottomed barges and scows could be moved by block and tackle, and by trial and error they contrived dams, locks, and weirs which canalized the rivers at these crucial points.

Then, as population pressure increased and liquid capital accumulated, North America raided Great Britain for still more capital and for the hydraulic engineers and masons who crossed the Atlantic fresh from their triumphs in the mother country. From the Ottawa south to the Santee, and from the Androscoggin west to the Wisconsin, vigorous North American communities mastered their transportation problems by linking the natural waterways into continuous channels from the interior to the Atlantic or to the Gulf of Mexico. What was perhaps the climax of effort and achievement was reached on the Pennsylvania Canal from tidewater to Pittsburgh. Although the project cost $16,500,000 (mostly borrowed in Europe), it was a financial success, and this in spite of the fact that thirty-six waterless miles at the crest of the Allegheny Mountains were conquered by floating the canal boats onto trucks which were hauled up and let down on rails by cables and stationary steam engines.

Fresh-water navigators in North America were just as ingenious in building vessels as those on salt water, beginning with the bark canoe or dugout and working on through the mighty *canot de maître*, York and Durham boats, sailing vessels, and all manner of flatboats, barges, and keelboats, to the steamboat. Bulky products clamored for markets and natural waterways were ready to bear them. First in order of importance were those inland seas, the Great Lakes, where the day of the sailing ship began when La Salle launched the *Griffon* near the outlet of Lake Erie in 1679. The interruptions of the St. Lawrence Rapids, the Niagara River, and the Sault Ste. Marie could be profitably circumvented when the reward was hundreds of miles of clear sailing for heavy loads with little expenditure of man power. The same considerations operated in greater or less degree on other waters, such as Lake Champlain, the Finger Lakes of New York, or the deep channel of the Hudson.

The Ohio and Mississippi systems presented unusual problems of their own which go far to explain the persistent eagerness of the northern part of the mid-continental valley to make water connections with the Great Lakes and to use the St. Lawrence. The Falls of the Ohio near Louisville, sandbars, summer shallows, and the snags and ever-shifting channels of the great rivers could be coped with, but the powerful currents, which made the down journey possible even for huge cargoes of coal from Pittsburgh, made the return trip so appallingly difficult that before the steamboat the up-traffic was less than a tenth of what went down. Most of the early river boats were broken up for lumber or firewood at their destinations and hundreds of boatmen made their way back for hundreds of miles on foot.

The introduction of the steamboat naturally had immediate effects on inland navigation. After twenty years or so of increasingly effective experimentation in Great Britain and North America, improved engines firmly established the new method of water transport on the Hudson in 1807, and it had reached the Quebec-Montreal river route by 1809, the Ohio by 1811, and Lake Ontario by 1816. While the steamboat could not be used without serious damage to the narrow shallow canals, it easily triumphed in the deep waters of lakes and great rivers, and it won its greatest victories when the intrepid boatmen of the Mississippi Valley spawned a breed of pilots who defied the shifting channels at the risk of their lives and ships, and who, by such legendary devices as setting a Negro on the safety valve during races between rival craft, contributed more than their share to the catastrophes of North American life. Ironically enough, however, by the time large numbers of steamboats were available in the upper Mississippi Valley, the canal builders had completed water connections with the eastern seaboard. In the Canadian-American Region, therefore, the steamboat must be thought of principally as an agency for speed and certainty in waters already amply, if erratically, served by sail.

A glance at the map on page 130 reveals the two great contests for the water-borne traffic of the Canadian-American Region, both of them merely new forms of the regional rivalries which had emerged during the last half of the seventeenth century. Now, as then, the St. Lawrence competed with the Hudson for the business of the Great Lakes Basin, and the Illinois and Ohio country tried to play off against each other the transportation facilities to the Atlantic Coast and to New Orleans. Yet these contests should not be allowed to eclipse the fact that the inland waterways broke down provincialism to a remarkable degree and facilitated the growth of some sense of nationality. The St. Lawrence and Welland canals stimulated the union of the Canadas in 1841. The Champlain canals drew western Vermont and northern New York away from forty years of membership in "the commercial empire of the St. Lawrence" into the American Union. And the Erie Canal, tapping as it did Lakes Ontario and Erie, built the foundations for the economic capital of North America at the mouth of the Hudson.

In spite of the canals which joined the Great Lakes to the Mississippi, in spite of the bold attempts of Pennsylvania to supplement its own river systems by canals built over the "humps" into New York, and in spite of the immense sums spent in the Canadas to drain the middle west to Montreal, the canals which New York built between 1792 and 1828 gave that state secure leadership in the conquest of the Appalachian barrier to transportation. The Hudson Valley was almost an ocean inlet as far as the Mohawk Gap, and from that point north to Lake Champlain, northwest to Oswego, and west to Buffalo the dividing heights of land were low and there were many streams to provide the channel or fill the man-made ditch.[5] The Champlain Canal was completed in 1823, the Erie in 1825, and the Oswego in 1828. By 1838 more grain came to Buffalo and the Erie Canal than to New Orleans. The Welland Canal, by which in 1829 the Canadian William Hamilton Merritt circumvented Niagara Falls, did more to swell the traffic of Oswego (and New York) than that of Montreal, because the route from Lake Ontario by the Rideau Canal (1831) and Ottawa River was roundabout and, even with canals at the most difficult points, the passage down the St. Lawrence from Lake Ontario to Montreal was risky for men, boats, and cargoes.

By 1850 the natural and artificial waterways of the Canadian-American Region from the Atlantic to Wisconsin had reached the peak of their usefulness relative to other forms of transportation. The staples of the interior—grain, lumber, flour, butter, pork, and lard—had brought higher and higher returns to their producers as the costs of transportation fell, and incoming cargoes grew in proportion. It became fashionable for the leisured to travel, once it could be done in comparative comfort, and the passenger vessels on the lakes, canals, and rivers of the region rivaled the gorgeous steamboats of the lower Mississippi in their plush, white paint, gay colors, and tinsel. Scores of European travelers made circular tours of the Middle States and Canada and rushed into print to tell of the natural beauties of the land, of Niagara Falls, of the barbaric manners of the tobacco-chewing inhabitants, and of the gargantuan repasts of coarse foods which were shoveled into the greedy mouths of restless people who seemed to glory in being "on the move."

Already, however, the railroad, which could run on schedule the year round, prophesied the fate of most of the waterways. Here and there, from Lower Canada and Nova Scotia to South Carolina, short railway lines had begun to operate in the 'thirties—to serve mines, to supplant other devices for getting round river obstructions, and to serve as substitutes for worn-out plank roads. The first thirty years produced a strange medley of experiments—all sorts of gauges for the distance between the rails; rails made of wood, or strap iron on wood, of iron, and (on the Boston & Lowell) of granite which speedily ground the wheels to

5. The Hudson-Champlain Pass is only 147 feet above sea level, for instance.

pieces; while stationary engines with cables pulled the cars up the steepest inclines and let them down the other side. By the middle of the century, however, the triumph of the railroad was assured, and in 1851 the first international through service connected Boston and Montreal. The winter-bound Canadian port was reaching out through the United States for the advantages of year-round ocean connections which its rival, New York, enjoyed by natural bounty.

CHAPTER VIII

PIONEERS AND DEMOCRATS
(1815–1850)

THE settlement of the interior of North America during the first half of the nineteenth century is too often pictured in dramatic but impossible colors. The persecuted European, usually fleeing from social, religious, and political discriminations in the British Isles, is herded into crowded, insanitary quarters below decks on a sailing vessel which takes many weeks to cross the Atlantic. The dazed survivors of this ordeal emerge at some port in British North America or the United States, are swindled out of most of their belongings by rascals lying in wait for them, but nevertheless proceed on foot hundreds of miles to the frontier. There they promptly lay hold of "that deadly tool, the American axe," hew out farms from the forest, and within a year or two have become good frontier democrats. Magically the neat town, with its green, its church, its courthouse, its town hall, and its little red schoolhouse springs into being, and some youthful rail-splitting genius starts off with a sack of meal, a slab of salt pork, and a copy of Blackstone to impress the will of the community on some distant legislature.

A little knowledge and common sense dispel most of the myth. Nearly all the Europeans who came to North America did so in order to better themselves economically. They were more accustomed to hardship than most of us, and accepted squalor, disease, and death more philosophically, because they themselves were the tough survivors of a thinning process at home. A large proportion of those who met them when they landed were relatives, friends, or the agents of philanthropic institutions, employers, or land companies, all of whom were interested in looking after them as well as possible. Few of them proceeded directly to the frontier, because they were of little use there. Highly skilled craftsmen gravitated to settled urban or semiurban communities. Many stopped in or near the seaboard cities. Self-confident rural immigrants who brought ready cash with them either purchased improved farms in the older regions or, more wisely, went to work for a time with established farmers from whom they could learn American agriculture. The largest proportion supplied the almost unceasing demand for semiskilled or unskilled labor—in simple manual tasks, with or without accustomed tools, at wharves, warehouses, brickyards, building construction, and, above all, as "navigators" or "navvies" digging canals or grading railroad beds.

When the time came to exercise the franchise, there were plenty of practiced native politicians who were adept at handling "the immigrant vote." All in all, with minor exceptions, the margin of settlement on the frontiers was made up of native or habituated North Americans.

It is not easy to find a close analogy for the outward spread of settlement on the continent, but perhaps the waves of the incoming tide along an irregular shore provide as good a one as any, breaking and spreading on the beaches, retreating for reënforcement, returning to occupy a little more, and finally inundating the broken shore line at an even level. The narrow ribbon of froth left far up the beach as each wave retreated might be taken to represent the little groups of men and women who were almost nomads, because they were hunters rather than farmers, and moved on when permanent settlement neared them. The main body of the pioneers was made up of very different elements, for the most part experts in an agriculture which appalled Europeans by its slovenly wastefulness, but which experience had shown would give rich enough returns in North America.

This moving flood of frontiersmen progressed or fell back in response to rises and falls in general prosperity, and it was composed overwhelmingly of younger sons and former hired men. "They play at leap-frog with their lands," said a British observer in 1806. M. L. Hansen, the great student of these population movements who has demonstrated that, for the most part, the Atlantic migrations and the migrations within North America were closely articulated elements of one huge dynamic process, hit upon a happy simile for the outward movements of the pioneers. The settled regions, he said, were like beehives whose occupants after a little stay were ready to swarm. Responding to internal pressure and external lures, they sent forth the knowledgeable men and women who planted themselves on the new lands and sent forth other swarms in turn.

"Mr. Malthus," wrote a settler in the interior about 1818, "would not be understood here." Since labor was scarce and sustenance plentiful, large families were the rule, often at the expense of worn-out wives, as country graveyards attest. By the time the young men were anxious to strike out on their own, the land values in their vicinity would probably have risen to such heights that the most generous father could not set up all of his sons with separate farms. But with the interior of a continent to choose from and with every skill necessary to conquer it, a patriarch could sell out at a profit to the less venturesome and move with his family to cheaper lands, or stay with one chosen son on the home farm while he "staked" the others elsewhere. The Pennsylvania "Dutch" of the United States and Canada, who know not Malthus or the neo-Malthusians, have been repeating this process for two hundred years and are still at it today.

It was the practiced farmer who provided the core of successful new settlements, as every land company that ever amounted to anything recognized. With him on the ground there could be assembled former hired men, substantial European farmers who had sense enough to be willing to learn new ways, and even a small proportion of unskilled Americans and Europeans who could master their inaptitude if they had the muscle and the willingness for hard work. But the wastage was enormous. The unfit either perished or found their way back to the towns and cities, or hung on the flanks of unskilled labor. No one will ever know how many immigrants and migrants were saved by the ubiquitous "construction gang" in North America. The annals of North American migration are always punctuated by accounts of how those who were marching outward had to steel themselves against discouragement from the tales of woe and disaster which were poured into their ears by those who were in retreat.

The pattern followed in the development of frontier farms was pretty much the same everywhere, except for some extreme differences in soil and forest cover, until the vanguard confronted the new set of problems presented by the comparatively treeless western grasslands and their tough sod. The first task was to clear of trees and brush a few small patches of land where vegetables and grains for immediate sustenance could be grown among the stumps. The best logs were used to provide the crude cabin, with bark roof, blanket doors, and greased parchment windows, which, improved here and there, served as human shelter (with a lean-to for the animals) until a sawmill was erected somewhere near and a proper frame house of clapboard, or siding and shingles, could be built. Some of the old log or squared-timber cabins survive to this day as cow barns or other farm buildings.

Meanwhile the great task was clearing the land, but this was made tolerable because it gave the pioneer his first cash crop in the form of the potash which he collected after burning whatever timber he did not need for construction, fence posts and rails, or firewood. Since the best lands were recognized to be those on which fine hardwoods grew, rather than the sandy soils which nourished the conifers, clearing was normally a long and wearisome ordeal. Usually the standing trees were girdled in order to dry them out and later felled so as to form long piles for burning. The collected ashes were then leached by packing them in containers through which water was poured. The resultant lye water could be used with animal fats to make soap or be evaporated into a crude potash which was worth about thirty dollars a barrel at any Atlantic port.[1] The other important tree crop, of course, was the syrup or sugar which could be manufactured every spring by evaporating the copious sap of the hard maple.

The remainder of the progression from backwoods to cleared farm lands can easily be imagined. Felled trees left stumps and roots, which meant that the first crops had to be harvested with sickle or scythe or cradle.[2] Oxen were better than horses for taming the unkempt farm. Their first assignment was stump-pulling, either with gin and block and tackle or with the root-cutting plow which was developed during the digging of the Erie Canal. The stumps with their flaring roots were sometimes dragged into closely tangled rows whose impenetrable chevaux-de-frise formed the first fences between the fields. These proved to be so durable that examples may still be seen in some sections of the eastern Canadian-American Region, often half hidden by the rocks and stones which past generations removed from the fields. Surplus stumps and debris were burned on the ground and their fertilizing ashes worked into the soil by its first honest plowing. Thereafter cultivation was of a normal kind as the increased production encouraged some individual or group to provide the finishing touch—the building and equipment of a gristmill to supplant the "hominy blocks" or other forms of hardwood mortars and pestles. For the most part, frontier livestock were mongrel breeds and led precarious lives.

A great deal of this pioneer enterprise was coöperative, with the "old hands" as directors and whole neighborhoods combining in what North Americans fittingly called "bees." There were bees for logging or clearing a farm, for sugar-making, for raising the heavy timbers of barns, for harvesting, for corn-husking, and for such women's occasions as apple-paring, wool-picking and carding, or the swift assembly of the materials in an intricately fashioned patchwork quilt. The beneficiary of a bee was expected to feed and entertain the helpers, which meant that "the womenfolk" worked in their kitchens for days in preparation. It also meant that the hard liquors which were so easily and cheaply distilled from corn, barley, and rye flowed with extravagant freedom, so much so that many of these bees broke down because the men got too drunk to work, or suffered serious accidents, or ended up with a "knock-down, drag-out fight, no holts barred."

1. Pearl ash, from which the carbon had been removed, was usually prepared in special establishments. Fortunately for the North American pioneer, the growing British textile industry needed large quantities of pot and pearl ash for bleaching.
2. An ingenious scythe to whose blade and handle a frame was attached onto which the cut stalks fell evenly enough to be easily gathered and bound into a sheaf when dropped on the ground at the end of the cutting swing.

There were, of course, some variations in these frontier ways in the eastern forested area of North America, but they do not greatly alter the general picture. Some men, for instance, took up poor lands, and some men were incurably poor farmers. The lumber industry had a way of encouraging farming on lands which were so thin and sandy that only the urgent local demand for hay and oats justified any man's working them. Then when the lumberman and his horses moved farther on, the farmer had to move too or relapse into a losing contest with the poor soil. Another anomaly was created by the Ohio and Mississippi river systems, particularly in the days before steamboats and canals. A frontiersman who struggled overland to some tributary of the Ohio found that he could load his family and goods into a river boat and be carried with slight effort hundreds of miles to the west and south. Those who yielded to this temptation were liable to end up in the south or southwest where they faced unfamiliar problems in almost everything from farming to housing.

In general, however, the occupation of the good lands which were bounded by the Canadian Shield on the north, the Appalachians on the east, the Ohio on the south, and the Wabash on the west, was a single, homogeneous, international adventure. As time went on, local and more general patriotisms affected some men's movements, but they could never dominate all. The older settlements, under unremitting pressure from their own natural increase, and from the Atlantic migrations which grew in a crescendo after the Napoleonic wars, sent out their columns of settlers to occupy the best untilled lands wherever they could be found. While the inland waterways exercised the most powerful influence in directing the course of settlement, there were many other forces in operation as well, notably in determining the points at which the pressure of arrivals from Europe was to be felt. The chief of these was commerce. Cargoes from North America to Europe were heavy, but the returning vessels frequently had relatively little to carry. Their owners, therefore, quite naturally installed temporary fittings to accommodate cargoes of human beings who were seeking the Land of Promise.

In spite of a flood of emigrants' handbooks or guides, and a lively controversial literature in Great Britain about emigration, a great proportion of the newcomers had very vague ideas of the lands to which they were bound. For those who had read them, Fenimore Cooper's romantic tales had a way of leaving more lasting impressions than sober, informative works, and any appreciation of the scale and character of North American geography was quite rare. Thus an Irishman with no love for British rule sought a grant of land "in upper Kennedy in North America," and a group of wistful Scots in northern Ohio who were longing for familiar British institutions, when they were asked why they did not simply cross Lake Erie to enjoy them, replied: "We didna ken the difference between the twa governments; at the time we came over here, it was a' America to us."

To a very large extent the emigrants were simply taken to the ports where the ship operators could count on cargoes. Thus the "second colonization of New England," by the Irish, whose early stages took place so imperceptibly that many old New Englanders believed it to be a secret conspiracy, was in considerable part a by-product of the New Brunswick timber trade. The timber ships brought the impoverished Irish to the mouths of the great New Brunswick rivers, where they could find little except temporary employment along the docks. To the same river mouths coasting vessels had come from the United States carrying supplies for the lumbermen and collecting the Maritime Province gypsum which was in steady demand to sweeten the farm lands at home. For a dollar or two the Europeans could purchase deck passage to a region of varied opportunities. The arrivals of these small groups at many different ports attracted little attention, and Church or kin quickly and inconspicuously attached the newcomers to countless "Little Irelands."

As the nineteenth century wore on and North American transportation facilities improved, established groups in the interior could do a good deal to attract friends, relatives, or countrymen, who arrived at any Atlantic port from Montreal to Philadelphia. The St. Lawrence waterway could carry a Scandinavian from Quebec to Wisconsin, or the Erie Canal and the Lakes a Scotsman from New York to the Canada Company's lands east of Lake Huron. On the other hand, the managers of construction jobs in the interior posted agents at the ports of arrival to recruit laborers for canal-digging and so on, with little regard for regional ties.

While all this interplay of geographical and economic forces made the American migrants and the European immigrants of the first half of the nineteenth century disregard political sovereignty on a scale surprising to later generations, it would be a mistake to believe that lack of an urgent sense of nationality was entirely characteristic. There were a good many incidents to the contrary, two of which attained considerable proportions and were ominous of a less easygoing future.

The first of these occurred in Upper Canada during and after the War of 1812. There the official class and the British minority gave vent to their relief over having escaped being engulfed in the aggressive United States by making it very difficult for Americans to become citizens and

NOTE

Railroads ——— Waterways ━━━

100   50   0   100
Miles

N.B.

Woodstock
St John R.
Grand Falls St John
Riviere du Loup
Saguenay R.
Quebec
LOWER (1841—1867) CANADA (1791—1841)
Montreal
Ottawa
Amprior
Ottawa R.
Arnprior
CANADA
UPPER (1791—1841) CANADA (1841)
Georgian B.
Collingwood
Huron Tract
Goderich
Sarnia
London
LAKE HURON
Port Huron
Bay City
Gd Haven
Milwaukee
LAKE MICHIGAN
Chicago
Kankakee
St Anne
MICHIGAN
Sault Ste Marie
Sault Ste Marie
LAKE SUPERIOR
MINN.
WIS.
La Crosse
Prairie du Chien
Wisconsin R.
Mississippi R.
IOWA
St Joseph
Missouri R.
Quincy
St Louis
Illinois R.
ILL.
Cairo
Ohio R.
Evansville
Wabash R.
IND.
Indianapolis
Louisville
Lexington
KENTUCKY
Cincinnati
OHIO
Columbus
Muskingum
Ohio R.
Wheeling
Pittsburgh
Zanesville
Cleveland
Sandusky
Toledo
L. St Clair
Detroit
LAKE ERIE
Buffalo
Rochester
LAKE ONTARIO
Toronto
Hamilton
Kingston
Niagara
PENN.
Harrisburg
Baltimore
Washington
Richmond
VIRGINIA
MD.
DEL.
Philadelphia
N.J.
New York
Albany
Hudson R.
Syracuse
Utica
N.Y.
Ogdensburg
L. Champlain
St Albans
Burlington
Plattsburg
VT.
Rutland
N.H.
MASS.
Boston
Gloucester
CONN.
R.I.
Providence
New London
Hartford
ME.
Bangor
Lewiston
Portland
Sherbrooke
Richmond R.
Penobscot R.
Kennebec R.
Chaudiere R.
Calais St John
ATLANTIC OCEAN

Map: Elements in the Eastern Canadian-American Region, 1815–1860

qualify as landowners. The representative Assembly, which reflected the feelings of the general population, fought hard against this policy, for it reduced land values and denied to Upper Canada what would have been her share of the most capable migrants who were moving westward along the Great Lakes. Moreover events promptly demonstrated that the substitute—the assisted and directed immigration from the British Isles which was officially supported between 1815 and 1825 and the voluntary British immigration which accompanied and succeeded it—could not remedy the loss of good settlers. The Assembly therefore returned to the attack in 1821, but did not secure victory until 1838, by which time the Erie Canal to Buffalo was "short-circuiting" the old Lake Ontario route which had carried so many Americans to Canada. The results were that Upper Canada put living flesh on its bones more slowly than upper New York and northern Ohio, and within the Province the anti-Americanism which had its roots in the Revolution and the War of 1812 was considerably enhanced, contributing a warm emotional element to local and larger politics in the process.

A second conspicuous contradiction of the usual expediency of the migrants was perhaps the most remarkable anomaly in the occupation of North America—the unpredictable American leap across the empty western half of the continent in order to settle Oregon and thereafter to try to goad Great Britain into withdrawing from the Pacific Coast. This exploit was effectively accomplished in five years, 1841–1846, at a time when the eastern half of the continent was still not solidly taken up. Nor did the venture have any substantial connection with the influx into the southwest which was to reach the lower Pacific just before the discovery of gold in California in 1848. Nevertheless it must be regarded as one facet of an aggressive American nationalism whose solid foundations were laid between 1815 and 1828. This was amalgamated by interested parties with the creed of Manifest Destiny, and made actual by recurrent filibustering expeditions against foreign territory in a great circle from Central America to the Maritime Provinces.

When viewed particularly instead of generally, the Oregon adventure grew out of the enthusiasm which this fertile, well-watered land aroused in the hearts of a small number of pioneers who, like the rest of their countrymen, had hitherto thought of most of the trans-Mississippi region as "The Great American Desert." The joint occupation of Oregon which had been agreed upon in 1818 had meant that the Hudson's Bay Company was the effective occupier for twenty-five years, with its fur-trade base at Fort Vancouver near the mouth of the Columbia and numerous outposts. Its superior organization and settled relations with the

Indians gave it an insuperable advantage over American traders who entered the region individually or in small groups. Indeed the American ventures frequently had such disastrous consequences that Dr. John McLoughlin, the humane Hudson's Bay Company's manager at Fort Vancouver, was repeatedly involved by them in dangerous and expensive rescue missions.

The writing on the wall for the future appeared between 1832 and 1836, when American Methodists and Presbyterians established missions to the Indians at two points just south of the Columbia. The missions did not amount to much, for the French-Canadian priests were much better adapted to the work, but the lyrical letters and speeches of the missionaries about the glories of the wooded Pacific slope infected the frontiersmen of treeless Iowa and Missouri with the "Oregon Fever."[3] By 1841 about four hundred Americans had arrived in Oregon, a little over a hundred more turned up in 1842, and in 1843 about one thousand newcomers swelled the American community sufficiently to outnumber the British. The die was cast and joint occupation was doomed.

The ousting of the Company was not a pretty affair. It could not be where ebullient frontiersmen were conducting an assured offensive. Old Dr. McLoughlin, who conducted himself with extraordinary detachment and generous judgment, and who later transferred his allegiance along with his domain to the United States, was vilified and victimized by the victors in inexcusable ways. The fur traders had originally hoped and expected that the Columbia River would be the dividing line, but doubts arose in the 'thirties and, when President Polk in his inaugural address of March, 1845, asserted American title to the whole of Oregon, thus underlining the Oregonian battle cry of "Fifty-four forty or fight," they resigned themselves to the retreat to Vancouver Island which they had already prepared for. Next year the British Government assented to a treaty which divided old Oregon by a line along the forty-ninth parallel from the Rockies to the Strait of Georgia and thence through the Strait of Juan de Fuca to the Pacific. Thus substantial, if freakish, agricultural settlement had dominated efficient, but thin, fur-trading occupation of a large section of North America. The United States was bursting its bounds, as inroads into Texas, Mexico, and California during the same years abundantly proved. For the next thirty years British North America was seldom free of the fear that, in part or whole, it might suffer the same fate.

3. They were having trouble in subduing the soils and unfamiliar obstacles, which were presented by the Great Plains. In addition, Washington Irving's *Astoria* (1836) and *Adventures of Captain Bonneville* (1837) were influential.

In the United States the vices of the expansive frontier have tended to be eclipsed by its virtues. Americans, like almost all other peoples, believed in themselves and in the benefits which they could confer upon others by the extension of their influence. This theme recurred constantly in many kinds of their recorded utterances from earliest times until it found its great oracle in Walt Whitman. From 1855 onward (somewhat after the event), that strange, powerful poet chanted Manifest Destiny at the top of his voice.

> Come my tan-faced children,
> Follow well in order, get your weapons ready,
> Have you your pistols? have you your sharp-edged axes?
>   Pioneers! O pioneers!

> For we cannot tarry here,
> We must march my darlings, we must bear the brunt of danger,
> We the youthful sinewy races, all the rest on us depend,
>   Pioneers! O pioneers!

> Have the elder races halted?
> Do they droop and end their lesson, wearied over there beyond the seas?
> We take up the task eternal, and the burden and the lesson,
>   Pioneers! O pioneers!

And so on for twenty-six stanzas, not to speak of hundreds of lines in other poems.[4]

James Bryce, that keen Scottish student of the United States whose historical and legal analysis of American institutions became a classic overnight in 1888, concurred in Whitman's belief that the frontiersman was the essential American.[5] "The West," he said, "is the most American part of America, that is to say, the part where those features which distinguish America from Europe come out in the strongest relief." Following him, it was the symbolically named American, Frederick Jackson Turner, who expanded the theme with assertions which were if anything more sweeping than Whitman's. To Turner, the frontier provided very nearly an all-embracing formula for explaining the history of American life. "The existence of an area of free land," he told the American His-

---

4. Whitman knew and admired Canada and Canadians, indeed his most loyal disciple from 1877 to his death in 1892 and one of his three literary executors was Dr. R. M. Bucke of London, Ontario. Whitman declared that Canadians were worthy of admission into the United States and he looked forward eagerly to this. It did not seem to occur to him that they had other ideas.

5. *The American Commonwealth* (London, 1888; rev. ed., 1910). It should be read in the unexpurgated first edition.

torical Association during the World's Columbian Exposition at Chicago in 1893, "its continuous recession, and the advance of American settlement westward, explain American development." He thereupon proceeded to amplify his thesis with ardent zeal in relation to such matters as Americanization, the growth of political and economic nationalism, and the evolution of political institutions. When, in 1920, a volume of his essays along these lines reached a much larger public, his confident hypothesis was enthusiastically seized upon to interpret everything American from poetry and painting to politics.

Such simple, comprehensive formulas usually have two consequences. On the one hand, they are adopted ignorantly or uncritically and stretched to embrace too much. On the other, these very excesses invite strong attacks. Darwin and Marx provide well-known examples, and Turner's thesis proved no exception, for, while he stimulated more interest and work in American history than any man before him, he thereby created his own effective critics. Among other instances, his common assumption that the frontier found the pioneer a European and then swiftly and dramatically Americanized him soon proved untenable. The most striking example, however, was the rapid adoption and then the whittling away of the rash tenet which Americans had quoted most often from Turner's essay and wanted most to believe: "The most important effect of the frontier has been in the promotion of democracy here and in Europe."

Interestingly enough the whole controversy about democracy and the frontier becomes relatively unimportant, and the substantial elements in it stand clear of the debris of shattered arguments, when the whole of the Americas is examined instead of merely the United States. French Canada and Latin America, for instance, provide some interesting and vigorous variations. Again, when the British elements in the democratic movements of British North America are brought into the picture, they awaken a demand for their proper place in the American picture as well. In fact it begins to appear that a great deal of what we like to call North American democracy was merely one phase of the assaults on political and economic privilege which reached substantial proportions in seventeenth-century England and Scotland; revived there and in the British colonies and appeared in France about 1760; and emerged, armed with systematic doctrine, from the American, French, and Irish revolutions of the last quarter of the eighteenth century. Democracy and nationalism dominated too much of the world during the nineteenth century for any reasonable man to claim that the American frontier played the major part in spawning either of them.

One can grant to the various North American frontiers "that coarseness and strength combined with acuteness and inquisitiveness," indeed grant the whole series of accented antitheses which Turner recited, and yet fall far short of the mark. The democrats of the United States and British North America—Jefferson, Benton, Jackson, Howe, Papineau, and Mackenzie, to name only a few of the leaders—were deeply in debt to Locke, Rousseau, Helvetius, Adam Smith, Bentham, and many another for the working philosophies behind their own creeds. And in the armies of immigrants, French and British Utopians, Irish republicans, and Scottish and English radicals and Chartists carried more than material baggage with them across the Atlantic as they moved from one kind of struggle against ensconced authority to another. Nor should it be forgotten that in France, Great Britain, the United States, and British North America during the first half of the nineteenth century the one unremitting demand of the democrats was for control of the purse, in other words, for control over taxation and the spoils of office. Patronage could never be separated from the campaigns for democratic government, indeed a cynic would deny the possibility of differentiating between them.[6]

Before the American Revolution, colonial assemblies from Nova Scotia southward had fought against the office-holding groups whose power was based on understandings with authority in Great Britain. During and immediately after the Revolution they tried to break the grip on authority and privilege which the propertied classes of the older settled areas retained by special franchises, by tardiness in conceding representation to more recently occupied areas, or by plain gerrymandering of the constituencies. Many of the new state constitutions were clearly intended to be democratic, but, except in Vermont, property qualifications for voting and office-holding considerably limited pure majority rule. "There are combustibles in every State which a spark might set fire to," said Washington after the repression of Daniel Shays's rebellion of 1786 in Massachusetts. Eight years later, as President of the United States, he had to call out the militia of four states to put down the Whisky Rebellion in western Pennsylvania which was the trans-Appalachian democrats' response to Alexander Hamilton's excise tax of 1791. Altogether, although the substantial propertied elements generally maintained and occasionally even increased their authority at the close of the

6. Witness the clear echo in Gladstone's famous, studied address on "Our Colonies," as delivered in its second version to the Mechanics' Institute at Chester, November 12, 1855: "It is plain they are not to be desired [by Great Britain] for patronage, properly so called, within their limits, because they will not allow us to exercise patronage."

eighteenth century, they were frankly alarmed by the growth of anti-oligarchical elements in the population which their own numbers could not balance.

It is natural to associate the insurgent democracy of the United States with Andrew Jackson's tumultuous inauguration to the Presidency on March 4, 1829, but it is wiser to recall the distress which was caused by the "Western Panic" of 1819–1824 and, as well, the break-up of the Jeffersonian Republicans into conservative and radical wings within the separate States during the 'twenties. Jackson, the brusque, forthright hero of New Orleans and Florida, was the choice of a small army of professional state politicians who saw a magnificent opportunity in the complete inability of that upright patriot, John Quincy Adams, to ingratiate himself with anybody. The election of 1828 was a malodorous affair in which the masses beat the classes. But the masses were not merely those frontiersmen who concluded their picturesque litany of bragging by announcing that they could "hug a bear too close for comfort and eat any man opposed to Jackson." The new President carried New York and Pennsylvania and the Atlantic Coast from Virginia down as well as most of the trans-Appalachian region.

It is doubtful whether the impulsive and unlearned Jackson ever appreciated how many elements were combined in the wave which deposited him among the mob at the east portico of the Capitol for his inauguration. Most obvious, of course, was the hatred of Senator Benton's chief bogey, the Money Power or "The Monster," as represented by the Bank of the United States. Jackson slowly strangled that dragon in spite of Nicholas Biddle's stubborn defense and the massive array of protections for property which Chief Justice John Marshall had built up in his decisions. But the generation which remade the United States between 1820 and 1850 received from its prophets and reformers dozens of other battle cries and creeds for the campaigns which it waged against privilege in behalf of social reform and the common man. It was a great age for all kinds of criers-down of inequality.

In spite of the fact that Great Britain did not venture upon political democracy until 1867, the parallels and interplay between her and the United States in equalitarian reform were close and persistent. The visit in 1833 of Garrison, the Abolitionist, to Wilberforce, the dying Emancipator, was typical of the transatlantic to-and-fro of practicing Utopians like the Owens, or the close communion between Emerson and Carlyle. The American campaigns against the established and conservative churches, which had materially equalized religious privilege in the States before 1800, and after that time took the form of intense sectarian competition in the west, paralleled the campaigns of the British Philosophical Radicals and the Non-Conformists against the established churches of the British Isles.

Closely related to religious toleration, of course, was the attack on privilege in education as exemplified by discriminating colleges and expensive academies. It was all very well to multiply small sectarian colleges in the United States, but the secular universities of Virginia, North Carolina, and Michigan on the one hand, and the University of London on the other, reflected the democratic temper of the times more specifically. The same thing might be said of the parallel outbursts of mechanics' institutes, libraries, and lecture programs. Emerson delivered his essays on *Representative Men* to workers in England before he published them in the United States. North America enthusiastically took up the English Young Men's Christian Association of 1844. The real battle, however, and the one in which the sweeping American victory eclipsed contemporary small British tactical successes, was over free or nearly free primary and secondary education. Here the people's parties in the separate States obtained something which they did not know how to handle, for success carried with it all sorts of related problems like common textbooks, as yet unwritten, and teacher-training schools, as yet unbuilt. Moreover the general population wanted utilitarian education, whereas the educators insisted on scholarship. Nevertheless before the middle of the century the United States had shown the world the possibilities of general public education. Fifty years later Great Britain was to lament that her own democratic urge had not been strong enough for her to follow suit.

It was not merely out of her own enthusiastic romanticism that the United States produced the swarm of early nineteenth century Utopian communities and new creeds which are commemorated in names like Brook Farm, New Enterprise, New Harmony, New Hope, Nauvoo, Oneida, and Salt Lake City. To believe so would be to overlook the widespread influences of Godwin and Mary Wolstonecraft; of Robert Owen of New Lanark and his son, Robert Dale Owen of Indiana; and of that veteran of the American Revolution, Saint-Simon, and his compatriot Fourier. The idealistic Europeans and Americans who labored in these humanitarian and philanthropic causes may have found a more fertile soil in North America than in Europe, but most of their intellectual nourishment came from abroad.

The transatlantic interplay stands out again in the beginnings of trade unionism. The same British statute, adroitly engineered in 1824 and 1825 by the master tailor and Benthamite, Francis Place, legalized trade unions and permitted the export of British machinery. The two crossed the Atlantic together, for the factory system which grew up in New England and the Middle States was never out of touch with the parent system in Great Britain. Thus the famous mill girls of Lowell, with their uniform dress and their literary journal, reflect Owen's New Lanark in Scotland; and the Workingmen's Association which was founded in 1828 at Philadelphia was the counterpart of the new British unions and their dreams of a workers' parliament. In Great Britain the unions fought the "dilution" which employers achieved through the labor of women and children and the encouragement of Irish immigration. In North America they had almost the same battles to fight.

On both sides of the Atlantic the working classes hoped to ease their situation by the ownership of land, but for a number of reasons, some common to both, and some particular to one or the other, these experiments came to little. The endless agitations in the United States for squatters' preëmptive rights, for lower prices on the public domain, and finally for free homesteads were tied up in complex and even contradictory ways with the aspirations of the urban workers, but the striking force behind them was rural. For forty years only piecemeal progress was made. It was not until the Civil War had removed the opposition of the south that the Homestead Act of 1862 offered a quarter section, 160 acres of public land, to any bona fide settler.

The most striking American democratic victory, as contrasted with British defeat, was in politics. From 1775 onward, in spite of a conservative reaction from 1790 to 1820 like that in Great Britain, the common man in the separate States made persistent headway in getting the vote and therefore in creating a class of professional politicians who catered for it and marshaled it, first locally in city or county, then in state politics, and finally, with Jackson, at Washington as well. It was in 1832 that the Democrats held the first national convention to choose by a two-thirds vote a presidential candidate. The electoral principle was given broader and broader application until it was used even in the selection of judges.

Meanwhile the ingredients of the spoils system were being blended together. Victory in the Revolution meant that the gift of public offices in State and Union was in American hands. Within the municipalities and States, where the distance between voter and government was shortest, the spoils system had developed before 1800. It was the child of two practical principles, rotation of office and the use of patronage for creating party strength. At Washington it began tentatively with Jefferson, but expanded rapidly during his term when it was found that "there is a wonderful tranquillity prevailing on the avowal and practice of this conduct." The Republicans whom he and Madison and John Quincy Adams ensconced in office were the particular targets of the Democrats' wrath in 1828.

As C. R. Fish has said: "When the people voted in 1828 that John Quincy Adams should leave office, they undoubtedly intended that most of the civil servants should go with him." They did, and in his message of December, 1829, Jackson at the same time wrote their epitaph and denied the United States an efficient civil service for almost a century to come when he declared that removal from office with change of administration "would, by promoting that rotation which constitutes a leading principle in the republican creed, give healthful action to the system." A shrewd British observer, K. B. Smellie, has put his finger on the efficient cause for the contrasted development across the Atlantic. "It may be said that it was the very slowness with which in England democratic government was substituted for aristocratic privilege that made possible the success of our Civil Service. It was rescued from private patronage without becoming public spoils."

When we turn from the give-and-take of democratic and social-reform movements between Great Britain and the United States to the ways in which the cogwheels of similar activity in the scattered British North American communities meshed with those of both the greater powers, we confront one important, persistent element in Canadian-American interplay. This is the time lag between North American developments in the northern and in the southern portions of the Canadian-American Region. Its operation has not been universal, and the interval has not always been the same, but during the first half of the nineteenth century northern conformity to what might be called the continental pattern of behavior lagged from fifteen to twenty-five years after southern in a large number of ways.

An underlying reason for this was that the Provinces were British and, faced by American expansionism, their defensive response was to persuade themselves that they were more British than they actually were. This in turn played into the hands of local oligarchies whose powers depended upon imperial authority in London. There the governing classes could not conceive of a method by which colonies could govern themselves and still remain colonies. They were implacably opposed to political democracy at home (*vide* Chartism) and therefore abroad, and, until after their own surrender to democracy in 1867, they were distinctly less aware than the British Americans of the full implications of cabinet government in the parliamentary system. The excesses which accom-

panied and followed Jackson's rise to power, and the similar features of
various European revolutions, convinced Whig and Tory alike in Great
Britain that democracy was a profound, pervasive evil.

A further obstacle to swift democratic achievement in the North
American colonies was the fact that the Provinces were sharply separated geographically and had developed strong local characteristics
which made coöperation nearly impossible. This prevented, for the most
part, any close parallel to the stimulating fusion of the democratic movements of the separate States which had occurred in the American election of 1828. The three Maritime Provinces were split apart by salt
water. Their whole region was divided from Lower Canada by Maine and
by rough Appalachian highlands. Lower Canada was segregated from
Upper Canada by the antipathy, even hostility, between their respective
cultural traditions in language, religion, law, and institutions.

Yet these communities ultimately displayed practically every phase
of the social and democratic agitations in Great Britain and the United
States. They attacked the Money Power of Halifax and Montreal. Upper
Canada was the principal terminus of the Underground Railway for
fugitive slaves from the American south. The Mormons and the Oneida
Community, among other romantic Utopian movements, recruited members and support in Upper Canada. The British American democrats attacked the religious and educational monopolies of the established Angli-
can and Presbyterian churches, founded small sectarian colleges, and
waged unceasing battle to secularize the universities and to provide public
primary and secondary schools. Trade unionism was backward, for so
also was the factory system, but mechanics' institutes, libraries, and
lyceums paralleled those of Great Britain and the United States. The
campaigns against privileged landlordism were exceptionally sharp and
well sustained in the Maritimes and in both the Canadas, and the united
Canadas could boast that they had instituted free land grants twenty-
one years before the United States.

These agitations were not, however, mere imitation of the United
States, but rather the British American variety of the assaults on privilege which were being delivered on both sides of the North Atlantic. In
the struggle French Canada gave birth to a quite distinct democratic
party, indeed the very conflict of race and tradition between the governors and the governed in Lower Canada made that party a perpetual
majority in the legislature. Numerous examples can be found of both
English- and French-speaking British North Americans appealing to the
United States as a criterion and citing American achievements or institutions or Jackson's speeches as models for emulation; but since there

was nowhere any substantial group which favored acceptance of the standing invitation to become part of the United States, it is clear that they were aiming either to irritate the professionally anti-American oligarchs or to provide practical arguments for specific reforms within an embracing structure of British colonial institutions. From the beginning to the end of their democratic agitations the British Philosophical Radicals were their principal allies.

Just as the Western Panic of 1819–1824 precipitated Jacksonianism, so did the Panic of 1837 and the depression which followed it precipitate the Rebellions of 1837 and 1838 in the Canadas. In both Lower and Upper Canada, recklessly courageous little groups of radical extremists responded to the British Government's flat refusal of their leaders' demands for self-government by resorting to arms against the privileged local oligarchies which profited by that refusal and exploited it against them. These outbreaks were relatively puny affairs, poorly led because unplanned and uncoördinated by the Upper Canadian leader, W. L. Mackenzie, and his Lower Canadian counterpart, L. J. Papineau (both of whom had to flee to the United States), and they were fairly easily, although unnecessarily brutally, stamped out. Yet they were rebellions, the ultimate form of protest against the intransigence of Lord John Russell and the British Government. These late echoes of 1775 forced the Whig Cabinet to send out an investigator, and an odd set of circumstances determined that he should be "Radical Jack" Lambton, Earl of Durham, the chief Benthamite goad to the reluctant Grey in Parliament during the campaign for the British Reform Act of 1832.[7]

Durham made many mistakes, some of them serious, in connection with his mission and with the *Report* which he submitted on his return, but later generations are agreed that he redeemed himself by lending his prestige to two Canadian ideas which ultimately, if reluctantly, became tolerable to British authority. These Canadian ideas seem to have taken form, during the months of Jackson's triumph in 1828–1829, from the discussions of a Toronto group which centered in W. W. Baldwin and his son Robert. Yet they owed nothing to the United States, for they suggested that the British cabinet system, under which the executive committee of Parliament may exercise power only so long as it enjoys the support of a majority, should be introduced in colonies. This seemed to mean independence to British parliamentarians, who, in accordance with John Austin's recent utterances on indivisible sovereignty, believed that colo-

7. Lord John Russell was "Finality Jack" because of his refusal to extend political democracy after 1832. It should be noted that Durham repeatedly used American achievements to bolster up his arguments in favor of Canadian nationality and self-government.

nial executives should be appointed by British authority. Robert Baldwin and Durham provided a simple way out of this impasse which has since been applied to British India and to the American Philippines. They would reserve to the British Parliament certain fields of government as imperial affairs, and in all others concede to the colonial legislature autonomy and the cabinet system of responsible parliamentary government.[8]

It was not until 1847 that this responsible government was achieved, for the British Government rejected practically all of Durham's recommendations except his ill-conceived proposal to unite the Canadas in order to subject the French Canadians to the existing numerical majority of English-speaking Canadians. Yet the British North American democrats finally succeeded, it would seem, for two reasons—the high quality of their native statesmen, and the "Little England," or anti-imperialistic mood in Great Britain which accompanied the substitution of free trade and navigation for the old mercantile empire.

Joseph Howe of Nova Scotia did the work so far as the Maritime Provinces were concerned, partly by brilliant ridicule of the old colonial system and of the unrealistic way in which Lord John Russell clung to Austinian concepts of indivisible sovereignty, but largely because he could win majorities in the Nova Scotian legislature and use them to deny support to any executive unless it would promote his ends. Louis Lafontaine, the farsighted leader of the democratic wing of the victimized French Canadians, deserves the principal credit in the united Province of Canada because he roused his followers from the sullen apathy and resentment which they naturally felt as a legislative minority, particularly after Durham's arrogant, scathing comments on them and their ways. By consenting to, and maintaining, a firm alliance with Robert Baldwin and the English-speaking democrats, Lafontaine brought about the ironical result that instead of the Union swamping the French, an Anglo-French democratic majority swamped the oligarchical parties of both halves of the Province.

During this long struggle for British colonial democracy, which had begun in earnest just before the War of 1812, probably the most authentic North American note was the continuous emphasis on control of the patronage. No one made any secret of it on either side of the contest and it is worth noticing that the plums of office were much richer than in the United States. The Lieutenant-Governor of Upper Canada, for instance,

8. Thus echoing the ineffective British proposals of 1778 for the pacification of the United States, and of 1782 for the pacification of Ireland, or, perhaps better still, the American Northwest Ordinance of 1787. See pp. 48, 67, 75, above.

had received over $20,000 a year, that is about ten times the average
salary of a state governor, or about the same salary as the President of
the United States, and the Chief Justice of the Province of Upper Canada
had earned half as much again as the Chief Justice of the United States.
Other salaries were in proportion. Howe, Lafontaine, and Baldwin un-
ceasingly made patronage the keystone of the arch of cabinet government and, once their constitutional goal was reached, the periodical
locusts of the spoils system became a regular feature of British North
American politics. The one striking divergence from North American
practice, and a useful one on the whole, was that the British colonists did
not extend the electoral principle to the choice of judges. In the Province
of Canada, they did, however, extend it to the upper house of the legislature, thus flouting the analogy to the House of Lords which Pitt and
Simcoe had dreamed of far back in 1791.

The Little Englandism which accompanied free trade in the British
Empire is so notorious that it needs little more than mention here. In the
light of their own pronouncements, it is fair to say that the prevailing
attitude of the British ruling classes in the late 'forties was that colonies
(except India) were expensive nuisances. The thing to do was to set them
solidly on their own feet and to be grateful if they walked off toward
independence. There were very few persons as wise as Lord Elgin, the
Governor of Canada. He rejoiced in agreeing with the Canadian political
leaders (and told the British Government so), that when the responsibilities of colonial autonomy came to light alongside its privileges, colonial statesmen would do their utmost to maintain the British connection.

Oddly enough, the Canadian democratic rebellions contributed substantially to the cluster of very dangerous situations involving Great
Britain, the United States, and British North America which were liquidated in 1842 by Lord Ashburton and Daniel Webster. Many of the
active participants in the rebellions, and sympathizers who lost hope
when the oligarchs triumphed, escaped to the United States, where they
were welcomed as martyrs of freedom. This would not necessarily have
had serious consequences except for the fact that the depression of 1837
had thrown large numbers of adventurous Americans out of employment
and this at a time when the expansionist mood was growing daily, when
border filibustering was almost becoming a special American profession,
and when anti-British feeling among the Irish in the United States was
bitter and strong. With alarming suddenness, from the Atlantic to Detroit, so-called "Hunters' Lodges" sprang into being to recruit and arm
for the freeing of British North America from British tyranny.

From 1837 to 1842, therefore, the border regions caused abundant anxiety. One breach of international correctness succeeded another. There were several destructive American raids into British territory, not unmixed with simple piracy and mayhem, and, when an American force assembled on Navy Island in the Niagara River, Canadian volunteers cut out their supply vessel, the *Caroline*, from a dock on the American shore and set her on fire. Later a Canadian named McLeod was rash enough to boast in a New York saloon that he had killed a man in that affair, thus getting himself arrested for murder and thoroughly embarrassing everyone interested in calming the tempest. The American federal authorities did their belated best to preserve correct relations, but President Van Buren's hand had been weakened by the economic depression and most Americans believed that Canadians wanted to throw off the British yoke. British tempers were sore over the current repudiation of millions of dollars of indebtedness by American public and private borrowers. British Americans quite naturally feared that they were going to be annexed according to the formula of Manifest Destiny as worked out in Texas and Oregon.

Probably the principal reason why an Anglo-American war did not break out about 1840 was that the two countries were each other's best customers. A secondary aspect of this situation goes far to explain the understanding upon which Webster and Ashburton based their remarkable achievements. Webster had visited England in 1839 in behalf of distressed American banking and commercial concerns and had surprisingly succeeded in selling Massachusetts stock and western lands. The discredited United States still had to have British capital. Webster met Ashburton, who was the head of the investment house of Baring, then under a cloud because it had distributed large amounts of American securities in Great Britain. Webster was able to serve both the Barings and his American backers by reassuring statements about the essential soundness of the States and by hints that the Federal Government would protect investors. He became Secretary of State in 1841, when the Whigs came in, and the two men who had such closely interlocked financial interests were chosen to make peace along the borders.

They did so by a series of clever compromises and shrewd manipulations of angry local feelings which two ordinary diplomats could hardly have brought about. It was at this settlement, for instance, that Fort Montgomery (commonly called Fort Blunder) at Rouses Point, New York, was restored to the United States by warping the boundary line northward from the forty-fifth parallel. When this very costly stone fortress had been near completion twenty-five years before in order to cover Lake Champlain against Canadian invasion, the site chosen was unhappily discovered to lie within the boundaries of Lower Canada! In 1842 Great Britain handed it back by accepting the distortion of an ancient territorial division, and the United States promptly set to work to bring the fort to completion. It is hard to imagine that kind of boundary adjustment taking place at the end of five years of extreme tension anywhere in the world except between the domains of Britain's offspring in North America.

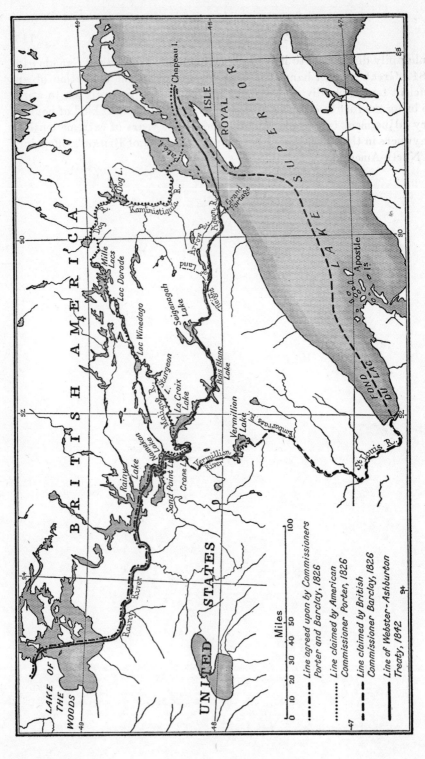

Isle Royal to Lake of the Woods

LAKE OF THE WOODS

BRITISH AMERICA

UNITED STATES

Rainy River

Rainy Lake

Namakan Lake

Sand Point Lake

Crane L.

Vermillion River

Vermillion Lake

La Croix Lake

Sturgeon L.

Maligne R.

Bois Blanc Lake

Embarrass R.

St. Louis R.

FOND DU LAC

LAKE SUPERIOR

Apostle Is.

Grand Portage

Pigeon R.

Arrow R.

Height of Land

Seiganegah Lake

Lac Winedago

Lac Dorade

Mille Lacs

Dog R.

Dog L.

Kaministiquia R.

Pie I.

ISLE ROYAL

Chapeau I.

Miles
0 10 20 30 40 50   100

—··—··— Line agreed upon by Commissioners
        Porter and Barclay, 1826
·········· Line claimed by American
        Commissioner Porter, 1826
— — — — Line claimed by British
        Commissioner Barclay, 1826
———————— Line of Webster-Ashburton
        Treaty, 1842

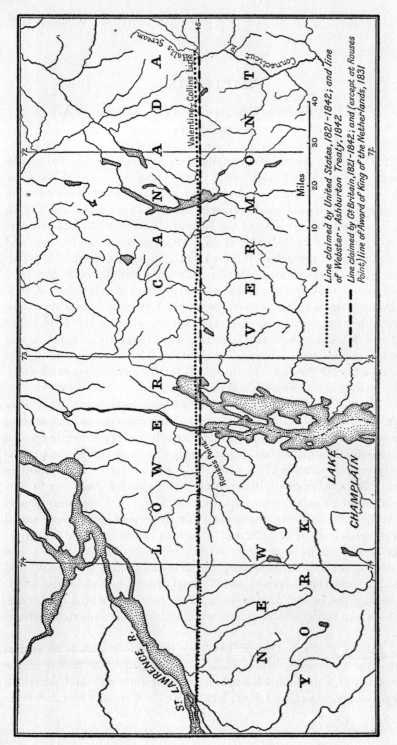

The Forty-Fifth Parallel

Line claimed by United States, 1821–1842; and line of Webster – Ashburton Treaty, 1842

Line claimed by Gt Britain, 1821–1842; and (except at Rouses Point,) line of Award of King of the Netherlands, 1831

CHAPTER IX

FREE TRADE, RECIPROCITY, CIVIL WAR
(1840–1865)

THE 'forties were feverish in Canada. When Great Britain baited the Union of Lower and Upper Canada in 1841 with guaranteed loans for public works, the Canadians decided to spend most of the money on enlarging the Welland Canal and completing the canalization of the St. Lawrence. Since the opening of the Rideau Canal in 1832, inbound cargoes had gone by it to the Lakes from the St. Lawrence and Ottawa, and only outbound cargoes had followed the risky route down the rapid-strewn St. Lawrence and its inadequate early canals. Now Montreal hoped to draw not only Canadian, but a large share of midwestern American products down to her harbor, for the St. Lawrence canals were to be ship canals abundantly supplied with water, whereas the Erie barge canal was a longer route to tidewater, was frequently congested, and from time to time rendered useless by drought. The American middle west was clamoring for the added facilities and for the competitive rates which the St. Lawrence waterway would provide.

The restrictive British laws of trade and navigation had never amounted to much west of the Richelieu. American commodities seeking European markets had at various times and in varying amounts crossed the rivers and lakes into the Canadas, becoming Canadian in the process and enjoying the benefits of the protected market in Great Britain. Intermittent efforts to impose British mercantilistic controls had come to very little in the long run, since the natural facilities for exchange were almost irresistible; and, in the opposite direction, American tariffs were scaled down progressively after 1832 and American commercial and transportation organizations were aggressive in seeking business. The ancient competition between the Hudson (plus Erie and Champlain canals) and the St. Lawrence (plus Rideau and Welland canals) had never died away, and, during the fateful decade when Great Britain adopted free trade, ingenious men in the United States were scheming for American advantage.

Sir Robert Peel's budget of 1842, by its bold free-trade measures, startled the Canadians, whose whole canal program was poised on the expectation of a protected British market for their own and American wood products, wheat, and flour. Next year the Canada Corn Act reassured them somewhat by restoring their substantial advantage in return for their setting up a moderate tariff against American grain. At the same time, however, it was conceded that if American grain was milled in Canada, the flour was to be considered Canadian in Great Britain, a provision which quickly produced an unhealthy speculative boom in the Canadian milling industry.

New York struck back almost immediately. In 1845 and 1846 the Federal Government was induced to pass drawback laws which authorized the restitution of duties on Canadian imports and exports which passed through the United States. The Erie Canal, which was paying good dividends and at the same time was being enlarged, thus served notice that it aimed to handle as much as possible of the business of Canada as well as that of the Lakes states. Montreal was in despair, but joy reigned in the western part of Canada, where the rural interest had been complaining for thirty years against the high freight rates to and from Canadian tidewater.

The Irish famine and Peel's courageous sacrifice of his own political career by repealing the protective Corn Laws in 1846 struck Montreal like lightning. While still reeling from the shock of their lost preferences, the merchants saw stealing up their great river an unending line of ships bearing thousands of the survivors of Ireland's disaster. With them came cholera and the utter lassitude which made the immigrants unable to help themselves. In 1847 about 100,000 fugitives from the throes of "John Bull's Other Island" strained to the limit the resources of private charity, cost the provincial administration over £150,000, and spread disease throughout the country. That same year world commodity prices crashed and the North Atlantic economy plunged into a depression which lasted until 1850. Finally it was discovered in 1849 and 1850 that, although the new canals made it distinctly cheaper to ship from the interior to Montreal than to New York, the opposite was the case when full transportation to Europe was in question. The difficulties and dangers of navigation on the St. Lawrence, even after it was opened to the world's ships in 1849, meant that fewer ships came to Quebec and Montreal than to New York, and that higher costs of pilotage, insurance, etc., increased their freight rates. To ship a ton of grain from Chicago to Liverpool via Montreal cost about $13.75 at a time when it could go by New York for about $10.50.

Such was the train of uncertainty, culminating in unalloyed disasters, which made the bewildered masters of Montreal grope for the devilish persons who had compassed their destruction. They persuaded themselves that they had found them in Lafontaine and Baldwin, and in the Governor in Canada and the Government in London who had faithfully acceded to their winning of colonial autonomy in 1847.

On Wednesday, April 25, 1849, Lord Elgin, the Governor of Canada, drove in to Montreal from his residence in the suburbs in order to hear the final reading of the bills which had been carried through the now autonomous Canadian Parliament by the Lafontaine-Baldwin Government. A tense city awaited him in the streets and in the galleries of the parliament buildings. When, late in the afternoon, he gave his formal assent to a bill which compensated even convicted rebels of the former Lower Canada for their losses and out-of-pocket expenses arising from the Rebellions of 1837 and 1838, there was an angry roar from the galleries and a pell-mell rush outdoors to spread the news. When the Governor returned to his carriage, a mob bombarded him and his entourage with refuse.

That night the whole city was systematically aroused to violence. After a wild meeting by torchlight on the Champ de Mars, the rioters marched back to the parliament buildings where the legislature was again at work. Volleys of stones smashed the windows, human battering-rams burst in the doors, and an orgy of destruction began. When the mob happened on the stationery storeroom, the papers invited their torches. Within a few minutes, fanned by a high wind, fire raced through the buildings and flames burst through hundreds of openings to fill the sky with burning fragments and momentarily to glut the mob with the thrill.

Rioting and destruction went on for days, in spite of the efforts of the military to protect the persons and property of the Government and the legislators. When the courageous Governor returned to the city on Monday, April 30, he and his companions were again assailed with stones and rotten eggs and escaped from the city by a ruse. Gradually the unrest subsided into sullen waiting to see whether the British Government would disallow the Rebellion Losses Act. Early in July it was learned that they would not. "It is said," declared an embittered open letter to Elgin, "that the policy of the present Cabinet is to get quit of Canada, and that your instructions were to endeavour to bring that about, now as you have done, by disgusting the British population of the Province. It was a dishonourable policy and your friends knew where to find a man for the dirty duty. Again I say, go home thou good and faithful servant, you have well performed the work assigned to you—go and receive your reward." With the four leading English newspapers of the city fanning angry passions, the conservative, hitherto professedly British, leaders of Montreal's mercantile community gave final vent to their rage early in October by circulating a vigorous manifesto which advocated the annexation of Canada to the United States.

The truth was, as D. G. Creighton has demonstrated, that the ninety-year-old commercial empire of the St. Lawrence had collapsed in ruins, and its manipulators could think of only one place to which to turn. The Rebellion Losses Act was merely the straw that broke the camel's back. A community, which by great daring and inventiveness had for three generations overcome the relative commercial disadvantages of Montreal, and had alternately fawned upon and attempted to bully British governments in order to maintain its far-flung apparatus, felt itself naked and helpless when Great Britain adopted free trade and navigation and turned over the government of Canada to Canadian democrats. In the meantime the economy of the United States had expanded so vigorously in every direction that it was drawing population away from all of the British provinces. For the moment the shaken leaders of Montreal could think of nothing better than incorporation into the irresistible colossus. In their despair, they announced that only one remedy lay open to them— "a Friendly and peaceful separation from British connexion, and a union upon equitable terms with the great North American confederacy of sovereign States."

The Montreal annexationists quickly realized, however, that they had gone too far in every way during 1849. They grew ashamed of their own extravagant utterances and tried to clear their skirts of the mobs' excesses. They learned that the French Canadians feared absorption in the United States far more than the continuation of what they were beginning to think of as a potentially beneficial connection with Great Britain. Habitual Montreal Tories found it hard to bear the reproaches which were fired at their heads from the Maritime Provinces and Canada West. Even New Brunswick, whose economic life had been thoroughly dislocated by the rapid reduction of the British preferential duties on colonial timber, deplored the contemplated treason. The signers and promoters of the Annexation Manifesto began to cast about for excuses, therefore, and quickly found a marvelously convenient one in the deplorable Fugitive Slave Law of 1850 which was so important a part of the last compromise between the slave and the free areas of the United States. The Montreal *Witness* grasped at the straw. "We have hitherto advocated annexation," it declared, "but rather than consent to the annexation of Canada to the United States, while the slave-catching law remains in force . . . we would be willing not only to forego all the advantages of annexation, but to see Canada ten times poorer and worse governed than she is."

Such excuses might serve to ease the sudden turnabout, but they carried too little weight to be of permanent worth. Gradually, however, the appropriate line of retreat emerged in the revival of proposals which had been made in the early 'forties for reciprocal free trade in natural products between the British North American provinces and the United States. At that time the suggestions had seemed to be merely one variety of the Canadian somersaults which had accompanied the revolution in British commercial and imperial policies. Now they seemed eminently reasonable, for while Britain had been freeing her trade and her colonies, the latter had, as early as 1847, successfully asserted their fiscal independence by setting up differential tariffs. It was a short step from this for the same provinces to bargain for free or preferential trade with the United States while at the same time imposing higher duties against other nations, including free-trade Great Britain herself. In 1848 a Canadian mission headed by William Hamilton Merritt presented the arguments for North American free trade in natural products before committees of both houses of the American Congress.

Three men—Merritt being one, and the other two Thomas Coltrin Keefer and Israel DeWolf Andrews—none of them Montrealers, had a great deal to do with bringing about this fundamental reorientation of the British provinces. All three had the capacity, as unusual then as now, of not allowing political sovereignty or maps made on Mercator's projection to eclipse the facts of geography. All alike could visualize the great region whose corners were Newfoundland, Lake Superior, the mouth of the Missouri, and the mouth of the Hudson, as it lay curved and compact on the terrestrial sphere, instead of flat and distorted as on the maps. All three thought of it in terms of the natural waterways, canals, and the best land channels for roads and railways, by which its wealth of products could most cheaply and freely reach the Atlantic. None of them ever lost sight of the fact that the more northern the ocean route the shorter the distance to Europe. Keefer even felt impelled to draw to the attention of the United States Congress the Hudson Bay entry to the mid-continent. "The distance from the shores of Superior to those of Hudson's Bay," he pointed out, "is no greater than that between the Hudson river, at Albany, and Lake Erie, at Buffalo; the sea-route to Britain is shorter this way than by the lakes and Montreal, New York, or Boston."

Merritt was born a New Yorker, but in 1796, at the age of three, migrated with his parents to the Niagara district of Upper Canada. A man of unusual energy and versatility, his imagination was fired by the building of the Erie Canal to emulate it by a canal based on the Welland River which would circumvent impassable Niagara. It took him from 1818 to

1829 to complete the task, first with local and American funds, and finally with subscriptions from the governments of the Canadas and Great Britain. As times changed, he proved adaptable enough to rise above his earlier scorn for anyone who would "compare the mighty St. Lawrence to a trumpery Rail Road."

Keefer was his protégé, the son born in 1821 to a neighbor on the Welland River whose family had moved in from the United States in 1792. He worked as an engineer on the Erie and Welland canals and, under Merritt, on those of the Ottawa River. By 1851 he was surveying the route of the Grand Trunk Railroad, that great supplement to the St. Lawrence waterway which was to run from Chicago across Canada and Maine to Portland. Long before he died in 1915 he had received the highest honors which his engineering colleagues in Canada, the United States, and Great Britain could pay him.

Andrews was born in Eastport, Maine, in 1813, the grandson of an eighteenth-century Massachusetts migrant to the lands of the expelled Acadians, whose Nova Scotian son had left the Minas Basin for the United States. As American consul at St. John, New Brunswick, during the troubled 'forties, Andrews became convinced that North American free trade would be to the benefit of all concerned, and in 1849 he persuaded the American Government to make him a special agent in order to inquire into this possibility in the British provinces. In Canada he turned to Merritt, who passed him on to Keefer, thus completing a triple alliance of men who by birth and experience could hardly help thinking in international terms.

Of the three men, Andrews played the most spectacular part, partly because he habitually did such spectacular things as to take a large suite of rooms for two months or more in New York's Astor House or at the National Hotel in Washington, but largely because, while it was all very well for the British provinces to want reciprocity, he had to combine scattered interests in the United States to make it appear that a majority of the American people wanted it as well. Andrews was a magnificent early example of the American genus *Lobbyist*. He contrived to get the American, British, and Canadian governments—and other public bodies as well—to pay him very large amounts for practically identical services and expenses. He subsidized the editors of leading newspapers and reviews, bought legislators, entertained lavishly, organized delegations and conventions at strategic times and places, and pulled wires in the legislative and diplomatic corridors of London, Washington, and the British-American provincial capitals. Bribery appears to have been his commonest procedure. Most of his associates became his creditors and he died in 1871, still a lobbyist, still trying to collect enormous bills from various governmental authorities for expenditures which he had not been authorized to make.

Keefer was Andrews' principal technical assistant from 1849 to 1853. He prepared a number of remarkable maps of the eastern Canadian-American region which by their projection gave a truer idea of the distances within the continent and between it and Europe, and by their attention to topography made obvious the best routes from the interior to the Atlantic Coast. At a time when statistics were rare and bad, he collected copious excellent ones. And into his memoranda for Andrews, from which the American agent composed two excellent reports for Congress, he wove some of the ideas which he had worked out in two published studies, *The Philosophy of Railroads* (1849) and *The Canals of Canada* (1850). These could be boiled down to the convictions that railroads and waterways must complement each other, that Canada must keep up with the States in railroad construction, that only navigation improvements on the St. Lawrence above and below Montreal were needed to make it the natural outlet of the mid-continent, and that better canals on the Richelieu–Champlain–Hudson route would make the island city a great summer entrepôt for both incoming and outgoing trade.

The active negotiations by the American, British, and British provincial governments from 1847 onward which finally produced the Reciprocity Treaty of 1854 make an intricate and fascinating story, but its details cannot be repeated here. For them must be substituted the somewhat simpler pattern of interplay among the varied economic and political interests which were involved. In considering that interplay one new general factor must be borne in mind. This was the cyclical return of prosperity which began in 1851 and which promptly reduced the sense of panic urgency which had been growing in the provinces. Reciprocity no longer seemed to be the only alternative to ruin. In fact all the provinces began to consider how they might retaliate against the American tariffs of 1842 and 1846 which had set up 20 per cent ad valorem duties against their grain, flour, timber, and other products.

The principal ingredients in the original American attitude toward reciprocity with British North America were general ignorance and apathy, both of which were accentuated by the political obsession with the now chronic sectional conflict between north and south. The actual passage of the Reciprocity Act, for instance, took place during that storm center, the debates on the Kansas-Nebraska Act. In addition the habitual anti-British sentiments of the nation were intensified by the prolonged Anglo-American strife over Nicaragua and an isthmus canal.

There were only two substantial special interests which tried to break through the general indifference. The Lakes states wanted the use and the competitive leverage which they could derive from the St. Lawrence waterways and from Canadian timber. One of their petitions to Congress complained in 1850 that their immense trade had been "forced to market through the Erie canal, four feet in depth and forty feet in width," whereas the St. Lawrence, "this great and natural outlet of the lakes seems designed by Providence as the great commercial channel by which the immense commerce of the lakes should find its way to the Atlantic ocean and the world." The second interest was New England's ancient insistence on free access to the whole North Atlantic fisheries, coupled with the equally ancient determination to carry on profitable smuggling on the side. Since the Convention of 1818 these insistences had taken the form of ignoring the restriction on inshore fisheries as much as possible and taking a chance on bluffing the way out if caught.

It was the second special interest rather than the first which broke down American indifference and compelled the Administration to act, for in 1852, in response to Nova Scotian pressure, the British Government sent out a small naval squadron to enforce the British interpretation of the Convention of 1818. This action seemed to President Pierce when he came into office in 1853 to contain in it the threat of incidents which might well lead to foreign war at a time when the United States was notoriously close to war at home. Committing his Administration to the solution of the fisheries problem, he sent Andrews off to the Maritimes, with abundant funds, to promote the idea of a reciprocity treaty as a bargaining counter for fisheries concessions. As Secretary Caleb Cushing wrote, when putting another $5,000 at his disposal, "The President is expecting you to produce the results." Andrews lavishly exceeded the financial means provided, but proved that he could manipulate Maritime legislators quite as well as American ones.

Once Congress was shaken out of its apathy by executive pressure, the usual clashes of economic interest developed among the states, along with fears of competition from provincial products. These differences dwindled into insignificance, of course, in comparison with the great tug-of-war between north and south. Quite unexpectedly, however, it was found possible to secure support for reciprocity from both north and south for entirely opposite reasons. The north was persuaded that reciprocity would be merely the preliminary step to annexation, which would increase the number of free states and compensate for the defeat suffered in the Kansas-Nebraska Act of May, 1854. The southern Democrats, on the other hand, who had hitherto feared the annexation of the

British provinces for just that reason, were persuaded that reciprocity would eclipse the danger by giving the provinces the economic basis for independence.

British policy in the whole matter was frankly expedient because of the Little Englandism which prevailed at the time. The one strong line of policy was that worked out by Lord Elgin in collaboration with Merritt and Baldwin. He started out with the argument that "unless reciprocity of trade with the United States be established, these colonies must be lost to England." Then, appealing to the prevalent British passion for economic retrenchment, he asserted that the prosperity which would accompany reciprocity would enable the provinces to pay for their own defense. In London these arguments were gradually interwoven with the desire to mollify the colonies for the shocks which they had recently received from the revolution in British commercial policy and with the anxiety to avoid either colonial debt repudiation or angry secession from the Empire. In addition, it was realized that the provinces had two excellent bargaining assets in the fisheries and the St. Lawrence waterway. With the Crimean War impending, and Russia and the United States becoming friends, the time seemed to have come for a general settlement of the outstanding issues in North America. Reciprocity negotiations appeared to be the best vehicle for the load.

The provinces naturally had their own peculiar interests to serve. Canada wanted reciprocal free trade for natural products in order both to break through the 20 per cent American tariff and to attract traffic to the St. Lawrence waterway. Nova Scotia was belligerently opposed to any treaty which modified the Fisheries Convention of 1818 as being "not only ruinous to the shore fishery of this Province, but most injurious to the national welfare and derogatory to the honour of the British Crown." On the other hand, free entry of Nova Scotian fish, coal, ships, and timber to the American market was worth considering, particularly if there was any danger that Great Britain might insist on settling the fisheries controversy without deferring to Nova Scotia. New Brunswick was naturally less concerned about the fisheries than about a market for her lumber and ships. Prince Edward Island, whose agricultural wealth made her a natural supply point (and smuggling center) for American fishermen, was quite willing to exchange the inshore fishery for free trade. Newfoundland, at first apathetic, woke up in time to see the advantage of the American market for her fish. In all these colonies, the British governors did their utmost to facilitate the Home Government's determination to reach a settlement with the United States.

The Reciprocity Treaty of 1854 was passed by Congress with suspi-

cious ease; in fact, the legislators themselves were not very clear as to
how or why it had been done. "Sectionalism vanished for the time," reported the well-subsidized *North American Review*, "and the act was
swept through Congress with an irresistible enthusiasm, of which our history affords no parallel." Actually it was the work of the American, British, and Canadian administrations rather than of the immediate representatives of the peoples concerned. Elgin went down to Washington and
wined and entertained the southern Democrats with infectious enthusiasm. The British legation gave a ball from which the company went home
"pleased with each other, themselves, and the rest of mankind." Meanwhile Andrews was at the National Hotel perfecting a masterpiece of congressional machine politics whose details can be imagined from the enormous expense accounts which President Pierce and Secretary Marcy
subsequently approved. Keefer's wry comment provides as good a summary as any. The official dignitaries, he said, "formed a tableau of political glory as brilliant and as deceptive as the variegated 'fizzle' which ends
a theatrical performance—made their bow to an admiring audience and
dissolved the long standing partnership, leaving Andrews to wind-up the
business—and pay the debts."[1]

A treaty which had passed so miraculously had to be a skilful structure of compromise. Its minimum term was ten years, with one additional
year of notice to terminate by either party. It provided for reciprocal
free access to the Atlantic coastal fisheries north of 36° (*pace* Florida).
The provinces secured free trade in all their important natural products,
including the Nova Scotian bituminous coal against which Pennsylvania
had protested until it was discovered that Cunard of Halifax and other
provincial users already imported American anthracite. A really deft
touch, for the benefit of the south, was the inclusion of naval stores, dried
fruit, and unmanufactured tobacco. The entire complex problem of
manufactured goods was wisely handled by leaving them out of the reciprocal arrangements made in the Treaty. The opening of the Canadian
canals and waterways was balanced by free navigation on Lake Michigan
and by the Federal Government's promise to urge the states to concede
equal treatment on their canals. The Maine lumbermen were allowed free
passage for their lumber down the St. John River. The Maritimes suffered the only substantial disappointments in their exclusion from the
American coastal trade and the refusal of American registration to
province-built vessels sold in the United States.

1. Andrews claimed that he spent $118,000 in securing the passage of the Treaty and
that he had also spent about $90,000 as President Pierce's agent in British North Amer-
ica. His inflated, complicated claims on various American, British, and Canadian public
authorities were by no means completely satisfied at his death.

Nova Scotia had not been represented at Washington, owing to a train of misunderstanding, and the province, already well practiced in making the most of any case it had, put up a vigorous, truculent opposition to the Treaty and to the manner of its negotiation. The British Government had wisely decided to signalize colonial self-government by referring the Treaty to each legislature for ratification so that this opposition had full expression. Once Nova Scotia realized that the inshore fisheries had already been opened to Americans and that the British naval squadron was being withdrawn, she fell into line. The American Government thereupon provided the coping stone of magnanimity by deciding that, since American fishermen had enjoyed free access during the season of 1854, the duties which had been paid in the interval between the signature of the Treaty and its final ratification by the British Parliament in February, 1855, on province fish and on the other free articles should be remitted. The provinces reciprocated. North America fairly glowed with satisfaction over its experiment in free trade. And, whether they realized it or not, the British provinces had been granted a ten-year reprieve from American expansionism.

The honeymoon of good feeling lasted for three years, with abundant expressions of satisfaction from all parties concerned, even from Nova Scotia. Then, gradually, an element in the situation which had been almost overlooked began to assert itself. This was the absolute necessity for Canada to raise substantial revenues in order to carry the public debts which had been incurred in building her transportation facilities. Looking backward from the present, it is easy to see that the very existence of both the Province and the later Dominion of Canada as entities separate from the United States has depended on such expensive transportation services that a large proportion of their cost has had to be met from the public purse. This was not nearly so apparent in the exuberant 'fifties, but it was then that Canadians for the first time began systematically to adopt the only procedure by which they could surmount this handicap, that is, the imposition of quite high tariffs on manufactured goods. Since that time, Canadians have paid substantially (although not always consciously or willingly) for the privilege of remaining Canadians by prices for a great many of the manufactures which they use and consume which are perceptibly higher than those in the United States.

The Canadian protectionist movement was necessarily an obscure one for many years after its beginning about 1845, for it conflicted in spirit with both the free-trade creed of Great Britain and the reciprocity negotiations with the United States. It was, of course, closely related to the rapid spread of small industries in Canada. The manufacturers, like their predecessors in New England, pleaded to the Government that, until they were strong in their own right, they must be protected against those elsewhere who had enjoyed a head start. So far as Great Britain was concerned, they felt that the violent dislocation to which they had been subjected in the 'forties justified any action which they felt necessary for their economic betterment. As for the United States, critics had only to be reminded that the Reciprocity Treaty had been expressly limited to natural products and that Canadian duties on manufactured goods were little more than half of the American rates. The Canadian protectionists' self-righteousness was reënforced because they could point with apparent public spirit to the decline in Canadian customs revenue which resulted from the Treaty.

In 1857 economic depression returned again to Europe and America alike. In 1858 the first Canadian protectionist association, the Society for the Development of Canadian Industry, was founded and went on record in favor of 25 to 30 per cent duties on manufactures which could be produced in Canada. The Government responded to their pleas in 1858 and 1859 by raising the duties, but to levels still below the analogous American rates. None the less the increased duties provoked a storm of ineffectual protest among British manufacturers who were thus rudely awakened to the realities of colonial self-government. Accompanying administrative devices, which were designed to encourage the direct importation of foreign goods to Canada instead of through the United States and to encourage Lakes traffic to by-pass Buffalo and Oswego and go on to Montreal, stirred up vigorous resentment in informed American centers. New York State quickly became the core of systematic agitation against the Reciprocity Treaty and succeeded in inculcating a fairly general, but largely erroneous, belief in the United States that Canada had violated the spirit of the agreement.

Yet it was the American Civil War which made irrelevant the question whether the United States and Canada might have adjusted their difficulties by a revision of the Treaty. That terribly prolonged conflict had such poisonous consequences in the relations among the United States and Great Britain and the British provinces that no treaty of mutual commercial accommodations would have had any chance of survival.

Long before the war broke out, British America had taken its stand on Negro slavery. By the beginning of the nineteenth century, practically all Negroes in the provinces had been freed because their owners could not depend on the courts to recognize such property rights. Nova Scotia had even anticipated the later Liberian experiment of American friends of the Negro by transporting to Sierra Leone about twelve hundred

Negroes of the loyalist migration.[2] By 1833, when the British Parliament formally emancipated all the slaves in the colonies, the British North American provinces, particularly southwestern Canada with its mild climate, had become to terrified American colored folk "the land that we Negroes call rock and our land of promise." In 1837 an Anti-Slavery Society was founded and systematic efforts at Negro settlement were well under way. *Uncle Tom's Cabin* was a best seller in both English and French versions. The Fugitive Slave Law of 1850 excited unanimous condemnation and had the effect of propelling more thousands of Negroes from their threatened position in the free states to the assured safety of the provinces. Appropriately enough, John Brown planned his famous raid in May, 1858, at Chatham, Canada West, close to the principal Negro settlements.[3] Before Lincoln's election and even after his declaration that his "paramount object" was to save the Union, British Americans generally, like the liberals and working men and women in England, insisted on attaching the great conflict to the moral issue of slavery.

In the first year of the war, however, an incident occurred which seriously undermined the friendly feelings toward the north which characterized the majority of British North Americans. It was one of the most dangerous episodes in the controversy between the United States and Great Britain over freedom of the seas and the rights of neutrals which has lasted from 1783 to the present day, and it occurred just when Great Britain, for reasons of prestige and of dependence on southern products, was least likely to be conciliatory toward the Union Government. In November, 1861, an American naval vessel stopped the British mail steamer *Trent* and insisted on removing Mason and Slidell, two diplomatic representatives of the Southern Confederacy. Instantly British tempers flared up. "I don't know whether you will stand it, but I'll be damned if I do," said Palmerston, and the British Government took immediate steps to reënforce with men and munitions the British North American provinces which might be expected to bear the brunt of the apparently imminent Anglo-American war.[4]

This dangerous crisis was liquidated without war. The Atlantic cable

2. In 1827 Great Britain paid the United States £250,000 for some 3,600 slaves taken to the Maritimes during the Revolution and the War of 1812.

3. After the Civil War, a large proportion of the Negro refugees in Canada returned to the United States in order to live in contact with the main bodies of their own people. The total in Canada alone about 1861 has been variously estimated at forty to fifty thousand, but the first census of the whole Dominion in 1871 recorded only 21,496, a number which had fallen to 19,456 by 1931.

4. A curious sidelight on this crisis is that, when some of the British officers were prevented by the winter closure of the St. Lawrence from reaching Canada quickly, the American Government allowed them to proceed from Portland across Maine by rail.

happened to break down. The dying Prince Consort induced Lord John Russell to moderate his protests. Montgomery Blair and Secretary of State Seward, reënforced by letters which Senator Sumner had received from Bright and Cobden, persuaded Lincoln and the Cabinet to yield after a long session on Christmas Day. Had war come, British North Americans, both English- and French-speaking, would unquestionably have aligned themselves with Great Britain. Even when the tension eased, the friendliness to the north of the liberal majority had been seriously impaired and the arrogance of the conservative minority had been heightened. Perhaps the children of western Canada summarized provincial public opinion pretty accurately. At the beginning of the war when they played "North and South," it was hard to get enough on the southern side. As the war went on and Anglo-American relations grew worse, fewer and fewer youngsters would consent to play Northerners.

Two acts, one British and one American, provided the ballast which enabled thoughtful provincial leaders to keep their ships of state on even keels—the Queen's Proclamation of May 13, 1861, declaring her "determination to maintain a strict and impartial neutrality in the contest," and Lincoln's preliminary Proclamation of September 22, 1862, that on January 1, 1863, all slaves in rebel territory "shall be then, thenceforward, and forever free." With these pronouncements to steady them, the statesmen of British America asked their people to arm, not for attack, but for defense of their neutrality. Let Joseph Howe of Nova Scotia serve as their spokesman. He wrote on Christmas Eve, 1862:

The Northern States are our immediate neighbors, and next to the Mother Country, ought to be our fast friends and firm allies. We claim a common origin, our populations are almost homogeneous . . . our commerce is enormous . . . our people intermarry, and socially intermix, all along the frontier. . . . All these neutral ties and intimate relations are securities for the preservation of peace.

It has sometimes been argued that British North American sentiments about the Civil War were most truly demonstrated by enlistments in the Union armies. In 1869, when Benjamin A. Gould published the results of his statistical investigations into the make-up of the northern armies, he reported that 53,532 of the soldiers had been born in British North America. About thirty-five or forty thousand of these seem to have been French Canadians. Calixa Lavalée, the composer of the Canadian national anthem of today, served in a Rhode Island regiment. One of Joseph Howe's sons also wore the Blue. These enlistments appear to provide abundant evidence that British North America affirmed its pro-Union sentiments in the most practical and sacrificial way.

Yet the statistics cannot be taken at their face value for several reasons. In the first place, emigration from all the provinces to the states had been quite substantial since 1830, and it had accelerated as American tariffs weakened the competition of the Maritimes in the fisheries and the forests, as the good lands south of the Canadian Shield filled up, and as aggressive land and transportation companies opened up the American middle west. The Panic of 1837 and the savage reprisals which followed the suppression of the Rebellions drove many thousands of western Canadians across the Detroit River, and the violent fluctuations of the 'forties in the economy of the British Empire induced many more to succumb to the well-advertised lures of the only middle west that was available to them. French Canadians, who had begun to find their way to New England even before the War of 1812 and who had always followed the moving forest frontier, responded to the pressure of their high birth rate on marginal lands at home by moving outward in all directions, first as seasonal labor seeking additional cash income for home obligations, and then as settlers in agricultural, unskilled, or industrial employment.[5] New England and New York attracted most of them, although devoted efforts by Church and State diverted some to new group settlements on British territory or among the old French stock in the Illinois country. Since there were about 250,000 Canadian-born persons resident in the northern United States in 1860, it is obvious that many must have enlisted voluntarily in the Union armies.

In addition large numbers of British provincials in the United States were conscripted in spite of the constant efforts of the British Minister at Washington to protect them. Furthermore the bounty system of recruitment and the arrangements whereby conscripted men could buy the services of substitutes created an even greater market for men in the British provinces than the one which John Bigelow was promoting at the same time in Europe. There was a constant stream of complaints in the British American press and in official correspondence against "crimping" and other unprincipled activities of professional recruiting agents on both sides of the border. Since the provinces were only too convenient

5. It seems not to be generally known that about this time Napoleon III fished in troubled Canadian waters by sending imposing missions across the Atlantic. He was assisted by the Anglo-French alliance during the Crimean War and by the Anglo-French Reciprocity Treaty of 1860. In response, French Canadians adopted as their own the tricolor flag of France and numbers of them enlisted for Maximilian's adventure in Mexico. They also raised troops of Zouaves for the defense of Rome against the Italian nationalists.

for "bounty jumpers," the American charges that the British Americans made a business of enlisting and then slipping home with various bounties or substitute payments doubtless had a good deal of foundation.

In the light of these considerations, Gould's figures do not contradict as substantially as they might seem to the defensive neutrality which the provinces strove to maintain. Since this neutrality and Great Britain's recognition of the South as a belligerent meant that British territory was open to northern "skedaddlers" and southern refugees alike, the role of neutrals was not easy to play and the provinces performed it only moderately well.[6] Their governments kept up detective services which Confederate agents complained made impossible any substantial activity on their parts, and they sent a constant stream of information about Confederate plans to Washington. Yet Halifax and St. John were regular bases of operation for Southern sea raiders and blockade runners, and Canada can hardly be excused for failing to take active precautions against the Confederate raids from British territory against the United States about which the Administration usually had some information in advance. They did not amount to much, but they could have been prevented.

In 1864 the United States Navy located the troublesome raider *Chesapeake*, an American vessel seized by the Confederates and abandoned by them at Sambro, Nova Scotia. The Northerners took her into Halifax, but failed in the courts to get her restored to her original owners. In the autumn of the same year Confederates seized two American vessels in the Detroit River with the intention of freeing Southern prisoners on Johnson's Island in Lake Erie, but gave up the idea and scuttled the ships. Another group of twenty-five Southerners under the command of Lieutenant Bennett H. Young attacked St. Albans, Vermont, on October 19, 1864, looted $200,000 from three banks, killed one resister, and wounded another. The Vermonters pursued the raiders across the border into Canada, where Young and twelve others were arrested, only to be freed two months later by a local police magistrate on the grounds that they could not properly be held under the existing laws. He also ordered that $90,000 found in their possession should be returned to them. The magistrate's behavior was profoundly disturbing to the Canadian Administration, but the plain fact was that Canada had not taken legal and police measures adequate for the maintenance of a correct neutrality. The indignation of Americans may easily be imagined. In spite of earnest efforts by the Canadian Government and Parliament, and by the courts

6. There was a place named Skedaddle Ridge in southern New Brunswick.

of New Brunswick, the St. Albans raiders had been neither punished nor extradited by the end of the war, but the Canadian Parliament did pay back the $90,000 and effectively tightened up its police controls.

These incidents were, of course, mere pinpricks compared to the millions of dollars' worth of damage which was done by Southern sea raiders (of which the *Alabama*, *Florida*, and *Shenandoah* were most conspicuous) and which the North entered against Great Britain's account because of the interpretation of neutrality which permitted such vessels to be built, armed, provisioned, and allowed to escape from British and British colonial ports.[7] In the case of the *Trent* affair, Lincoln had given in, but he is said to have explained his surrender in a characteristic parable. This was an elaborate story about a man who, believing that he was dying, allowed himself to be persuaded to make a most affecting peace with his worst enemy. Then, when his weeping, departing visitor had almost reached the door, the sick man rose up on his elbow and said, "But see here, Brown, if I should happen to get well, mind, that old grudge stands." As the North gradually ground out its costly victory over the South, the attitudes of President Lincoln and Secretary of State Seward progressively hardened toward Great Britain.

After the *Chesapeake*, Johnson's Island, and St. Albans incidents, the American Administration was ready to act. On November 23, 1864, notice was given of its intention to terminate the Rush-Bagot Agreement for naval disarmament on the Lakes. On December 17 rigid passport regulations were established for the British American borders. On January 16, 1865, Congress, after a thorough and somewhat dispassionate debate, instructed the President to give notice of the termination of the Reciprocity Treaty. The first two reprisals were dropped in March, 1865, but on the seventeenth of that month formal notice was given that the Reciprocity Treaty would terminate one year later. A new and rather grim period had opened in the relations of the United States and British North America.

7. Interpretations of neutrality are subject to change. Compare the neutrality laws and behavior of the United States between September 1, 1939, and December 7, 1941.

CHAPTER X

TRANSCONTINENTAL CANADA
(1865–1871)

THE United States emerged from the Civil War powerful, truculent, and expansionist. The South must be taught to knuckle under. Great Britain must be put in her place. The west beyond the Mississippi must be conquered by the railroad. An ebullient domestic industry must be protected against foreign competition. And the British North American provinces must learn that their destiny was membership in the triumphant Union of the States. Jonathan Mitchel Sewall's chant of 1778 echoed and re-echoed from political orators' throats.

> No pent-up Utica contracts your powers
> But the whole boundless continent is yours.

"I know," cried Secretary of State Seward to a Boston audience in the summer of 1867, "that Nature designs that this whole continent, not merely these thirty-six states, shall be, sooner or later, within the magic circle of the American Union."

About 1865 the new United States began to exact from Great Britain a grudging, but steadily growing, respect as a world power. As Richard Cobden said of his country's politicians: "The alteration of tune is very remarkable. It is clear that the homage which was refused to justice and humanity will be freely given to success." Great Britain was still far in the lead industrially and the United States had to look to her for markets, for capital, and for other economic services, but the amazing American organization of natural resources, transportation, and manufactures during the war was clear warning of what the future would bring. The Union Army was the most powerful in the world. Political and civil employment might rapidly absorb its members, but its equipment and its reservoir of skill and experience in the new kind of warfare remained easily available. The American Navy, although in bad condition and inferior in numbers to the British, had by its ironclads and monitors converted its rivals into quaint anachronisms for many kinds of naval service. The United States felt tough and strong and determined to collect full recompense for the enormous damage done to her commerce—284 vessels representing a loss calculated to be $25,000,000—by the Confederate sea raiders whose activities the British had been arrogant and foolish enough to facilitate.[1]

The war had failed to halt entirely the growth of railways and the occupation of western lands, although it had temporarily diverted and diffused some of these immense expansive energies. None the less the frontier of settlement had moved steadily northwest across Wisconsin until its spearhead up the Mississippi was lodged deeply in the new state of Minnesota, pointing directly at the valley of the Red River of the North which led in turn to the Selkirk Settlement in Hudson's Bay Company territory. In other words, the great northern column of mingled Canadian and American migration, after having been diverted at Lake Huron by the Canadian Shield to a pathway south of the western Great Lakes, was almost ready to be diverted back again into British territory by the high, dry lands in the United States west of the Red River.

Except far south in Texas, the continent was practically without white settlers from the ninetieth meridian, just east of the Red River Valley, to the Pacific Coast. Along the western ocean the discovery of free gold in California in 1848 had drawn in from all over the world a motley population which quite overshadowed the previous Oregon and Hudson's Bay Company settlements. In fact gold launched northward from Sacramento a new spurt of the mineral exploitation of the Cordillera which had begun on the Isthmus of Panama over three centuries before. From Sutter's Mill the Argonauts began weaving in the mountain valleys and passes a network of prospecting and placer-mining which gradually covered this whole broad Cordilleran belt until it petered out on the sea beaches of Alaska two generations later.

The international boundary along the forty-ninth parallel which had been agreed upon in 1846 was, of course, no barrier to the prospectors. By the early 'fifties they were making small strikes in the Fraser Valley, in 1858 they "struck it rich" there, and a "rush" into British territory followed. This influx of predominantly American population did much to precipitate the substitution of British colonial government for Hudson's Bay Company rule both in Vancouver Island and in the new mainland Province of British Columbia. James Douglas, once Dr. McLoughlin's lieutenant in Oregon, left the Company to become Governor of both colonies and to wrestle remarkably successfully with the problems of making the gold diggers live up to British ideas of law and order.

1. During the summer of 1866 the House of Representatives unanimously amended the Neutrality Act of 1818 so as to permit Americans to sell ships to belligerents. Although the Senate did not act on the measure, its potential threat to the British merchant fleet in time of war was not unheeded.

Succeeding "strikes" and "rushes" drew the miners northward and ever deeper into the mountains, but Douglas built roads to the diggings and his administrators kept the peace among rough customers who still used American coinage and celebrated the Fourth of July. The beginnings of the representative government which he distrusted were instituted just before Douglas retired in 1864, the two colonies were united as British Columbia in 1866, and in 1867 Seward completed arrangements for the American purchase of Alaska. Now only a British colony, inhabited largely by Americans, interrupted the dominion of the United States over the Pacific Coast from Mexico to the Arctic Ocean.

The ominous new note for British North America in the postwar expansion of American settlement was the accelerated tempo which was introduced by the railroads. It had taken two and a half centuries to occupy the east, but about a generation would be enough for the west. In the northern mid-continental states the colonization devices of the land-grant railways which had been shaped in the southwest by the Kansas Pacific and the Santa Fé were being developed to a high art, particularly where they were cleverly combined with the Free Homestead Act of 1862. Even during the Civil War, Illinois, Wisconsin, Minnesota, and Iowa added 788,000 persons to their population, chiefly at the expense of the older frontier states. New lands and towns exerted a mightier attraction when the railroads were there to lure men on by the mushroom growth of land values which they stimulated. Chicago had emerged clearly as the railway center of North America.

Down in the southwest the Texans had discovered a gold mine in the countless herds of half-wild "longhorn" cattle which had been left behind by the retreating Spanish Americans. Just before the Civil War they had learned that herds of thousands of these animals could be driven in a self-supporting way across the unfenced country to markets where they would bring many times their cost. After the war, "cow towns" sprang up all along the railroads, and hundreds of thousands of animals, with their custodians, ground out the famous cattle trails which led from the ranges of the southwest toward the cities of the north and east. The sordid, exhausting, monotonous lives of the cowboys, punctuated by brief, explosive sprees in town, began to be translated into interminable plaintive ballads which were based for the most part on the most melancholy of eastern song tunes.

The leap from the Mississippi to the Pacific was a prodigious one, particularly since so much of the area between was desert and mountain, but an Eldorado proceeded to give the world its first lesson in how precious metals could make railway builders achieve the otherwise impossible.

Camels had been tried and discarded. Stagecoach lines were expensive in proportion to their carrying capacity and vulnerable to Indian attacks. The railroad was so obviously the answer to a crying need that the charters of the Union Pacific and Central Pacific for a line from the Missouri to San Francisco Bay were granted during the second year of the Civil War and Congress was then and later persuaded to provide more than the actual cost of building the joint venture. Rails stretched all the way across the continent by May 10, 1869, and new lines were reaching out toward the northern Rockies and the Pacific Coast. The Northern Pacific, chartered in 1864 to run from Duluth to Puget Sound, seemed like a steel arm destined to embrace the Hudson's Bay Company's Red River Settlement and British Columbia as new northern territories or states of the triumphant Union. The breathing-space of the Civil War was over.

The north held industrialists as well as railway builders, land speculators, and mortgage houses, and now, while the south lay prostrate, they need not worry about such nonsense as free trade or low tariffs. They had most of a continent as a market and they meant to exploit it for themselves. The Great Lakes and waterways, the railroad, and the iron, steam-driven ship were being woven into a web of transportation which would carry American grain, cotton, and meat to Europe with unparalleled speed and cheapness. The south was being systematically looted in the name of Reconstruction. Why should the British provinces expect to be "let in on" the new American Golconda? The Reciprocity Treaty was ended and if the colonials wanted to share they must ask to be taken into the United States.

In fact, the north was not averse to evening up a little for the recent Confederate raids from Canada by letting the Canadians have a taste of their own medicine. The means were at hand. As early as 1864 a widespread, semimilitary Irish-American organization, known as the Fenian Brotherhood, was planning to exploit popular anti-British feeling and the talents of thousands of unemployed soldiers in order to filibuster against the British provinces, just as the Hunters' Lodges had done thirty years before.[2] One wing of the Brotherhood wanted to concentrate its efforts on the British Isles, but in 1865 the larger, so-called "Canadian" wing, headed by John O'Neill, split off more or less on its own in order to engage in seven years of activity against the provinces. It claimed in justification that the colonials were only waiting to rebel and that the United States would be glad first to recognize and then to absorb a new American republic, following the Texan precedent.

2. George W. L. Bickley's southern and western filibusterers who were known as the Knights of the Golden Circle had been brought into disrepute by the Civil War.

The British colonists had other notions. Indeed it was a Canadian ex-Fenian, Thomas D'Arcy McGee, whose eloquence and statesmanship did an immense amount to unite the scattered provinces in a drive toward associated nationhood. From the time of the premature Fenian alarm of November, 1864, in western Canada, to O'Neill's last futile raid against Manitoba in 1871, the British North Americans were resolute in resistance. Great Britain sent out arms and substantial reënforcements, the militia and volunteer forces rose to unprecedented proportions, and stern-faced men, sometimes armed only with staves, patrolled the borders from the Atlantic to Lake Huron.

The most serious invasion came in June, 1866, when about six hundred Fenians crossed the Niagara River, captured and entrenched the village of Fort Erie, defeated a militia force at Ridgeway, and were driven out by the volunteers only after they had done a great deal of damage to property in the Niagara district. Although detachments of Fenians continued to be distributed at various points from Maine to Minnesota, the only other systematic attacks were weak raids from Vermont and the Red River Valley. Yet it was a costly business, even with generous aid from Great Britain, for the provinces to guard their frontiers for seven years while American federal and state authorities, ever mindful of the Irish vote, behaved in a conspicuously dilatory and tender way toward the Fenians. It was not until 1870 and 1871 that American authority began to be exerted decisively. Today not a few Canadians have so thoroughly forgotten the Fenians that they are puzzled by the monuments and memorials to the dead, or amused by the truncheons, staves, and more formidable weapons which earlier generations have handed down to them, but the provincials of the 'sixties had good cause to be afraid.

In fact fear of the United States was the principal cause of the germinal federation of four eastern British North American provinces in 1867. In the course of the grand debate on this matter which began in the Canadian Parliament in January, 1865, George Brown listed Canadian anxieties.

The civil war . . . in the neighbouring republic; the possibility of war between Great Britain and the United States; the threatened repeal of the Reciprocity Treaty; the threatened abolition of the American bonding system for goods *in transitu* to and from these provinces; the unsettled position of the Hudson's Bay Company; and the changed feeling of England as to the relations of great colonies to the parent state.

During the next five years he could have added to his list not only the overt activities of the Fenians, but the blunt annexationist pronouncements which were being made by leading American politicians.

The most notable of them was the American Secretary of State, William H. Seward, who had urged Lincoln in April, 1861, to try to avert civil conflict by expansionist ventures in North and Central America and who returned to his theme even before the Civil War had ended. Just as Caleb Cushing had sent off I. D. Andrews in 1853, so Seward dispatched Robert J. Walker, an equally able propagandist, to persuade the provinces that without the Reciprocity Treaty their only course was to join the United States, a doctrine which was reiterated freely by *The Times*, Seward's willing organ in New York. The Secretary's pledged avoidance of interference with the Fenians and his purchase of Alaska in 1867 were quite obviously integral parts of his design, and he privately urged an American banker to advance it by buying out the Hudson's Bay Company's rights in the northern half of the continent.

While Seward was thus trying to squeeze the provinces into the Union, less highly placed men were freely uttering specifically belligerent threats, particularly when they were appealing for the Irish vote. Leaders of that type were Senator Zachariah Chandler, chairman of the Military Affairs Committee, and H. W. Davis, chairman of the Foreign Affairs Committee of the House of Representatives. Davis's successor, N. P. Banks, introduced the Taylor bill of July 2, 1866, in which provision was made for the admission of each of the British provinces into the Union upon request. This bill, which practically coincided with the Fenian invasion of the Niagara district, died in committee after its first and second readings, but it won for Banks and the radical Republicans many votes from the Irish controllers of many constituencies.

The campaign was renewed in 1868 and 1869, after the impeachment and trial of President Johnson were over, with the added incentive that the several provinces were in process of federating into a single tempting transcontinental entity. The new leader was Senator Charles Sumner, chairman of the Foreign Affairs Committee, who was aiming at the presidency. He had become persuaded by the "Little England" attitude of his friends and correspondents in Great Britain that the Mother Country was quite ready to let British North America go. He also believed that the provinces could not get along without the Reciprocity Treaty. In April, 1869, therefore, he denounced in the Senate a proposed convention for the settlement of the "*Alabama* claims" against Great Britain, demanded preposterous damages in the form of "indirect claims," and indicated that Great Britain could pay the bill—at least two, and possibly eight, billion dollars—in the form of her North American colonies. He later told his constituents that he meant exactly what he had suggested. Senator Chandler was his echo, for he declared to Congress that he held Great Britain responsible for half the cost of the Civil War and that he "put on file a mortgage upon the British North American Provinces for the whole amount."

President Grant told his Cabinet and his intimates categorically that one of his chief aims was to effect Sumner's design. Accordingly, when Secretary of State Hamilton Fish was approached by the British Minister at Washington about certain incipient Fenian raids, he replied: "Well, why not withdraw entirely from Canada and remove the pretext for these Fenian threats? At the same time we can settle the *Alabama* Claims immediately." All sorts of Americans, from Carl Schurz to John Lothrop Motley, were urging the same bargain, without any consideration of how the British colonists might feel.

Fish, who was the real statesman of the otherwise lamentable Grant Administration, was shrewd enough to realize that the deal was not quite so simple as it looked. "Great Britain is quite willing to part with Canada when the latter requests it," he told the Cabinet, "but will not cede it, in any negotiations, as a satisfaction for any claim." Yet even his judgment was open to question so far as British willingness was concerned, and it remained a profound mystery to him and to other Americans that the Canadians, under unremitting pressure from the United States, had chosen rather to cling more closely to their Mother Country than to ask her to let them go.

The federal Dominion of Canada which had come into existence on July 1, 1867, was the product of a long historical process which had begun in the eighteenth century, but which became practical, in fact urgent, politics only after 1850. It was a thoroughly natural idea to neighbors of the United States, and the railway not only made it possible, but desirable as well. Most of the basic promotion of the plan was the work of leading statesmen of all parties in the Province of Canada, but by 1863 John Alexander Macdonald, George Brown, Alexander Tilloch Galt, and Georges-Étienne Cartier had discovered that there was a weak but analogous movement toward union of the three Maritime Provinces which was enjoying British support. Charles Tupper of Nova Scotia, Samuel Leonard Tilley of New Brunswick, and William Henry Pope of Prince Edward Island thereupon coöperated with the Canadians in dovetailing their own Maritime Conference at Charlottetown in 1864 into broader discussions there and at Halifax and St. John, and into a final constitutional convention at Quebec during October, 1864. In less than two months this group of remarkable men worked out in secret a series of resolutions which subsequently provided the main outlines of a sound and durable constitution for a federal Canada. Almost at once, however, the movement ran into determined opposition from Newfoundland, Prince Edward Island, Nova Scotia, and New Brunswick, whose economic and fiscal structures could not easily be fitted to those of the Province of Canada. In consequence federation was not achieved until 1867, when Canada, divided into the Provinces of Ontario and Quebec, joined New Brunswick and Nova Scotia, with Newfoundland and Prince Edward Island dissenting. Indeed the two Maritime Provinces which entered the federation did so in spite of sturdy domestic opposition and largely in response to very skilful and strong pressure from Great Britain.

While the roots of this stubborn British colonial insistence on survival as political entities separate from the United States reached far back into the past, its success during the crucial years after the Civil War can only be understood in the light of the curiously interlocked and often contradictory elements of the federation movement in British North America and the British pressure which forced it to bear fruit. All these developments were bedeviled and confused to a degree which has made them perplexing down to the present day because, during the decade after the Civil War, the ruling classes in Great Britain, unconsciously rather than consciously, directly reversed their thinking and action about their Empire.

From the beginnings of free-trade ideas during the last quarter of the eighteenth century there had developed a crescendo of anti-imperialism in Great Britain which reached its peak in 1865 when Viscount Bury in his *Exodus of the Western Nations* proclaimed the natural law of colonial independence as demonstrated by the experience of six European nations in the Americas. This anti-imperialism, or Little Englandism, was never absolute. India, as has been noted, and indeed most of the British territories occupied chiefly by non-European peoples, were conspicuous exceptions, even to a thoroughgoing Little Englander like John Bright. In addition, leaders like Lord Durham and Lord Elgin argued that the concession of autonomy to the colonies inhabited by European stock would have the effect of creating a free and friendly association with the Mother Country which would be, by every standard, more beneficial to all concerned than the combination of authority and subordination. Nevertheless a perfect spate of parliamentary eloquence, pamphleteering, and historical or pseudohistorical writing had by 1870 equipped the anti-imperial movement with a full panoply of what passed for philosophical armor. It had become the law and the gospel to Conservative and Liberal alike.

Looking back on this paradoxical behavior of the world's greatest empire, one is tempted to believe that Napoleon was shrewd in seizing upon the shopkeeper motif in British life. As the commercial and industrial classes increased their influence at Westminster, a passion developed for better national bookkeeping and closer economy. Peel and Gladstone so elevated the annual budget that it became the supreme example of the statesman's art. In this climate of opinion, colonies, like everything else, had to pay, and it seemed absurd to both Gladstone and Disraeli that the British taxpayer should provide protective garrisons for self-governing colonies, particularly when those colonies imposed tariffs on British goods.

Bury summed it up: "One by one, the last rags of the commercial system have been torn away. We receive no tribute; we expect no advantage . . . yet we undertake the burden of defending them against attack." Disraeli exploded in characteristic fashion. "An army maintained in a country which does not permit us even to govern it! What an anomaly!" To the Canadian, Galt, who at this time was laboring in England to bring about Canadian federation, there was only one conclusion to be drawn. "It is very grievous to see half a continent slipping away from the grasp of England with scarcely an effort to hold it." To many members of the House of Commons, British North American federation was simply a decent way of creating a polity which should be big enough to assume responsibility for its own defense. If it became and remained independent, the bonds had been loosed in a respectable way, and the aggrandizement of the United States would be checked. At any rate the British North America Act, which created the Dominion of Canada in 1867, passed through Parliament like "a private bill uniting two or three English parishes," according to John A. Macdonald, and the British military forces were withdrawn in 1871.

While it is easy enough to recognize the almost universal sway of anti-imperialism in British ruling circles at this time, it is quite another matter to decide just why it did not prevail in the specific form of bidding the self-governing colonies farewell. It is certainly permissible to suggest that perhaps the anti-imperialists did not mean quite what they said, yet too many of them said too much for this to be a very persuasive explanation, unless they hoped to have an empire for nothing. Somewhat more to the point was the fact that the colonies did not want to say farewell, but their wishes could carry relatively little weight in determining the policy of a country most of whose politicians knew next to nothing about their empire. One is thrown back, therefore, upon certain rather subterranean forces which at this time were being brought powerfully to bear upon the most influential circles in Great Britain and in British North America.

The great problem in estimating these forces, which may be crudely summarized as financial imperialism, is that they became influential on governments in little-known ways some time before they were allowed to come out into the open in more appealing guises. In addition, long before they could dominate British policy by their own weight, their influence could be expediently allied to policies which arose from quite other motives and thus achieve a decisive result. The most striking feature of the whole matter is that this new imperialism not only quickly captivated its natural adherents, the Conservative party, but gradually imposed its will upon its avowed enemies, the Gladstonian Liberals, as well. Unquestionably most members of both the Liberal Government of 1865, which engineered Canadian federation, and the Conservative Government of 1866, which pushed it through, thought that they were acting in orthodox Little England fashion, but some members of both groups were consciously or unconsciously responding to influences which were directly the opposite. So much so, that the British North America Act may be regarded as the point at which Great Britain commenced to circle away from the tranquil, reassuring path of anti-imperialism toward the exciting arena in which all of the great nations of the world were warming up for an imperialistic free-for-all. By 1875, for instance, Disraeli was able to make his Suez Canal coup with a complete assurance of its emotional appeal to popular approval.

In the case of British North America, the foundations for British financial imperialism had been built up over a long period. British investors owned provincial obligations, Hudson's Bay Company stock, and canal and railroad securities, many of them guaranteed by the British or the provincial governments. Now, both the Hudson's Bay Company and the Grand Trunk Railway were in grave financial difficulties, and the underlying strength of the provinces themselves seemed threatened by the termination of the Reciprocity Treaty with the United States. Inevitably, therefore, the politicians on both sides of the Atlantic found that they could not separate the fortunes of big business from the maintenance of public credit in British North America. For instance, when Galt in the autumn of 1860 secured a judgment of £3,000,000 against the Grand Trunk in behalf of the Government of the Province of Canada, he wrote to S. G. Ward, the Boston agent of Canada's British bankers, that he was "in the position of the man who had the good luck to win the elephant."

The British and British North American stages were thus set for the super-lobbyist; the time was ripe for the new kind of leading actor, the agent of finance rather than of industry or commerce, the man who could "reorganize," "consolidate," and otherwise manipulate tottering debt structures once he had established the necessary understandings with the public authorities and the leading private interests. Contrary to common belief North America did not invent these gentry; indeed it was in Great Britain during the railway age that they invented the schemes which were exported to the rest of the world along with British capital. At any rate it was Edward W. Watkin of the International Financial Society of London who in 1861–1863 came to the rescue or "reorganization" of both the Grand Trunk and the Hudson's Bay Company, and who, appropriately enough, was knighted when his efforts had been crowned by the federation of the British North American provinces in 1867. There were others, too, like Edward Hornby and John Rose, who were involved in the work and who also received titles of honor, but such men see to it that the details of their operations must be left largely to the imagination of succeeding generations.[3] Suffice it to say that under Watkin's guiding hand a grand design gradually emerged with the blessings of the British and provincial governments and of British bankers and railway builders. Reduced to its simplest terms, it involved the salvation of the Grand Trunk by expansion, both from Chicago to the western lands of the Hudson's Bay Company, where a road and telegraph line were to anticipate a railway to the Pacific, and, in the east, by connecting with a new Intercolonial Railway from Rivière du Loup in Quebec to the Maritime Provinces. This line was to follow an all-British route along the Gulf of St. Lawrence and meet the existing New Brunswick and Nova Scotia short lines from St. John and Halifax at Moncton and Truro. Never again would Great Britain have to depend on American railways or overland winter roads if the Canadian interior needed military aid during the winter. Southern New Brunswick might in times of peace avail itself of American connections with the Atlantic terminal of the Grand Trunk at Portland, but the assumption was that Canada would use Halifax as its principal winter port. "Build the road," Macdonald of Canada told the Nova Scotians, "and Halifax will soon become one of the great emporiums of the world. All the resources of the West will come over the immense railways of Canada to the bosom of your harbor."

The appropriate political and economic underpinning for so vast a structure could only be a federation or a union of the provinces, for the structure itself was in part an admitted abandonment of the old monopolistic Montreal dream of draining the mid-continent, in favor of a new

---

3. It was later, in 1875, that Samuel Butler was in Montreal on Grand Trunk business and composed the famous "Psalm," with its refrain, "O God! O Montreal!"

design of coöperative exploitation and complementary intercolonial trade across the northern half of the continent. The truth was that the Province of Canada had grown to a point where it had to expand, and the barrier of the Canadian Shield made immediate extension eastward easier than to the west. American hostility, as evidenced by the abrogation of the Reciprocity Treaty and threats to withdraw the privilege of bonding goods across United States territory, apparently ended the prospect of economic gain by trade to the south. So clearly was Canadian growth the root of the railway-federation project that the various proposals for union among themselves which the Maritime Provinces half-heartedly put forward at this time have been convincingly explained almost exclusively in terms of Canadian expansion, that is, either as a preliminary, or as an antidote, to incorporation in a larger whole of which the former Province of Canada would form the dominant part.

Watkin tactfully put his project in one way:

The result of mature consideration . . . was, that, at that time, 1863, the best route for a Railway to the Pacific was, to commence at Halifax, to strike . . . to Sarnia; to extend that system to Chicago; to use, under a treaty of neutralization, the United States lines from Chicago to St. Paul; to build a line from St. Paul to Fort Garry [Winnipeg] by English and American capital, and then to extend this line to the Tête Jaune [Yellowhead] Pass, there to meet a Railway through British Columbia starting from the Pacific.[4]

A. A. Dorion, a lively French-Canadian opponent of federation, put it in another:

This project [for an Intercolonial Railway in 1862] having failed, some other scheme had to be concocted for bringing aid and relief to the unfortunate Grand Trunk—and the Confederation of all the British North American Provinces naturally suggested itself to the Grand Trunk officials as the surest means of bringing with it the construction of the Intercolonial Railway. Such was the origin of this Confederation scheme. . . . Another necessity of Confederation [was] some westward extension of the Grand Trunk scheme for the benefit of Messrs. Watkin and Company of the new Hudson's Bay Company.

One need not pursue this "hen or egg" controversy farther in order to realize that the British North American "Fathers of Confederation," who showed such remarkable political capacity in framing the constitution for the new Dominion of Canada at their two short Conferences in Charlottetown and Quebec in 1864, were not the only agents in creating a new transcontinental North American nation. In the background were

4. Note how British Columbian gold, like Californian, could call forth a railway across thousands of miles of almost empty territory.

the most intricate interplay and counterplay of forces—fear of truculent American expansionism, general British indifference coupled with intense special interest, considerations of strategy and of European communications with the treasure house of the Far East, old hates and new hopes, and the great, impersonal, international engine of earth conquest, the railway itself, complete with its whole retinue of attendants.

Among the several British North American colonies, only the leaders of the Province of Canada were sure that they wanted federation. Indeed they felt that they had to have it, both for economic salvation and in order to break the chronic political deadlock between French and English liberals and conservatives which legislative union and local autonomy had brought about in the 'fifties—the "Double Majority" system. To form a successful Canadian government then it was necessary to unite majorities of both English- and French-speaking representatives, and this too frequently proved impossible in the light of the natural antipathies which persisted. On the other hand Newfoundland discovered that it belonged to the Atlantic, instead of to the continental, system. Nova Scotia felt much the same way, but was somewhat bewildered by the cluster of changes in the carrying trade of the Atlantic area which accompanied the transition from wood and sail to iron and steam, and by the abrupt termination of reciprocity with the United States. New Brunswick's similar diffidence was intensified because the proposed Intercolonial Railway was to run along the St. Lawrence instead of up the St. John Valley, and a powerful faction insisted on preferring the "Western Extension" which would link up the province with the railways of Maine and New England. Prince Edward Island was afraid of being locked into a structure which would bring to an end the agreeable combination of agriculture, fisheries, and smuggling with which her location had endowed her. The whites and métis of the Red River Valley had grumbled and struggled against Hudson's Bay Company rule and had overcome its prohibition of trade with the United States, but they were sure that they preferred its understanding of their peculiar ways of life to the crass, overbearing ignorance of a lot of decadent, urban easterners—Canadian or American. And out on the Pacific Coast many British Columbians felt that it would be more sensible to fill the gap in the American ribbon of settlement and sovereignty along the coastal slope than to gamble on the possibility that the Canadians might bridge the gap of two thousand miles which lay between them.

Yet the Canadians, backed by Maritime minorities, did secure British legislation which set up a Canadian federation on July 1, 1867, in spite of the other provinces' objections. In the first stages they succeeded because the British Government put its full weight behind a number of rapid and high-handed maneuvers on the part of the provincial governors which whirled New Brunswick and Nova Scotia into the federation beside Ontario, the former Upper Canada, and Quebec, the former Lower Canada, in spite of themselves. Nova Scotia was so angry at being dragooned in this way that she sent eighteen antifederationists out of nineteen members to the first Dominion Parliament and dispatched Joseph Howe to London in a vain attempt to arrange for secession.

British determination held firm, however; the Canadian Prime Minister found inducements with which to mollify Howe and his disciples; and at once the new Dominion began to reach out in fulfilment of the motto on its coat of arms—"*A mari usque ad mare.*" The Red River Settlement, after melancholy misunderstandings, confusion, and bloodshed, became the core of the Province of Manitoba in 1870. British Columbia joined the federation in 1871 when its leanings toward the United States were offset by British pressure and by the Canadian promise to begin within two years a railroad which would be completed in ten. In 1873 Prince Edward Island, crumpling under the burden of ill-advised efforts to keep up with the rest of North America in railroad construction and ferry connections with the mainland, was ready to find shelter and support within the Canadian Dominion. Newfoundland was not to be won.

What seems to have happened in British North America, then, is that fear of the United States and British pressure served to weigh down in favor of federation an almost even balance between inertia, indifference, or even antipathy on the one side and certain tendencies toward growth and collaboration on the other. Some of the latter tendencies, as has been seen, were echoes and responses to half-understood developments in technology, finance, and political economy in the outside world. Others were indigenous to the region itself or were the human impulses natural in the leaders of toughened little North American communities, some of which had been rooted for over two hundred and fifty years and all of which were fairly solidly committed to an identity separate from the United States.

It was perhaps surprising that the Montreal annexationism of 1849 was too utterly dead to revive at the termination of the Reciprocity Treaty sixteen years later. Yet dead it was, for the main bodies of population simply did not want to become Americans. Only in British Columbia was there anything that might be called a strong pro-American group and even there pro-Americanism was to a considerable degree an instrument to keep Canada suitably on edge, in much the same way as British

North Americans elsewhere had on other occasions used it to agitate Great Britain.

In general, traditional dependence on the Mother Country and traditional fear and dislike of the United States, combined with a disinclination to change and an unwillingness or inability to shed familiar cultural garments, were quite naturally so strong that it would have required a profound cataclysm to have projected the colonists into the American Union. Quebec, in particular, threatened as it felt it was by English-speaking Canadians so far as the maintenance of its ways of life and thought was concerned, was still more afraid of engulfment in the omnivorous, all-digesting culture of the United States. Better make a bargain for autonomy in these fundamentals as part of a smaller federation which would not be able to ignore the power and the geographical position of the French-speaking province.

The North Americans who worked so hard from 1858 to 1866 for Canadian federation had the United States as an inspiration and a warning while they dreamed and planned to bridge the continent. What Americans had done they felt they could do, and in their constitution they would remedy the central defect of the American constitution which the Civil War had revealed. Their intention, declared the Canadian Governor, Lord Monck, in 1866, "was to constitute a strong central authority the power of which should be supreme and pervading throughout the Union with provincial bodies of a completely subordinate and municipal character for the administration of purely local affairs." The Dominion, in the words of D. G. Creighton, a modern scholar, "was to become a great corporation" and to be "the heir in direct succession of the old colonial system. . . . Self-government, on the British Parliamentary model, should operate in the provinces; but it was to be self-government with limitations not unlike those which Lord Durham had proposed nearly thirty years before."

Time was to defeat their hopes, but at the moment those hopes were the measure of the sense of a national mission which pervaded "the Big Seven"—Galt, Macdonald, Brown, Cartier, and McGee of Canada, Tilley of New Brunswick, and Tupper of Nova Scotia. The same sense of mission, particularly for the salvation of the west from American expansion, actuated an idealistic little group in Ottawa—the new capital—and Toronto, whose motto and party name, "Canada First," was intended to elevate the national cause above local and sectional loyalties. No one can estimate exactly the influence of these emotional drives, but no one can read the glowing Celtic eloquence of D'Arcy McGee's speeches without realizing how stimulatingly his actual words must have come to the ears of his thousands of listeners.

These men were also confident that they could create a prosperous transcontinental economy. Even before federation had been achieved, official representatives of Canada, the Maritimes, and Newfoundland had met at Quebec in September, 1865, with Britain's blessing, in a "Confederate Council" in order to plan their economic life after the termination of the Reciprocity Treaty. Without waiting for British approval, the Canadian Government thereupon appointed three commissioners to investigate the possibility of reciprocal trade agreements with the West Indies, Brazil, and Mexico, and instructed one of the commissioners to investigate similar possibilities in the countries bordering on the Mediterranean. Equally confident independence marked the conferences on the possible renewal of the Reciprocity Treaty, conferences which took place in January and February, 1866, at Washington, between provincial representatives and the Committee of Ways and Means of the House of Representatives. At the conclusion of these fruitless negotiations Galt, in behalf of the Province of Canada, bluntly said:

We shall probably make such concessions to other countries as we were prepared to make first to you—our best neighbours. We shall tell our people that the market of the United States is practically shut. We shall direct their attention to the supply of the Lower [Maritime] Provinces with flour and breadstuffs, and shall endeavour to find in the West Indies and the Mediterranean a market for our lumber and fish.

Finally, it is clear that these men felt entitled to act on a larger stage than those which their separate provinces provided. As Joseph Howe of Nova Scotia said in 1855, at the conclusion of the twenty years of activity which had made him the most redoubtable colonial statesman of the Empire, "I have a very natural desire to earn distinction beyond the narrow limits of the Province in which I was born." In 1858, defeated in this ambition, he added ruefully: "Statesmen who figure in the great centres of intellectual life, whether in Europe or America, can alone be expected to command general attention." Any of the others, except perhaps Francis Hincks of Canada who won a colonial governorship, could have told the same story, particularly the Canadians, who were at the limit of their patience after years of the exasperating futility of the "Double Majority" system in their Provincial Parliament. These men and their like had been successfully measuring swords with British statesmen for a full generation. They had wrestled successfully with domestic and external problems whose weight and complexity would have taxed the full capacities of any statesman whom they knew in the English-speaking world. Some of them saw their Dominion of Canada "as," in Milton's glowing words, "an Eagle mewing her mighty youth"; but Macdonald, the principal architect and builder of the new structure, leaned less to rhetoric and more to the work ahead. "We are all mere petty provincial politicians at present," he said; "perhaps by and by some of us will rise to the level of national statesmen."

CHAPTER XI

CORNERSTONE OF TRIUNE UNDERSTANDING
(1871–1878)

By a kind of natural irony the expansive nationalism of the United States had driven the discordant British North American provinces into a national federation, but the Dominion of Canada of July 1, 1867, was only a blueprint defiance of American Manifest Destiny, and it remained little more even after the incorporation of Manitoba and British Columbia in 1871. Two great questionmarks shadowed its future. One of them, as to the Dominion's capacity to develop into an effective transcontinental economy, was not to be answered in the affirmative for another twenty-five years. The other, as to what degree of tolerance the new structure was to receive from the United States, had to be answered at once. Canadians then and thereafter were prone to bewail the fact that the decision in this matter was a by-product of the liquidation of serious Anglo-American disputes at a time when Great Britain was abnormally compliant. Yet it is extremely doubtful whether Canada could have done nearly so well for herself if she had had to confront the United States alone.

During the early days of the Dominion, a good many thoughtful Canadians were justified in doubting whether Great Britain rated Canadian rights above Anglo-American understanding. These Canadian misgivings had a long ancestry, beginning with the surrender of the mid-continent to the new United States in 1783, and coming down through other territorial and fisheries settlements to the unexpected loss of the territory north of the Columbia River in the Oregon settlement of 1846.

Canadian political leaders knew that British leaders like Gladstone, Granville, Cobden, and Bright expected the new Dominion to become part of the United States. Nevertheless most of these Canadian statesmen were determined to oppose the British policy of "loose the bonds and go" to the limit of their abilities.[1] Only a little group of "mere Canadians," headed by Galt, as yet had the courage to startle the general population by suggesting that the Dominion might pursue an independent course, and no responsible Canadian politician outside British Columbia dared to flout public opinion by openly advocating annexation to the United

1. Tennyson's angry denunciation of Little Englandism:

> And that true north of which we lately heard
> A strain to shame us, loose the bonds and go.

States. In these circumstances, Canada may seem to have been unlucky in beginning her career on the international stage as the puny third party to a grand settlement between two Great Powers, but she had to realize her standing in an unfriendly world some time and she had a leader in Macdonald, now Sir John A. Macdonald, who was able to drive home the first lesson at surprisingly small cost.

The great, dangerous issue between the United States and Great Britain was of course the *Alabama* Claims. Here national honor was at stake as well as the financial consideration, for the United States naturally insisted that Great Britain acknowledge publicly that she had been in the wrong to loose the armed raiders. For years this was too bitter a pill to swallow; indeed Lord John Russell, the principal actor in the events, could not bring himself to the admission until after he had retired from public life. Accordingly it had been fortunate for international peace that, after the Civil War ended and Lincoln was assassinated in the spring of 1865, the Congress of the United States had found itself almost fully occupied by problems of reconstruction, a rapid flux in party politics, and the impeachment of President Johnson. Until this interlude was terminated by Grant's campaign of 1868 and his inauguration as President in March, 1869, the United Kingdom was able to pretend to ignore a situation which was heavy with potential mischief.

One other Anglo-American issue might have been regarded as a sort of make-weight for British righteousness and American sin, but its relative unimportance to Great Britain made it little more than a pawn. Congress had been so obstructive and dilatory in providing funds for the property compensation awarded under the Oregon Treaty of 1846 that it had dishonored the Treaty. In addition, inhabitants of Washington Territory had taken it on themselves to settle the unspecified boundary through the Haro Archipelago between Vancouver Island and the mainland by "squatting" on San Juan, the westernmost island of the group.

Inevitably friction developed there, in spite of efforts at peaceful joint occupation pending settlement. An American shot a British pig, there was fence trouble, the idle troops relieved their boredom in dangerous ways, strategic considerations began to loom large, and 1870 was to be a census year in the United States. Were the inhabitants of San Juan to be counted Americans? The British Government wanted to arbitrate the boundary. The United States refused.

Meanwhile a swarm of problems affecting the relations of the United States and Canada had been gathering, and, while they undoubtedly seemed of secondary importance to the leaders of Great Britain and the United States, they could not but be vital to Canada.

The new Dominion's position was most delicate and precarious. On the one hand, practically all Americans who were interested at all assumed that Canada must immediately or quite soon be embodied in the United States, either by bullying, or by an American bargain with Great Britain, or by a systematic American diminishment of her ability to stand on her own feet economically. On the other, the governing class in Great Britain, not yet dominated by the still subterranean "new" imperialism, was profoundly ignorant of, and uninterested in, Canada, and therefore conceived its problem to be merely the ethical one of abandoning the Dominion in a decent, dignified way. Yet the concession of colonial autonomy in the 'forties had made this somewhat difficult, for it was generally agreed that the Canadians could not be turned over to the Americans against their will.

Grant's Secretary of State, Hamilton Fish, was the only prominent

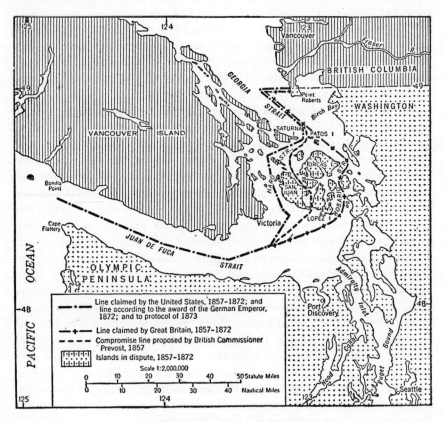

The San Juan Boundary

American who had come to understand the British attitude by 1869, largely because he had begun to accept almost at their face value the statements of his friend Edward Thornton,[2] the British Minister at Washington. In June, 1869, Thornton told him flatly that England "did not wish to keep Canada, but could not part with it without the consent of the inhabitants." Fish thereupon decided that the thing to do was to settle the Anglo-American issues promptly, encourage Great Britain to liberate Canada, and then "kick or kiss" the Dominion into the Union.

In these circumstances Canada pursued the only practical course, that is, her leaders systematically sought out and tried to exploit every Canadian issue, right, or advantage in which either the United States, or Great Britain, or special groups in either country, might have a material or moral interest. In British and American eyes Canada was thereby capitalizing her "nuisance value," but it is doubtful whether any leading Canadian saw matters in that light. One obsession eclipsed all other considerations. Somehow or other both of the Great Powers must be kept from overlooking Canada's rights and legitimate aims.

The termination of the Reciprocity Treaty in March, 1866, had practically set Canadian-American relations back to where they had been before 1854. The North Atlantic fisheries once more came under the Convention of 1818. New England gas companies now had to pay duties on Nova Scotian coal or buy from Pennsylvania, and Canadian lumbermen found that their pork and cornmeal from the middle west had gone up in price. Forgotten complications reappeared in the water-borne traffic of the Great Lakes, the other inland waterways, and along the Atlantic Coast. A great snarl of major and minor annoyances fouled the easy economic intercourse of the past decade. The Fenians and the annexationists threatened the whole of British North America from Atlantic to Pacific, and the absurdity of Washington's offer in 1866 of free trade only in unwrought millstones and grindstones, rags, firewood, and gypsum made it clear that the United States was waiting for a ripe plum to fall from the branch.

During the next five years, or from 1866 to 1870, the Canadians lined up and developed their bargaining assets. In the forefront they placed their moral right to redress from the United States for the losses and expenses incurred from the Fenian menace. In second place they set the right to exclude American vessels from the inshore fisheries and from recourse to Canadian ports for bait, ice, and supplies. Finally there was the well-known anxiety of the states near the Great Lakes to use the Canadian waterways as a supplement to, and competitive lever against,

2. He was knighted in 1870.

American rail and water transportation facilities. It was hoped that this might somewhat offset the resolute protectionism of the industrial Middle States and New England and facilitate the reëstablishment of reciprocal free trade in natural products.

Past experience had shown that the self-centered giant to the south was most sensitive to interference with the fisheries. Naturally, therefore, even before federation, Canada and Nova Scotia mildly asserted their rights by exacting a fee of fifty cents a ton from American vessels for licenses to fish inshore and to land for bait, ice, and supplies. When Nova Scotia showed her sense of injustice by raising the fee to a dollar a ton, Canada followed suit. Following federation, Prime Minister Macdonald handed over the portfolio of Marine and Fisheries to an aggressive New Brunswicker named Peter Mitchell, who at once busied himself in still more vigorous defense. In 1868 he raised the license fee to two dollars a ton and reduced from three to one the number of warnings before seizure of offending vessels.

It was about this time that the Canadians began to realize that their efforts to assert their rights were being almost completely thwarted. Whereas in 1866 four hundred and fifty-four American vessels out of about eight hundred paid the required fee, less than three hundred paid in 1867, only sixty-eight did so in 1868, and in 1869 only twelve of one hundred and sixty-two vessels which were stopped for examination possessed licenses. The Americans simply refused to admit that the Canadians would dare to exclude them, and the British Navy, which had the task of policing the shores, was much too tender and anxious to avoid trouble to disillusion them. In these circumstances the Dominion Government decided that the only thing to do was to drop the licensing system, build six police schooners at the cost of almost a million dollars, and strictly enforce the Convention of 1818 during the season of 1870. Its task was not made easier by Prince Edward Island, still outside the new Dominion, which refused to abandon its unorthodox role of ignoring the Convention of 1818 for the sake of trade and smuggling with the Yankees.

The blaze of indignation which Canadian seizures under this policy provoked in New England did much to raise American annexationism to its peak in 1870, particularly during the period leading up to the autumn elections. General Benjamin F. Butler, Representative for Massachusetts, who had visited Prince Edward Island two years before in order to strengthen the Islanders in their resistance to entering the Canadian federation, ranted and roared in spectacular fashion, urging that the United States withdraw the bonding privilege and pass a nonintercourse act. President Grant in his Annual Message of December 5, 1870, gave abundant attention to the fisheries and to the "unfriendly way" in which Canada, the "semi-independent but irresponsible agent" of British jurisdiction in the North Atlantic, had been treating American fishermen. He asked for power to suspend the bonding privilege and to refuse to Canadian vessels entry to American ports. General R. C. Schenck, interviewed at the time of his appointment to succeed Motley as American Minister to England, summed up the Administration's views pretty aptly when he said: "England feels annoyed at the conduct of the Canadians, and will probably send out a delegate to the Government of the Dominion, with instructions to put a curb on their arrogance, and bring them to a sense of the duty they owe to the people of the United States."

Although the new Dominion's assertion of its rights along the North Atlantic was well founded in itself, it was also closely linked to broader considerations. In 1854 it had been the fisheries which had provided much of the leverage for securing commercial reciprocity. It was hoped that they would do so again. In fact this was so obvious that the American lobbyist, Israel D. Andrews, and one of his former acolytes, G. W. Brega, scenting another chance to employ the talents which they had displayed twenty years earlier, made repeated, if vain, approaches to British and Canadian authorities. Leaders in Ontario and Quebec brought forward the familiar arguments for freer commerce across the borders and for mutual concessions on the canals and natural waterways which had been so flatly rejected by the American protectionists in 1866.

Moreover, eleven years of the Reciprocity Treaty had taught Nova Scotians and New Brunswickers to see a little farther than the fisheries. They were now prepared to surrender free access in return for reciprocal free trade in coal and lumber, American registry for Canadian-built ships, and mutual concessions in the coasting trade. Accordingly it would seem that Sir Francis Hincks, Dominion Minister of Finance, summed up his country's case quite accurately early in 1871 when he wrote to Macdonald:

Really we have no object in refusing them [the fisheries and use of the St. Lawrence], on the contrary the fisheries are a mere expense. Our equivalents that should be pressed are full reciprocal trade—If we yield on this England *must compensate us*. But we cant yield the fisheries without *at least* free importation of our fish & free or low duty coal lumber & salt particularly the first.

Viewed dispassionately, the Dominion's chances seemed slight at the end of 1870. Control of the situation was passing into the stronger hands of the United States and Great Britain. Hamilton Fish, the one person who might have been said to have his hand on the throttle, was now confident that he could go ahead. He had established the necessary ascendancy, where international relations were concerned, over President Grant, for the latter had been humbled by some of his own experiments in that difficult field. He had seen Motley, Senator Sumner's friend and the American Minister to England, dismissed by Grant. Most important of all, he had given Sumner enough rope to hang himself by the extravagance of his threats against Great Britain and Canada. The autumn elections of 1870 had diminished the influence of the Radical Republicans, but the unbalanced Sumner, in deadly feud with Grant over Motley's dismissal, rushed on to his destruction. When Fish consulted him in January, 1871, about the proposed form of negotiations with Great Britain, he replied by submitting a series of preposterous demands. Among them, the last straw deserves to be reproduced in full.

The greatest trouble, if not peril, being a constant source of anxiety and disturbance, is from Fenianism, which is excited by the proximity of the British flag in Canada. Therefore the withdrawal of the British flag cannot be abandoned as a condition or preliminary of such a settlement as is now proposed. To make the settlement complete the withdrawal should be from this hemisphere, including provinces and islands.

From the Falklands to the Arctic the Union Jack must be hauled down. Such fantastic reasoning seemed so close to derangement that Fish was able without difficulty to contrive that Sumner should be supplanted as chairman of the powerful Senate Committee on Foreign Relations when the new Congress assembled.

Fish had been encouraged to press forward toward his goal largely because of his intimate understanding with the British Minister, Thornton. Great Britain had recently been rendered more amenable by the threats to her position in the world which were embodied in the Franco-Prussian War and in Russia's unilateral denunciation of the Black Sea neutrality provisions which had been imposed upon her at the end of the Crimean War. Gladstone's first reform ministry, which had just assumed office, was almost ready to acknowledge Great Britain's fault in the Civil War in order to foster Anglo-American friendship.

Yet history owes a page to the man behind the scenes in which the leading actors played their parts. He was the recently created K.C.M.G., Sir John Rose, a Scottish-Canadian. In business and law in Montreal he had made a fortune which he had invested in a London branch of the financial house which Levi P. Morton, a suavely aggressive banker-politician from Vermont, had recently set up in New York. A discreet and able, if acquisitive, man, not overly popular among leading Canadian politicians, he had been one of the Montreal annexationists in 1849, and had married a former Vermonter. He had his fingers in such pies as the Grand Trunk, the Hudson's Bay Company, the new Pacific railways of the United States, and the refunding of the huge American national debt which had been piled up by the Civil War.

Like the Ashburton of the House of Baring who had got along so well with Daniel Webster in 1842, Rose slipped easily into the role of go-between for the American and British leaders who were exploring the paths to peace. The Canadians feared that, as had often been the case when colonials went to live in London, he had become so much "more English than the English" that he could not be counted upon as a defender of Canadian interests. They also had scraps of information which made them believe that the fate of Morton, Rose & Co. hung upon what course the American Government would adopt in connection with its preferred claims against the builders and management of the Pacific railway, in which the firm had lost heavily. Actually Morton and Rose were hoping that they might avert disaster by arranging for instalment payments to the Treasury in return for facilitating the flotation of a new United States funding loan in London, after which specie payments could be resumed.

Today one can only speculate as to how these business interests may have affected the Anglo-American agreement to settle differences in 1871, but obviously peace would make a better bond and specie market than a prolongation of the disputes. We do have explicit evidence that, when the United States, by its ill-advised and uncandid revival of the "indirect claims" at the Geneva Tribunal in 1872, shook the money markets of the world, Rose in London and Morton in Washington played very influential parts in inducing Fish and the Grant Administration to invent a way of retreat in the face of general condemnation and fear of renewed Anglo-American tensions.

Rose had made his first "unofficial" approaches to Fish in July, 1869, when he had come to Washington, avowedly about the $650,000 which the Oregon Claims Board, on which he and his friend Caleb Cushing of Massachusetts had served, had awarded to the Hudson's Bay Company. At that time Rose had to report in Canada and England that Fish, although interested in the possibility, did not think it practicable to link with the settlement of the *Alabama* Claims the whole gamut of matters at issue between Canada and the United States. The general course of events during the twenty months between Grant's inauguration and the fall elections of 1870, particularly Fenianism and annexationism of the Sumner mode, showed the would-be conciliators that the time for Anglo-

American negotiations was not ripe. In fact, Rose's mission of 1869 was followed by the beginnings of retaliatory Canadian policies. President Grant, in his Message of December, flatly opposed reciprocity, but he did urge the payment of the Hudson's Bay Company award.

Fish tried to set the ball rolling again in conversations with Thornton during September, 1870. Their culmination came on September 26, as recorded in his diary.

Disclaiming any official character or purport in the suggestion, I asked whether Great Britain would settle all the questions pending between the countries at once. That the United States had refused the arbitration of the *Alabama* Claims, and Great Britain would not settle except upon arbitration. The United States declined a partition of San Juan or arbitration. That if the United States abandoned their opposition to arbitrating the *Alabama* Claims, Great Britain might agree to the American claim of the San Juan boundary line. All commercial claims may be referred to arbitration. The inshore fisheries be opened to American vessels, and in return a more free trade be allowed in certain articles between the United States and its [Great Britain's] colonies.

This at least temporary abandonment of annexationism by Fish was the cornerstone of further negotiations between Washington and London, which went on behind a screen of such overt acts as Grant's Message of December, with its contradictory mixture of threat and conciliation. Once the Gladstone Government had schooled itself to the humiliation of admitting that Great Britain had been wrong in its interpretation of neutrality during the Civil War, Granville, the Foreign Secretary, sent Rose back to his task, again "unofficially." He reached Washington on January 9, 1871, and made some ingenious suggestions by which sensitive British national honor could be mollified, on the basis of which he reached an agreement with Fish the same evening. Arrangements for the sitting of an International Joint Commission in Washington to settle all Anglo-American differences were rapidly completed, with the blessings of the British Cabinet and a dependable understanding with the Senate.

The public announcement on February 9, 1871, was welcomed enthusiastically in the United States and Great Britain, but there was immediate evidence of much heartburning in Canada. There it was rightly suspected that, as in most serious international negotiations, the basic issues had been settled in advance. Rose, after testing sentiment about himself in Ottawa, wisely refused to serve on the Commission, leaving the unwelcome role of representing Canadian interests, alone in a group of ten, to the only alternative choice suggested by the British Government, Sir John Macdonald. Although Prime Minister of Canada, his status would be that of servant of Great Britain.

The reluctant Macdonald was no fool. He knew that his country's interests could not escape being among the principal burnt offerings to Anglo-American understanding and yet he saw clearly that Anglo-American understanding must be the basic objective of any realistic Canadian foreign policy. He must therefore play the lone dissident at the coming reconciliation, to the very limit of American and British tolerance. He must not really threaten the grand Anglo-American settlement and yet he must hamper it sufficiently to create an interest among both British and American commissioners in quieting Canada's relatively unimportant rights and claims.

Finally, he knew, he must somehow persuade Canadians at home, less realistic than himself, that the broken meats which he might carry home from the rich men's table were appropriate dishes for Canada's needs. It was a frightening task, bordering on the ignoble, but Macdonald performed it with consummate skill, although he knew that his countrymen would blame him for the shattering of what seemed their just hopes, and that generations must pass before Canadians acquired the detachment necessary in order to view his achievement and Great Britain's in the proper light.

The progress of the High Commission, which did its work between February 27 and May 8, 1871, was almost exactly what might have been expected. The British delegation behaved with that nervous anxiety to please which is likely to accompany the unaccustomed role of admitting a serious fault. The Americans betrayed their newness in the seats of the mighty by an incapacity for imaginativeness or magnanimity. The Canadian fought a lone hand, for the British did not dare to go very far in using his resistance as a counterpoise to the Americans' constant warnings that whatever was done must be acceptable to the Senate.

Throughout it all, Macdonald was almost fatally handicapped by the underhand behavior of Lord Lisgar, the British Governor General of Canada, who repeatedly hamstrung him by betraying to the British Commissioners Macdonald's confidential correspondence with the Canadian Cabinet. Meanwhile the whole Commission worked pretty steadily and hard in spite of a lively round of hospitality. The main decisions and the outlines of the settlement, however, were hammered out by Hamilton Fish and Lord de Grey in frequent private conversations.

Once an agreement had been reached on the phraseology of the British "expression of regret" for having facilitated Southern depredations on Northern commerce, and on Great Britain's commitment to certain stated principles of neutrality whose acceptance the Americans successfully insisted must precede the submission of the claims to arbitration, the main business of the Commission was over and all hands turned to the task of making Canada give up the inshore fisheries. It was in vain that Macdonald put forward all his counters, for the free-trading British harbored the erroneous belief that American protectionism was a passing phenomenon of the Civil War. "I told Lord de Grey," he reported to the Canadian Cabinet, "that we had not even taken into consideration any other equivalent [for the fisheries] but that of enlarged commercial intercourse in the direction of reciprocity, and as nearly approaching the old Reciprocity Treaty as the exigencies of the U. S. Revenue would permit." But he soon found that there was no chance whatever of securing substantial commercial reciprocity with the United States.

All that he could do was to fight a stubborn rearguard action, using as his shield a cable from Lord Kimberley, the Colonial Secretary, of which the British Commissioners were completely ignorant until Macdonald produced it when they finally cornered him. It read: "Her Majesty's Government never had any intention of disposing of the fisheries of Canada without her consent." Finally, however, even this protection was battered to pieces by blows from de Grey and by explicit orders from the British Government. Macdonald then capitulated, but he now clutched a new British promise of March 20 "to insert a clause in the Treaty providing that its provisions must be subject to ratification by the Canadian Parliament." The Joint High Commission then degenerated into rather hurried bargaining over secondary issues. On May 8, 1871, there emerged the Treaty, of which, as the London *Daily Telegraph* observed, "everyone is glad and nobody proud." Macdonald signed and whispered to Fish: "Well, here go the fisheries."

The Treaty of Washington provided that both the *Alabama* Claims and the San Juan boundary would be arbitrated, the former by an international tribunal of five at Geneva, the latter by the German Emperor. The Treaty opened up mutually the Canadian inshore fishery and the American, north of 39°, for a term of ten years plus two years for notice of termination. It also conceded the free entry to the United States, during the same term, of Canadian sea fish and fish oil. This was really an excellent arrangement for the Maritime Provinces, but, since it had been argued convincingly that British North America had yielded more than she got in connection with the fisheries, a third arbitral tribunal of three was to sit at Halifax in order to determine whether the United States should in equity make specific cash payments to Canada and Newfoundland.[3]

3. A suggestion made by Fish to de Grey on April 12, but an assumption expressly "not admitted" by the U.S.A. in the Treaty.

The St. Lawrence was opened in perpetuity to American shipping, as were three remote Alaskan rivers, the Yukon, Porcupine, and Stikine, to Canadian. Canadians were guaranteed equality with Americans in using the canal across the Flats of Lake St. Clair. Great Britain agreed to urge on the Canadian Government, and the United States to urge on the affected state governments, that all the canals be at the service of Canadian and American shipping on equal terms. Lake Michigan was to be open to Canadians for the term of the Treaty. Canada and the United States guaranteed to each other the transit of goods in bond for the same period and some relatively unimportant concessions were made concerning the coastal trade. A satisfied Senate ratified the Treaty by a vote of fifty to twelve on May 24, leaving the implementing legislation to some future date. John Bassett Moore, the distinguished American jurist, in writing about the Treaty as recently as 1937, placed it second in importance only to the Treaty of 1783 in American history, and said: "It was the greatest treaty of actual and immediate arbitration the world has ever seen; and it still holds that preeminence."

The startling omission from the Treaty was that of any mention of the Fenian Claims. The Americans had bluntly refused to discuss them on the technical ground that they had not been included by Rose and Thornton in the preliminary understanding with Fish. To this the British Commissioners had mildly acquiesced. When Macdonald protested to his colleagues, it was intimated to him that the British Government would compensate Canada for the damages and expenses suffered because of Fenians operating from the United States! This proposal was perhaps less extraordinary than it seemed, for on the one hand, in British eyes it was part and parcel of a larger pattern of bargaining, and, on the other, it harmonized in a sort of way with Gladstone's view of the Irish problem, for it could be argued that Canada had suffered for British sins. Macdonald stiffly refused any money payment from Great Britain, but suggested that it would be convenient for Canada, and distinctly more compatible with national dignity, if the British Government would guarantee a large loan for the railway to British Columbia.

Signing a treaty was one thing, but getting it ratified and implemented by the necessary legislation and money votes in five legislatures proved to be much more difficult. Indeed it was not until more than seven years later that the United States brought the long, wrangling negotiations to their close by paying, under protest, the first instalment of the Halifax Commission's award for adjustment of inequalities in the fisheries concessions.

A detailed balance sheet of the sins which were committed against honorable international dealing, although easily drawn up, would not make agreeable reading. The Grant Administration and the Congress had the worst record, partly because Great Britain's surrender was heady wine to a rather disreputable group, and partly because the campaign in 1872 for Grant's second term had to be fought in the face of the Liberal Republican revolt. Perhaps the most regrettable American action was the unexpected revival at the Geneva arbitration of claims for indirect damages, including the cost of the Civil War for about two years, with 7 per cent interest, a sum which Gladstone calculated to amount to about eight billion dollars. Charles Francis Adams, the American Commissioner, himself devised the Tribunal's irregular retreat from this impossible position. Sir Alexander Cockburn marred the relatively blameless British record by snatching up his hat and rushing from the room the moment Count Sclopis had finished reading the Geneva Award of $15,-500,000 against Great Britain for the *Alabama* Claims, and by subsequently refusing to sign the published Award. Ensign H. Kellogg, the United States Commissioner, refused to join Galt of Canada and Maurice Delfosse, the Belgian Minister at Washington, in signing the Halifax Award of $5,500,000 against the United States for the fisheries.[4] The involved efforts of the United States from 1871 to 1873 to get the inshore fisheries without giving the *quid pro quo* in free admission of fish and fish oil from Canada, Newfoundland, and Prince Edward Island make an unsavory story. An added note of disingenuousness was provided in October, 1872, by the German Emperor, who had reasons of his own for accepting the full American claim in the matter of the San Juan boundary.

The one really commendable achievement was Macdonald's. He went back to a Canada which was inflamed beyond reason by the omission of the Fenian Claims and by other disappointments. Great Britain seemed to have given everything, even Canada, to the triumphant Republic. As one newspaper put it, "the Treaty of Washington appears to be another step in the direction of what designing American and supine British statesmen have conjoined to make The Inevitable." Yet, although he knew that his parliamentary majority had been crumbling during his absence, Macdonald had the nerve and astuteness to keep silence for two months so that his critics, and particularly his leading Liberal opponents, would commit themselves solidly against the Treaty.

I want to endeavor so to manage it as to let the Globe [the chief Liberal paper] write under the impression that I have assented to the Treaty. Brown

---

4. Since the Commission for settling general American and British claims against each other which met in Washington from September, 1871, to September, 1873, awarded almost two million dollars to Great Britain and disallowed all the American claims, the United States received on all three accounts about eight million dollars.

[the editor] will then pitch into the Treaty and into me for sacrificing the interests of Canada. He will afterwards find out when it is too late that he is on the same side as myself and will not be able to retreat. My chief object in doing this is, that if Brown finds that I was opposed to the Treaty he will try to find reasons for supporting it. He may take up the loyalty cry and state that it is the bounden duty of Canada to sacrifice something for the sake of insuring peace to the Empire.

This strategy worked almost perfectly. By late June, Macdonald had his opponents so nearly where he wanted them that he allowed the news to trickle out that he had opposed the Treaty to the last and had only signed it at the bidding of the British Government and in the Imperial interest. He then adroitly drew attention to the clause which required ratification of the Treaty by the Canadian Parliament and quietly left matters to stew.

His task was not made easier by the Governor General and the British Government, both of whom tried to withhold the promised loan guaranty until *after* the Canadian Parliament had been induced to ratify the Treaty. It was not until the United States had incensed Great Britain by resurrecting the "indirect claims" at Geneva, that the British surrendered in part on March 18, 1872. They would guarantee a loan of £2,-500,000 (not the £4,000,000 requested) for Canadian railways and canals, and Canada would not be bound to surrender the inshore fisheries until the United States had committed itself to the legislation for free admission of fish and fish oil. Canadian passions had somewhat burned themselves out by this time, and, with this consoling exit presented to it, Parliament was induced to ratify the Treaty in May, 1872.

Thanks to the United States' delaying tactics in the matter of appointments to the Halifax Tribunal, and to Macdonald's defeat in Parliament in 1873, Canada received one more demonstration that commercial reciprocity could not be arranged with the United States. The new Liberal Government, headed by Alexander Mackenzie, in 1874 allowed the self-confident George Brown, editor of *The Globe* in Toronto and traditional mentor of the party, to go to Washington with the proposal that the Halifax Tribunal be abandoned in favor of a reciprocity treaty. When Brown proved to be very gullible and easy to play along, Fish adroitly led him on from February to June in an extraordinary series of tariff concessions, which included important categories of manufactured goods, and in a variety of other engagements, whose principal usefulness to Fish was their revelation of Canada's economic insecurity after the Panic of 1873.

This incident closed abruptly when Fish exposed the proposed treaty

to a protectionist Senate, but Canada enjoyed an ironical revenge when
circumstances beyond his control forced Fish into accepting the un-
wanted Belgian, Delfosse, as the third member of the Halifax Tribunal
in 1877. That gentleman displayed what was probably his belief that
Great Britain had been forced to pay too much under the *Alabama* Award
by assessing the surprising balance of $5,500,000 against the United
States in the matter of the mutual concessions in the inshore Atlantic
fisheries. It seems almost unnecessary to add that the response of the
enraged United States was to terminate the fisheries clauses of the Treaty
at the first opportunity, on July 1, 1885.

Yet these discouraging bickerings could only temporarily obscure what
time has revealed to be the great and enduring achievements of 1871 at
Washington. Of these unquestionably the greatest was the acceptance
of the United States as a major Power by Great Britain and the laying
of the foundations of an Anglo-American understanding which was based
on substantial mutual respect. There were even some glimmerings of
what was to prove to be a common outlook on world politics. Circumstance and tradition of course continued to hamper easy Anglo-American
relations by providing the usual plethora of shallow gibes and reproaches; but, when a new crisis developed twenty-five years later, the
underlying agreement emerged stronger than in its beginnings and it
continued to gain in strength.

In purely North American terms, Washington signified that the United
States had accepted the barrier to Manifest Destiny which was represented by the transcontinental Dominion of Canada and by its ownership of inshore rights on the Atlantic. Perhaps it would be truer to say
that the United States fell into a general apathetic indifference toward
Canada. This mood was always faintly colored by the common assumption that sooner or later the Dominion would tumble into the lap of the
United States, and from time to time special "pressure groups" tried to
do something to speed up the process, but it proved impossible to rouse
Americans as a whole to concern themselves about a country which they
felt they could safely take for granted. Meanwhile the essence of being a
Canadian was quite naturally the determination to preserve Canada's
independence of the United States.

At the time of the Treaty the most thoughtful Canadians were deeply
puzzled by the behavior of Great Britain. Must they conclude that she
really wanted them to go, or could they detect and could they encourage
some faint stirrings of a new and vigorous sense of empire? To Macdonald it seemed a toss-up whether twenty-five years hence Canada would
be independent or a part of the Empire. To Galt, Blake, Mackenzie, and

their Liberal friends the more likely alternatives seemed to be independence or membership in the American Union, but they too clung to the hope of remaining British.

Macdonald has no greater claim to statesmanship than in the shrewd, warm-blooded appeal which he made in a great speech of May 3, 1872, when he urged the Canadian Parliament to ratify the Treaty. The prophetic note which he struck was intended for British as well as Canadian ears.

Let Canada be severed from England—let England not be responsible to us, and for us, and what could the United States do to England? Let England withdraw herself into her shell, and what can the United States do? England has got the supremacy on the sea—she is impregnable in every point but one, and that point is Canada; and if England does call upon us to make a financial sacrifice; does find it for the good of the Empire that we, England's first colony, should sacrifice something, I say that we would be unworthy of our proud position if we were not prepared to do so. (Cheers.) I hope to live to see the day, and if I do not that my son may be spared to see Canada the right arm of England, (cheers) to see Canada a powerful auxiliary to the Empire, and not a cause of anxiety and a source of danger.

Whatever the future might bring, Canadians had learned in the hardest way a lesson which, like any proud people, they were always to be most prone to forget, namely, that in a world of Great Powers Canada was a minor one. But they had also rediscovered the working principle which had emerged during the reciprocity negotiations of 1854, that is, that both Great Britain and the United States had certain specific interests in Canada which could on occasion be stimulated to activity, and actually intensified, by playing one off against the other, to Canadian advantage. As any other country would in the same circumstances, Canada rejoiced in the possession of two strings to her bow.

Yet neither string must be twanged until it broke, for then all added advantage would be lost and Canada would have to resign herself to the fate of an isolated secondary Power. Moreover she might lose what was potentially the most powerful guaranty of the kind of world in which she could live and grow most freely. Anglo-American understanding was henceforth to be, if not always acknowledged, the cardinal principle of Canadian foreign policy, for if Great Britain and the United States began to pull in opposite directions the vulnerable Dominion of Canada was bound to be the first casualty.

CHAPTER XII

WESTWARD THE COURSE OF EMPIRE
(1850–1900)

ABOUT 1850–1860 it had begun to be obvious all along the moving frontiers of settlement in North America that, while the western half of the continent promised new rewards for enterprise, it also bristled with obstacles, most of which were new and strange. In the eastern half, slightly modified European practices had served quite well. Quality had been blithely subordinated to quantity. New commodities, like tobacco, maple sugar, Indian corn, and pumpkins, had been easily absorbed into ordinary living. The abundant forests had in many ways made settlement easier. The Indians could be subjugated when necessary or be pushed farther west. But west of the Great Lakes and the Mississippi, North America was so unlike the European or eastern North American homes of most of the migrants that mastery of it demanded great feats of imagination, stubborn enterprise, and inventive adaptability. Meanwhile the eastern hives of population were ever ready to launch forth new swarms.

By 1855, for instance, the good lands of what was then Canada were about gone. Along the margins of the inhospitable Canadian Shield there were farmers, or farmer-lumbermen, whose livelihood depended in large part on the services which they rendered to the Juggernaut car which was laying low the pine forests and always moving on. Here and there, wretched victims of ignorance—usually newcomers because the natives were too wary—had been left stranded on the rocky ribs of doomed farms along the so-called "colonization roads" which mistaken public policy had, with the lumbermen's blessing, driven into the wilderness. Meanwhile the really substantial northern column of land seekers had crossed the waterways between Lakes Huron and Erie and moved toward the Illinois and the Mississippi, giving the sands of the Michigan Peninsula a respectfully wide berth.

The Shield, then, was a barrier to settlement both in Canada and in northern Michigan, Wisconsin, and Minnesota, where it projected into the United States. Yet it was also rich in opportunities of different kinds. The stands of pine were remarkably compact, and up near Lake Superior were copper mines which had been worked by the Indians long before Cartier heard of them in 1535. More important still, for an onrushing age of iron and steel, were the astounding stores of rich, easily worked iron ores which were being uncovered at intervals all the way from the Sault to Duluth and beyond. Strangely enough these were virtually all in the territory of the United States. But Lake Superior's mineral treasury could not be tapped effectively until man mastered by a canal the "Sault" and the rapids of the St. Marys River leading down to Lake Huron, and even then he must go on to carry out a technical revolution in marine loading, unloading, and in shipbuilding. The construction of railways across the rough, watery, practically uninhabited expanses of the Shield was still another problem.

Nor was the mid-continental column of settlers to be allowed merely to rely on old ways in exploiting the marvelously rich soils which continuously receded before their eyes. New problems, like the inadequacy of all save the new, expensive steel plows for breaking the thick sod of the prairies, and the years needed to rot it after it was turned under, were at first only faintly appreciated, but they began to pile mountain-high as soon as the land seekers lost touch with the forests and the humid margins of the Shield. How get along without abundance of wood for building, fencing, and fuel? How reach down to the deep water table with wells and how man the pumps to raise the water? How work out the techniques of dry-farming, and find grains both sturdy enough to resist plant diseases and swift enough in growth to ripen in a shorter growing season? How deal with bison, wolves, coyotes, prairie dogs (marmots), mounted Indians, and belligerent cattlemen?

The bowl of the continent rose and dried out as men traveled westward from the central valley or from the margin of the Shield and mounted toward the abrupt eastern escarpment of the Rockies.[1] Sometimes the aridity was so severe that the land was desert or the near-desert suitable only for cattle ranges. Only if one followed the Red River of the North into British territory did watered lands extend continuously northwestward to the foothills of the mountains. The Oregonians had skirted desert on their way to the Pacific Coast; the persecuted Mormons had plunged into it in 1847 and by bold experiments in irrigation had established a commonwealth in the Salt Lake Basin; and the overland Argonauts to California had not only traversed the western desert and mountain area at its broadest, but had anticipated the mineral promise of the forbidding barrier between the interior and the Pacific.

Yet the barrier of mountains and desert plateaus was there, a thousand miles across at its broadest, and lowest, east of southern California, and,

1. There are three principal levels, or steppes, in the Canadian-American great plains, separated by the Manitoba Escarpment and the Missouri Coteau, both of which run northwestward across the international boundary.

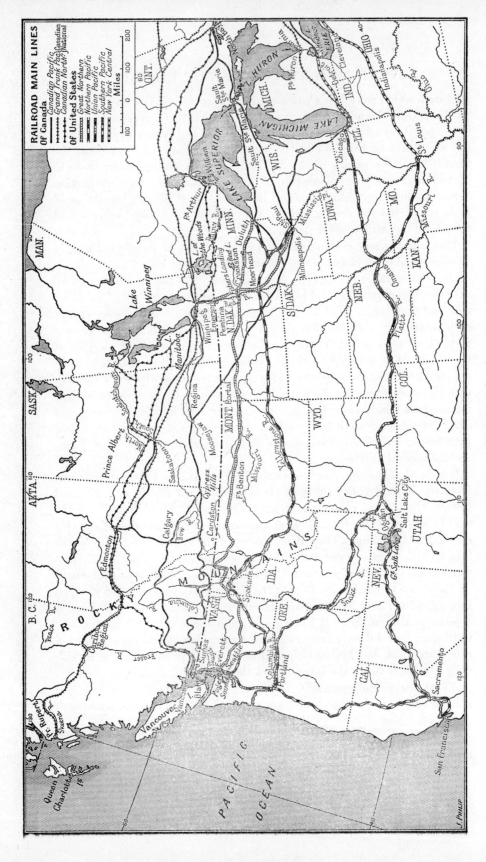

Transportation and Settlement in the Western Canadian–American Region, 1861–1914

if narrowing to a mere four or five hundred in well-watered southern British Columbia, there piling up in range after range with average crest lines of from eight to twelve thousand feet. Even the passes in this region were from 5,300 to 7,100 feet above sea level.

When on May 10, 1869, the last spikes, of western gold, silver, and iron, were driven into railway ties at Promontory Point, Utah, and locomotives of the Union Pacific and Central Pacific drew close enough together for a man on each to break a bottle of champagne over the cowcatcher of the other, it was demonstrated that the railroad could conquer the Rockies. When placer-mining led to lode-mining and the tilted, tortured rocks revealed not only gold and silver, but coal and base metals, it was apparent that railroads in the region could pay. Yet there can seldom have been a more complex problem, or series of problems, than those which the great mass of the Rockies presented when it came to achieving a profitable balance between costs and depletion on the one hand, and sustained returns on the other. Fortunately, determined men were learning how to occupy the empty lands to the eastward.

The moving frontier of agricultural settlement in the western Canadian-American Region has been called the "Sod-House Frontier" because a large proportion of its pioneers, like the dwellers on the plains and steppes of Europe, made their buildings from tough segments of the matted vegetation on the surface of the prairies. A special plow, drawn usually by several oxen, was used to slice out a continuous ribbon, two to four inches in thickness and twelve to fourteen inches wide. This was then cut up into appropriate sizes and shapes. Wooden poles were used for door and window frames and as rafters upon which brush was piled before slabs of sod were arranged to make a roof. Where sod happened to be thin or the contours of the land especially favorable, dugouts were often constructed, and either form of earthen building was excellent winter shelter, although both were almost intolerable without better roofing during thaw or rain. At such times, umbrellas and tarpaulins were useful indoors. Covered wagons served as temporary dwellings, and the invention of tarpaper helped to convert leaky, drafty dwellings into snug refuges from wind and weather.

This sod-house frontier was like a great westward-growing crescent, based on the upper Mississippi, with its projecting horns in Kansas and the Canadian prairies, and with the dry uplands of Nebraska and South Dakota indenting a hollow between. The less wood immediately available, the more sod there was in buildings. Thus Kansas and Nebraska were most typical, whereas northern Iowa, Minnesota, and Manitoba profited by the proximity of the forested Shield. Though the rivers there ran the

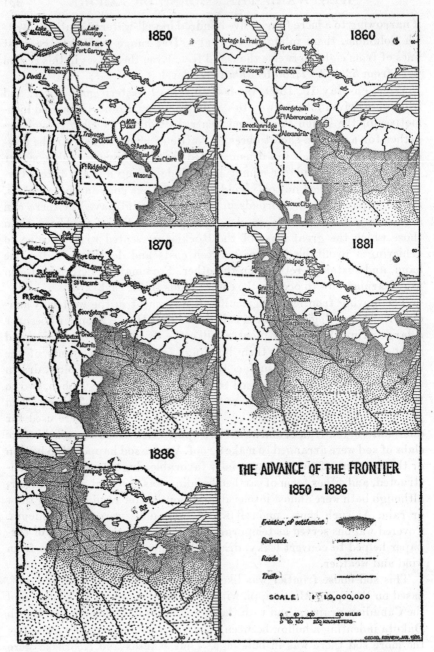

The Advance of the Frontier
1850–1886

Reproduced through the courtesy of Professor A. H. Moehlman and of the *Geographical Review* published by the American Geographical Society of New York

wrong way for easy transportation of lumber, roads often became bottomless pits of gumbo mud, and railways were at first nonexistent, yet lumber could be hauled long distances with some ease in winter. The lack of wood began to be felt again in Dakota and was critical farther west in the United States, but it was not so serious when the westering column swung up into Canada and hugged the parklands of the Manitoba Basin and the valleys of the Assiniboine and Qu'Appelle.

Men and women endured these hardships because they were bewitched by the discovery of rich, finely divided, dark or black soils, which might continue in undiminished fertility two or three feet down. Since the region was dry, the humus was not washed out. The "sod-busting" pioneers of Illinois and Iowa had in the 'thirties and 'forties converted such soil into corn (or corn whisky) and into "fifteen or twenty bushels of corn on four legs," in the form of huge hogs which could carry themselves to market and usually did.

West and north of these states, however, the distance from market and the more severe climate necessitated a shift from corn and hogs to wheat and cattle. There, even with the steamboats of the Mississippi, Missouri, and Red rivers to aid them, and, after 1855, with the aggressive railroad crossing the Mississippi—at Davenport, Iowa—as well, the farmers who ventured into western Minnesota, the Dakotas, and Manitoba during and after the Civil War found that they had let themselves in for all the problems of high-plains agriculture in their most trying forms. A full generation of trial and error, immigration and emigration, boom and depression, was to pass before they and their descendants had acquired mastery of most of the obstacles except the occasional invincible catastrophes of hail, premature frost, or utter drought. Wave after wave from the eastern reservoirs of farmers rolled westward, shattering themselves upon unsuspected obstacles, and receding, leaving little pools of the stubbornest and luckiest, until repeated assaults had broken down the barrier reefs. In most districts of the North American far west there were two, three, or four human assaults and retreats before the conquest was achieved. The losses among the speculators, the ignorant, the inept, the lazy, and the merely unlucky were awe-inspiring to those who finally fought through to success.

Speaking generally, the triumph over the problems of high-plains agriculture was an international affair. The column of westward migrants which swung south of the Great Lakes and skirted the Canadian Shield contained many Canadians.[2] After the incorporation of Manitoba in the Dominion in 1871, and even more during and after the construction of

2. See the maps on pp. 202 and 223.

the Canadian Pacific Railway (1880–1885), many settlements—North American, European, and mixed—were founded on the Canadian prairies. Nevertheless, for a number of reasons, distinctly the larger part of the early wrestling with plains agriculture took place in the United States. As we shall see, American economic nationalism, in the shape of the systematic protectionism which persisted after the Civil War, succeeded much better than its Canadian counterpart, thereby attracting hundreds of thousands of Canadians to the United States, largely to less exacting regions than the great plains. In spite of recurrent difficulties the United States was expanding its energies between 1873 and 1895. Canada slowed down almost to a halt.

One result was that the pressure on empty American lands was incomparably more insistent than that upon Canadian. Fortunately for Canada the stubborn resistance of western Minnesota and the Dakotas to agricultural subjugation greatly reduced American ambitions and capacity to annex the Canadian prairies at a time when Great Britain and Canada would have found it very difficult to defend them. By 1895, when world commodity prices took an upward turn and hundreds of thousands of Americans joined the influx which peopled the Canadian plains, Canada was secure against annexation because of the experience of her long-suffering western pioneers, the railways which bound together her transcontinental economy, and the assurance that she could sell her wheat profitably in the world market. She also was in a position to benefit tremendously from the skills and experience of incoming Americans who were quite ready to become Canadians in order to acquire almost the last good free, or nearly free, farm lands of North America. The whole advance of agricultural technology and its servants between 1865 and 1895 was available for the rapid subjugation of the Canadian far west.

As W. P. Webb has made abundantly clear in his classic, *The Great Plains*, when North American civilization emerged from the woods beyond the Mississippi, it may have faced unprecedented problems, but it had to support it the already exploited and the exploitable potentialities of the Industrial Revolution. Accordingly a great part of the conquest of the far west can be credited to the British achievement of the railroad and to ingenious Yankee inventors of other specialized apparatus. In addition the resourceful and daring manufacturers of agricultural machinery in the middle west were ready to gamble on new inventions in order to facilitate the large-scale agriculture which the Great Plains invited, indeed, practically demanded.

Nevertheless the abiding conquest, the conversion of the grasslands into huge farms capable of supporting the population at a decent standard of living, was the product of the farmers' own unremitting trial and error and of the specific demands which they laid upon manufacturers for the specialized machinery which their novel farming required. The whole varied assault on the west forms a confused story, with many local successes and failures, slow pooling of knowledge, and many kinds of experiment and contest going on at once. It was for the most part an intensely individualistic enterprise with all the cut-throat competition and human wastage which that kind of endeavor involves. The historian must resolve it arbitrarily in order to make it at all clear, but the smooth account which results would have surprised and probably angered most of the harassed individuals who acted out the great drama.

To begin with it is necessary to realize that the railway, although immensely serviceable, did not in itself conquer the Plains. Jay Cooke's failure and the Panic of 1873 are merely conspicuous examples of the fact that railways across the plains could not and did not pay until long after the 'seventies and 'eighties when they were being built. Private investors and all manner of public bodies, from municipalities to national governments, were left "holding the bag," and even the railway builders themselves, whose inside knowledge made them adept at realizing and draining off construction profits, were frequently ruined by the collapse of what had seemed legitimate hopes. Railways had to be unprofitable where human beings had not yet learned how to live.

Nonetheless, since the railways did supplant the covered wagon in transporting the migrants and their equipment, and were available to export the products when the settlers had learned how to wrest them from the soil, the underlying structure of railways in the western Canadian-American region must be taken into account. The idea of the Northern Pacific, which came next after the Union Pacific and Central Pacific by reaching the Coast on Puget Sound in 1883, had been born in Boston thirty years earlier. It was originally to have taken the form of an expansion of the Grand Trunk through Canada to Sault Ste Marie, thence south of Lake Superior to the prairies, and by some route to the Pacific, near the international boundary in order to serve both countries. This idea persisted in various forms as late as 1880. As assembled and built between 1870 and 1883, however, the railroad was wholly American, starting at Duluth, and running almost due westward across the High Plains to Spokane and the Coast, well to the south of the international boundary.

Meanwhile complicated controversies had developed around the regions between the upper Mississippi—already connected with Chicago by rail—and Manitoba, and between the latter and the Ottawa Valley.

The objective in each case was to connect the most promising areas of the Canadian-American northwest with the Atlantic seaboard, and hot debates raged as to whether the parts of the Canadian Dominion which were separated by the Canadian Shield should be joined by a line within Canadian territory or, more economically and profitably, by a line south of Lake Superior.

A piquant note was introduced when a group of Canadians and ex-Canadians formed a syndicate in 1878 which picked up, at little cost to themselves, the control and the remnants of two chartered Minnesota railways which had been ruined by the grasshopper plagues of 1873–1875. From this nucleus they set to work, reaching up from St. Paul and Minneapolis to Manitoba, and planning thereafter to build a Pacific line in Canada or in the United States north of the Northern Pacific. The Canadian Government opened a line from Winnipeg to meet this railway at the border in November, 1878, and had built another from Manitoba to Fort William on Lake Superior by 1881.

Then followed a confused melee among the western railway builders which was an amusing and pointed commentary both on the mingled American and Canadian stock in the northwest and on the futility of thinking of it other than as a single geographical region. The Canadian syndicate, having made substantial fortunes for themselves out of their St. Paul, Minneapolis & Manitoba Railway, were confident enough in 1881 to accept Sir John Macdonald's invitation to build a Canadian Pacific Railway. A wet cycle in the west from 1877 to 1880 had heightened their hopes. At once, however, they found it impossible to agree on the route for the Lake Superior section.

James J. Hill, late of Ontario, argued forcibly that there could be little local traffic north of the Lake, whereas south of it a line would not only pass through the iron- and copper-mining regions, but could connect profitably with the syndicate's St. Paul line to the prairies. When it became clear that the Canadian Government would not stand for this, Hill resigned from the Canadian Pacific directorate. Failing in an attempt to gain control of the Northern Pacific, Hill then set about expanding the St. Paul line into the Great Northern, a Pacific railway running from termini at Duluth and St. Paul close to the international boundary. This line reached the Coast at Everett, Washington, in 1893.

While the ex-Canadian was thus engaged in the United States, an ex-American, William C. Van Horne, was successfully building the Canadian Pacific within Canadian territory in less than five years (1881–1885), in spite of picturesque threats and substantial opposition from the angry

Hill. Van Horne's conquests of the Canadian Shield between the Ottawa Valley and Fort William and of the Canadian Rockies between Calgary, Alberta, and Vancouver, British Columbia, were the greatest achievements in North American railroad engineering up to that time—"one of man's most marvelous accomplishments," in the words of the closest student of these matters, W. J. Wilgus. The Canadian Pacific, after crossing the Shield between Ottawa and Winnipeg, continued slightly northwest to Calgary, south of the well-watered Saskatchewan Valley route which had originally been surveyed. This location involved the abandonment of the moderate Yellowhead Pass—3,733 feet above sea level—west of Edmonton, and the crossing of two very high ranges—the Rockies and the Selkirks—by the Kicking Horse Pass and the Rogers Pass which were 5,300 and 4,316 feet above sea level, respectively. Maximum grades of 116 feet to the mile and extraordinary curvatures were balanced against the shorter route and greater nearness to the border. The clear intention was to deny to American railways profitable access to the Canadian west.

Hill had not been made any happier by Clause 15 of the Canadian Pacific contract of 1880 which practically prohibited the building of competing railways—Canadian or American—in Canada south of the main line, and thereby prevented the future Great Northern from tapping Canadian territory. His wrath began to ebb in 1888, however, when Clause 15 was terminated, following unremitting pressure from Manitoba and the Company's financial embarrassments. Thereafter Hill's branch lines to the Canadian border—about a dozen in number—were able to make useful connections with Canadian railways and even to penetrate Canada, whereas the older Northern Pacific secured only two entries. The Canadian Pacific took some of the gilt off Hill's gingerbread in 1889 and 1890 by acquiring one important American railway system as a link between east and west south of Lake Superior, and another across Maine, thus completing a remarkably efficient transcontinental system with a summer terminus at Montreal and a winter one at St. John, New Brunswick. Hill's competition, however, finally forced the Canadian Pacific to build its own expensive Crow's Nest Pass line from Medicine Hat, Alberta, across the ranges of southern British Columbia to Vancouver.

Thanks to these engineering conquests and to the funds which optimistic private investors and interested public authorities were willing to pour into the treasuries of railways which could not immediately pay, it can be said that the far west was always, before about 1895, oversupplied with railways. Three lines ran all the way to the Pacific north of the pioneering Union Pacific and Central Pacific, and branches and lesser railways awaited the passengers and freight which could only be created by the conquest of the semiarid grasslands.

These lands had been occupied by forbidding mounted Indians whose capacities as warriors were beyond anything which Easterners had previously known. The horse, first introduced to the southern plains about 1540, had been steadily passed on northward, replacing the dog for transportation purposes and establishing the Indians, who lived among the countless buffalo, in a thoroughly enviable position. Their mounts made the buffalo easy victims and the buffalo supplied almost all their needs. These brilliant cavalrymen, armed with lances, shields, and quivers of arrows which they could shoot forth with astonishing rapidity, bade fair to deny the plains to the oncoming farmer, who at first was usually an infantryman armed with a single-shot rifle. At last the traditional American Indian policies of long-drawn-out extermination, or expulsion farther west, would no longer serve.

The Industrial Revolution, in the person of Samuel Colt of Connecticut, produced the six-shot revolver as the effective reply to the Indian's quiver of arrows. In 1842 down in the southwest, where the Indian scourge had long been fiercest, the mounted Texas Rangers raised from the obscurity in which it had been buried for seven years what they described as "the only weapon which enabled the experienced frontiersman to defeat the mounted Indian in his own peculiar mode of warfare." Five years later the United States Government took up the weapon on a large scale and within a generation the six-shooter had become a conventional article of dress among the cattlemen and soldiers of the Great Plains.

Yet the Indians stubbornly persisted in their two and a half centuries of resistance to the advancing whites. Since the official American Indian policy of the time amounted to an ugly combination of graft, treachery, ignorance, and would-be terroristic ruthlessness, wars were inevitable.[3] A Sioux rising in Minnesota in 1862–1863 started with massacres totaling more than seven hundred whites, and ended with several serious pitched battles and the hanging of Indian prisoners. The Arapahoes and the Cheyennes between the Arkansas and the North Platte, cheated of their lands, went on the warpath against the frontier folk in 1864 and were only partially subdued by the massacre of large numbers after they had surrendered and were defenseless. Congress took a hand promptly after the Civil War, but its so-called "Peace Policy" of 1865–1867 was

3. Instead of being in the hands of a single, expert administration, Indian policy was a contentious issue between corrupt and inefficient civil servants of the War Department and the Department of the Interior.

a failure except in so far as it split up the tribes and herded many into reservations, and the borders from Texas to Nebraska blazed with local wars in 1868–1869 and again in 1874–1875.

Meanwhile the mining rushes to Montana, Idaho, and the Black Hills of Dakota were blatantly violating the most cherished hunting grounds of the Sioux, in spite of their protests. The Government forced treaties of surrender on them which it backed up by a string of forts from Minnesota to the Rockies. Inevitably, however, violence was added to violence until occasional raids became a series of pitched battles in 1876 and 1877. The shattered remnant of the Sioux warriors under Sitting Bull fled to Canada, not to return until 1881. Their last flare-up accompanied the religious revival known as the Ghost Dance craze of 1888. It was ended when Hotchkiss rapid-fire guns exterminated an Indian village occupied chiefly by women and children. Thereafter the Plains Indians were penned up in their reservations, chiefly land of little use to the whites, and the white man's frontier was quiet at last.

All this while there had been no Indian trouble of any serious consequence in Canada, a circumstance which has not failed to excite attention. Frederick Merk, an American historian who has been especially concerned with the contrast, offers the following explanation in his *Fur Trade and Empire:*

London paternalism and St. Louis individualism gathered each its own fruits. The territory of the Hudson's Bay Company, inhabited by a numerous and diverse Indian population, was an area of peace and order. . . . On the American side of the line, violence and murder were the order of the day. . . .

This striking contrast between British and American Indian relations was no mere temporary phenomenon disappearing with the passing of the fur trade. It persisted as long as the red man and the white faced each other in the coveted land of the Far West. Trapper and trader gave way on both sides of the international boundary to miner and cattleman and they in turn to the pioneer farmer. These harbingers of a new day on the American side entered a region of already established strife and perpetuated there traditions two centuries old of Indian massacre and border retaliation. On the Canadian side civilization entered a region reduced by the Hudson's Bay Company to a tradition of law and order and the history of this frontier was one of almost unbroken peace.[4]

This interpretation of what might be taken as the underlying principles in the contrast, particularly before 1880, ought probably to be supplemented by other factors. To begin with, the French of Canada had been the children of the Counter-Reformation of the seventeenth century,

4. Reprinted by permission of the President and Fellows of Harvard College.

that is, a Christian missionary people. They had lived with the Indians, intermarried with them, and labored to save their souls for Christ. In the west, therefore, the French and the French half-breeds, or métis, formed a buffer between the Indians and the advancing whites. It can have been no accident that the only two appreciable explosions of violence which occurred, in 1870 and 1885, during the occupation of the Canadian west were puny, short-lived, half-breed revolts led by the métis Louis Riel. In both cases the half-breeds were particularly distressed by the unbending way in which the public land-surveyors laid down rectangular lines of division which disregarded their own established holdings and the adaptation of these to the lie of the land and the winding courses of the rivers. The "in-betweens," resenting and fearing the ignorantly conducted onrush of what seemed to them a decadent and ignoble eastern civilization, tried to assert an independence which would hold it at bay. The great mass of the Indians, grateful to have others, who presumably understood the situation better, fight their battles for them, did not rise.

Again, while it is true that Canadian Indian policy was more enlightened, less urgent, and more honorable than American, yet it would be foolish to regard the policy in itself as proof against the inevitable frictions between Indian and white. What seems more to the point is that, thanks to the barrier of the Canadian Shield, the irresistible pressure of an advancing white population came up against the Plains Indians first in the United States, thereby generating violence and war. At the same time a relatively small number of settlers, who were pressing less urgently against them in Canada, found it both convenient and wise to adopt the paternalistic attitude of their predecessors, the fur traders.

There were no such disruptive mining rushes across Canada as those to California, Colorado, Nevada, South Dakota, Montana, and Idaho. By the time population pressure became severe in Canada, the foundation of life for the Plains Indians—the buffalo herds—had been destroyed, and they shrewdly judged from what had already happened in the United States that they were at the white man's mercy. These circumstances must be remembered when one thinks of the Indian's acceptance of evenhanded, judicious control from a few Canadian missionaries and, after 1874, from a handful of North-West Mounted Police, as contrasted with their astonishingly stubborn, if clearly futile, resistance to the might of the United States Army.

The practical extermination of the buffalo, like the complete extinction of the passenger pigeon, seemed incredible even to those who took part in it. These animals had almost disappeared from east of the ninety-fifth meridian by 1850, but they were innumerable west of that line; one herd, for instance, numbering half a million. By 1876 they had disappeared from the United States and by about 1880 from Canada. No pestilence carried them off; no storms destroyed them. Their doom was sealed when the railways invaded the plains, when "robe hunters" embarked on twenty-five years of mechanical slaughter with repeating rifles, and when the American Army decided that Plains Indians without the buffalo would be humbled. Up in Canada bewilderment reigned among the Indian and half-breed hunters and pemmican makers when the seasonal migration of the northern herds from the United States dwindled and died away, and strange legends circulated, attributing the catastrophe to this or that baneful influence emanating from the pioneers who were invading their plains. If they could be expelled, "the buffalo would return."

As the buffalo were exterminated in the grasslands, cattle took their place. At the end of the Civil War in southwest Texas alone, there were probably five million, worth only three or four dollars a head there, but thirty to fifty dollars in the north. Free grass extended from the Gulf of Mexico to the North Saskatchewan, and thanks to the warm Chinook winds which melted or kept down the snow on the northern grasslands in the shadow of the Rockies there seemed no end even to the winter range. The continental Cattle Kingdom was born in the winter of 1864–1865 when some stock, turned loose to starve on the Laramie Plains of Wyoming, pawed through the snow like buffalo and *fattened* on the northern grass. A famous cowboy song, with a cantering rhythm, epitomizes the story:

> Whoopee ti yi yo, git along little dogies.
> It's your misfortune and none of my own.
> Whoopee ti yi yo, git along little dogies,
> For you know Wyoming will be your new home.

The Cattle Kingdom spread north across the plains about as rapidly as the buffalo disappeared from them. The "longhorns" were gradually killed off or bred out in favor of Hereford and other crossbreeds which made better beef and carried less dangerous horns on less agile bodies. The cowboy and his special craft came into being. Branding and semi-annual roundups protected a new kind of property rights and the law was gradually adapted to this new business. Indians and cattle thieves were summarily taught that cattle were not buffalo, free for any man's taking. This western Eldorado boomed in a dizzy spiral until 1885, when prices crashed and a three-year depression sifted out the speculators and the frivolous all the way from Texas to the Canadian North West Territories.

Actually this crash coincided rather neatly with what might be regarded as the preliminaries to a territorial partition of the far west between cattlemen and farmers. The Cattle Kingdom, as Webb points out, had been created during the lull which occurred while eastern agriculture paused circumspectly on the humid lands "east of 98°" because it did not know how to deal with the plains. But during the years while the cattlemen were reigning as "lords of creation" and the "cow towns" along the western railways were almost as spendthrift as the mining towns farther west, the agricultural pioneers were learning, at very high cost to themselves, the tricks and devices by which they might mine grain from the level, rich soils of plains. These lands were arid or semiarid and were criss-crossed by rivers so deep below the prevailing land level and so violent in their fluctuations as to be practically useless for irrigation.

Cattleman and farmer would have agreed that the barbed-wire fence and the metal windmill would be appropriate memorials of the contest between them. The wire, which cattle and horses gradually and painfully learned to avoid and which pioneering farmers could afford to put up in treeless regions, was worked out in 1873 by J. F. Glidden of De Kalb, Illinois, and put on the market by him and his neighbor and competitor, Jacob Haish, in 1874. A total production of 600,000 pounds in 1875 had become more than 80,000,000 five years later.

The Halladay self-regulating windmill, which held to the wind and maintained a uniform speed regardless of the wind's velocity, was a Connecticut invention of 1854, but it was not until the 'seventies that it and its like began to be combined with drilled wells in the west. The drills bored down, from thirty to three hundred feet, a six-inch hole, within whose sheet-iron casing a bucket four feet long, equipped with a valve in the bottom, was raised and lowered by the mill at a rate which delivered small quantities of water in a steady stream.

The "Fence-Cutter Wars" of the 'eighties between cattlemen and "nesters" were for the most part contests for water in a dry land. The ranchmen, legally or illegally, fenced off streams, water holes, and the pastures which they needed in order to keep their better-bred stock free from adulteration. The farmers, whose predecessors of the days before barbed wire had often found that a "free homestead," when fenced in the treeless area, cost more than land purchased in the humid east, now set up cheap barbed-wire barriers around their watering places and around their crops. Often enough these blocked cattle trails or cut up range which the "high-riding" cattlemen had grown accustomed to treating as their own. At any rate the clashes were frequent and bloody, the destruction of property on both sides was great; and over huge areas in the

United States and Canada it seemed as if the cattlemen's troops of reck-less cowboys, backed by acquiescent public authorities, were likely to be victorious.

Yet the contest ended with the cattlemen for the most part pressed back onto the arid and semiarid lands, where heavily alkaline soil forbade farming, or where the black soil thinned out, or where the rainfall was less than ten inches a year, or into the mountains where they promptly fell into a new contest with their new enemies, the sheep herders. The farmers won because they painstakingly learned how to make the grass-lands yield grain in regions where only from ten to thirty inches of rain fell on an average in a year.[5]

The northern Great Plains formed a region which was dry in winter and received from 60 to 70 per cent of its moisture between April 1 and August 31. It was treeless because tree leaves transpire moisture and tree roots go deep. It was grassland because grass leafage resists transpira-tion and the matted vegetation and shallow roots suck in rain almost as fast as it falls.

Since the farmers' conquest of the Great Plains was the lasting con-quest, and since it was they who made the region yield sustenance and surplus in behalf of the permanent population, history owes them a circumstantial account of what they faced and how they mastered it. Their assault had all the elements of an apparently interminable siege. One false move, or a natural catastrophe like hail, and a year's efforts might be lost. Without an unfailing supply of man power endowed with the capacity and willingness for oft-repeated trial-and-error methods in the face of implacable resistance, they would never have won through. Their human and material losses were enormous and are almost unre-corded. Their victory was one of the most remarkable, if still most pre-carious, which Man has achieved over Nature.

A. S. Morton summarizes the agricultural assault on the Canadian Plains in terms which might well apply to the whole region. It begins, he says, "with ignorant optimism, passes on to disillusionment and even to despair, then shows the adjustment of the settlers' methods of farming to the necessities of the climate; it ends with what might be called a modest victory over nature and a prosperity moderated by the vagaries of the climate and of the price of wheat in the world market." The main opera-tions of the evolution which he describes dragged out over the full genera-tion between the end of the Civil War and the end of the century. After all, it had taken the entire decade 1812 to 1822 to establish the little Selkirk Settlement on the Red River, while that colony had been gener-

5. Or as little as eight or nine in northern regions where evaporation was least.

ously underwritten by a philanthropist and, in an economic sense, remained secondary to a flourishing fur trade.

It would be tedious and unprofitable to do more than list some of the minor variations in the struggle. The mantle of grass-bound black soil naturally ran thin in some areas and, when broken by the plow, could be, and was, blown away. Considerable areas were sterilized by deposits of mineral salts, on the alkali plains. Coal seams in the Souris Valley of Manitoba and in southern Alberta were an unexpected blessing to regions short of wood for fuel. Evaporation grew less and the frost risk grew greater as the farmers traveled north. Floods, hail, grasshoppers, plant diseases, and even drought or frost struck with a regional capriciousness which must substantially qualify any generalizations.

Yet it can be said that the painful and slow discovery of the over-all possibilities and the best methods of dry-farming formed the hard, central core of the long campaign and that the lessons learned were the basic guarantees of the final victory. Clearly the main objective was to deliver as much as possible of the annual rainfall to the roots of the growing crops, but eastern experience in this matter was far more misleading than useful. Some greenhorns, for instance, actually plowed up the western soil in the spring and left the furrows to dry out.

No one today can piece together the whole story of how the new knowledge was accumulated and shared. Rainy cycles lured men into normally arid areas from which drought sternly expelled them. Philanthropists and speculators from Europe and the east frequently substituted large expenditures of money for serious investigations of what must be learned from the land and the climate. On the other hand thousands of unrecorded stubborn men and women, quite frequently the hardy peasants who had begun to pour in directly from Europe, struggled through to success. It is claimed, for instance, that about 1863 some Scandinavians near Bear River City, Utah, discovered part of the basic techniques of dry-farming by accident. Salt in irrigation water having ruined their fields, in desperation they deep-plowed and planted some naturally fallowed neighboring dry lands which, to their amazement, yielded well. Yet it was thirty years later before the whole gamut of dry-farming devices had begun to become conventional throughout the west.

The basic pattern of western dry-farming came to comprise the deep-plowing of the finely divided soil in order to create a thick spongy layer with easy capillarity to the plant roots, and frequent shallow cultivation of the surface thereafter in order to form a blanket of finely divided mulch which would minimize evaporation. In the hotter regions, when rain fell in the summer months, all hands and all machinery must be rushed into swift and continuous action in order to loosen and divide the soil before the moisture could escape. A crust on the soil, besides being caked too hard to break up finely, was perforated or cracked and allowed moisture to evaporate which a loose, fine, soil cover would retain.

What proved to be the most important device, however, was to summer fallow each year a third or a half of the farm. This land was thoroughly plowed during the June-July wet season in order to turn in the stubble, and harrowed or cultivated at intervals thereafter in order to keep down weeds and "volunteer" grain and to protect the moisture in the spongy subsoil. In the following spring the seed planted in this land was well covered, in the early years by shallow plowing, but later by a seed drill which placed it deep enough for its roots to become established in the water sponge which had been saturated the year before and protected during the dry winter. Last year's moisture was needed, for the melting snow was barely sufficient to promote germination and on an average only 5 per cent of the year's scanty rain fell during the April sowing season. Wheat planted on such summer-fallowed land would grow mightily in the face of droughts which withered less favored crops away.[6]

Various refinements of these techniques, such as the use of specialized grass and clover cover crops, existed here and there, but in the more northern areas they were, on the whole, of distinctly less importance than the final problem, that is, the development of a sturdy, quick-ripening, spring wheat.[7] The old Red River variety was thoroughly unsatisfactory, for it took about 140 days to ripen, which meant that even when sown in late April it might be caught by mid-September frosts, and occasionally there were frosts as early as August in Manitoba. In addition, its slow maturing meant that it was easily weakened by the plant rust which ordinarily developed during the warmth and damp of August.

The wheat which gave the plains their first start as a world granary was as international as the region. Back in the early 'forties, David Fife, a farmer near Peterborough, Canada, had asked a neighbor, who was going home to Scotland for a visit, to bring him back some new kinds of

6. It might be convenient to note here that an unending conflict with aridity has continued during the twentieth century and has been aggravated since 1919 by two periods of drought which raised the problem of wind erosion to vast proportions. The dust-mulch device has almost been abandoned and the present tendency seems to be toward alternate strips of sown land and fallow, with the fallow merely undercut by shallow slicing in order to kill the weeds and to protect the soil with a trash cover. While every effort is made to leave as much fiber in the soil as possible, the prevalence of the wheat fly, which infests stems and stubble, has necessitated the use of broad trap rows of wheat or grasses, with a bare space between them and the crop. Experiments continue in search of wheats resistant to insects and disease.

7. There were some areas between the Platte and the Saskatchewan where favorable conditions permitted winter wheat, but spring wheat predominated.

wheat. The friend almost forgot the mission, but hurriedly collected a little from a ship which was unloading at Glasgow at the time when he sailed from there. Fife planted the samples in the spring of 1844, but, since most of the lot was apparently winter wheat, only three stalks came up. Fife fenced them, his wife saved two out of the three from greedy cows which came foraging near the house, and Fife discovered that he had accumulated forty seeds of a red grain, probably Russian in origin, which would mature ten days earlier than any other he had ever seen.

This wheat, useful chiefly as a "mixer" with conventional grains, spread across Ontario, was taken up in Ohio, advanced with the agricultural frontier up the Mississippi to Minnesota, and was restored to Canadian territory again in Manitoba during the mid-'seventies when three grasshopper years in succession forced the Manitobans to call on their neighbors for seed grain. Red Fife made the Canadian-American section of the plains its own.

Growing this wheat was one thing, but persuading housewives to use its flour was another. They and the millers had been accustomed to use winter wheats and the white flour which these yielded. About 1870, therefore, the millers were put on their mettle to get a white flour out of hard Red Fife. A minor revolution in milling, maturing, and bleaching had to take place in the great flour mills of Minneapolis and Lake of the Woods, a revolution which spread over the world, floating on the currents of the ever-expanding exports of North American hard spring wheat. The world's housewives not only received as white a flour as ever, but one of baking qualities superior to any in the past.

As a matter of course there continued to be efforts to improve wheat for the plains. Naturally, because of the increasing frost problem as settlement spread northward, the most urgent and persistent of these took place at the Dominion Government's experimental farms, which were established at Ottawa and in the west during the 'eighties, but American farmers as far south as Iowa eagerly awaited their bulletins of progress. The presiding genius of these experiments was William Saunders, whose work was carried on into the twentieth century by that of his gifted sons, A. F. and C. E. Saunders—who was knighted—and other workers. A. F. Saunders brought in Ladoga from Russia, which matured from seven to ten days faster than Red Fife, but milling tests in 1892 proved very disappointing. He also tried Red Calcutta, but it yielded poorly and the heads shattered easily.

Following these failures the Saunders family embarked on the painstaking, long-drawn-out experiments in crossbreeding Red Fife with these and other Russian, Indian, Australian, and African grains which en-

dowed the west after 1900 with a succession of fine northern wheats—
Marquis, Garnet, Reward, and the present favorites, Red Bobs and
Thatcher. These had maturing periods of from 98 to 105 days. Reward,
for instance, yielded practically twice as many bushels (in terms of pound-
age) to the acre as the original mainstay, Red Fife, and this was high-
protein grain of excellent milling quality. By allotting such grains to the
varying regions in terms of their efficiency when measured against the
known drought, insect, disease, and frost risks, first-class wheat could be
grown over most of the plains from their semiarid margins to the Peace
River district at 56° north latitude.

Thus the farmers finally achieved the ways of establishing themselves
on the plains and thereby of denying any land which they could profitably cultivate to their competitors, the cattlemen. Yet these two groups
of exploiters were not the only effective agents in opening up the western
half of the continent and laying the foundations for its continued occupation. Miners and lumbermen were also alive to the bounties which the
west had to offer and it was they who raced across the plains, plunged
into the mountains and swelled the prosperity of the Coast itself. They
did not rival the farmers in terms of established population, but they
wrested wealth at an astounding rate from regions which were very forbidding to the tillers of the soil.

The western mining frontier was far too complex an affair to be fully
described by any simple pattern. It ranged the Coast and the mountain
areas from within Mexico to the interior of Alaska and involved the
precious metals, the base metals, and coal. It turned water power and
steam power to its purposes and laid unparalleled burdens on all kinds
of transport from the pack horse or the multiple team to the specialized
mountain locomotive or the aerial cableway. For its prosperity mountains were tunneled for huge distances, either for railways or to drain to
lower slopes mines so deep in the earth that tons of ice had to be imported
in order to relieve the men at work. Powerful steamboats were marvelously
assembled on long, narrow mountain lakes far beyond the ends of steel,
and these and detached stretches of narrow-gauge railroad demonstrated
that the western miners could work out ways of their own for moving
heavy machinery and other apparatus across the roadless mountain
masses.

The placer-mining of 1848 and earlier had become mere froth on the
boiling kettle of lode-mining. From Colorado and Nevada the new kind
of prospector worked his way northward through the ranges to reach a
sort of natural focus in the far northwest, "The Mining Advance into the
Inland Empire," to use W. J. Trimble's title phrase. Here in Montana,

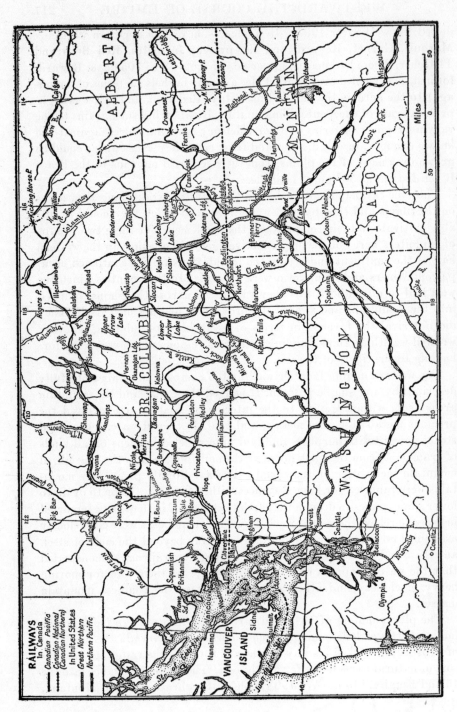

Railways in Southern British Columbia and the Adjacent United States

Idaho, Washington, and British Columbia, a great nexus of mining and smelting activities came into being, with almost all its roots in the United States because until 1897 the dozen or more rich mining districts in southern British Columbia south of the Canadian Pacific main line were accessible almost exclusively, and largely by Hill's Great Northern, from the United States. In 1897–1898, the Canadian Pacific drove a zigzag line from Lethbridge, Alberta, through the coal fields, over the Crow's Nest Pass—5,500 feet above sea level—toward the Pacific, and began to reclaim the region for Canada.

In its early, burgeoning days this international treasure house was the scene of successive exploits which bordered on the fantastic. Rich ores could always be found and usually the capital necessary to exploit them was available. Labor was plentiful, at a price, for work in mines, mills, and smelters which was frequently quite murderous according to modern standards of industrial health protection. The most remarkable feats and extravagances were those connected with transportation—pianos and pier glasses and rare wines destined for evanescent mining towns perched high on mountain shelves; coal and coke and heavy machinery drawn over hump-backed roads, round rapids and falls, and floated for many miles on the rivers and lakes; ore wastefully sorted, stamped out, and concentrated at mines remote from the railways, but emerging so rich as to repay the extraordinary costs of transporting it hundreds of miles to the smelters. Even the revolutionizing railway could only gradually moderate the feverish temperature of the mining regions. Cities like Spokane, Boise, Butte, and Helena retain not a little of it even in the present day.

The mines encouraged agriculture wherever it was practicable; the railroads emboldened it to persist; the rivers and streams of the mountains, unlike those of the plains, could be utilized for irrigation. As a result, although mining communities rose and declined, a steadily increasing agricultural population proceeded to develop the mountain slopes, plateaus, and valleys. Wheat under dry-farming in Montana, Alberta, Washington, and Oregon; gigantic potatoes in Idaho; irrigation for sugar beets in Alberta and the neighboring states; fruit-farming in the many lovely mountain valleys on both sides of the boundary—all these did something to heal the raw gashes made by the miners and to people an empty region permanently.

The miners were also influential in stimulating the lumber industry of the Coast. With improved steam navigation on the oceans it would ultimately have developed anyway, but the enormous demands for mine timber and for railway and other construction provided an immediate and insistent market. But the lumbermen from the Maritimes and New England, Ontario and Michigan, Wisconsin and Minnesota found forests in Idaho, Washington, and British Columbia which in magnitude of trees and roughness of terrain called for the mythical strengths of their gigantic patron deity, Paul Bunyan, and of his equally gigantic blue ox, Babe.

Where the east and the mid-continent had evoked the peavy hook, river dam, log chute, and the strengths of men and animals, the west required the steel cable, the donkey engine, and the railway. Western timber toppers often had to saw off and drop to the ground what in the east would have been a respectable tree in itself before they felled a tree trunk, each one of whose lower logs required most of the carrying capacity of a railway flatcar. Small wonder that the sawyers in the mills along the Pacific from California to British Columbia refused to regard eastern lumbering as anything but child's play. Rapidly, but inevitably, their output rose as the forests of the east were eaten up by the saws.

Viewed as a whole, the human conquest of western North America between 1865 and 1900 was an amazing achievement. It planted abiding populations on an unexpectedly large proportion of an area which had been generally described as the Great American Desert, or had been thought of as uninhabitable mountains. This land was made to produce sustenance for its successful occupiers, and even surpluses, which were spent either to build up its amenities and services or to import the luxuries and some of the color of the softer civilizations elsewhere.

Yet when one looks into the long succession of booms and depressions, the flows and ebbs of population, the lands conquered for a year or two only to be relinquished in a year or two more, the base-metal mines roaring this year and silent next, all of which characterized the region and the period before about 1895, it is apparent that the conquest of the west was a narrow victory. Men's lives balanced precariously between feast and famine, as the businessmen of Kansas City, Minneapolis, Winnipeg, Billings, Calgary, Spokane, Portland, Seattle, and Vancouver were ever ready to attest. When W. J. Bryan, "the silver-tongued boy orator of the Platte," stirred stolid farmers of the Middle Border into "radicalism" and declared: "You shall not crucify mankind upon a cross of gold," he was voicing the discontents of a generation of hard-working men and women who had stood about all that they could stand.

Vaguely, if at all, did that generation of westerners realize that they were the innocent victims of the steady decline in world commodity prices which went on from the Panic of 1873 to 1895. Only when prices began to rise again in 1896 did the land begin to pay full interest on the capital of human endeavor which had been invested by the farmers, the cattlemen, the miners, and the lumbermen of the west. Incidentally, it is not a little ironic that when our generation casts a romantic glance back at the pioneers of the west, it nearly always ignores the farmers. Dime novels, "western" pulp magazines, and the moving-picture industry find their colorful actors among the Indians, cavalrymen, Mounties, cowboys, miners, railway builders, and lumbermen. Only a gifted literary artist like Rolvaag—a European by the way—sees that the real heroes were the pioneers on the soil.

In order to round out our picture of Canadian-American interplay at this time, it should be added that the twenty-five years following 1873 were probably the grimmest quarter century in the history of Canada. Neither courage nor enterprise was lacking, witness for instance the construction of the Canadian Pacific, but witness also the stunning collapses of the Manitoba and British Columbia booms which followed hard after its completion. The old burden of the transportation services which were needed to hold the Dominion together had been increased by the construction of the Intercolonial and by mortgaging the future in the west. The United States market, even for the ores from American mines in British Columbia, was being progressively closed by shrewdly designed tariffs. Transportation, in spite of the recent improvements in ocean carriage, was not yet cheap enough to make the British market remunerative.

The protectionism which Macdonald introduced in 1878, partly for revenue purposes, pleased Quebec and Ontario manufacturers, but angered consumers in the same provinces when they compared the prices which they paid for manufactured goods with those paid by their American cousins a few miles away. Its effects went far to persuade Maritimers and Westerners that Confederation had cast them in the roles of hewers of wood and drawers of water for the money barons of St. James' Street, Montreal, and King Street, Toronto. The American cartoonist's cow that stood on a map of the United States, eating corn in Kansas and being milked in Wall Street, had close Canadian analogies.

The recital of Canadian woes could easily be extended, but it can more conveniently be summarized in the statement that the average Canadian standard of living during this period fell below the average in the United States, and, since there were no barriers to migration, many "surplus" Canadians naturally sought the higher reward for their labors which they could secure across the boundary. All over eastern Canada parts of the population, roughly equivalent in total numbers to the natural increase plus the immigrant newcomers, discovered that they must move on unless they were prepared to become a sort of economically depressed class, a margin or substratum of the established folk. Naturally most of them moved on. More than half of the Canadians whom various circumstances

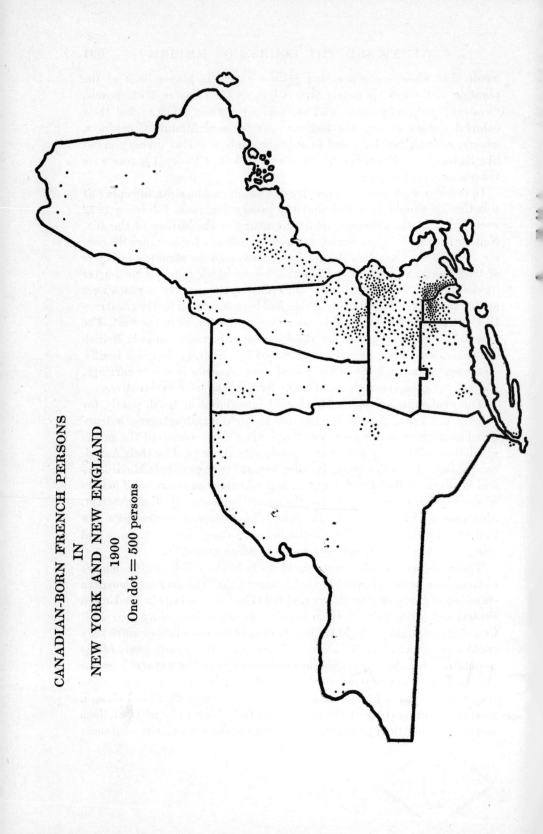

CANADIAN-BORN FRENCH PERSONS
IN
NEW YORK AND NEW ENGLAND
1900
One dot = 500 persons

CANADIAN BORN PERSONS
IN THE
NORTH CENTRAL STATES
1890
One dot = 250 persons

Prepared with the assistance of the United States Bureau of the Census, Washington

uprooted from their birthplaces between 1851 and 1901 managed to find new niches elsewhere in the Dominion, but nearly half of them entered the United States.

Immigrants were pouring into Canada after 1851 in hundreds of thousands, but the periodical censuses of immigrant population showed that after 1861 they were pouring out again into the United States about as fast as they entered. In addition, what had hitherto been a relatively minor outward seepage of native Canadians became a real torrent some time in the 'seventies. This combined emigration of immigrants and native Canadians for the *decade* 1881–1891 exceeded one million persons at a time when the total population of Canada was less than five millions. By 1895 the situation was so bad that had it continued Canada's population would speedily have become stationary.

When old Sir John A. Macdonald died in the summer of 1891, after a lifetime of high statesmanship, sometimes low politics, but always single-hearted devotion to the nation which he had done more than any other man to create and maintain, the future of Canada looked dark indeed. Had he lived only five years longer, his eyes of faith would almost certainly have detected the sudden turn of the tide which launched Canada on a spectacular rise to a condition which was at least to equal his most roseate expectations.

Until that time came, however, the general plight of Canada might not unfairly be taken as symptomatic of the plight of the economically marginal regions of the United States, where hard-working men and women were sick with hopes deferred and whence the less determined retreated to the shelter of richer regions. In spite of Canada's backbone and skeleton of railways, as yet the disjointed segments which made up her settled regions seemed, with the exception of Quebec, more like outward projections from the settled regions of the United States than the integrated parts of a single transcontinental nation. Until rising prices, assured markets, and expanded enterprise should fuse the parts into one, they were not unlike the distressed American areas where unrest and "radicalism" kept showing themselves in such a disconcerting way. In spite of the boundary and the tariff walls, North America in the 'eighties and 'nineties had a good many of the characteristics of one great continental field for economic endeavor, with some sections where reserves had piled up for the lean years or where new industrial enterprises were profitable, and others where lean years meant leaner living and stark endurance unless one simply decided to give up and run for shelter.

CHAPTER XIII
THE MATERIALS OF A TRIANGLE
(1896–1940)

THE world economy, burdened by the depressions of the 'seventies and 'eighties and wounded by the Panic of 1893, felt new life flowing into all its veins and strengthening all its sinews when prices turned upward in 1896. With new gold from the South African Rand, the Klondike, Alaska, and Ontario adding to the basic medium of exchange in unparalleled quantities, man's economic enterprises expanded everywhere into an accelerating boom which went on, with brief interruptions, until 1920, and gave millions of the world's peoples an abundance beyond anything that they had known. In this exuberance no great region was as favored as North America. Toward it the migrants of Europe and Asia turned their faces and for the former, at least, the gates were opened. From it flowed immense streams of products, chiefly to Europe, there to provide cheaper, better bread, meat, and textiles for the poor and, for the middle class and the rich, new and exciting varieties of the fruits of the earth.

During this expansive quarter century (1896–1920), the economic triangle of buying and selling, investing and dividend-paying, migration and production, into which Great Britain, the United States, and Canada poured their efforts, became the mightiest thing of its kind on earth and seemed destined to remain so. Individualism was still practically unbridled, so that competition was the order of the day, but the three areas proved to be complementary in so many ways that they coöperated in spite of themselves.

Interestingly enough this economic coöperation persisted in spite of a curious procession of changes in the economic activity of the members. The United States rapidly assumed and expanded many of the industrial functions which Great Britain had once performed for her and for other parts of the world, and Canada, in a kind of breathless haste, not only took over much of the former American role of pouring forth raw and semimanufactured products for the world market, but became increasingly capable in highly specialized industry. In a rapid crescendo, much hastened by the War of 1914, Great Britain found herself relying more and more heavily upon "invisible exports," that is, upon the income from her foreign investments and from the services and apparatus which she had built up for the distribution of her own and others' goods and money to the four corners of the earth. For both the United States and Canada,

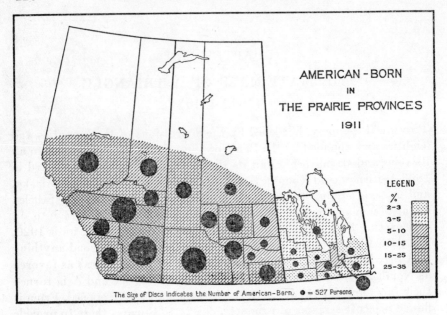

AMERICAN - BORN
IN
THE PRAIRIE PROVINCES
1911

LEGEND
%
2-3
3-5
5-10
10-15
15-25
25-35

The Size of Discs indicates the Number of American-Born. ● = 527 Persons,

(Dominion Bureau of Statistics, Ottawa)

as coöperators or competitors, the Mother Country was the most important market and entrepôt in the world. Thus, while the three components
of the triangular equation were constantly shifting in quantity and quality, yet the maximum expression for the whole or for any one of its parts
depended on their continued interaction.

The restless peoples of Europe and North America dramatized the
boom of 1896–1914 by their mass movements across the Atlantic and
within the North American continent. The twin streams of humanity
which entered the mouths of the St. Lawrence and the Hudson were the
greatest in history. Inside North America two magnets of profitable
enterprise, one west and one east, set up a clockwise international migration which deposited over a million Americans on the Canadian prairies
and about a quarter of that number of Canadians in the industrial northeast of the United States. By these movements the population of Canada,
for the first time in her history except perhaps during the loyalist migrations, grew faster than that of the United States; indeed between the
censuses of 1901 and 1911 a gain of 34 per cent made her the fastest-
growing country in the world.

Fertile lands supplied the clue, for about 1890 the United States found
that she had little left in the way of free or almost free acres of arable
land which a single resolute man or family could subjugate. Farmers in

the solidly occupied agricultural areas of the United States and Canada might not be able any longer to set up their sons with farms of their own on lands near home, but on the Canadian prairies there was still an abundance of rich wheat lands to be had, free from the Dominion Government, or at small cost from the Hudson's Bay Company, or from the Canadian Pacific and other railways, or from land companies which had cannily assembled desirable locations. These agencies, responding to the keen land hunger, and to the price rise and the reduced costs of transportation by land and sea which made far western wheat-raising profitable, did everything possible to capitalize the opportunity. They advertised and opened offices in promising American, Canadian, and European regions; they conducted free tours of inspection for the interested; public authority and private interests combined in order to cut initial transportation charges to far below cost for the sake of the activities and the traffic which would come with settlement; and ingenious, if sometimes foolhardy, financial arrangements lured the newcomer to take a chance on the last great unexploited area of North American farm land. Fortunately for the migrants the promise was lavishly fulfilled, and the Canadian west received a basic stock of experienced, resourceful, English-speaking, North American farmers. In terms of free homesteads alone, the amount of land entered for settlement was astounding. Chester Martin has calculated that in the year 1909 the area entered was larger than Vermont; in 1910, twice the area of Connecticut; in 1911, more than New Hampshire plus Delaware; in 1912, about the area of Maryland; and in 1913, more than Massachusetts.

The statistics of immigrant arrivals in Canada from 1897 to 1914 reveal an interesting proportion. Great Britain provided 1,154,709, the United States 1,026,678, and other countries 842,689, but in 1914, for the first time, "other countries" slightly surpassed the United States and almost equaled the United Kingdom. Had war not intervened, Canada, in spite of continued American entries, would presumably have felt the impact of Continental European emigration almost as sharply as it had been experienced since about 1883 in the United States. As it was, the Canadian west was mottled by group settlements from all the countries of northern and central Europe; construction camps were crowded by the same folk and by the so-called "birds of passage" from southern and eastern Europe who hoped to return home with their savings; and the cities and industrial centers of the east arrested still more before they could join in the agricultural conquest of the west.

The immigration into the United States furnished the other side of the medal. There almost a third of the thirty-two million immigrants of

1820–1914 arrived during the last decade, but the growth of population
had slowed down to about 20 per cent between decennial censuses. The
striking phenomenon was the relative supplanting of British and German
migrants by Italian, Austro-Hungarian, and Russian, which became
consistently apparent after the 'eighties. With the passing of the American frontier, these folk furnished the man power for the great construction work and the mighty industries of the northeastern quarter of the
United States. A relatively small flow of Canadians came south to join
them in the industries of New England, New York, and the middle west,
or in response to the pull of the metropolis as it was exerted by Boston,
New York, and Chicago. A study made by the United States Bureau of
the Census of data collected in 1910 showed that the percentage of Canadian residents exceeded that of the general white population of the United
States in the professions, in the upper ranks of labor and the services,
and in the servant classes—a range which would include the President of
Cornell University, the systematically recruited Canadian trained nurses
all over the United States, the French Canadian of the New England mill
town, and the Maritime-Province girl in the Boston basement kitchen.

As always in North American history, the distribution of the incoming
peoples was a reverse movement of the distribution of outgoing goods.
Just as sailing vessels coming from Europe for fish or tobacco or lumber
had once filled their holds with human beings, so again the steamships,
when they sought cotton, wheat, meat products, fruits, and base metals.
The picture had become a little less simple because of the revolution in
ocean shipping which began with cheap steel in the 'seventies and accelerated with expansion engines, multiple propellers, refrigeration, and the
turbine. Now the ocean greyhound, straining for the Blue Ribbon of the
North Atlantic and the prestige and first-class passenger lists which
went with it, might carry huddled in her lower decks, second class and
steerage, several times as many humble toilers as the total of the privileged in the luxury above. Nonetheless, the old pattern persisted for the
most part, with immigrants inbound and goods outbound along the same
routes.

On land, the response in the expansion of railroads was tremendous.
In the eastern half of the continent the networks thickened in order to
take care of the industrial and urban growth which was spreading steadily westward toward the amazing combination of iron ore, coal, limestone
(for smelting), petroleum, and cheap water transportation now revolutionizing life on both sides of the Great Lakes Basin. In the western half
of the continent and in access to it, it was Canada rather than the United
States which startled all beholders, for the Dominion recklessly added,

with lavish Federal and provincial support, a second and a third railway system from the Atlantic to the Pacific in the decade before 1914. American railway mileage, which had doubled between the recovery of 1878 and the Panic of 1893, added another 90,000 miles to reach its peak of 254,000 miles in 1916, more than a third of the world's total. Canada jumped from 6,226 miles in 1878, to 15,000 in 1893, to 37,400 in 1916, and her mileage continued to grow until it amounted to 42,916 miles in 1935.

Important links in each country's rail systems crossed the territory of the other. Thus three American trunk lines used the short cut across Ontario between Buffalo and Michigan; a variety of western Canadian lines invaded North Dakota, Minnesota, Wisconsin, Illinois, and Michigan on their way to Lake ports or to southern Ontario; and other lines reached out across New England from the Montreal region to the winter ports of St. John, Portland, and New London. In the far west feeder lines of the Northern Pacific and Great Northern tapped the Canadian wheatlands and mines. In the east the New York Central, the Delaware & Hudson, and the Wabash took coal to the industrial centers of coal-less Ontario and Quebec. Great bridges and tunnels mastered border waterways. Car ferries and special shipping made use of rivers and the Great Lakes. Each country took for granted the services of the other's customs and border officials, services which were at once so efficient and so casual that traffic proceeded smoothly, almost without interruption.

Strangely enough very few Americans or Canadians had the least conception of the importance of their most valuable joint possession, the Great Lakes, unless they happened to have watched the continuous procession of freighters coming down through the canals at Sault Ste Marie or passing, on an average for the whole season, at fifteen or twenty minute intervals, on the St. Clair and Detroit rivers. The Lakes carried annually more than the total ocean-borne foreign trade of the two countries. During the feverish seven and a half or eight months of open navigation, racing against winter, several times as much tonnage passed the Sault as was handled at Panama or Suez in a full year.[1] Coal and manufactured goods, such as agricultural implements, moved up the great waterway, but many vessels went up in ballast, because twice the upward tonnage came down in the form of iron ore from the mines of northern Michigan and Lake Superior and wheat from the prairies. Coal, lime-

---

1. In 1941, 111 million tons of freight passed through the Sault canals. The corresponding tonnage of 1939 through Panama was 28 millions and through Suez, 30 millions. The total annual movement, on the Lakes, of bulk freight (iron, coal, limestone, and grain) has been: 1900, 35 million tons; 1910, 80 million tons; 1920, 107 million tons; 1929, 138 million tons; 1941, 169 million tons.

stone, lumber, flour, and package freight crisscrossed the whole chain of lakes in many directions. Yet, strictly speaking, most of the traffic was coastal traffic for one country or the other, the great American routes being those between Lake Superior or Lake Michigan and the Lake Erie ports, and the great Canadian routes those between Lake Superior and the Georgian Bay railway connections with Montreal.

The "upper laker" symbolized this traffic. It was in effect an ingeniously constructed, long, shallow, self-propelled, steel barge, with an average cargo capacity of from 7,000 to 9,000 tons. It might be over six hundred feet long and carry 16,000 tons, but it seldom exceeded sixty-five feet in beam and thirty-three in draft when fully loaded, because of the difficulties of navigation in locks and harbors, and because the shallows of the St. Marys River at the Sault, of Lake St. Clair, and of the Amherstburg Channel of the Detroit River restricted safe upbound drafts to between seventeen and twenty-one feet, depending on the quite remarkable annual and seasonal fluctuations of the water levels. The vessel's navigating bridge topped a brief deckhouse at the very bow, its great funnel pierced another from an engine room below at the very stern, and as many as twenty hatches covered the hopper-like holds of a slightly flexible, double-bottomed hull between. There were no interfering masts or booms or hoisting apparatus,[2] for the many compartments of these ships were so covered and curved that they might be loaded and unloaded by very elaborate dumping or scraping and hoisting machinery at the ore docks and grain elevators. Here the speed of operations was fantastic. Ore could be loaded at an average of 4,000 tons an hour and unloaded almost half as fast. Corresponding figures for grain between elevator and ship were 50,000 and 23,500 bushels.[3] Coal was loaded by hoisting the railroad car and turning it upside down into a chute. The "lower laker" or "canaller" was a somewhat more conventional craft than its big brother, although it too might be "tailored" to pass the St. Lawrence canals with their fourteen-foot draft and their shorter locks.[4]

This great apparatus of railways, inland waterways, and ocean serv-

2. Except on the self-unloaders for limestone, introduced in 1908.

3. The records in these matters, e.g., loading at 8,464 tons of ore an hour, have been achieved by such elaborate devices as holding a freighter in against the dock by half-a-dozen tugs lest the inrush snap her moorings and pile her up across the slip, but it is interesting, nonetheless, to consider the following average figures for 1932–1941. For each loading, the ore carriers, with cargoes averaging 9,300 tons, remained in port four hours and twenty-nine minutes; and for each unloading, ten hours and eight minutes. A European unloading record for iron ore, established at Liverpool in 1937, averaged 250 tons an hour.

4. The accepted maximum dimensions for such ships were 261 feet length, 44 feet breadth, and a cargo tonnage of from 2,000 to 2,500, until the new Welland Canal of 1930 permitted "upper lakers" to pass through to Lake Ontario.

ices was the unremitting concern of the farmers of the United States and Canada, for transportation costs seemed to them to be the principal reducible element in the mysterious and suspicious processes by which they as producers received only a third or a quarter of what their products cost the consumer. Wheat was the characteristic example, for, in terms of western large-scale farming, the difference of a few cents in the price per bushel meant rags or riches, but there were as well substantial, organized agricultural groups representing the cotton growers, the corn and hog producers, and the cattlemen, so that altogether the politicians were seldom free from farm pressure for the regulation of transportation costs.

Generally speaking, the legislators of Canada and the United States responded, by setting up public authorities to iron out discriminations and other inequalities, at about the same times and in about the same ways. The remarkable circumstance was that, although the two countries were competitors in production and transportation for the same markets, there was only occasional and minor friction between their transportation services. American interests quite frequently complained of unfair Canadian competition and lamented the fact that American law did not permit the integration under substantially the same ownership of transcontinental rail services with Atlantic and Pacific ocean services as did Canadian, but overt retaliatory policies were almost nonexistent. No doubt the root of this mildness lay in the handicaps under which Canada labored in the long, unremunerative rail haul across the Canadian Shield and in the insuperable inferiority of Montreal and the St. Lawrence when in competition with New York. Montreal could and did rise to be the second greatest port in North America, but could not better that position.

In continental terms, and even more so in purely Canadian ones, the new keynote of the times was wheat. North American agricultural methods yielded less than half the amount per acre which Germans and Britons extracted from their soils, but more and more untouched North American acres were brought into bearing after 1895. American annual production, which had doubled between 1865 and 1880, hung fire until the mid-'nineties, when another spurt raised it to an average of 700 million bushels. The war of 1914 and the uneconomic methods which it fostered brought the immediate postwar average quite close to 900 million bushels. Canada's total was much smaller, but since her population and domestic consumption were only about one-twelfth of the American, her production and its growth were much more significant in the world market. The 42 million bushels of 1891 had become 132 million by 1911, doubled in the next five years, and had reached the 400-million-bushel level by 1922, the crop year in which for the first time Canadian wheat exports exceeded those of the United States. This tenfold growth in thirty years gave Canada an entirely new place in the world economy. In both 1939 and 1940 the 500-million-bushel level was substantially exceeded, although the long-term average was a little over 300 millions.

Actually North American agriculture had become commercialized to an overwhelming degree, although there were marked differences in this between the United States and Canada. In the former, for instance, the corn (maize) crop and the hay and forage crop were both more valuable than wheat and its close rival, cotton, thus signalizing the great importance of meat-packing and dairy products. The outstanding difference, however, was that the United States, with its rapidly growing, dense, urban and industrial population consumed the greater proportion of its agricultural production, while Canada did not. In fact, by the twentieth century, in spite of a well-established policy of agricultural protection, the United States was importing substantial amounts of Canadian farm products.

The over-all North American pattern of agricultural production was of mixed farming in the east, cotton and tobacco in the south, corn and hogs in the middle west, and wheat, cattle, and sheep in the far west, with specialized crops scattered about. The Canadian west and the American south felt that almost their entire prosperity was based upon the world, that is, the British, market, as did cheese makers, tobacco growers, meat packers, and apple growers in lesser degree, but most of the rest of the agricultural producers looked to home markets. The pattern of the future for the whole continent was indicated, when, some time about 1890, manufacturing became a more valuable economic activity than agriculture in the United States. The same thing happened in Canada about 1920.

Agriculture was of course a leading handmaid of manufacturing in both countries, but it seemed less important in an age of iron and steel and electricity than mining and the production of power. In these the United States was endowed in a fashion which seemed grotesque to the European visitors who came to inquire into the sources of her strength. Somehow, rich iron ore, base metals, and soft coal, which could be mined from open pits by steam shovels, were the last straw to foreign competitors. To be sure much of the extractive industry was more ordinary than this, but the abundance and the convenient distribution of the materials for an industrial civilization were amazing to less fortunate foreigners. The shift westward between 1860 and 1920 of the center of American manufacturing from a little east of Pittsburgh to a little northwest of

Columbus, Ohio, signalized the basic industrial nexus around the Great Lakes upon which the startling growth of the five states north of the Ohio and east of the Mississippi was based. Coal, petroleum, iron, limestone, and water transportation were its principal components. And, in addition, even the far-distant Rockies were found to contain good coal for the smelting of their gold, silver, copper, and base metals.

Canada was distinctly less fortunate. Her petroleum in southwestern Ontario, first exploited by deep drilling two years before Colonel Drake's famous well of 1859 at Titusville, Pennsylvania, had begun an abrupt decline about 1891, and the apparently enormous oil resources of Alberta were as yet very modestly exploited. Her good coal lay farthest east in New Brunswick, Nova Scotia, and Cape Breton, or almost farthest west near the boundary between Alberta and British Columbia. Until very recently Canadians could find no such easily exploitable iron ranges within their portion of the Canadian Shield as those with which it richly endowed northern Michigan, Wisconsin, and Minnesota.[5] Consumers of coal and iron in the urban, industrial region of the upper St. Lawrence and lower Great Lakes had to buy from the United States, except for the coal which came out in ballast from Great Britain or was brought up the St. Lawrence from Nova Scotia. The great steel and coal combine of Cape Breton Island, which by 1914 was producing 90 per cent of Canada's enormous needs in steel rails, used iron ore from Newfoundland.

Fortunately for Canada the watery, rocky Canadian Shield, which was so effective a barrier to contiguous settlement and to a closely integrated national economy, was a storehouse of hydraulic power. During the 'eighties the complementary inventions of the dynamo and the turbine invited the conversion of this water power into electricity, an invitation which was enthusiastically accepted in Canada. Year by year the Niagara, St. Lawrence, and Ottawa rivers were called upon to supplant more and more steam power in industrial, urban Quebec and Ontario, while deep in the wilderness of the Shield, often far from rail transportation, swift waters were impounded in order to deliver by wire, for papermaking and mining, the power which would otherwise have been lacking. The people of Ontario, resenting their great dependence on the United States for coal, created between 1900 and 1906 a great public authority, the Ontario Hydro-Electric Power Commission, which bought, produced, and sold the "white coal" on an expanding scale which soon surpassed all private competitors.

5. A new method of electrical detection, employed in order to discover whether the iron formations which lie at the surface of the Shield in Minnesota continue deeper down in Canada, located a large, rich deposit near Lake Superior and production began in 1944.

For Canada's relative deficiencies there were, on the whole, some large compensations. The mining areas of British Columbia were at least as well situated and supplied with coal or hydroelectric power as those in the American Rockies. The Klondike gold rush into the rich placer-mining regions of the Canadian Yukon, which began in 1896, could be set over against the later phases of the same free-for-all in American Alaska, although northwestern Canada failed to reveal any such Golconda of lode-mining as was developed around Juneau, halfway down the Alaskan Panhandle. The mother lode of the Yukon has never been found.

What thrilled Canadians with the greatest hope for their future, however, was the gradual revelation, by railway construction gangs in the wilderness, that a weird hodgepodge of minerals in the Canadian Shield could transform it from a mighty obstacle to Canadian development to a great national asset. The asbestos discovered by railway builders near Thetford, Quebec, in 1876, made Canada the world's principal producer. The builders of the Canadian Pacific Railway uncovered at Sudbury, Ontario, in 1883, the ores of a nickel-copper complex which were ultimately to give Canada almost a world monopoly of nickel, that alloy for steel, copper, aluminum, and other metals whose importance has expanded year by year. Twenty years later, when the Province of Ontario pushed north from Toronto the Timiskaming & Northern Ontario Railway as an approach to the agricultural possibilities of the Clay Belt between the Canadian Pacific and James Bay, its construction gangs uncovered the famous "silver pavements" of Cobalt. This rich discovery of 1903 furnished the capital and the experience for a rapid sequence of silver, gold, and copper discoveries in the region which has transformed the wilderness around the northern half of the boundary between Ontario and Quebec, has scattered mining developments in a great curve all the way from central Quebec to Great Bear Lake on the Arctic Circle in the far northwest, and whose end is not yet in sight.

The nickel mines produced copper, gold, and silver as by-products and enough platinum and related ores to make Canada the world's leading producer of those rare metals. To top off the picture with a last exotic bounty, in 1930 Gilbert La Bine staked claims on Great Bear Lake for a mine which was not only rich in silver, cobalt, and copper, but whose pitchblende produced enough radium and uranium to break the former world monopoly and the incomprehensible prices which it had maintained.

The industrial structure which was reared upon North America's advantages in natural resources and transportation need not be described in detail. The materials were crying to be used and the ingenuity was not wanting. The United States sometimes led the world in new developments in technology, was sometimes merely respectably abreast, and occasionally fell rather unaccountably behind. In general, however, the old mandate of North America held good, for, compared with Europe, quality continued to be subordinated to quantity. Labor was always relatively scarce and expensive, so that in industry, as in agriculture, it was profitable to spend great sums on machinery which would take the place of men's hands and brains. The use of mechanical power was lavish in the extreme, particularly after the replacement of the old steam-driven shaft, belt, and pulley by the individual electric motor geared to drive each separate machine in the line of production.

Needless to say the so-called "rationalization" of industrial production was thoroughly congenial to American circumstances, indeed it was practically native, for the Yankee makers of clocks and guns in the early nineteenth century had been quick to realize the advantage of standardized, interchangeable parts, and it was a mere extension of this practice to divide almost any process of fabrication into the making of identical separate parts and their gradual assembly. Henry Ford and other automobile manufacturers were less conspicuous for their originality than for their daring, as they increasingly subdivided manufacture to a point where any man who could learn by brief experience could help to turn out a highly complex product which might not be so supremely efficient as its European rival, but which completely eclipsed it in the matter of price. The American locomotive, agricultural implement, textile, shoe, or motor car might be an outgrowth of European inventiveness, and often was a somewhat rough-and-ready version of its finest prototype across the Atlantic, but it served and it was cheap—so cheap that Americans could have such things in greater abundance and could afford to scrap them or to throw them away at a point where a Briton or a German or a Frenchman would still have lavished labor and resourcefulness on their repair.

Canadian industry was interlocked with American in various ways, partly contributory, partly derivative. The contributions, which were notable, arose from the fact that the American market for inventiveness and industrial skills was ten or fifteen times as great as the Canadian, so that the Canadian railwayman, inventor, mining expert, manufacturer, or businessman who had special knowledge or aptitude which was wanted in the United States usually ended up there, easily blending with his cousins and leaving little trace of his foreign origin. Actually, relative to wealth and population, Canada's industrial investment in the United States was larger than its American counterpart in Canada, indeed American branches of Canadian business concerns had a way of becoming larger than their parents; but when set against the American total they were about as completely lost to general view as the corresponding human migrants. No one has yet gone to the trouble of publishing a study of leading Canadians in the United States, as has been done for the Germans and the Irish, for instance, but the high proportion of Canadian-born among the elect in any edition of *Who's Who in America* or in *The Dictionary of American Biography* indicates that the project would be a significant one.

The reverse process, American industrial penetration of Canada, was of course much more obvious because settled Canada was a so much smaller region. Its roots lay far back in the eighteenth and early nineteenth centuries when millers, stove makers, distillers, sugar refiners, iron workers, and wagon builders followed the tides of migration into the Maritime Provinces, Quebec, and Ontario. Thereafter, with the habitual easy passage of men and goods across the border, every new or useful manufacture in either country was bound quickly to come to the attention of the other, first as an importation, and then in replica or adaptation locally made. In the days before display advertising, the North American county fair, the periodical "World's Fairs" which emulated England's Exhibition of 1851, and the Canadian National Exhibition at Toronto (the world's largest annual fair) were probably far more effective agencies for this kind of distribution than the columns of press and periodicals. At them, the crowds in the Hall of Machinery, the Transportation Building, and the Manufacturers' Pavilion were likely to be at least as big as those at the Live-Stock Show, the Women's Building, and the Carnival of Fun or Midway. Both Canada and the United States welcomed some British manufactures, particularly exclusive patented articles and highly finished goods, but for mass consumption the cheap, rapidly modified North American product was more congenial. The early nineteenth-century American axes, scythes, and sickles which supplanted the output of Birmingham and Sheffield were forerunners of many other articles to come, for they were specifically designed to meet local ways and needs and they did not have to pay their way across the Atlantic before finding their consumers in the interior of a continent.

Since both countries were resolutely protectionist, about the same industries existed in both. The domestic American plants were certain to be larger, indeed their immensely greater and denser home market encouraged a large-scale production which brought costs down so low that the corresponding Canadian enterprises demanded and got very high tariff protection. Since they were especially vulnerable to American "dumping," they had to have special protection against that. The Canadian consumer paid the difference, largely because he wanted his country to remain separate from the United States.

The most conspicuous end product of these forces was the American branch factory in Canada, which was in itself an ironical commentary on the futility of American and Canadian attempts to preserve independent economies. Most of these factories were distributed within the densely populated southern salient of Canada between Montreal and the Detroit River which was surrounded, as it were, by the corresponding American industrial regions. The heaviest concentrations were around Montreal, at the industrial focus between Toronto and eastern Lake Erie which was created by the Welland Canal and Niagara power, and on the Canadian side of the Detroit River. Clearly it was easier to maintain contacts between the principal industrial sections of the United States and Canada than for either of them to reach out to more sparsely settled areas. Thus American firms customarily quoted prices to their own consumers "east of the Mississippi," the Canadian counterpart being "east of Winnipeg."

The American invasions in lumbering, mining, transportation, and manufacturing, while clearly apparent before Canada's systematic protectionism of 1878, were greatly stimulated by it and by subsequent tariff increases. In 1886, for instance, a Canadian export duty of two dollars per thousand feet of logs accelerated the construction of American sawmills in Canada. Yet, on the whole, the movements were in essence responses to new economic opportunities, whether a gold rush to Nova Scotia or the Pacific Coast; a shift from exhausted American forest lands to unexploited Canadian; the seizure of key materials like the base metals, asbestos, phosphate, or mica; or almost any variety of enterprise in transportation, communication, or manufacture. There were even American companies for catching bullfrogs in Ontario for New York restaurants and for converting Maritime-Province lobster shells into fertilizer.

The authors of the one thorough investigation of this great field of international investment[6] have compiled a revealing analysis of the 1,350 American firms which were active in Canada at the end of 1934. They found that "5 per cent of them began operations before 1900, 11 per cent were established from 1900 to 1909, 22 per cent from 1910 to 1919, 36 per cent from 1920 to 1929, and 26 per cent from 1930 to 1934." As they appropriately observed, "neither war nor depression was able to halt the movement," but it should be added that these mounting percentages somewhat eclipsed two circumstances, the natural mortality of business enterprises, and the persistent Canadian habit of buying the Americans

6. *Canadian-American Industry*, by Herbert Marshall, F. A. Southard, and K. W. Taylor (New Haven, 1936).

out, just as Americans liked to buy out Canadians who were doing well south of the border. By 1934, however, American-controlled companies did almost a quarter of the manufacturing in Canada, and in some fields their share was very large, as, for instance, automotive goods, 82 per cent; electrical apparatus, 68 per cent; rubber goods, 64 per cent; nonferrous metals, 50 per cent; nonmetallic minerals, 44 per cent; machinery, 42 per cent; and chemicals, 41 per cent. Only a part of this production was for Canadian consumption. A great deal went to the United States and a large proportion was destined to British, British dominion, and British colonial markets under imperial tariff preferences which were extended to Canada—if the article had a high Canadian "content" in materials and labor—but not to the United States.

Canadian enterprises in the United States, when expressed as percentages of the American whole, would of course be insignificant. Perhaps, therefore, the best brief revelation of the way in which the United States and Canada were economically intermeshed lies in the amounts of money each was willing to entrust to the other. The American investments in Canada and the Canadian in the United States are summarized below, with the British investments in Canada and vice versa added for convenience and comparison. Another useful criterion is that the national income of Canada has recently been about one-fifteenth of that of the United States.

Investments in Millions of Dollars

Year	American in Canada	British in Canada	Canadian in U.K.	Canadian in U.S.A.
1900	167.9	1050.1	In all countries	97.2
1910	486.9	1958.1	In all countries	215.2
1920	2128.2	2577.3	In all countries	894.0
1926	3161.2	2597.8	59.6	778.0
1930	4298.4	2766.0	67.7	933.1
1937	3932.4	2684.8	40.9	1097.6

This testimony to confidence, insofar as its Canadian-American expression was concerned, was the largest and most remarkable thing of its kind in the world. It reflected three North American booms—the price rise of 1896–1913, the commodity boom of 1914–1920 which was created by the War of 1914, and the general production boom of 1922–1929. The depressions of 1907, 1913, 1921, and 1929–1933 had relatively small effect on it. Economists liked to sum it all up by saying that between 1895 and 1939 Great Britain moved from being the world's greatest creditor to the point where she was making inroads on her capital; that the United States was transformed by the War of 1914 from a "mature debtor country" into a creditor; and that Canada became a "mature debtor" between 1914 and 1929 and was showing signs of moving toward a creditor position when the War of 1939 upset all calculations. It was noticeable that in that war Canada clung to a "pay-as-you-go" policy, refusing to borrow abroad, repatriating foreign-held Canadian securities, and making enormous outright gifts or noninterest-bearing loans to Great Britain. The United States, under lend-lease and commodity exchange agreements, pursued similar policies.

Money, of course, was little more than the symbol of the triangular economic relationship. Goods were its lifeblood. Their movements, therefore, give the best idea of why the three countries remained locked in an interplay whose vitality could triumph over generations of economic isolationism, depressions, and wars. While it is rank heresy to say so to interested Americans, Britons, or Canadians, the whole apparatus of tariffs, quotas, and preferential duties among these nations, plus the exclusions, diversions, and enhanced prices of goods which it has produced, has been far less important than the irresistible floods of goods which have flowed "through, by, or over" those nationalistic locks, dams, and weirs. Since that is the case, it may be permissible to consign tariff wars and such matters to a more appropriate place among the political interrelationships later to be discussed, and to concentrate here on the exchanges of goods which transcended them.

A neat way of summarizing the over-all interchange would be to note that Canada normally bought more from the United States than she sold to her and paid the balance with the sterling credits which materialized from selling more to Great Britain than she bought from her. This summary, however, takes no account of the direct Anglo-American trade, which until recent years was ordinarily somewhat larger than the Canadian-American interchange. Most Americans had always been conscious of the overwhelming importance of their trade with Great Britain, but it was not until the early twentieth century that a few of them glimpsed the importance of Canada as a market and a source of supply. Gradually but unmistakably the total value of Canadian-American trade began to approach the magnitude of Anglo-American until, by about 1935, it seemed certain that it would henceforth at least equal and probably surpass it. This remarkable development passed almost unnoticed in the United States even when it was signalized from 1935 to 1938 by prolonged and far-reaching negotiations among the three countries in their successful attempts to adjust their reciprocal trade by means of treaties.

To begin with, the United Kingdom, because of its tremendous industrialization, its comparative abandonment of agriculture, and its almost complete lack of tariff protection, was the market par excellence for American and Canadian raw materials, or processed goods like flour, metals, and tobacco. The so-called world price for wheat, cotton, copper, beef, pork, cheese, and wood products was pretty much the price which was set in the world's warehouse which was Great Britain, and, if they read no other foreign news, the commodity brokers of Butte, Winnipeg, Chicago, Montreal, Richmond, and Houston never failed to look for certain prices quoted from Liverpool, Manchester, Bristol, and London.

Gradually, however, the tremendous capacity of the United States to consume its own products began to assert itself and even a few unaccustomed domestic deficiencies began to appear.[7] This change was so unexpected that the politicians found themselves dealing with an embarrassing lag in the attitude of the voters. It had been all very well to exclude Canadian agricultural products by high tariffs during the 'nineties, for instance, but by 1910 American millers had to call on Canada for enough hard spring wheat to keep their increased production of flour up to standard. The situation was equally embarrassing in wood products and gradually mounted to sheer dependence in the case of newsprint. To cite another example, with an electrified nation growing up around them by leaps and bounds, American copper producers lost a good deal of their old interest in European prices. Except for cotton, Canada was quietly sharing more and more largely the place of the United States in the British market. She even grew "Kentucky" and "Virginia" tobacco along the north shore of Lake Erie. But as the United States relinquished her share of the world market in raw and slightly processed materials, her natural resources, notably coal and iron, made her a more and more menacing manufacturing rival to the homeland of the Industrial Revolution. Britons were too proud and too deeply rooted in free-trade principles to erect protective duties for their iron and steel industries, but they found themselves introducing, rather shamefacedly, tariffs against certain mass-produced American machines like motor cars and typewriters. The United Kingdom had never been completely free trade and now, facing overpowering competition, she found herself slipping back, after an interlude of a century, into protectionism.

Canada had never been a free-trade country and after the termination of the Reciprocity Treaty in 1866 she had received an almost uninterruptedly harsh schooling in protectionism at the hands of her competitor,

7. Imports exceeded exports in 1937 for the first time since 1888–1889, the characteristic "favorable" balance having been established about 1874.

the United States. This was severe from 1865 to 1909, was moderated quite substantially down to 1920, but then mounted to the avowed and unprecedented pugnacity of the Hawley-Smoot Tariff of 1930 and the fiscal tariffs of 1932 which seemed expressly set up to keep out Canadian copper and lumber. Beginning, therefore, with an admitted dependence on import duties in order to pay for the transportation services which held her separate regions together,[8] and an industrial protectionism which Macdonald had designed to round out the national economy, Canada found herself committed to tariff retaliation. The Dominion even threw out an apparently secure Liberal government and repudiated its policy in 1911 *after* an American President had manipulated an unruly Congress into passing an act which embodied the long-sought commercial reciprocity which later judgment held would have been of economic advantage to Canada. In brief, Canada and the United States conducted an almost continuous tariff war from 1865 to 1935 and yet trade between them grew until it was the largest exchange between two nations in the world.

What was the explanation of this anomaly? Basically, of course, it meant that for the sake of maintaining a separate nationality Canadians were willing to pay higher prices for some goods, that is, accept a slightly lower standard of living than that of the United States, but since the latter was so far above any European national standard, perhaps that did not matter very much. Far more significant was the fact that economically the two countries were Siamese twins who could not live without each other. In facing the world they might be rivals, but in relation to each other they were complementary. The very nearness of their related parts made for an ease in the movement of goods to the consumer which was the despair of outside competitors. Even the Panama Canal served Canada in the same ways as it served the United States and just about as cheaply. An almost uninterrupted boom has characterized the whole Pacific Coast since the Canal was opened in 1914, and Canadian and American sections of the Atlantic region have felt the competition of products from the Pacific region in like degree. Each national economy could supply the other with vital satisfactions of its needs better than anyone else could. Common sense and real dependence, therefore, triumphed substantially over the extravagances of economic nationalism when it became apparent that Canadians would have some American products at almost any cost and Americans vice versa. That is why the free lists, the free quotas, and the low-duty categories of American and Canadian tariffs have in the long run proved to be more important than

8. See above, p. 158. Since 1916 increasing reliance on revenue from income taxes has diminished the fiscal importance of tariffs.

the general height of the tariff walls which they have set up against the world and against each other.

In 1929 the value of Canadian-American merchandise trade reached its peak at about $1,400,000,000. It collapsed along with all the other pricked balloons during the Great Depression, but recovered so that by 1939, on the eve of a war, it was almost $900,000,000. In terms of exports, the ratio of the United States to Canada was about eight or nine to five. Capital investment, as we have seen, tended to flow in from the United States, but in gold and silver the direction was reversed. American summer visitors spent more in Canada than Canadian winter visitors did in the great American cities and in California and Florida. It was the movement of commodities, however, which was chiefly revealing. Up from the United States moved coal and petroleum for fuel; iron ore and iron and steel for construction; cotton for textiles and rubber for tires; from 75 to 90 per cent of Canada's imports—not requirements—of machinery and machine tools; citrus fruits, dried fruits, early fruits and vegetables for the varied North American diet; and motion pictures, books and periodicals, and radio programs for entertainment or instruction.

Down from Canada (recall that this involved American-controlled businesses in Canada) went wood products and about 80 per cent of the newsprint needs of the United States; practically all of the nickel and asbestos consumed there; aluminum and other nonferrous metals; grain; meat; fish; and an increasing flow of the chemicals and fertilizers whose production was a profitable side line of the Canadian mining, forest, and hydroelectric power industries. Conceivably, at great expense, the United States might have got along without anything Canadian except nickel. Canada might have dispensed with everything American, even cotton. Yet it takes little imagination to realize the revolutions which would have occurred if either country had shut off the products of the other.

Since man does not live by bread alone, the remarkable economic interlocking of Great Britain, the United States, and Canada which has been outlined above would never serve alone to explain the political coöperation which was painfully achieved among them between 1895 and 1917. The behavior of nations bears close analogies to the emotional surges, the anomalies, and the self-defeating actions of individuals. Intangibles and imponderables play havoc with any purely economic interpretation of history. In this case Great Britain had to learn to accept the United States as an equal for the first time and had to watch Canada assert the same independent power of control over her external relations as she had so long been enjoying over her domestic affairs. The United States had to go through a period of blustering behavior and international irresponsibility before she could adapt herself to the power and weight in the world with which her enormous growth had endowed her. Canada had to learn that freedom of action carried consequences in the way of responsibility, and that it required unremitting vigilance and skill to make the best of being a junior partner to Great Britain and the United States. The intricate interplay of these forces can best be displayed against its economic background in the succeeding chapters.

CHAPTER XIV

A TRIANGLE TAKES FORM
(1880–1917)

THE somewhat reluctant respect for the United States which Great Britain acquired between 1861 and 1871 was almost bound to persist, in spite of all kinds of friction, misunderstanding, and chauvinistic altercations. Its strength for survival lay, on the one hand, in recognition of the growing weight in the world of the American Republic, and, on the other, in a dim but increasing understanding of the complementary roles which the two countries might play in the Atlantic region and in the world as a whole. Histories of the United States and Great Britain have paid too little attention to the early emergence of this new factor in international affairs, for fairly obvious reasons. For one thing, national histories are usually parochial. For another, in both countries a great many exciting things were happening whose color and drama rather easily eclipsed the more humdrum, grudging growth of an understanding which persistent tradition made not a little strange, and even unwelcome, to Mother Country and Independent Daughter alike.

Meanwhile Canada was not standing still. From the 'seventies onward, she was systematically cultivating a novel political hybrid, a cross between the principles of the American and the British North American revolutions, until it yielded the strange fruit known to the world as Dominion Status. In this complicated and often rather obscure process, her principal minority people, the French Canadians, played a considerable part, not always consciously, but nonetheless at least as effectively as during the achievement of cabinet responsibility during the 'forties.

The Canadian peoples were being driven on by a strong inner need to handle their own affairs, externally as well as internally. Like other minorities in the world, the French Canadians, responding to the real or imagined woes of subjection to external authority, were consciously bent upon extending the autonomy which they enjoyed within the Canadian federal system into some equivalent within the British Empire and the world which would give them at least the capacity to withhold participation in any armed action other than the direct defense of their own country. The English-speaking Canadians, reënforced every year by more and more immigrants from the British Isles, felt within themselves an emotional loyalty to the Mother Country, but they too sought complete autonomy.[1] The Conservative leader Sir Robert Borden, for instance, fought for this even more pertinaciously and precisely than did his French-Canadian Liberal predecessor, Sir Wilfrid Laurier, and Sir John Macdonald would have applauded them both. What drove Anglo-Canadians toward the same goal as French Canadians was the well-justified fear which had been revived during the 'sixties that, in a pinch, Great Britain would not refuse to sacrifice Canadian interests to Anglo-American understanding.

The persistent, central problem in Canada's external relations amounted to a kind of bookkeeper's puzzle, that is, computing a balance of how much Canada gained by any improvement in Anglo-American understanding as against how much she gave up in order to make it possible. Between 1871 and 1911 Canadians were gradually forced by the actions of Great Britain and the United States to insist upon estimating these balances themselves, insofar as their intrinsic strength allowed them to, reënforced by any additional leverage which they might acquire by getting their much stronger associates to bid against each other for Canadian concessions.

These uneasy, immediate obsessions, coupled with their inferior material strength, quite naturally made Canadians somewhat short-sighted and disinclined to take a broad view. They were likely, for instance, to leave out of their calculations the significant fact that both Great Britain and the United States had boldly embarked on imperialistic courses not long after the Washington negotiations of 1871. Each of them was isolationist, either in the sense of Salisbury's "magnificent isolation," or in the American tradition of "no entangling alliances," but this did not prevent them from grasping substantial shares during the international partition of the more defenseless areas of Africa, the Caribbean region, Asia, and the Pacific. Canadians, as a people, might well have been quicker to realize that Canada was being spared from territorial aggression while Caribbean, Central American, Pacific, and Asiatic territories were being gobbled up by the United States, and they might have been more realistic about reminding themselves that this escape was at least partly owing to the sheer power of Great Britain and the aegis of the Foreign Office. The countries of Latin America, so brusquely handled by the United States for forty years following their brief wooing at the Pan-American Conference of 1889, could have given the Canadians a few pointers by comparison.

1. Irish-Canadians seemed to lose their anti-British bias, perhaps because a large proportion of them came from Protestant Ulster, and never had it.

The New Imperialism of the United States, like that of Great Britain, was the product of a slow and subterranean growth and was directly related to an industrialized nation's search for new markets and raw materials. It was fortunate for Canada that Britons became empire-conscious again during the early 'eighties, whereas Americans, in spite of some imperial fumblings during the 'seventies and 'eighties, did not transfer their energies from domestic matters to the heady excitement of a reborn Manifest Destiny until the middle of the 'nineties. The result was that the older hand at the game could adopt a kind of cordial, patronizing tone toward the younger which Rudyard Kipling reflected perfectly in February, 1899, when he addressed the United States on the subject of its potential spoils from the recent war with Spain:

> Take up the White Man's burden—
> Ye dare not stoop to less—
> Nor call too loud on Freedom
> To cloke your weariness.

Or, as a wry editor out in Nebraska put it: "In other words, Mr. Kipling would have Uncle Sam take up John Bull's burden." While this kind of thing was going on between the big fellows for the advancement of the "backward" peoples, Canada might be inconsiderately treated by either or by both, but she hardly need fear being engulfed in the American empire as long as she was a gleaming member of the British.

The path to Anglo-American understanding was a very thorny one, for there was abundant Anglophobia in the United States and plenty of what James Russell Lowell had described as "a Certain Condescension in Foreigners"[2] to feed its flames. The Irish vote, which had been such a serious obstacle to conciliation immediately after the Civil War, acquired additional leverage because of the Home Rule issue in Great Britain, the almost even balance between Republicans and Democrats at home, and the seesaw of party power which characterized the 'eighties and 'nineties and recurred about 1910.

In addition, the Monroe Doctrine, that little understood and changeable "principle" of American foreign policy, was violently resuscitated. Its mixed American and British birth had been obscure, and its authority was negligible for a generation after its enunciation on December 2, 1823. President Polk had tried to give it a new twist in 1845 during the Oregon dispute by forbidding European diplomatic intervention in the Americas, as well as colonization and armed intervention. It had been directly or indirectly appealed to without much practical effect in vari-

2. In the essay of 1868 under that title.

ous Caribbean and Central American issues, in the ill-starred adventure of Napoleon III and Maximilian in Mexico,[3] and even in forwarding the American annexation of Hawaii. But in 1895 it suddenly exploded into an all-out warning to the world that the United States meant to regard "Hands off the Americas" as practical international law, to be enforced by its single might, no matter how serious an innovation that might be in international relations, and regardless of what the other nations might think of it. Richard Olney's unilateral declaration concerning Venezuela, sent to England on July 20, 1895, was the cornerstone of the multilateral inter-American policy of the United States today.

The Anglo-American disagreements which had arisen before the Venezuelan crisis had not been particularly ominous. James G. Blaine, as Republican Secretary of State under Garfield in 1881 and under Harrison from 1889 to 1892, was somewhat maligned by the nickname "Jingo Jim" except during his bids for the presidential nomination, for in office he was more moderate and statesmanlike than his Presidents or their Congresses. He cherished the hoary "ripe fruit" theory about Canada and believed that he could weaken the stem by countering in every possible way Canada's endeavors to exploit her rights in the fisheries and by closing the American market to Canadian goods; but he revealed an eye prophetic of the future by his revival of inter-American conferences in 1889. During his second term as Secretary of State, he inherited the problem of the killing at sea, by Canadians and others, of seals belonging to the valuable Pribilof Islands herd. In this matter the first Cleveland Administration, in spite of Secretary Bayard's repeated warnings, had got itself into the anomalous position of denying the traditional American thesis of the freedom of the seas by trying to make the Bering Sea a mare clausum. Blaine could extricate his country only by means of an arbitration treaty of 1892, under which in 1893 an international tribunal in Paris decided against all five American contentions, thus rendering the United States liable for compensation totaling some $473,000 to the victims of past seizures.

Thomas F. Bayard, who served President Cleveland as Democratic Secretary of State from 1885 to 1889, was the first prominent American statesman to realize and to declare that the United States must deal with Canada as an autonomous nation. On the basis of several of his pronouncements he has a substantial claim to have revived John Jay's principle of good neighborhood as a thesis of American foreign policy. It was his misfortune, however, to be an active worker for Anglo-American and Canadian-American friendship under fatally unpropitious circum-

3. Seward systematically sustained the Doctrine, but did not refer to it by name.

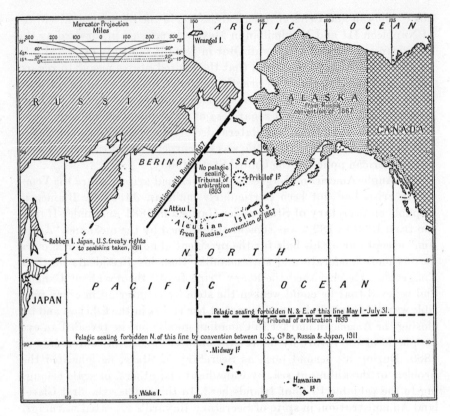

Sealing Restrictions Established by the Paris Award, 1893,
and the Treaty of 1911

stances. He and Lord Salisbury, with the active coöperation of Sir Charles Tupper of Canada, managed to set up at Washington during the winter of 1887–1888 a distinguished and able joint commission to remedy the dangerous situation which had been created by the American termination of the fisheries clauses of the Treaty of Washington.[4] Canada, in an obvious but vain attempt to revive some measure of commercial reciprocity, had exploited this restoration of her inshore rights by wholesale seizures of American vessels and by other actions which were calculated to reprove American presumptions in emphatic, provocative ways.[5]

4. Bayard and Joseph Chamberlain, both bent on conciliation, controlled the proceedings.
5. Probably the most extraordinary was the administration of an emetic to some American seamen by authorities at Prince Edward Island in order completely to nullify an illegal purchase of potatoes.

The Bayard-Chamberlain Treaty which emerged from the sittings of the Commission was a respectable compromise which might well have removed most of the causes of strife arising from the fisheries, but 1888 was an election year and a doubtful one at that. Every facet of Gladstone's recent campaign for Irish Home Rule was familiar in the United States, and Chamberlain was the leader of the defection from the Liberal party which had defeated it and installed Salisbury and the Conservatives in office. Anti-British feeling was studiously stimulated, therefore, to such heights that, for the sake of the Democratic Administration, Chamberlain had to be prevailed upon to conceal his engagement to Miss Mary Endicott, the daughter of the American Secretary of War, until after the election. The partisan Republican majority in the Senate quite openly tried to capitalize "the ancient grudge" by rejecting the Treaty late in August, contrary to the President's recommendation, thereby inducing Cleveland himself to send down a strongly anti-Canadian Message as part of a last effort to win the election.

This, unfortunately, had to be the moment chosen by the British Minister to Washington for a piece of ineffable stupidity and an unwarrantable intrusion into American domestic affairs. Sir Lionel Sackville-West fell into a well-laid trap by allowing himself to be gulled into telling an unknown California correspondent that Cleveland's recent Message must be interpreted in the light of the political situation, and that he believed the President to be at heart friendly to Great Britain! His letter, released by the Republicans on the eve of the election, and his jaunty discussions of the matter with certain avid newspapermen, helped mightily to send Cleveland, Bayard, and Anglo-American understanding into the discard, in spite of the President's swift dismissal of the irresponsible diplomat for having impugned his motives and those of the Senate.[6]

The Venezuelan Affair of 1895 was distinctly more serious than this comedy of errors. Although Cleveland, who had an impressive record as a foe of expansionism, was once again President, he and his Administration had been swept along with the times and with the temper of the American people toward a new assertion of hegemony in the Americas. Although the frontier had just passed away within the boundaries of the United States, its methods and moods could be carried outward into the arena of world politics.

The matter in question arose from the undetermined boundary be-

6. The letter was published on October 21, the dismissal took place on October 30, and the election was held on November 6, 1888. The Mexican Minister avoided a similar trap.

tween Venezuela and British Guiana. This involved both the region close to the mouth of the Orinoco, and such extravagant Venezuelan claims to parts of the hinterland where gold was believed to be plentiful as would have engulfed half of what had been regarded as British Guiana since 1815. Great Britain, ironically enough, had repeatedly offered Venezuela a settlement, based upon the only expert survey, which was essentially the same as the one which emerged at the end of the excitement in 1899; but she had flatly refused to arbitrate, even at the formal request of the United States in 1887, lest the arbitrators split the difference between the now widely discrepant claims. The Venezuelans thereupon broke off diplomatic relations and, in collusion with American speculative interests, began a clever, lavish, and well-timed invocation of the Monroe Doctrine in the United States.

This campaign, accelerated by the landing of British troops in Nicaragua, came to a head in 1895, when the jingoes of both American political parties drove Cleveland and Secretary Olney into their startling amplification of the Monroe Doctrine. Olney wrote to London, asserting that Great Britain was violating the Monroe Doctrine, and demanding an explicit answer as to whether she would submit the boundary settlement to arbitration:

Today the United States is practically sovereign on this continent and its fiat is law upon the subjects to which it confines its interposition. Why? . . . It is because, in addition to all other grounds, its infinite resources combined with its isolated position render it master of the situation and practically invulnerable as against any or all other powers.

Lord Salisbury took four months to answer Olney's ten-thousand-word note, but he finally did so with a stiff demonstration that President Monroe's utterance of 1823 did not apply to the circumstances of 1895, that it was not part of accepted international law, and that it could not be relevant to "the determination of the frontier of a British possession which belonged to the Throne of England long before the Republic of Venezuela came into existence." Great Britain chose to regard the incident as closed and lacked the imagination to see that it could not possibly be. Cleveland had to act. He did so in a Message of December 17, 1895, which, in effect, urged Congress to appoint a boundary commission, determine the line, and defend it, if necessary, by war. Congress enthusiastically agreed.

All this was heart-warming, but extravagant, for the United States was unable to defend her own Atlantic Coast because of her naval inferiority to Great Britain, let alone protect Venezuela. The stock markets promptly crashed. Voices of reason began to make themselves heard in the United States and a remarkable wave of conciliatory feeling and action swept over Great Britain from Trade Unions to House of Commons. Great Britain surrendered to Cleveland's threat, accepted the good offices of the United States, found herself able to work out a treaty of arbitration which admitted in advance her principal contentions, and, in October, 1899, agreed to an award which gave Venezuela ample control of the mouth of the Orinoco and a little new hinterland.

Thus, for the second time within twenty-five years, the British people had sacrificed their prestige to their belief that war with the United States was unthinkable, and they did so in more forbidding circumstances than those of 1871. Any student of international relations can draw up a list of reasons for the British surrender, such as the incipient South African troubles and the rise of Germany at a time when the United Kingdom had no allies. It has been argued that Anglo-American friendship was absolutely necessary to her. Probably the most persuasive interpretation of the circumstances is to think of Great Britain as having slowed down in her imperial growth and standing on the defensive against a potential Continental counterpoise to her weight in the world, thus creating an opportunity for the United States, as a lucky outsider, to embark on imperialism herself with little risk of disastrous consequences.

Yet it must be contended that this kind of calculation in pure power politics is too shallow, too much like wisdom after the event, to be entirely convincing. If Great Britain stood alone, so did the United States, for by her assertion of the power to dictate international law she had angered the Continental Powers and incensed the larger Latin American republics. At the moment she was only potentially a World Power, for her jingoes had so utterly neglected her army and navy that if war had come she would have been incapable abroad and almost defenseless along her own coasts.

In these circumstances, and considering also the deliberate provocations launched at Great Britain, it must be an inadequate explanation to credit the British submission merely to far-sighted shrewdness as to the shape of things to come. Imponderable forces were at work, as they had been in the days of Burke and the Revolution, during the independence movements in Latin America and during the American Civil War, and as they were to be again. Great Britain and the United States had common interests in the Atlantic region and in the world and were to discover these and more, but they also had a host of less tangible things in common— language, tradition, and perhaps most important of all, the elevation of the citizen above the state—which made many of their peoples respond to instinctive urges toward coöperation and understanding. As yet, these tendencies had been far more apparent in Great Britain than in the United States, as was natural during the latter's exhilarating coming of age, but already they were percolating downward through the mass of the American people from the utterances of preachers and teachers and members of the ruling political and economic classes.

Not all of these imponderable sympathies were creditable. When, in 1899, Great Britain embarked upon the conquest of the Boers and the United States upon the subjection of the Filipinos who had thought they were going to be independent, and when the generals of both the imperialistic nations displayed more interest in winning over the public at home than in facing the enemy abroad, the immortal Mr. Dooley of Chicago bestowed his left-handed benison on Anglo-Saxon imperialism:

I tell ye, Hinnissy, ye can't do th' English-speakin' people. Oursilves an' th' hands acrost th' sea ar-re rapidly teachin' th' benighted Lutheryan an' other haythin that as a race we're onvincible an' oncatchable. Th' Anglo-Saxon race meetin's now goin' on in th' Ph'lippeens an' South Africa ought to convince annywan that, give us a fair start an' we can bate th' wurruld to a tillygraft office. Th' war our cousins be Sir Thomas Lipton is prosecutin', as Hogan says, again' th' foul but accrate Boers is doin' more thin that. It's givin' us a common war lithrachoor.

A little later, he professed to be mystified by the sudden change in that professional Briton-baiter, Senator "Hinnery Cabin Lodge":

Now where's Hinnery? Where's the bould Fenian? . . . Faith, he's changed his chune, an' 'tis "Sthrangers wanst, but brothers now," with him, an' "Hands acrost th' sea an' into some wan's pocket."

He began to "sigh f'r th' good old days befure we became what Hogan calls a wurruld power" and to suspect that the time might soon come when "th' subjick races" would rebel against the Sahibs, "beloved iv Gawd an' Kipling."

Whatever were the ingredients in Anglo-American understanding, it emerged after the Venezuela crisis, clear for the whole world to see. Almost at once it began to prove itself strong enough to survive the stresses and strains of profound readjustments in the roles played by the two countries in the western Atlantic, the Caribbean, Central America, Europe, the Pacific, and the Far East. In spite of the surprising maneuvers performed by Theodore Roosevelt in his various capacities[7] during this

7. Assistant Secretary of the Navy, 1897–1898; colonel of the Rough Riders in the Spanish-American War; Governor of New York, 1898–1900; Vice-President, March–September, 1901; and President until 1909.

basic rearrangement of the balances in world politics, both he and the controllers of British policy operated more and more confidently on the assumption that they could work better together than apart. Needless to say this tacit principle was seldom publicly paraded. But if Great Britain would admit the potential equality of the United States and back her up while she found its expression in such forms as the Great White Fleet and the seizure of the Panama Canal Zone, the United States would relieve Great Britain of naval responsibilities in the western Atlantic and, in L. M. Gelber's phrase, "in her own interest cover the rear of the British Empire against a foreign invader."

When a rebellion against Spain occurred in Cuba, and the American yellow press, reënforced by the destruction of the U.S.S. *Maine* in Havana Harbor, stimulated a popular insistence on war which broke down President McKinley's resistance, Great Britain was conspicuously friendly. "Neither here nor in Washington," A. J. Balfour told Ambassador Hay, "did the British Government propose to take any steps which would not be acceptable to the Government of the United States." In Europe she offset the hostility of the Continental Powers, particularly Germany, incensed as they were by the international practices that the United States stood for. They objected especially to American activities in the Far East and to the ban on European colonization in the Americas which was contained in the Monroe Doctrine. When Roosevelt and Admiral Dewey carried the war to the Philippines and Germany sent a more powerful fleet than Dewey's to Manila, the British naval commander there was so patently sympathetic to the Americans that a timely movement of his ships was popularly interpreted as a warning to the Germans not to interfere with the American attack on the city. It was with Great Britain's blessing that in 1898 and 1899 the United States rapidly acquired by conquest, purchase, or other means Hawaii, part of Samoa, Puerto Rico, the Philippines, Guam, and Wake, and brought Cuba under a kind of protectorate. During the same years the two countries in effect coöperated by laying down the Open Door Policy for China in a not-too-successful or entirely sincere effort to preserve their commercial advantage and to cope with the threatening international free-for-all for the dismemberment of the decadent Manchu Empire.

The next token of respect paid by Great Britain in the course of her wooing of the United States was a very substantial one, and it was elicited by methods which may have accurately reflected American capacity to capitalize inherent strength and others' embarrassments, but which were plainly discreditable even by the lax standards of the international behavior of the day. Theodore Roosevelt, by his mixture of protracted (perhaps calculated) adolescence, territorial acquisitiveness, and appeal to the gallery, was an appropriate President for times when the Congress of the United States drove an honorable man like John Hay to frenzy by its determination to let no solemn engagements stand in the way of the nation's getting whatever it wanted.

The two most frequently quoted remarks of Roosevelt, "Speak softly and carry a big stick" and "I never take a step in foreign policy unless I am assured that I shall be able eventually to carry out my will by force," tend, on the whole, to misinterpret the situation in a way agreeable to his egotism. The truth was that a host of domestic and external circumstances had launched the United States on an almost uncontrollable international rampage, during which the Rough Rider may have been in the saddle, but could hardly be credited with the explosive energies which were at work between him and the ground. Mr. Dooley's favorite image for Roosevelt after the Spanish-American War was as the ebullient motorman of a runaway trolley car.

When the United States committed herself to empire in the Pacific and Asia, the building of an Isthmian canal became an imperative for a nation whose new navy had still to grow to one-ocean size and was fatally handicapped by the distance round the Horn. But in 1850 Great Britain and the United States had agreed in the Clayton-Bulwer Treaty to coöperate in facilitating the construction of an Isthmian canal and to bind themselves individually never to fortify or exercise exclusive control over such a canal.[8] The Treaty had always been unpopular in the United States, but by 1900 it was regarded as intolerable. In January of that year Congress made it perfectly clear that it would simply disregard the Treaty by providing for exclusive American construction of a canal. Within less than a month, Secretary of State John Hay and Lord Pauncefote, the British Ambassador, had signed a new treaty allowing the United States to build, own, and neutralize, but not fortify, an Isthmian canal. The South African War was in the midst of its most humiliating phase.

Even this prompt surrender could not satisfy the Senate, most resolutely backed up by the arguments of Roosevelt, then Governor of New York. It proceeded to amend the Treaty so drastically that Hay felt obliged to hand in his resignation and the British Government felt impelled to reject the Treaty in March, 1901. Congress displayed little or no concern over this. In Great Britain the sands of "magnificent" isola-

---

8. Another provision, designed to prohibit both from colonization in Central America, involved Great Britain by implication in recognizing the noncolonization thesis of the Monroe Doctrine.

tionism were visibly running out as the discreditable South African War dragged toward its conclusion and as Germany's naval challenge became clear. With the world in flux and no allies, what better friend than the United States? A second Hay-Pauncefote Treaty, acceptable to the Senate, was concluded in November, 1901, and Great Britain then went the whole way by withdrawing all save token fleets and garrisons from the Caribbean.

Roosevelt, President since McKinley's assassination in September, 1901, now let himself go in a somewhat inexplicable fever of impatience. As he said, "I took the Canal Zone and let Congress debate," although there is every indication that he could have achieved his ends about as quickly by more honorable means than shady negotiations with the old French canal company, the cheating of Colombia by promoting and protecting the revolution of its Department of Panama, and the extortion of the Canal Zone from that puppet for a grossly inadequate sum. It took a full generation, much greater payments as conscience money, and lengthy conciliation to repair even in part the damage thus needlessly done to its own reputation and interest by the American nation and its new President. What D. C. Miner has aptly called "The Fight for the Panama Route" necessitated a lot of peacemaking during the next forty years.

While this gigantic poker game between Great Britain and the United States was going on, Canada had been sitting in, drawing cards, and occasionally venturing a bet, but it was progressively brought home to her that the stakes were much too high for her to have any chance of winning, or even of splitting, a single stake. In fact, when the luck finally turned toward her during the years 1910–1912, the only gesture which could console her after forty years of being overridden in the game by Great Britain and the United States was to refuse to play, at any rate temporarily, with either.

Canada had two old interests and one new problem at issue with the United States after 1878. The inshore rights connected with the fisheries, now of dwindling relative importance to both countries, had been regulated, after the American denunciation of the Treaty of Washington arrangements, by a fairly satisfactory modus vivendi of 1888, under which at least some American vessels paid moderate tonnage duties in return for the privileges which they sought.

The campaign for commercial reciprocity had almost expired in the face of resolute American protectionism, in spite of spasmodic Canadian efforts to keep it alive. The truth was that closer commercial relations with the United States, under whatever appealing name or guise, had become indelibly tainted with annexationism in Canada and there were many whose political or economic interest it was to keep the taint apparent. Canadians were becoming not quite sure of how much reciprocity they wanted or dared to risk. In the United States, S. J. Ritchie of Akron, Ohio, who had large interests in Ontario railways and in the Sudbury nickel-copper deposits, and Erastus Wiman, a Canadian financier in New York whose stake in Canadian telegraphs was considerable, kept the issue alive in Congress and elsewhere. Goldwin Smith, a brilliant, disgruntled Oxford don who had settled in Toronto and whose shrewd, skilful pen reflected a lifetime spent in unpopular causes, boldly bade Canadians seek their inevitable future within the United States.

Yet, even if Canada was staggering through decades of adversity, her people were nonetheless too habitually anti-American for either political party, except when in Opposition, to gamble everything on close commercial relations with the Republic. Canada, compelled by fiscal needs to be protectionist herself, had come to like it. Both parties made vain "pilgrimages to Washington" in order to secure some degree of easier entry into American markets, but each accused the other of risking the national existence by so doing. Actually, however, there was a good deal of truth in Goldwin Smith's contention that the Liberals were "the continental, their opponents the anti-continental party," for their inheritance of nineteenth-century liberalism made them favor free trade[9] and a maximum of autonomy, and suspect manifestations of aggressive British imperialism. The Conservatives, on the other hand, were almost outright protectionists and characteristically responsive to the swelling chorus in the Mother Country on the theme of "Greater Britain." To them an active British connection was the one efficient guaranty against absorption in the United States.

The turn of the tide of popular, rather than party, opinion in Canada against reciprocity with the United States occurred about 1895–1897 after the repulses suffered at the hands of Blaine and in the McKinley tariff of 1890 and the Dingley tariff of 1897. It was just then that prosperity began to beckon, that Laurier's Liberals at last supplanted the Conservatives and had to assume responsibility for their doctrines, and that their finance minister, W. S. Fielding, invented Imperial Preference as a mild and noncommittal response to Joseph Chamberlain's designs for an imperial customs union.

Canada's new course in commercial policy was clearly charted during the autumn and winter of 1898–1899, when a Joint High Commission

9. Edward Blake, the Leader of the party from 1880 to 1887, anticipated their ultimate surrender to protectionism by a good many years.

representing Canada, Newfoundland, the United Kingdom, and the United States spent a good many weeks in Quebec and Washington trying to reach agreement on the many matters at issue among them. The Commission failed on several grounds, but it is a striking fact that the Americans were taken by surprise when the Canadians rejected their suggestion that a mutually advantageous reciprocity treaty might be salvaged from the wreckage. John Hay was very angry at Laurier for this unexpected reversal, but the Canadian Prime Minister, who admitted that the Canadians might have made "a very fair treaty," rather boasted to his House of Commons of their resistance and justified it on the grounds "that the general feeling in Canada today is not in favour of reciprocity." Canada's transcontinental economy was at last beginning to function, and to function in terms of success in the British market, which in a decade had advanced from taking about as much Canadian produce as the United States to taking almost twice as much. It was the part of wisdom to wait until it was clear whither that course would lead.

The new problem which had grown up between the United States and Canada was the determination of the boundary between Alaska and British Columbia. Its settlement was, next to the War of 1812, probably the most unfortunate single incident, the worst setback to reasonable understanding, in the whole gamut of Canadian-American relations. The negotiations from which it emerged, even granting that they were inextricably involved with crucial American and British adventuring and bargaining all over the world, and took place during an easily misinterpreted Anglo-German blockade of Venezuela, reflected discredit on all three parties to the dispute. The Canadians had a slight case juridically, which might have won them something if Great Britain and the United States had been willing to treat it as a make-weight during the Panama Canal affair, but, after failing in that, they went ahead unsupported anyway, only to end up by cloaking their own political error in bitter accusations against their overpowering American and British associates. President Roosevelt marred a foregone conclusion by treating Canada almost as outrageously as he had treated Colombia. Great Britain not only connived at the American dishonoring of a formal agreement for a judicial settlement, but her unhappy representative committed the unpardonable sin of giving himself away.

The point which Americans and Britons quite naturally like to forget, but which Canadians remember so vividly as to eclipse all other considerations, is that it was the *manner* of the Alaska Award, far more than the *matter*, which left behind it a generation of bitterness. The people of the

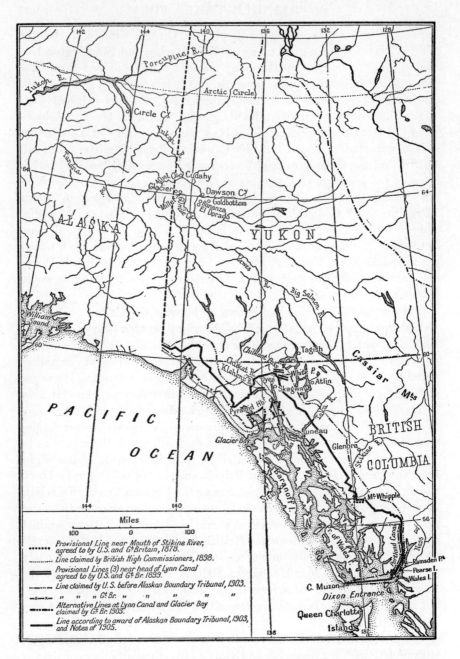

The Alaska Boundary and the Klondike

Dominion could hardly be expected to tell themselves that the very qualities which enabled President Roosevelt to "ride the tiger" of American
expansionism precluded in him the touch of imagination or magnanimity
which might have lessened or even obviated this unfortunate result.

The matter in question was complex in its details, but clear enough in
general outline. The boundary, it was agreed, depended basically upon a
loosely drafted Anglo-Russian Treaty of 1825 which surmounted the
problems presented in a coast line deeply indented by narrow fiords, and
in a coastal margin made up of a rugged sea of mountains with no distinct ranges, by providing alternative principles. Very little of the region
had been explored. The line from near the head of the Portland Channel,
therefore, was to "follow the summit of the mountains situated parallel
to the coast," but if this, as it proved, nonexistent, crest should stray
more than ten marine leagues (about 30 miles) from the ocean, then the
line "shall be formed by a line parallel to the sinuosities of the coast" at a
distance not exceeding ten marine leagues therefrom. The general intention, however badly phrased, clearly was to give to Russia, and, after the
purchase of 1867, to the United States, a thirty-mile-wide "panhandle"
to the main mass of Alaska, along the windings of the coast, from 54° 40'
north latitude to the point where this inland boundary should cross 141°
west longitude.

As early as 1872, because of scattered gold discoveries in the British
Columbian interior behind the Panhandle, across which lay the only
practicable access to them, the Canadian Government had initiated a
series of efforts to have the boundary determined, but various Congresses
refused to appropriate the funds for the American share of the effort.
The pot really began to boil, however, in 1895, when the great Klondike
gold rush started, for the prospectors' route was by way of the Lynn
Canal across the Panhandle to the White and Chilkoot passes and the
Canadian interior. The immensity of the traffic created the American
towns of Dyea and Skagway near the head of the Canal, and there were
inevitable difficulties about customs and jurisdictions, since no one knew
where the boundary was. The Lynn Canal ran inland eighty miles or
more, so that if the Treaty could be interpreted, either under the moun-
tain-crest or the coastal principle, so that the boundary cut across it
instead of circling thirty miles inland from its head, the ports of access
to the new Canadian gold fields would be on Canadian soil.

It seems clear that the principal reason why Canada ran the risk of
attempting to extract from the United States some such entry to the
interior was that she expected Great Britain to obtain it as part of the
compensation for allowing the United States to build and control the

Isthmian canal. In the Joint High Commission of 1898–1899, for instance, when all the Anglo-American issues were on the table, the American commissioners professed to believe that there was at least a slim chance that Congress might be persuaded to lease Pyramid Harbor on the Lynn Canal to Canada, but the Canadian commissioners did not pursue this possibility and the Americans refused the counterproposal of arbitration on the terms of the recent Anglo-Venezuelan treaty. Canada's awakening from her too-confident optimism came, of course, during the rude scrimmage of 1900–1901 when Congress and the McKinley-Roosevelt Administration destroyed the Clayton-Bulwer Treaty without giving Great Britain any *quid pro quo*. When Canada begged Great Britain at that time to bargain for the Alaskan entry, she was told bluntly that nothing could be done. As a result of Great Britain's wholesale surrender, the Dominion had bound herself to a doubtful contention with no substantial Canadian or British bargaining asset to back it up.

Such was the background for the discreditable Roosevelt coup of 1903. After prolonged and complicated negotiations at the three capitals during 1902, Great Britain and the United States implicated Canada by signing the Hay-Herbert Convention of January 24, 1903, in agreement to establish a tribunal of six "impartial jurists of repute," three appointed by each party, to consider judicially (not, as the Canadians had hoped, by arbitration) the several problems of interpretation of the Treaty of 1825. The Senate was induced, by substantial assurances of victory from the President through Senator Lodge, to approve the Convention in February. Hay and the President were confident "that the Canadian claim has not a leg to stand on and that compromise is impossible." Laurier, who had been in London and had interviewed the President in Washington about terminating the dispute, was evidently fearful of the issue, but he did his best to make his Cabinet understand the situation. Without waiting for a Canadian assent, the two major powers hurriedly exchanged ratifications. Roosevelt professed to regard the Tribunal merely as a device by which Great Britain could escape from the difficult position in which Canada had placed her.

The tragedy was that the President could not let well enough alone, but had to make assurance many times sure. Whereas the Canadians honored the Convention scrupulously by appointing George Armour, a justice of their Supreme Court,[10] and Sir Louis Jetté, a former justice of the Quebec Supreme Court, and Great Britain appointed Lord Alverstone, her Lord Chief Justice, Roosevelt's nominees were his Secretary

10. He died in London and was replaced by Allen B. Aylesworth, a leader of the Ontario Bar who had recently declined a seat on the Supreme Court of Canada.

of War, Elihu Root, who had just reënforced the Alaskan garrisons,[11] Senator Henry Cabot Lodge, whose public utterances alone made his impartiality unthinkable, and Senator George Turner of Washington, the state which had led a relentless opposition to Canadian claims. Of them, only Root could be considered a "jurist of repute." Not only did the President tell these men in detail what their arguments must be, but he informed them that if the American case failed he would ask Congress to vote the funds necessary for him "to run the line on our own theory," that is, challenge war. Finally he arranged through several channels to convey precisely this decision of his to the Prime Minister and members of the British Cabinet, for transmission to Lord Alverstone, at appropriate intervals before and during the sittings.

Needless to say, when the Tribunal met, the unfortunate English Chief Justice, who knew that his vote alone could avert an outright break with the United States, granted the principal American contention, that is, that the boundary went round the heads of the inlets.[12] This was juridically sound, although the Canadians had alarmed the Americans by the effectiveness of their arguments against it. Unfortunately he went farther at the insistence of the American commissioners, who could not resist pressing their advantage even beyond the instructions of their President, and he voted (unjudicially) with them in favor of an unprecedented division of four islands at the mouth of the Portland Channel which gave the show away, for the Tribunal had neither heard nor read any formal argument to that end. The two Canadians, who might possibly have swallowed their medicine on the general decision, knew by the division of the islands that they had been right in suspecting their British colleague of political rather than judicial considerations, and they refused to sign the Award. This gesture was almost inevitably expanded by the Canadian people into a condemnation of all the decisions of the Tribunal. To President Roosevelt, the Award was "the greatest diplomatic victory during the present generation." In Canadian eyes, the rights of the Dominion had been sacrificed again, this time dishonorably, to Anglo-American understanding. The President's tactics and Alverstone's had eclipsed the fact that their plight was in large degree the result of their having miscalculated the effectiveness of equitable considerations in power politics.[13]

11. Some eight hundred soldiers as against about forty Canadian police constables. Root accepted the commissionership under protest.

12. He also conceded a coastal strip nearly as wide as that demanded in the American claim.

13. Time provided a curious twist. At the Paris Peace Conference of 1919, George Louis Beer, the colonial expert of the American delegation, actively but unsuccessfully sponsored a proposal that the Panhandle be ceded to Canada, both in order to liquidate Canadian dissatisfaction and to facilitate some British surrenders in the Caribbean.

With President Roosevelt's reëlection in 1904, American pressure on Great Britain and Canada began to ease, in fact, the President began to rest upon the laurels of prestige and territorial acquisition which he and the United States had won. He still believed in carrying a Big Stick, for, as he pointed out, "If we quit building our fleet, England's friendship would immediately cool," but he seemed to enjoy some of the amenities of Anglo-American friendship.[14] Elihu Root had now become Secretary of State and, in an effective understanding with the new British Ambassador, James Bryce, his reputation grew rapidly from being merely that of an astute legal counsel and politician to one of broad and wise statesmanship. In 1905 he went to Newfoundland to look into the vexed fisheries situation. In 1906 he made a studied tour of Latin America in order to repair some of the damage done there and in the same year he made a systematic list of matters to be settled with Canada. He visited Ottawa in 1907, as Bryce made a point of doing every year, and coöperated vigorously with Britons and Canadians, in informal as well as formal ways, in order to salve some of the wounds of 1903.

Meanwhile, the circumstances of the Alaska Award enormously accelerated the determination of Canadians to handle their own external affairs. The benefits accruing from Anglo-American understanding which were to stand out crystal-clear fifteen or twenty years later were outweighed in Canada by the soreness felt over the Dominion's sacrificial role at Washington in 1871 and during the *rapprochement* of 1895–1903. In fact almost any Canadian could put together a list of real or imagined injuries whose total approached the proportions of the American's "ancient grudge" against Great Britain. Laurier put the matter precisely to the House of Commons in October, 1903. "It is important," he said, "that we should ask the British parliament for more extensive powers, so that if we ever have to deal with matters of a similar nature again, we shall deal with them in our own way, in our own fashion, according to the best light that we have." Time and altered attitudes toward Canada in both Great Britain and the United States were to reveal that this policy was less daring than it seemed at the time.

In fact the push and pull which were exerted upon her by her two great associates lie very near the heart of Canada's greatest contribution to the stream of world history—her invention of Dominion Status. This discovery was a complicated one because of that very push and pull, because of the peculiar position of the French Canadians, and because in the working of British and Canadian political institutions the actual prac-

14. By a queer turn in the comedy of human affairs, he received the Nobel Peace Prize in 1906 for his services in terminating the Russo-Japanese War.

tices and conventions of the day are often most misleadingly reflected by the enacted law. It is out of the question here to do more than sketch the inner framework upon which Canadian nationality was being constructed, but the basic elements in its growth between 1871 and 1914 illustrate clearly the practical status which Canada was attaining in her international relations long before it was formally enunciated after the First World War.

Looking backward, Dominion Status seems to have been inherent in the transplantation of Britons and their political institutions to North America. Madison realized this as early as 1800 when he said, "The fundamental principle of the [American] revolution was that the Colonies were coordinate members with each other and with Great Britain, of an Empire united by a common executive sovereign."[15] As we have seen, the Baldwin group in Toronto had the same insight twenty-five or thirty years later. Durham implied it when he wrote about "the necessary consequences of representative institutions." Howe waxed ironic over British refusal to recognize it. Macdonald wanted to call the federation of 1867 the Kingdom of Canada in order to signalize it.

If this be understood, it is possible to cut through whole forests of discussion over the exact contributions of the two political parties and of their leaders to the evolution of the new status. The Liberal leader, Edward Blake, in his own right and by inheritance from his forerunners, was more conspicuous than his Conservative opponent, Macdonald, in making precise, objective advances along the road; but Macdonald, no matter what flag-waving appeals he made to imperial loyalty for domestic political ends, also saw the necessity of Canada's controlling her external relations, and he worked for twenty years toward that end with keen realization of the responsibilities which it would entail.[16]

World politics, however, determined that it was upon Wilfrid Laurier, who was Prime Minister from 1896 to 1911, that there fell the heaviest and most urgent burden of leadership in this matter, and, as a French Canadian, he carried with him a keener, subtler insight into the distinct attitude of his own people toward the problem. This remarkable man again and again showed himself to be more intimately acquainted with the spirit of British political institutions and with the highest refine-

15. Compare the Balfour Declaration of 1926 which finally recognized what had long since become the relationship which involved Great Britain as well as the Dominions. "They are autonomous Communities within the British Empire, equal in status, in no way subordinate one to another in any aspect of their domestic or external affairs, though united by a common allegiance to the Crown, and freely associated as members of the British Commonwealth of Nations."

16. "The Suez Canal is nothing to us," he said, for instance, in refusing to send troops for the Khartoum Expedition of 1884.

ments of nineteenth-century British liberalism than almost any of his English-speaking parliamentary colleagues. In fact he had served his political apprenticeship in Quebec as early as 1877 by releasing his people for useful political action through a skilful differentiation between liberalism in the British tradition and the Continental liberalism against which the Papacy and the ultramontanes were waging implacable war. Throughout his long career Laurier fought, and fought successfully, with his compatriots' support, the reactionary elements of his Church in Canada. He was not, as is often thought, simply a great French Canadian. He was a great Canadian and a great man.

Yet his people, whose North American lineage was longer than that of the English-speaking North Americans, were in, but not of, the main currents in North American life. Their attitude toward the rest of Canada, the United States, Great Britain, and a France which had strayed sadly from the golden, far-off traditions of the Most Christian King, was the characteristic attitude of minorities everywhere—passionately defensive and persistently noncoöperative. Every expedient concession to alien ways and patterns of action must be compensated for by some new or some intensified devotion to idealized forms of seventeenth-century French culture and of the glorious tradition of the Counter-Reformation. French Canada was out of step with the rest of the world, but out of step by conscious choice, not through inherent backwardness. Having no imperative sense of obligation to anyone save their own North American ancestors and themselves, her people were almost deaf to national or international appeals. *"Canadiens français, soyons nous-mêmes!"*[17]

Laurier began his career as Prime Minister during the burgeoning of what might be called Chamberlain imperialism. When he attended Queen Victoria's Diamond Jubilee and the Colonial Conference in 1897, he was knighted, fêted, and wooed by the hosts of those who planned to enhance falling British prestige by building the substructure of a consolidated empire. In the circumstances, which he humorously admitted were rather difficult, he kept his head and refused to commit his country to more than voluntary coöperation. As representative of the Senior Dominion, his opposition to centralized authority proved effective. Two years later he had the South African War on his hands, with thousands of Anglo-Canadians clamoring to serve and the body of French Canadians quite disinterested. He realized that when Great Britain was at war, Canada was also, but French Canadians argued that passive belligerency ought to be quite possible. Laurier chose this occasion to assert Canada's "liberty

17. This slogan, "Let us be ourselves," by its analogy to Sinn Fein, "Ourselves Alone," signalizes the classic attitude of a minority people.

to act or not to act, to interfere or not interfere, to do just as she pleases, and that she shall reserve to herself the right to judge whether or not there is cause for her to act." Yet he facilitated the recruitment, equipment, and dispatch to South Africa of about seven thousand volunteers, with the national Treasury meeting about $3,000,000 of the expenses involved.

By the time of the Colonial Conference of 1902,[18] Chamberlain was pressing Laurier hard by offering Canada a voice in determining the foreign policy of the Empire in return for contributions to the British Navy. Laurier, still fighting for a free hand in the likely event of world-wide commitments, and now facing the unmistakable beginnings of a formally isolationist political party in French Canada, found his way out by declaring that Canada would assume responsibility for her own naval defense. It proved difficult to make the British Admiralty see things in this light, but in 1910 the Canadian Navy emerged in the form of two antique cruisers.[19] Laurier had won the elections of 1900, 1904, and 1908 largely on the strength of Canada's expansive prosperity, but Henri Bourassa and Olivar Asselin were steadily building up the forces of a fiery isolationist nationalism in the Province of Quebec, using both British imperial intentions and Catholic Quebec's continuous controversies with Protestant Ontario over public education as fuel to feed the flames.

While Canada and Great Britain were achieving a kind of equilibrium of forces in this way, something quite similar was developing in Canadian relations with the United States. The efforts of Root and Bryce from 1906 onward, with the cordial coöperation of Roosevelt, were beginning to bear fruit, although Laurier was capable of being rather conspicuously diffident. Early in 1908, however, he sent Mr. Mackenzie King down to Washington for an informal exchange of views with the President, Root, and Bryce before going on to London as the bearer of confidential messages, concerning Japanese immigration, from Roosevelt as well as from the Canadian Prime Minister, to Sir Edward Grey, the British Foreign Secretary. This direct Canadian representation at Washington was an interesting portent of the future.

A host of outstanding Canadian-American issues had been liquidated by the end of 1911, two of which were of outstanding importance. In 1909, following several years of successful work by an exploratory joint International Waterways Commission and much diplomatic encourage-

18. The conferences among representatives of Great Britain and the larger English-speaking colonies, which were held at intervals from 1887 onward, had been called "Colonial," but in 1902 the new term, "Imperial," was in process of adoption.

19. The Conservative leader, R. L. Borden, said that he entirely agreed with this policy.

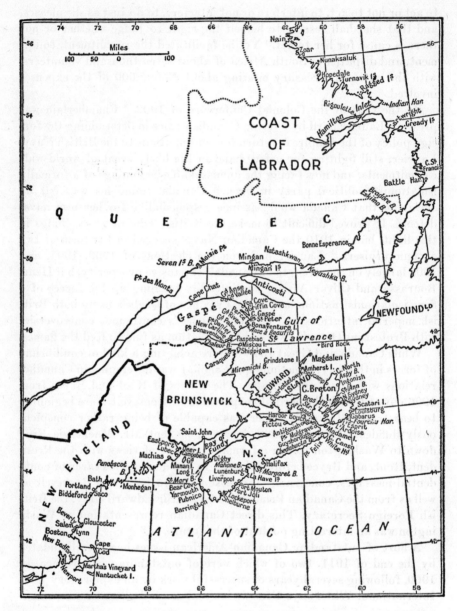

Fishing Ports of Labrador, Quebec, the Maritimes, and New England

ment from Bryce and Root, the United States and Canada established through the Boundary Waters Treaty an agreed-upon and equitable code of principles to govern the use, for transportation, power, and irrigation, of the thousands of miles of lakes and rivers between the Atlantic and the Pacific which geography compelled them to share. They also set up a permanent International Joint Commission, with equal representation, in order to decide judicially and peacefully, and on technical engineering grounds, all problems as they arose. Such problems might even be presented by individual citizens. Bayard's principle of treating Canada as a distinct political entity had at last been conspicuously accepted by the United States.

This Commission has justly earned a great reputation by its habitually unanimous disposal of the many matters brought before it. Under certain permissive clauses it can handle arbitrally any Canadian-American problem submitted to it by both governments. Its province has, however, been principally highly technical and difficult waterways business, although it has, with equal success, handled the adjustments required by the effect upon American forests, crops, and soils of smelter fumes blown across the border from Canada.

The second great achievement was the submission, under an Anglo-American general arbitration treaty of 1908, to the Permanent Court of Arbitration at The Hague, of the whole question of American rights under the Convention of 1818 in the coastal fisheries of Newfoundland and Canada. In effect the claims which the United States had pressed and used so unremittingly since 1783 were submitted to disinterested judgment. This immense arbitration, which was disposed of in about three months of the summer of 1910, concerned Newfoundland rather more than Canada, but it was an unquestioned advance toward sound Canadian-American relations to have so much of a long-vexed problem finally cleared up. The practically unanimous judgments of the Court upheld the British interpretation of the old Convention of 1818 and rejected the American case, but they also forbade any unreasonable exploitation of their rights by Newfoundland and Canada.

The stage was now set for two conspicuous symbolic declarations of independence by Canada, one from the United States and one from Great Britain. Apparently Canadians yielded to irresistible inner compulsions in making these two gestures. It was as if they had to show that they could no longer be dragooned and subordinated. Henceforth their country insisted on being treated as a partner instead of as a subordinate, and, although it must obviously be a junior partner, it meant to delimit precisely what it would or would not do, unless overborne by force.

The first symbolic declaration was made in 1911 after the Taft Administration and the Laurier Government had secretly worked out a legislative agreement (not a treaty) for commercial reciprocity. Its mildness
on the American side and its receptiveness to the free entry of natural
products reflected the increased reliance of the American economy on
Canada for materials and markets, surprised Laurier, and completely
discouraged R. L. Borden, the leader of the Opposition in the Canadian
Parliament. Yet there speedily welled up an irresistible revolt against this
apparently foregone conclusion which was probably the most dramatic
episode of the kind in Canadian history. Public opinion and Laurier's
honorable refusal to exploit his parliamentary majority by applying
powers of closure forced the Government to go to the country on the
issue and it was roundly defeated at the polls.

Many forces were combined to achieve this result. The organized,
often specious, and expensive propaganda on both sides of the boundary
was unprecedented. Canadian industrialists and financiers were the backbone of the opposition as a matter of course. A whole series of inept
references to Canada's inevitable annexation by the United States, made
by the President and others during their strenuous efforts to get the
Agreement through Congress, furnished the most effective possible ammunition for emotional Canadian appeals to rally round the flag.[20] Deep
down, moreover, was the new confidence in Canada which had been created by her marvelous prosperity and by the favorable interlocking of
her production with the British market. This was neatly reflected in the
attitude of the transcontinental railways as it was summed up in the
remark of the ex-American, Sir William Van Horne of the Canadian
Pacific, when he emerged from retirement among the Old Masters which
he had been collecting: "I am out to do all I can to bust the damned thing."
At any rate, the Reciprocity Act was left to slumber impotently in the
American statute book until 1922, while Canadians savored the deep, if
transient, joy of having at last told Americans that they could get along
without them.

Canada's symbolic declaration of independence from Great Britain
was a less clear-cut affair, but in its way no less significant. Laurier's
own shrewd comment on his defeat furnishes a clue: "It was not reciprocity that was turned down, but a Catholic premier." This reference to
the hostility of the ultra-Protestants of Ontario also involved the re-

---

20. E.g., Taft's reference to Canada at "the parting of the ways," and Champ Clark's
"I hope to see the day when the American flag will float over every square foot of the
British North American possessions clear to the North Pole." The yeasty support given
to Taft by the Hearst Press was a boomerang so far as Canada was concerned. Taft
was also known to Canadians as Roosevelt's chosen instrument and heir.

sponse which they provoked in Quebec, for there two forces effectively undermined Laurier's hold. The first was the old ultramontane distaste for a Liberal Catholic leader, marvelously reënforced by Ontario extremism. The second was the isolationist nationalism made vocal during the South African War and raised to effectiveness at the polls by Laurier's creation of a Canadian Navy in 1910. Laurier's defeat was assured when Bourassa's Nationalists, in an unholy and utterly contradictory alliance with Borden's Conservatives, took thirty of the sixty-five Quebec seats away from the Liberals.

Having achieved its purpose by dislodging Laurier, this unnatural alliance began to defeat itself almost at once, because its English-speaking members wanted to aid the threatened Mother Country, while the French Canadians emphatically did not. In addition, Canada was having to chart her course from a new position, for in 1911, on the occasion of a coronation and an Imperial Conference, the Foreign Office had acquainted Laurier and the other Dominion delegates with the high policy of the Empire, although Asquith had refused to consider Dominion participation in framing it. Borden, who succeeded Laurier as Prime Minister that autumn, himself well understood the implications of this move, for he, as well as Laurier, had clearly pointed out the inescapable relationship between armed effort and foreign policy. A voice in the latter involved a share in the former and vice versa. He himself visited London in 1912, and, in the light of the dangerous international situation and of Germany's new naval appropriation, made a tentative bargain that, if Canada found the money for three British battleships, the Mother Country would concede to her minister-resident in London a seat on the all-important Committee of Imperial Defense and inform him of every important step in foreign policy.

But when Borden introduced in Parliament his legislation to appropriate $35,000,000 for the building of the British ships, he had to face, not only Liberal declarations of faith in the Laurier policy of a Canadian Navy, and denunciations of Borden's reversion from Dominion status to "colonialism" and "Downing Street control," but also the resolute defection of his recent allies, the Quebec Nationalists. The Cabinet was split, and party lines were in utter chaos because French Canada was making her obstructive power felt. Borden was able to force the bill through the Commons by means of an extra session in 1913 and by the use of closure proceedings such as Laurier had disdained in the matter of reciprocity two years before, but when the Liberal majority in the nominated Senate estimated that it could safely reject the bill, he was not unwilling to let the matter rest. The Senate majority pointed out that he had no popular mandate for the policy, and made its assent conditional on a referendum, but Borden did not respond to this suggestion. He himself was not yet satisfied that London was at all willing to understand what Canada meant by an imperial partnership and meanwhile the Dominion was being shaken by an unexpected economic depression.[21]

Canada's perhaps rash repulses of the United States and Great Britain in 1911 and 1913 can be explained in the economic and psychological terms which have been suggested, but in addition her geographical isolation and her sense of security must be taken into account. In those years it was the rare Canadian, except the inarticulate "New Canadian" fleeing from the military conscription and authoritarian rule of central and eastern European countries, who had any immediate sense of the devilish brew which was ready to boil over in Europe. Morocco, the Balkans, Tripoli—these meant nothing to him, and the Anglo-German naval race was a far-off contest whose dangers thrilled rather than frightened him. Moreover, after a hundred years of peace with the United States and incalculable mingling of the peoples, even if it had been peace interrupted by friction, threats, and actual invasions, the Canadian did not believe that the United States would annex the Dominion by force.

Actually Canada was basking in the delights of her astounding growth and of her apparent ability to shake off both her thraldoms, and doing so in an unself-critical and shortsighted mood. Unfortunately this mood was nourished by the underlying conviction that, if the international weather grew bad, she was sheltered from harm by two oceans in the first place, with the umbrella of the British Navy and the enveloping waterproof of the Monroe Doctrine at hand as well. Strictly speaking the original Monroe Doctrine did not apply to Canada, but it would have been a daring person, any time after 1895, who would attempt to define the chameleon-like Doctrine, and Canadians did not try. They seldom mentioned it, in fact, for they did not like to remind themselves of any obligation to the United States, but a casual remark of Laurier's reflected a common Canadian assumption, particularly after Great Britain's naval withdrawal from the West Atlantic, following the crisis of 1900–1901. In 1902, during an interview with Lord Dundonald, who had been brought out to Canada to be head of the militia, Laurier said: "You must not take

21. The development of Canadian nationality after 1867 might be described by saying that while Macdonald fought British indifference by constructing a nation, while Laurier fought centralization by refusing commitments, and while Borden fought condescension by balancing responsibility against a share in policy-making, all three aimed to enable Canada to chart her own course in the Empire and the world. The effective variables were Canada's ability and willingness to exert influence and assume responsibility, as was revealed after 1918.

the militia seriously, for though it is useful for suppressing internal disturbances, it will not be required for the defense of the country, as the Monroe Doctrine protects us against enemy aggression."

From this mood the War of 1914 gave the Dominion and its peoples a rude, and in a sense timely, awakening. This war, in which Great Britain had stepped to the side of France, at first united Canada to a degree unpredictable as little as a month before it broke out. Borden cabled Canada's offer to help even before Great Britain was formally engaged, and Laurier explicitly lived up to the prediction which had accompanied his reservations during the South African War. "Every Canadian admits," he had said in 1900, "that he would be ready to contribute our treasure and our blood, and the resources of Canada at the disposal of this country, for the rescue of England, were she engaged in a life and death struggle."

During thirty-two months while Canadians were redeeming that promise on a scale which astonished themselves, the people of the United States were trying desperately to reconcile the irreconcilables of their position in the world. They were undergoing their first stiff course of political self-education since the Civil War, and they were glimpsing the responsibilities that accompany power. Practically all the precepts and traditions of their national life bade them stand aloof; their intimate knowledge of the horrible character of the warfare made them soberly aware of what entering it would mean; and the British blockade flagrantly violated their cherished principles of neutrality and the freedom of the seas. But politically the United States could not cut free from the North Atlantic nexus if she wanted to; economically she had bound up her fortunes with an Allied victory; Germany's submarine warfare was even more intolerable than Britain's stringent blockade; and in the imponderable realm of ideas and aspirations she knew she stood much more closely with France and Great Britain than with their enemies. On April 2, 1917, President Wilson asked Congress to accept the state of war which the repeated sinkings without warning of unarmed merchant ships had thrust upon the United States. The Senate agreed two days later and on April 6, the House of Representatives concurred.

The decision had been slowly and solemnly reached. The United States did not enter the war on the crest of any such tide of heart-warming emotion as had Canada. But gradually a great cluster of external and internal forces had become fused into an irresistible compulsion to exert the American will in determining what had escaped the bounds of Europe and become a world struggle. The United States did not enter that maelstrom out of love for France and Great Britain or in order to emulate her

Canadian cousins, but it should be apparent that it was natural, almost inevitable, for her to find herself at their side. In the curious and not always trustworthy memoir of that arch-nationalist, Henry Cabot Lodge, he points out that if it had not been for Great Britain's surrender of her Isthmian rights in 1902, and, still more important, the successful settling of the Alaska boundary in 1903, "the attitude of the United States towards England would have been of such a character as to have embarrassed us most seriously when the Great War of 1914 broke out." Lodge realized that foreign as well as domestic circumstances practically compelled the United States to enter the war, and he appreciated how important it was for her to do so alongside congenial allies, but he was to do more than any other individual toward wrecking the Peace after it by the shallowness which led him to place party politics above international cooperation.

CHAPTER XV

NORTH AMERICAN WITHDRAWAL
(1918–1932)

IT was ironic that during the years immediately following their joint enterprise in war, ordinary social intercourse between Americans and Canadians was blighted by conflicting conceptions of the share which the various Allied Powers had played in it. Countless futile arguments took place without impressing upon Americans much effective realization of the heroic efforts which had preceded their own contribution and without persuading Canadians that in 1917 American naval assistance averted the imminent collapse of the Allied cause because of submarine activity, that American money came into play just when Allied financial resources were exhausted, and that a million and three-quarters of fresh American soldiers gave Foch the margin which enabled him to knock out Germany in 1918 by four months of continuous offensive on the Western Front. Matters were made worse because both peoples had been systematically misinformed about the achievements of their forces in relation to the total Allied effort.

The significant circumstance behind these misunderstandings was that the war had been nothing like so searching an experience for the United States as it had been for Canada. The Republic took its eighteen months of involvement and eight months of costly land warfare almost in its stride. The Dominion nearly exhausted its capacities, human and economic, by plunging into the war from 1914 to 1916 on an expanding scale which it was barely able to sustain during 1917 and 1918. The Americans had six months of adversity in the field and four months of triumph. The Canadians had been fighting for three and a half years with fluctuating fortunes before they entered upon the victorious Hundred Days which carried them into Mons on the morning of the Armistice. That was why, with about one-thirteenth of the population of the United States, Canada suffered two-thirds as many casualties.

The magnitude of Canada's armed efforts, paralleled as they were in the production of munitions and supplies and in public and private expenditure, made it undesirable any longer to allow her to be regarded as a British dependency. The time had come to affirm to the world at large the autonomy in domestic and external affairs which she had achieved in relations with Great Britain and the other Dominions before 1914. Throughout the war Sir Robert Borden had resisted every inclination of

Great Britain to assume that Canada would take orders, and had pains-
takingly built up the precedents and practices of partnership. The Cana-
dian forces overseas were subject to a Canadian Cabinet Minister in
London. The Canadian Prime Minister sat as an equal with five British
Cabinet Ministers and other Dominion Prime Ministers in the so-called
Imperial War Cabinet which directed operations from 1917 onward.

The natural consequence was that the Dominions secured separate
representation, analogous to that of Belgium, at the Peace Conference,
served on the British Empire panel of delegates, and signed the various
peace treaties separately. Indeed Borden was successful in postponing
British ratification of the treaties in behalf of Canada until after they
had been ratified by the Dominion Parliament, following prolonged debates. Finally Canada received separate membership in the Assembly of
the League of Nations and assurance of membership in its Council.[1] In
A. G. Dewey's words, "Dominion nationalism emerged from the shelter of
the Imperial Conferences, where it had enjoyed the privacy of a strictly
family matter, and asserted itself before an international assembly."

Thus, after 1918, Great Britain, the United States, and Canada, lately
bound together in the successful pursuit of a single purpose, were free to
follow separate courses or to combine in efforts to establish and maintain
peace on the troubled globe. As might have been expected from her greater
maturity in world affairs and from her proximity to harassed Continental Europe, Great Britain attempted to found her postwar foreign policy
on the broadest possible international machinery and on the controlled
rehabilitation of Germany. Although she had not lost her imperial acquisitiveness, and although she had a way of regarding the League of
Nations as a sort of holding corporation for the settlements imposed at
Versailles, she aimed at international peace and prosperity which should
be based upon the elastic processes of a revived world trade rather than
upon the military conceptions of security which were cherished by France,
ever conscious of her vulnerable land frontiers.

Great Britain's handicaps were her economic exhaustion and her domestic maladjustments, as signalized by her taxpayers' revolts against
postwar commitments in various parts of the world and by the disturbances which accompanied the workers' defense of the higher standards
of living and of security which they had won during the past ten or twelve
years of social legislation. Great Britain simply could not raise the
money needed to maintain relatively her old position as a world power,
particularly in the Indian Ocean and the Pacific; but, if the League of

---

1. Realized in 1927. Canada was also a member of the International Labor Organization.

Nations could be made to work, it might be possible to "freeze" her post-war empire against serious sudden disruptions. It would be particularly helpful if the Dominions could be won over to some scheme of unity in imperial policy; but surprisingly little hard thinking was devoted to this project in the United Kingdom, perhaps because the managers of high policy there realized how difficult it would be to achieve. In the meantime rising tides of nationalism in Ireland, Egypt, and India strained British resourcefulness to the breaking point.

On grounds of analogy the United States might have been expected to take over a good many of Great Britain's traditional attributes after 1918. Indeed an informed minority, composed of financial leaders and of what Senator Lodge called "the vocal classes of the community," spent the next twenty years trying to persuade their countrymen to assume the role which they felt that events had thrust upon the United States. Her unique gold store amounted to over 35 per cent of the world's visible supply, she was the greatest industrial producer in the world, and she had acquired a mercantile marine. A debtor to the tune of three billion dollars in 1914, she had become a creditor for sixteen billions by 1922, not to speak of over ten billions of governmental loans to foreign governments. A century earlier, when Great Britain had found herself in much the same position, she had embarked on the free-trade and the free-gold market which had facilitated her rise to economic leadership in the world. President Wilson doubtless had the British analogy in mind when, in vetoing a tariff increase early in 1921, he wrote: "If there ever was a time when America had anything to fear from foreign competition, that time has passed. If we wish to have Europe settle her debts, governmental or commercial, we must be prepared to buy from her."

Far different was the temper of Wilson's opponents. Even before the war was over, the nation's voters had rejected his explicit appeal for their approval and continued support by returning hostile Republican majorities to both Houses of Congress. Three weeks later Theodore Roosevelt announced that "Mr. Wilson has no authority whatever to speak for the American people at this time" and carried to his deathbed his plotting with Senator Lodge to defeat Wilson "and his Fourteen Points and his four supplementary points and all his utterances every which way." Within two years the Treaty of Versailles was rejected, the League was rejected, an emergency tariff increase was under way, and high barriers had begun to rise for the first time against immigration. By 1921 the United States had chosen a Magnificent Isolation beside which Lord Salisbury's conception during the 'nineties would have seemed pale indeed.

The defeat and destruction of Wilson during the period embraced by the congressional elections of 1918 and 1920 provide a theme for tragedy with which a genius like Shakespeare might transcend *King Lear*. The conspiracies against the President were so tortuous, the passions involved so primitive, and the changes and chances of the conflict so precarious, that students of the battle whose issue held such consequences for the whole world have never been able entirely to agree in explaining it. Did the reverential awe with which Wilson was greeted by the submerged millions during his European progresses, or his own sense of righteousness, enlarge his self-sufficiency to the Messianic proportions which gave his enemies such broad purchase for their leverage? Did the explanation of Senator Borah's leadership of the isolationist "irreconcilables" of the Senate against the President and his works lie in principles which he was unable to express with consistency, or did he succumb unconsciously to the prestige which he derived from conspicuous political nonconformity? Was it blind, implacable hatred of Wilson or a narrow quest of party advantage which made Senator Lodge, himself once an avowed proponent of a league of nations, translate his Italian-American constituents' exasperation over Fiume, and his Irish-American constituents' demands for Ireland's independence into the attribution of isolationist sentiments to the whole American people?

Whatever the answers to these questions, it seems safe to say that in 1919 the majority of Americans were clearly in favor of ratifying the Peace Treaty and the League Covenant contained in it. Even in the Senate, where the immense prize in contest was the amount of prestige which Wilson and the Democrats might derive from the success of the President's international policies, three-quarters favored a league of some sort. But Wilson, who had rashly boasted in March, 1919, that he would come back from his second visit to Europe with "so many threads of the treaty tied to the covenant [of the League]" that they could not be separated without the destruction of both, would not admit of any serious modifications of the Versailles settlements of June 28, 1919. His opponents, who in the early summer of 1919 privately agreed that public sentiment was overwhelmingly in favor of acceptance, could hope at that time for little more than some minor victories via the traditional Senate practice of appending reservations during the process of ratification.

Had the Treaty and the League been forced to the vote with reasonable promptness during the special session of Congress which began on May 19, 1919, they would probably have passed without substantial reservations, for public opinion was insistent.[2] But Lodge was chairman

2. The main outlines of the settlements were well known by the end of February and the Senate received an unofficial copy of the Treaty on June 9.

of the Committee on Foreign Relations and he gambled everything on his power to delay. He spent two weeks reading the whole Treaty aloud, held six weeks of often fantastic hearings in committee, and by various devices kept the Treaty from the floor of the Senate. By September the President, although in poor health, felt that he must appeal directly to the people lest, puzzled by the delay and already preoccupied with their own postwar problems, they relapse into traditional American isolationism. Three weeks of this effort, although marked by enthusiastic response, brought about his physical collapse and practical elimination from the political stage—the result which his friends had feared and which he had knowingly risked.

Thereafter the destruction of Wilson's cause proceeded slowly but inexorably. On November 19, 1919, the Treaty, with fourteen reservations by Lodge,[3] was defeated at the President's request. An aroused public quickly forced the Senate to return to its task. This time there were fifteen reservations, and once more the President commanded enough following to secure their defeat.[4] He then vetoed a joint resolution of Congress which merely declared that hostilities were at an end, thereby putting the issue to the voters at the polls of 1920.

In a weird election, which was marked by an ambiguous Republican platform and by flatly contradictory utterances on the League question from its candidate, the American people called a halt to the interminable Wilson-Lodge duel and blindly committed their destinies to the Republican party, so called, of which one half said it supported Harding in order to keep the United States out of the League and the other half said it did so in order to get into it. The Democrats had made matters worse by a weak candidate and by fumbling intimations of compromise. Harding promised the people "normalcy," and, ill-served by the political leaders in both parties for two troubled years, they voted overwhelmingly for whatever that might mean. The war with the Central Powers came to its inglorious end by a declaratory resolution of Congress on July 2, 1921, and treaties were signed with Germany, Austria, and Hungary the following month.[5]

3. His committee had originally proposed forty-five amendments and four reservations.

4. The vote, 49 yeas to 35 nays, failed under the two-thirds rule for treaty ratification by the Senate.

5. Other consequences of the American withdrawal were the nullification of the joint security treaty for the protection of France, nonparticipation by the United States in the reparations settlement, and refusal of responsibilities in the League's mandates system. Repeated efforts to have the United States adhere to the World Court have been defeated, although Americans have acted as judges on it. The United States joined the International Labor Organization in 1934.

For many years after 1918, Canadians, who are accustomed to find compensation for material inferiority to the United States in assumptions and assertions of moral superiority, congratulated themselves that in international relations they were not as Americans were, for they had ratified the Versailles Treaty and had taken up active membership in the League. Looking backward from 1938, J. W. Dafoe, the Winnipeg newspaper editor who had given his great talents and the best years of his life to educating his fellow citizens in the responsibilities of nationhood, commented rather wryly on this mood:

The comfortable idea took possession of the Canadian mind that the war era was over and that permanent peace was guaranteed by the League of Nations, an institution for which they had a vague detached regard resting upon a mysterious belief that it had occult means for keeping the peace without any obligation resting upon its member nations to see that it had either the power or the will to enforce any such programme on a turbulent world.

This general outlook, colored as it was by native North American isolationism, reflected in part the stubborn intransigeance of an embittered French Canada, which had begun to lose its enthusiasm for the war sometime during 1915, and had suffered from a virulent case of "minorityism" during the succeeding years of unreserved Anglo-Canadian effort. Laurier supported the war, but his Nationalist enemies, notably Henri Bourassa and Armand Lavergne, quite early began to undermine the cause in French Canada by using uncensored information, received through the still-neutral United States, in order to cast doubts on Allied war aims. They also fanned the flames of a bitter, if congenial, conflict between Quebec and Ontario which had begun in 1912 when Ontario had made it plain that English must be the language of instruction in her schools. The children of the growing French-Canadian influx into the neighboring province were to be taught in French if necessary, but must meanwhile study English so as to make the change in language of instruction as early as possible. By early 1916 the French-Canadian press was reporting the war against Ontario "Prussianism" at greater length and with hotter passions than the war against Germany.

The problem of French Canada became literally a national one during 1917, when Borden decided that Canada, like the United States, must adopt conscription. In order to achieve this he and his principal lieutenant, Arthur Meighen, felt compelled to employ unprecedented and questionable methods in connection with the franchise and with the creation of a coalition government, thus giving Quebec added excuses for opposition. Laurier, aged seventy-seven, bravely traveled across Canada explaining why he thought conscription unwise, but he accepted the verdict of the Khaki Election in its favor and urged his people to obey the law against which they had voted en masse.

Actually conscription was a pretty complete failure in Canada, for the country had by 1918 practically reached the end of the man power available for the depleted armed forces, for the expanding war industries, and for aid to the farmers, miners, and lumbermen of whom so much was demanded. Evasions of, and resistance to, conscription took place all over the Dominion, particularly in trade-union circles and among the bewildered farmers, and western appeals against the law were carried in vain to the Supreme Court. These scattered instances were, however, quite eclipsed by the solidarity of Quebec's opposition, which burst out into mob violence in the face of Ottawa's impetuous and maladroit efforts to dragoon French Canadians into the army. The wound to Canadian unity, which was caused by the impact of Anglo-Canadian determination upon French-Canadian indifference, became a festering sore. The French Canadians felt that they had nowhere to turn save inward, and their separatist tendencies, which have already been noticed in connection with Laurier and Dominion Status,[6] became all the more deeply ingrained.

But Quebec had sixty-five seats in the Dominion Parliament with which to make her weight felt in the direction of the country at large. Inasmuch as Parliament was in perpetual hot water from 1921 to 1926 because no party could establish a safe majority, it should be remembered that the French-Canadian members, drawn from Quebec and other parts of the Dominion, could and did bring pressure to bear in every possible way which might free Canada from commitments abroad and from the risk of involvement in another "foreign" war.

Canada's negation, whether bred from an underestimation of the difficulties of collective security, or from a minority's sense of injustice, was clearly reflected in her postwar international behavior. Sir Robert Borden, for instance, had anticipated American objections to Article X of the League Covenant by submitting, during the drafting of the Covenant at Paris, a memorandum demanding its deletion or material amendment.[7] This Article, which President Wilson later called "the heart of the Covenant," seemed to Borden, by its guaranty of "the territorial integrity and existing political independence of all Members of the League," to involve both a perpetual assumption that existing delimitations were

6. See above, pp. 262–265.

7. This was in mid-March, but in February Borden's Minister of Justice (one of the four Canadian plenipotentiaries), C. J. Doherty, had circulated a condemnatory memorandum among his Canadian colleagues.

just and expedient, and an automatic obligation upon Canada to repress even justifiable attempts to alter them. Borden was not prepared to surrender a portion of Canada's newly won international autonomy in order to create an overriding international sovereignty for maintenance of the status quo, but his objections were overruled at Paris.

That Borden's views were not peculiar to himself was clearly demonstrated during the debates in the Canadian Parliament over ratification and particularly over Article X. Mr. C. G. Power, an English-speaking Liberal member for Quebec, was merely more picturesque than other critics, drawn from both parties, when he said:

Our policy for the next hundred years should be that laid down by George Washington for the guidance of his countrymen—absolute renunciation of interference in European affairs—and that laid down by the other great father of his country in Canada, Sir Wilfrid Laurier—"freedom from the vortex of European militarism."

Mr. Rodolphe Lemieux, also a Liberal from Quebec, said: "In military matters we are governed also by and from Ottawa, and not by and from London; and we do not want to be governed by and from Geneva." Mr. L. T. Pacaud, another Quebec Liberal, declared: "By the adoption of Article X we are stripping this Parliament of its most valued prerogative; we are placing the Canadian people at the beck and call of a Council not responsible to the nation for its actions." Yet in Canada, as in the United States, majority opinion favored ratification of the Treaty and the Covenant. It triumphed, partly because of the effective coalition majority in Parliament, and partly because the members in opposition were too inexperienced in the implications of Canada's new international status to know how to build up in Parliament and the nation a countermovement sufficiently powerful to make Borden revert to his original stand concerning Article X.

Nevertheless the Canadian delegate to the first Assembly of the League in 1920 did make the motion that Article X be deleted from the Covenant; and subsequent Canadian delegations carried on, until the Fourth Assembly in 1923, an unremitting effort, which received substantial support from other secondary nations, to have the offending Article amended or formally interpreted so as to restore freedom of action to members which might be called upon to enforce it. The final Canadian effort of 1923, which required unanimity for its success, failed in the face of one adverse vote (Iran) and a number of abstentions.

While this peculiarly Canadian cause was being pursued in the League, Canada was also opposing there the prolonged efforts of France and her friends to frame some substitute for the Anglo-American protective guaranty to France which had disappeared with the defection of the United States.[8] The striking feature of this opposition, aside from its evidence of North American isolationism and from Senator Dandurand's revealing statement to the League Assembly in 1924 that Canada lived in "a fireproof house far from inflammable materials," was the invariable Canadian explanation that her refusal to coöperate arose in large part from the close Canadian-American relationship.

In 1924 the Canadian Prime Minister, replying to the proposed Draft Treaty of Mutual Guaranty, pointed out, *inter alia*, that "apart from indications that the Government of the United States of America was not likely to find the plan acceptable in principle, Canada has already indicated disapproval of the terms of Article 10 of the Covenant as implying an obligation upon her to intervene actively under that article." A year later Mr. King, in opposing the provisions for economic and military sanctions under the Geneva Protocol, declared that "among the grounds for this conclusion is the consideration of the effect of the non-participation of the United States upon attempts to enforce the sanctions and particularly so in the case of a contiguous country like Canada." Canadians must therefore share a kind of primary responsibility for the rather widespread contradiction between what League members had covenanted to do in general and what they intimated that they might be counted upon to do in particular instances.

In the meantime an extraordinary event, or series of events, had taken place, which brought out in high relief the peculiar relationships among Great Britain, Canada, and the United States. In 1921 Arthur Meighen, Conservative Prime Minister of Canada, singlehandedly persuaded an Imperial Conference to reverse itself and suspend the renewal of the Anglo-Japanese Alliance.[9] This feat created a favorable opportunity for Charles Evans Hughes, President Harding's Secretary of State, to invite the Powers to a conference at Washington for naval disarmament

8. The Canadian Government had so delayed the presentation to Parliament of the British treaty for aid to France that it had not been ratified by Canada when the American Congress ended the whole tripartite proposal by rejecting the interlocked Franco-American treaty.

9. The role of the late Mr. Loring Christie of the Canadian Department of External Affairs in this whole incident remains to be elucidated. He was strongly influenced by Borden, who had repeatedly and emphatically lectured the Imperial War Cabinet during 1918 as to Canada's insistence on Anglo-American coöperation. For instance, to quote Borden's own account of one occasion, "if the future policy of the British Empire meant working in cooperation with some European nation as against the United States, that policy could not reckon on the approval or the support of Canada. Canada's view was that as an Empire we should keep clear, as far as possible, of European complications and alliances."

and for redressing the balance of power in the Pacific. The London incident must be regarded as an exceptional, indeed practically unique, instance of Canadian capacity to bring her two great colleagues together by making one of them change her mind. In addition it should be noted that the Dominion obtained the leverage which multiplied her power because Ottawa's view of the Alliance coincided with Washington's at a time when London caught a glimpse of the possibility that the United States might be wooed from her isolationism.

Another consideration, which should not be eclipsed by Japan's behavior after 1930, is that a series of liberal Japanese administrations, by their meticulous international behavior from 1919 onward, did much to encourage the belief that international relations might be adjusted by collective negotiations instead of by war and by threats of war. That belief, enshrined and fostered as it was by the League of Nations, probably reached its culmination in 1927 and 1928, when Briand's proposal for the outlawry of war was enthusiastically affirmed by almost all the nations, while they tacitly ignored the fact that the Pact of Paris to which they subscribed contained no provisions for its enforcement.

The Anglo-Japanese Alliance, originally of 1902, had been carefully adjusted in later years so as to preclude any possibility that its operation might involve an Anglo-American war. It had served brilliantly as insurance for Great Britain in the Pacific and India during the War of 1914, but the war-time premiums paid had taken the form of British toleration toward a marked increase of Japanese territorial and economic aggression in China. This involved American as well as British loss of prestige, but there seemed no way out save a conflict which neither country was prepared to sustain. At the London Conference, which met during June and July, 1921, Great Britain, Australia, New Zealand, South Africa, India, and the other parts of the Empire which were represented were anxious to renew the Alliance and to keep Japan's friendship. Meighen, much assisted by the venomously extreme opposition of Prime Minister Hughes of Australia, gradually made good the view which he had urged on the British Government by correspondence as early as February. This was that, since renewal amounted to approval of Japanese aggression, and almost certain estrangement of the United States, the Alliance must be superseded in favor of multilateral Pacific agreements to be arrived at in international conference.

This Canadian case, as presented in London, was a perfect blend of the components in the national outlook. Belief in, and commitment to, the League's principles of collective security made the bilateral Alliance repugnant, in spite of its "tailoring" to fit League requirements and to exclude British obligations against the United States. Thus Canada, on her own grounds as a League member and a North American nation, shared, on considerably different grounds, the opposition of the United States to the Alliance. The very foundation of Canada's foreign policy must be the cultivation of Anglo-American friendship, for she would be the first victim of their falling out. If she could bring them together at a general Pacific conference, the chances would be good that they would see more nearly eye to eye than any other two Powers. If they did, Canada's problems would be solved at one stroke.

Meighen carried off this coup on July 1, his country's birthday, when the nimble-witted Lloyd George, distressed by the schism between Canada and the rest of the Empire, and sensing the possibilities of Anglo-American understanding, threw the whole ponderous British case into the discard and fell in behind the Canadian, leaving the more stubborn Australian in the lurch. A week later the Canadian, now British, proposal had blended with the rapidly matured, similar plans of Secretary Hughes, and informal invitations had gone out to the Powers to meet at Washington.

The taxpayers of the five Great Powers, the four Minor Powers, and the British Dominions which were represented at Washington regarded the Conference principally as a triumph for disarmament. The clue lay in Secretary Hughes's success in persuading the Great Powers to scrap a large number of completed ships and others in construction, and to halt the race in capital ships, by the famous $5:5:3:1.75:1.75$ ratio, respectively, for Great Britain, the United States, Japan, France, and Italy. Ironically enough it fell to the isolationist, but loyal Republican, Lodge to secure the necessary Senate support for the Four-Power Treaty, which substituted for the Anglo-Japanese Alliance an agreement among Great Britain, Japan, France, and the United States to respect each other's existing rights in the Pacific and to settle future disputes in joint conference and by joint action. He also drove through the Senate, at the price of a reservation against armed force, alliance, and obligation to join in any defense, the Nine-Power Treaty which bound the signatories to respect the sovereign independence and territorial integrity of China and to uphold the principle of the Open Door. His task was made much easier by Japan's simultaneous, specific, and honorable adjustments of elements in her relations with China and the United States which conflicted with the new atmosphere of peace and mutual respect in the Pacific.

In the spring of 1922 every Power had retreated from its most extreme pretensions, and the world was at least temporarily a better place because of the settlements reached at Washington. The future seemed bright, but its actuality depended upon the resources of statesmanship when the status quo should be threatened, for only collective support could implement paper promises against any dissident Power or group of Powers.

In fact retreat from outward extensions of national interest was the order of the day, apparently in response to rebellions from harassed taxpayers. The United States began to extricate herself from Latin American, as well as from Far Eastern, implication. The task was a complicated one because of American investments in Mexico, Central America, and the Caribbean islands for the production of such commodities as Mexican oil and bullion, Central American bananas, and Cuban sugar. Nicaragua occupied a special position because she contained the only practical second route for an Isthmian canal. Gradually, however, one difficulty after another was liquidated, and the emblems of domination, whether Marines, munitions movements, or economic controls and reprisals, disappeared from Santo Domingo, Nicaragua, and Mexico.

The pinnacle of this movement, at least in principle, came in the form of a State Department memorandum of December 17, 1928, which provided both an echo of Wilson's abjuration of territorial aggression at Mobile in 1913 and a confession of retreat by the Hoover Administration from the recent aggressive tactics of President Coolidge and Secretary of State Kellogg. Although not made public until 1930, it showed that the permanent custodians of policy possessed better judgment than some of the politicians. Its author, Mr. J. Reuben Clark, flatly laid it down that the "Roosevelt Corollary" of the Monroe Doctrine, by which in 1904 that President had claimed a police power to put down "chronic wrongdoing" in the Western Hemisphere, was an aberration. "The Doctrine," said Clark, "states a case of the United States *vs.* Europe, and not of the United States *vs.* Latin America." In his Inaugural Address of 1929 President Hoover disavowed any American "desire for territorial expansion, for economic or other domination of other peoples," and Secretary of State Stimson communicated the sense of the Clark memorandum for the reassurance of the Latin American countries.

Meanwhile Canada had also been conducting systematic withdrawals from involvement in external responsibilities, in addition to those already noted in connection with the League of Nations. In 1922 a Liberal Cabinet refused a sudden cabled invitation from London to send troops to defend against the Turkish Army the Internationalized Zone at Chanaq on the Dardanelles, saying that Parliament would have to be summoned to approve of such a serious step.[10] When a new Treaty with Turkey was negotiated at Lausanne in 1923, Canada was not invited and she neither

10. Canada had participated in negotiating and signing the Treaty of Sèvres, which set up the Zone.

signed nor ratified the Treaty. That same year, having independently negotiated with the United States a Treaty for the protection of the Pacific halibut fisheries, the Canadian Government refused to allow the British Ambassador to sign it, in the old fashion, along with the Canadian negotiator.

By 1925 Canada's relation to the Locarno Treaty made it even more clear that she intended to decide for herself about her foreign obligations. The Dominion was not represented during the negotiations, but there was written into the Treaty an express reservation,[11] to the effect that it involved no obligations on the Dominions or India unless they chose expressly to assume them. Not only did Mr. King's Liberal Administration refrain, but it was also in 1925 that his Conservative opponent, Arthur Meighen, argued in a public address at Hamilton, Ontario, that Canadian troops should not be sent overseas without the sanction of the Dominion Parliament after a general election on the issue.

In such circumstances the Balfour Declaration of the legal and constitutional equality of Great Britain and the Dominions, which emerged from the Imperial Conference of 1926, was a mere recognition of things as they had come to be. Part of the British Empire changed its name to fit its shape by becoming the British Commonwealth of Nations. Stripped of its technicalities the Statute of Westminster, which converted the Declaration of 1926 into law, amounted to the legal provision that henceforth neither Great Britain nor any Dominion might exercise its sovereignty so as to bind any other of the group without its express consent. Legally and constitutionally, therefore, Canada now possessed the independence which she had long been exercising, and it was characteristic of her intentions that she began immediately after 1926 to exchange diplomatic representatives with other countries, including Great Britain herself.

The Dominion's whole campaign from 1918 onward to assert her separate entity was an exhilarating and satisfying experience for most Canadians, Conservative and Liberal alike, but very few among them as yet realized the full implications of this assertiveness. The whole adventure rested on assumptions which the future might modify or destroy. The League might not be able to prevent war; Great Britain might find the United States more important to her than Canada; the United States might extend the Monroe Doctrine in a compulsive, instead of a protective, sense over the Dominion. Canadians, and especially the minority-minded French Canadians, still had a lot to learn about what could hap-

11. Article IX.

pen to isolated secondary powers if the settlements reached at Versailles and Washington began to break down.

During the decade after 1918 the United States and Canada had made it very clear that they could and would withdraw from external commitments, but the past centuries of interplay between them meant that there would be sad consequences on both sides when the logic of the process carried them to the point of trying to disengage from their mutual mesh the gears of one which were interlocked with those of the other.

The outstanding peculiarity of this situation was that the United States so far exceeded Canada in terms of population, wealth, and productive capacity, and was so engrossed in domestic concerns, that the overwhelming majority of the American people simply took Canada for granted as a sort of worthy, dependable, but rather backward, country. A number of small, tightly organized, American "pressure groups," which were moved by self-interest to inform themselves about opportunities in Canada or about Canadian competition, were able to pursue their ends almost unnoticed. Thus it came about that Americans in general, whose attitude toward Canada might fairly be described as benevolent condescension, had almost no idea of the tremendous and often wounding impact of many of their nation's policies upon their weaker neighbors to the north. John MacCormac published a book in 1940 entitled *Canada: America's Problem*. Any knowledgeable Canadian could have told him that, even in 1940, a more revealing title would have been *The United States: Canada's Problem*.

Perhaps the most vivid illustration of how Canada fared in single competition with the United States was provided by trade relations. It is amusing to speculate upon what might have happened had the Canadian Parliament in 1919 or 1920 revived and passed the Reciprocity Bill of 1911, thereby bringing into play the corresponding Act which still stood in the American statute book, but this was too much to expect of a predominantly Conservative coalition government, and, anyway, the Republican Congress of 1918 would have made short work of repeal. American determination to build high the tariff walls was perfectly apparent before the end of Wilson's term, and, once he was out of the way, the builders got to work on the Emergency Tariff of 1921. Their great stimulus was the precipitous collapse of prices during 1920 which produced a short, but acute depression. In these circumstances it was easy to make even the farmers believe that barriers must be raised in order to prevent foreign countries from dumping their products in the United States and thereby depressing ruinous prices still farther. Americans had not yet learned that the only ways to keep up farm prices were limitation of production or treasury subsidies, in addition to import controls.

By 1922 the whole curious apparatus of "logrolling," or exchange of favors, by which an American Congress made a tariff, was at work to produce the Fordney-McCumber revision. The rates which it set on agricultural products were higher than ever before in the nation's history, and those on manufactured goods were either close to prohibitive or, in the case of so-called "key industries," like coal-tar products and dyes, were frankly so. The President was authorized, on the recommendation of the Tariff Commission, to raise or lower duties by not more than 50 per cent, a power which was subsequently exercised rather sparingly, but practically always upward.

Canada was at first too seriously involved in her own postwar problems to reckon up the consequences for her of the Fordney-McCumber Tariff.[12] She went through the same shocking deflation as the rest of the world, but since her degree of prosperity depended largely upon the export of precisely those raw or processed natural products which were hardest hit by the collapse in prices, and since the borrowing and inflation which she had employed in financing the war inflicted very heavy burdens on her rather narrowly specialized economy, her postwar depression lasted from the end of 1920 to the end of 1923.

In the circumstances the Canadian governments of the early 'twenties took the postwar outside world pretty much as they found it, concentrating meanwhile on domestic problems. Chief among these was the war legacy of two bankrupt transcontinental railway systems which Sir Robert Borden had had to take over and combine with the existing publicly owned and operated lines to form the Canadian National Railways. This system, with an operated mileage at December 31, 1922, of almost 22,665, was burdened with such an enormous debt that fixed charges prevented it from paying its way. The American-born Sir Henry Thornton, formerly of the Pennsylvania Railroad, and the Great Eastern Railway in Britain, took over the management in 1921 and made a surprising best of a bad job until depression wrecked his work after 1929, but the national treasury had had to meet the annual deficits.

To the average Canadian during the postwar years, the most irritating symbol of his country's difficulties was the depreciation of the Canadian dollar in terms of the American. During the war, and down to the withdrawal of the American Government's "pegs" from the international ex-

12. Except that the Maritimes were deeply shaken by the sudden practical exclusion of their fresh and frozen fish, and potatoes.

change market in November, 1920, the depreciation had not been serious, but during the next two or three years the dollar was sometimes worth only 82 American cents and consistently remained well below parity. The roots of the trouble were only partly Canadian. The United States was keeping her imports of Canadian products to a minimum. Canada, therefore, sold her goods for the most part to Great Britain and to other countries whose currencies were depreciated in New York. Thus the Dominion, having borrowed since 1914 chiefly in the United States, and being unable to sell enough goods there to pay both for her extensive purchases and for interest payments, was at a very great disadvantage until the pound sterling was put back at its former gold value in May, 1925. The Dominion resumed her own gold standard on July 1, 1926. There was a moral for Canadian isolationists in the fact that their dollar had for so long dangled helplessly midway between the exchange values of the American dollar and the British pound.

Actually Canadian governments had seen the writing on the wall and had taken some steps in heed of its warning. They could not do much to escape from the New York money market by turning to London, because that center was showing its displeasure over the losses incurred in the recent railway bankruptcies, and anyway sterling was too weak in New York to be of much help to Canada there, but they could, and did, do as much as possible of their borrowing from their own people. They dared not lower tariffs on foreign manufactured goods to the point where American and British factories could snuff out Canadian factories, but they began to get rid of special war tariffs and sales taxes so as to increase their citizens' purchasing power. After the Liberals came into power in 1921 each annual budget showed additional modest reductions in tariffs, particularly where these were such as to please the Western Progressives, an agricultural bloc which held the balance of power in the House of Commons from 1922 to 1926.

All in all the Dominion could fairly claim to have shown rather better sense in tariff matters than the United States, but this was attributable to her greater relative dependence on export trade. Canada had by 1927 rocketed up to become the fifth largest trading nation in the world, and was exporting about 30 per cent of her total annual production.[13] She had established a system of trade commissioners all over the world, and she was exercising to the full the control over her commercial treaties which she had won in 1907. It had been in that year, also, that Fielding's

13. Following Great Britain, the United States, Germany, and France. In 1930 her leading shares of the world's export trade were: newsprint, 63 per cent; wheat, 32 per cent; aluminum, 31 per cent; copper, 14 per cent; lead and zinc, 12 per cent.

device of Imperial Preference had been transformed into the henceforth characteristic "three-decker" Canadian tariff, under which the high general rate was flanked by an intermediate rate, which was customarily used for most-favored-nation treaties, and by the still lower British preference rate. As has been noticed, this last rate was valuable to the Mother Country chiefly in competition with European rivals, for Canada's nearness to the United States and her appetite for articles of common North American use meant that she would always buy more from the United States than from Great Britain, provided that she could acquire the necessary American dollars.

After Canada had absorbed the shock of American postwar tariffs at the cost of perhaps two added years of depression, both countries prospered greatly, with their immense productive capacities resting securely on an almost even "plateau" of world prices. In 1928 this began to deteriorate in certain primary products,[14] and next year it collapsed, to the accompaniment of an unparalleled crash in the American stock markets which rocked the credit structures of the entire world.

Canada was of course fundamentally harder hit than the United States by this series of catastrophes, but her woes became agonizing in 1930 when the American Congress set to work upon the Hawley-Smoot Tariff. Almost every agency of production in the United States clamored for higher protection and got it, with the total effect of raising the general ad valorem rate on dutiable products to 40 per cent, that is, about 20 per cent above the Fordney-McCumber level. More disturbing to Canada than the increases, however, was the narrowing of the free, or nearly free, list with the specific object of keeping out Canadian field crops, dairy products, livestock, lumber, and copper.[15] Canadians, with all their world markets in collapse, despaired of being able to amass the $4,000,000 a week which they needed for their net interest and dividend payments abroad. Maturing capital obligations in New York were an even greater bugbear. The only thing they thought they could do was to pare to the bone their purchases from the United States.[16]

The Hawley-Smoot Tariff opened a five-year tariff war which severely damaged Canada, and which is now believed to have been of no discernible benefit to the United States. The victims in both countries were the unlucky consumers. C. W. Wright's general views seem very much to the point. In most branches of American industry he finds that the higher

14. Thereby forcing Canada off the gold standard again.
15. Other removals from the free list were hides, leather, and timber.
16. Actually, having been a net exporter of capital throughout the boom, Canada's position was unexpectedly "cushioned" until September, 1931.

costs of materials, notably raw materials, hindered development. He feels certain that the farmers would have been distinctly better off if there had been no protective duties of any sort. On the other side of the border the peculiar disproportion which existed (as in New Zealand and Australia), between population and domestic consumption on the one hand and production for the world market on the other, made every obstructing item in American protectionism vitally important in the uphill struggle to preserve the Dominion's credit in New York.

In 1930 the pugnacious Richard B. Bennett, "the one-man Cabinet" who headed the Conservative party, turned out the Liberals on the strength of promises to put "Canada First, then the Empire," and to end unemployment by "blasting" a way into the markets of the world. He began his operations by raising even higher the duties already proposed by his Liberal predecessors in order to counter the Hawley-Smoot Tariff, and by introducing a number of variable administrative devices which made it extremely difficult for Canadians to buy goods from the United States. He then transferred his activities to an Imperial Conference in London, where he bluntly bade an astounded Labor Government adopt protection so that all the members of the Commonwealth could thereupon set tariff rates 10 per cent higher against non-British nations than against each other, thus creating an imperial tariff wall round the maze of walls protecting the separate parts of the Commonwealth. That was more than orthodox free traders like J. R. Macdonald and Philip Snowden could stomach. J. H. Thomas, the irreverent Secretary of State for the Dominions, flatly called it "humbug."

Next year, however, the British bastion fell, unable to hold out alone against the disruptive forces in the world economy. A so-called National Government, elected to "save the pound," not only had to sever it from gold, but also felt obliged to set up a low emergency tariff in order to prevent the world's last free market from becoming a dumping ground for the distressed world's goods. The British tariff gave Empire goods a temporary exemption, pending the Imperial Economic Conference which was to be held at Ottawa in 1932.

It might have been thought that the American Government would have been impressed by the almost certain implications of Great Britain's revolutionary change of direction, even if Canada's unique relationships to it and to the United States happened to be overlooked. But in 1932 a kind of panicky obtuseness reigned in the United States after three years of bewildering new experiences, and, with one or two notable exceptions, all that the Republicans could suggest in the way of remedies for American ills was to administer larger doses of the old medicines. That can be the only explanation why, on the eve of the Ottawa Conference, Congress tacked on to a revenue act prohibitive duties against petroleum products, coal, lumber, and copper. Nothing could have been better calculated to strengthen Canada's hand in the imminent business of persuading the British delegation to Ottawa that it was hopeless to proceed with their avowed aim of loosening up world trade by bringing Dominion and foreign tariffs down to the vicinity of the British level.

At any rate the British plan was defeated after a stubborn struggle. Accounts of what went on during the heat of that Ottawa July have been scrupulously watered down and censored, but, even granting that the British Government was overwhelmingly secure in office and that it was pretty confident that public opinion at home had settled down to regarding a combination between the "paper pound" and protectionism as a natural phenomenon, it seems clear that the British fought for their policy of mild protectionism until the bitter end. Instead of the Conference achieving its purposes by lowering the already high Dominion tariffs for the benefit of Empire countries, it created imperial preferences by raising the rates still higher against foreign countries. Instead of one all-inclusive treaty, twelve separate treaties, mostly bilateral, emerged from the melee.

Speaking generally, Great Britain, two-thirds of whose exports normally went to non-British countries, and who knew precisely what that meant in terms of imports and balances of payments, gave everything and received little in return. Apparently the British delegation, in conceding to the various Dominions practical monopolies of the United Kingdom's market for the products of farm and forest and mine, without in return getting under the barriers which protected Dominion industries, decided that for five years, at least, it could pay that price in order to preserve some economic semblance of imperial unity. Canada had been frankly out for all that she could get, particularly British discrimination against competitive Russian products, but until the United States also went off gold, her takings were chiefly in depreciated British pounds.

The United States was not formally represented at the Ottawa Conference, but her devotion to high tariffs was one of the primary forces which brought the Conference together.[17] It was appropriate, therefore, that the next few years revealed her to have been the principal non-British victim of the system which was erected there. Her postwar tariffs had worked against her, for they had cut her off substantially from her two

17. An ironic feature of the Conference was the presence there of lobbyists in behalf of tariff protection for American branch factories in Canada, distinctly more against their parent industries in the United States than against competition from elsewhere.

most important trading associates, Great Britain and Canada. The following approximate comparisons between 1929 and 1933 are significant:

	1929	1933	Ratio (Per Cent)
Total trade of Canada with the United States	$1,372,000,000	$430,000,000	31
Total trade of Canada with Great Britain	624,000,000	271,000,000	43
Total trade of the United States with Great Britain	1,178,000,000	423,000,000	36

Thus American economic isolationism had forced Canada, and Great
Britain also, into distortions of a triangular movement of goods and
money which had been advantageous to all three countries in the past.
In terms of self-interest, the United States must now change her course
in such a way as either to break down, or to break into, the Ottawa system.

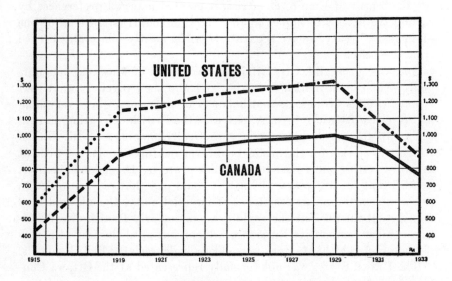

Comparative Standards of Living: Canada and the United States
(H. A. Logan, University of Toronto)

By 1932 the consequences of isolationism in the economic relationships
of the United States and Canada were patently serious, but the same
forces, having been applied to control of human migrations, had brought
about even more perturbing results. Here again a policy of the United
States which had been designed for one purpose effected another. Here

again the stronger country half unwittingly exerted a force upon the weaker with which for a long period the latter could not cope. And here, finally, when the depression came, both countries carried the isolationism which had been coloring their attitudes toward non-American migrants to its logical extreme as affecting each other. In 1930 they abruptly narrowed to minute proportions the ebb-and-flow of peoples between them which had begun in the Illinois country and Louisiana at the end of the seventeenth century and had continued ever since, save for brief interruptions, all across the continent from Atlantic to Pacific.

Between 1914 and 1930 the mingling of the Canadian and American peoples had probably been the greatest in history. It was accompanied and colored by three unique North American phenomena—the existence of international industrial areas at several points along the border, attempts to enforce the prohibition of alcoholic beverages, and the North American habit of ranging far and wide for recreation in motor cars or other means of transport.

The most important of the border areas were those clustered round the hydroelectric power and the "upper lake" shipping of the Niagara region, and those containing the practically identical automotive industries and their satellites on both sides of the Detroit River. Smaller or less closely integrated areas existed in the forest industries of the St. Croix and other Maine–New Brunswick valleys; in the manufacturing region of Montreal and upper New York; in the flour-milling area comprising Winnipeg, the Twin Cities, and Lake of the Woods; and in the great blend of mining, forest exploitation, specialized farming, and commercial fisheries near the international boundary in the Rocky Mountain and Pacific regions. In all these areas, and on the wheat-growing prairies, there was a good deal of seasonal migration of workers, as well as a willingness to ignore the boundary in taking up new ventures. Around Niagara and Detroit, however, there were, in addition, thousands of "border commuters," that is, men who habitually lived in one country and worked in the other. A large proportion of them were men who happened to have established themselves on one side of the line, but who, for a great variety of reasons, found that they could sell their skills for a higher price on the other.

A considerable number of the "border commuters" lived in Canada because it was less difficult to get alcoholic beverages there. The severity of the American prohibition enforcement from January, 1920, to March, 1933, meant that smuggled liquor was expensive and "home-brew" was bad. In Canada the nature of the federal constitution had allowed Quebec to draw back from the very brink of the national war-induced prohibition at the end of 1918, and permitted the manufacture, if not the sale, of spirits, beer, and wine in the other provinces. The success of the Quebec Government's retail monopoly, the inevitable "leakage" of the Canadian-manufactured beverages, sometimes after their alleged legal export to the United States, and the deterioration of public order which accompanied "bootlegging," produced a turnabout in Canada after 1924. By 1927 the governments of most of the provinces were controlling, and profiting from, the legal sale of alcoholic beverages.

The discrepancies between the two countries in this matter inevitably produced trouble along the border, in spite of the provisions of a treaty for search and seizure which was concluded in 1924. Rumrunning became a large enterprise, involving on the part of both American and Canadian nationals huge investments, small armies of agents, and extensive official corruption. In opposing it both governments spent large amounts of public money. On balance, however, Canada undoubtedly profited materially from making it easier for Americans to break their own laws, which somewhat tarnished her legal triumph over the United States in the most spectacular incident of many, the American sinking of the Canadian schooner *I'm Alone*, some two hundred miles out to sea. It is worth remembering, however, that, after 1930, when the Dominion largely succeeded in strangling the traffic, it and its profits were merely transferred to French St. Pierre and Miquelon, and also that the agents who smuggled liquors out of Canada cheated the Canadian Treasury on an enormous scale for over ten years by smuggling back into Canada commodities which were subject to high duties and excise, even including cheap American industrial alcohol for the Canadian bootlegging trade.[18]

The Canadian "oases" in "dry" North America undoubtedly intensified an already strong American tendency to seek recreation in Canada. The movement was an old one, much accelerated just before the Civil War by improved railroad facilities and by steamboats on the Great Lakes and St. Lawrence. The inexpensive motor car converted it into a common American habit. All parts of Canada, even the remote Mackenzie Basin, Hudson Bay, and the Arctic, went into the tourist business by building roads and hotels, or by providing other facilities. The resultant influx of Americans had agreeable effects on Canada's international balance of payments, for the Americans characteristically spent about twice as much in Canada, summer and winter, as the Canadians did on their winter pilgrimages to California and Florida, or on their visits to the great American cities.[19] During the depression year 1931–1932, accord-

18. As revealed during the customs scandal and investigation of 1926–1928.
19. This proportion takes account of the statistical error in the Canadian estimates which was discovered in 1940. See *Canada Year Book* (Ottawa, 1941), pp. 475–476.

ing to rather incomplete border records, Canadians paid some 10,500,000 visits to the United States, and Americans about twice as many to Canada, that is, there were at least 30,000,000 border-crossings in all.

This striking movement of tourists, since it offered little challenge to the forces of isolationism, had been allowed to persist. The involved processes which were gradually brought into play against outright change of residence were a different matter. Their beginning during the War of 1914 lay in American fears that the Republic, with no more free lands and with much unemployed production, would be inundated by a tide of millions fleeing from war-wracked Europe. In 1917 a bill establishing a literacy test and some other limitations had become law over Wilson's veto, the first substantial product of various campaigns for restriction which had been going on since 1882. Once Wilson was out of the way the Act of May, 1921, limited admissions from European, Australasian, Near Eastern, or African countries to three per cent of the total number of persons born in the country in question and residing in the United States in 1910, thus allowing about 350,000 such admissions annually or about a third of the prewar average. The more drastic Act of 1924, designed even more sharply to favor British, Irish, German, and Scandinavian stock over southern and eastern European, went back to the 1890 ratios of foreign-born nationals and reduced the percentage to two, or about 160,000 persons a year.[20] In 1929, under a clause of the 1924 Act, a flat annual total of 150,000 admissions was established to be allotted according to the ratios of national *origins* of the whole population as revealed in the Census of 1920.

Superficially these laws did not apply to Canada, but in practice their results were so profound as to eclipse in the memories of Canadians the more crucial ordeal through which they had gone between 1873 and 1896.[21] Canada had been exercising a mild selective process among intending immigrants since 1918, not in terms of national origins, but of literacy, capital resources, and aptitude for occupations in Canada where the demand for labor was greater than the supply. Under these regulations and responding to the partial transfer of the Atlantic Migration from the United States to Canada, the average admissions from 1919 to 1930, inclusive, amounted to 123,000 a year. This total of almost a million and a half seemed a respectable addition to the eight and three-quarter millions of population at the end of the war, but appearances were deceptive. Thanks to the shaping of the new American immigration

20. It was this Act which deeply offended Japan by its blunt exclusion of Japanese immigrants.

21. See above, pp. 221–224.

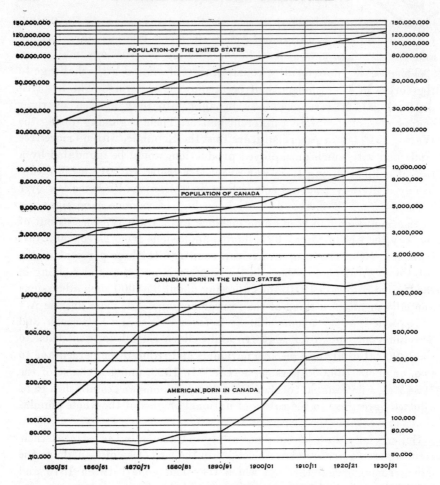

Population of the United States and Canada: 1850/51 to 1930/31

(Bureau of the Census, Washington)

laws, Canada might be gaining population from Europe, but the same laws were draining off her population to the United States at such a rate that she suffered on balance a loss of over a million persons from her potential population during the decade 1921–1930.[22] It was the character of these emigrants which made their loss particularly hard to bear.

Immediately after the war the Canadian depression had lasted two years longer than the American. When the American recovery began in 1921 the renewed appetite for labor could not be satisfied by the quotas of

22. A small proportion of this loss was accounted for by returns to Europe.

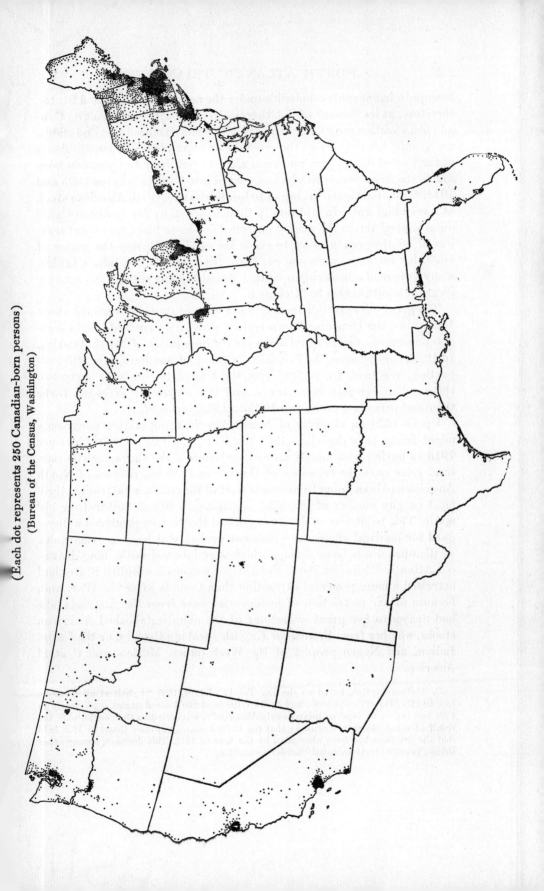

(Each dot represents 250 Canadian-born persons)
(Bureau of the Census, Washington)

European immigrants admissible under the new laws. The United States, therefore, as its "boom" of the 'twenties developed, began to act on Canada like a suction pump, particularly in the industrialized east and middle west. Unfortunately, from the general Canadian point of view, the doors of the United States were now open almost exclusively to Canadian-born and to the American-born who had poured into Canada between 1895 and 1914.[23] Canada, therefore, began to lose her native North American stock at a very high rate. In addition to these losses many foreign-born Canadians slipped across the weakly patrolled border or hired the expert services of bootleggers in order to evade the officials. During the winter of 1923, for instance, when the St. Clair River was frozen into a bridge, many owners of motor cars operated almost regular services in carrying illegal entrants across to Michigan.

The great outward tide from Canada was not slowed down until about 1926, when the Dominion's own revived prosperity enabled her to compete on somewhat more equal terms for the population of North America. In 1926, for instance, the Dominion, although Canadians were still emigrating, regained, by return from the United States, over sixty-two thousand of her lost inhabitants, and this movement averaged forty thousand persons a year from 1925 to 1930, inclusive.

Up to 1930 an observer of North American population movements might fairly have described the Canadian-American relationship since 1918 as having been merely an odd variation of the characteristic pattern. Ever since the founding of Halifax in 1749 the peoples of North America had been going to whatever part of the continent attracted them most on any number of grounds—economic, political, cultural, or climatic. This habit was so deeply ingrained that it had produced a disregard for political allegiance which was probably at least as remarkable as the uprootings from Europe which were involved in the long-drawn-out Atlantic Migration itself. For various reasons the United States had exercised a more powerful attraction than Canada after the War, and, because of her restriction of immigration save from the Americas, she had drawn to her great accretions of the oldest-established American stocks, whether from French- or English-speaking Canada, or the Latin, Indian, and Negro peoples of the West Indies, Mexico, and Central America.

23. The assumption, based on the Jay Treaty of 1794, that "it shall at all times be free to His Majesty's subjects, and to the citizens of the United States . . . freely to pass and repass by land or inland navigation etc." was carried to the courts, with the result (*United States* v. *Karnuth*) that the United States Supreme Court in 1928 held that the privilege had been abrogated by the War of 1812. This decision, among other things, practically terminated "border commuting."

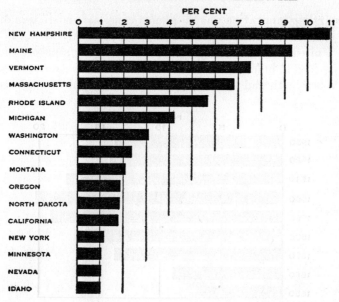

Percentage of Population Canadian-Born, by States: 1930
(Bureau of the Census, Washington)

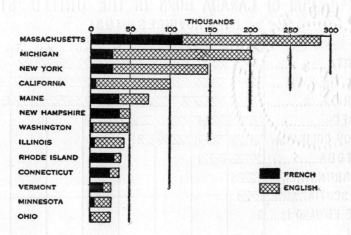

Canadian-Born, French and English, for 13 Selected States: 1930
(Bureau of the Census, Washington)

The startling innovation was the almost complete prohibition of immigration and international migration in 1930. In that year both Canada and the United States, stricken with ever-mounting numbers of unemployed, decided to hold their own for their own and to keep out nearly all others. When birth and citizenship tests were applied to applicants for

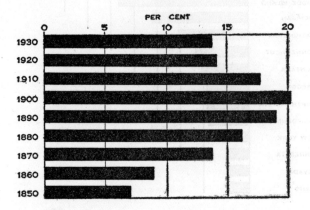

Percentage of All Canadian-Born Who Were in the United States: 1850 to 1930

(Bureau of the Census, Washington)

POPULATION OF CANADA BORN IN THE UNITED STATES
BY PROVINCES, 1931

(Dominion Bureau of Statistics, Ottawa)

poor relief, thousands of persons who had become public charges were repatriated north and south across the border, as well as to Europe and elsewhere.[24] Many illegal entrants to the United States were discovered and, in cases where these had once acquired Canadian domicile or similar standing, they were likely to be returned to Canada. The two governments worked in harmony during these readjustments, for their policies were essentially the same. They even worked out controls for non-Americans who wanted to use Canada as a way station pending quota admission to the United States. So far as can be learned the exchange of population between the United States and Canada has been almost negligible since 1930, with the movement enlarging the Canadian population down to 1936 and the American since that date.

Not all the movements can be learned, for the simple reason that neither country maintained a close patrol of the whole border. Since 1938 the proportions of unrecorded border crossings have probably been small enough to be negligible, but during the grim drought which devastated the North American dry-farming area from 1929 to 1937 or 1938 the movement must have been substantial, for abandoned farms marred the wheat belt from Texas to the Prairie Provinces. The hundreds of thousands of persons who were dislodged by this great catastrophe either flocked to the cities or sought better-watered regions, usually within the mountains, on the Pacific slope, or in the Peace River district of northern Alberta. Having loaded what they could into their motor vehicles (sometimes drawn by horses) or wagons, they took to the road, and they were little inclined to go out of the way to observe border formalities. Since there were more big cities in the United States than in Canada, higher subsidized prices for farm products, better roads, and lower passes through the mountains, the fair supposition is that more Canadian refugees from drought entered the United States than vice versa.

Recently the official statisticians of population in Canada and the United States—R. H. Coats, M. C. MacLean, and L. E. Truesdell—have worked out and recorded in great and interesting detail the measurements of the international migrations since 1850. From these it is possible to present a numerical picture of the final, "frozen," outcome of the last century of North American mingling.

In 1930 the number of Canadian-born in the United States was about one-sixth as great as the native population in Canada. Three and a third million persons of Canadian birth or Canadian parentage, living in the United States, represented a quarter of the total Canadian stock (by

24. In 1931 Canada began to lose population to the United Kingdom and has continued to do so in small proportions.

birth and parentage) in North America. About one-third of them were French. Over seven-eighths of the Canadian-born emigrants lived in the States along the border, with southward projections down the Atlantic Coast to New York, and down the Pacific Coast to California. Detroit, with 95,000 Canadian-born residents, was closely followed by Boston and New York. On the opposite side of the ledger, 345,000 American-born constituted in 1931 the largest single non-British immigrant group in Canada and about 30 per cent of all foreign-born residents. They were widely and evenly distributed over Canada and they were both more rural and became naturalized much more readily than Canadians in the United States. American stock in Canada (about 820,000 by birth and parentage) represented less than one-fourth of one per cent of the total on the continent. Interestingly enough, both the Americans in Canada and the Canadians in the United States stood appreciably above the general population in material, educational, and professional ways.

Canadians customarily speak of this situation as a "national deficit" or a "cruel loss," yet these terms invite criticism. Indeed it can be argued that the Canadians who stayed at home may literally have gained because one-quarter of their stock went to live in the United States. The explanation is to be found in the maintenance and improvement of the North American standard of living. Largely because of their immense financial obligations for the systems of transportation which alone can bind the Dominion together, Canadians have normally enjoyed a slightly lower standard of living than Americans. Yet as long as the Republic lay open to them, the discrepancy could be kept small because those who found opportunity lacking at home could move to the United States and by their departure release some of the pressure upon opportunity and remuneration in Canada. The middle and older generations of Canadians today, in almost any occupation, can recall the kind of relief that was felt when some one of their co-workers created a vacancy by leaving for the United States; and the officers of many a Canadian university, when they have reckoned up the destinations of their graduates, have felt less anxiety about their overproduction of professionally trained persons, because so many of them have been able to find employment south of the border. Now that the Republic is no longer a safety valve for "surplus" Canadian population, time may reveal some unexpected consequences of the novel ban on interchange of population which was laid down in 1930.

The nations of the earth seem to have reached the limits of withdrawal into their own shells during 1930 and 1931, and already there were signs that these policies of *sauve qui peut* meant the return of war. The vacuums which had been created in the arena of world politics by passive evasions of collective responsibility plainly invited inthrusts of irresponsible aggression. The passion for national economic self-sufficiency, by wrecking the world economy, had created tensions so severe as to make revolution certain in some places and with difficulty avertible in others. The substantial stoppages of human migration across the face of the globe had dammed up energies which threatened to vent themselves in violent ways.

The United States and Canada, perhaps the most fortunate nations on earth, had played conspicuous parts in the disintegration of the world community, and they could not expect to escape the consequences by shutting their eyes and exulting in their geographical insulation. Between them they had not only distorted their own natural relationships, but had forced Great Britain into uncongenial paths as well. Within Canada, French-Canadian particularism, whose most extreme form was now a demand for secession from the Dominion and for the creation of the separate state of "Laurentia," was making English-speaking Canadians exaggerate either their Britonism or their Americanism. The circle of vain flight from responsibility for achieving an over-all Canadianism was completed when the orthodox French-Canadian *élite*, repelled by modern French culture and fearing the prestige of American ways among the masses, sought their enhancement from the Vatican. Yet, at the same time, these three Canadian quests for spiritual reënforcement, when added to more material gropings for outside alliance, indicated that by 1932 Canada had realized the perils of trying to stand alone, and was ready to act accordingly. Her great neighbor, largely because she felt so strong even in depression, had a long, hard row to hoe before her people would admit that isolation meant destruction.

CHAPTER XVI

MAELSTROM

(1932–1942)

As we approach the present our inferences grow more and more subject to distortion. Circumstances which bear one kind of fruit in tranquillity yield another kind in days of apprehension and still another in time of war. Secrecy and censorship veil huge areas of behavior so thoroughly that the same group of known events can be put together in half-a-dozen explanatory patterns, none of which will remain completely valid twenty-five years from now, and some of which will appear ridiculous. Any attempt to make the course of events intelligible, therefore, is like an exercise in algebra where the values of many of the components are unknown and where even time-tested formulas produce at best tentative results.

In 1931 a number of man-made whirlpools on the earth's surface started a series of mad gyrations which ended up ten or eleven years later with the whole globe drawn into one gigantic maelstrom of war. In these processes the United States and Canada played stubbornly separate parts until the dominant forces submerged their differences and drew them both into vigorous collaboration with Great Britain. During the prelude, however, the interplay of similarities and differences, and their varying degrees of intensity, produced a puzzling picture, and it is likely to be many years before the full significance becomes apparent of how Canada, the most dependent of the three nations, was both attracted and repelled by the other two.

The two North American peoples seemed practically identical to the casual visitor of 1931 or 1932. In general they were of the same human stock except for their proportions of French and Negro elements. They lived in the same kinds of dwellings, relished the same foods and drinks, dressed alike, drove the same kinds of cars, and used the same household appliances. They both played and watched the same games—golf, bridge, baseball, hockey, and water sports. New York was their theatrical capital, and New York plays "on the road" always visited Canada. Canadian conductors led American orchestras and vice versa. Hollywood exported its films but imported Canadian players, singers, and technicians. In 1932 Canadians in self-protection set up their own national radio broadcasting commission, but it could not drown out sound waves from the United States for those who preferred them, and anyway the best productions on either side of the boundary were freely "piped" by telephone to be rebroadcast on the other.

Great movements of advanced students signalized the cultural interplay. Under a well-informed provincial system of scholarships, young men and women from Quebec studied everything from agriculture and forestry to library and museum administration in the United States. English-speaking Canadians could be found in all fields of scholarship at the better American universities from Atlantic to Pacific. Americans filled the quotas which were open to them for professional training in medicine and dentistry at Halifax, Montreal, and Toronto. They visited Nova Scotia to study coöperatives, Quebec for language and theology, Montreal for Gregorian chant and plain song, and Toronto for such varied pursuits as medieval studies and Chinese archaeology. Winnipeg was the publishing center of the continent for Icelandic and Ukrainian belles lettres. The teaching faculties in most of the great institutions of higher learning in both countries drew upon both.

American philanthropy disregarded the boundary line. The rich foundations established by Carnegie, Guggenheim, and Rockefeller directed their funds as freely and skilfully over Canada as over the United States. Their most conspicuous contributions were made to education, whether in medical and other scientific schools, coöperatives, assistance to learned societies and to individual scholars, or in the publication of original studies for whose support the smaller country lacked a sufficient public.

Yet in spite of these and many other circumstances, the negative, preponderant essence of being a Canadian quite naturally amounted largely to the assertion that one was not an American; indeed to be an orthodox French Canadian meant rejection of identity with the United States, English-speaking Canada, France, and Great Britain. Only Rome could enhance the emotional satisfactions of saying "*je suis canadien.*" For most English-speaking Canadians, the same enhancement was derived half-consciously from an emphasis on real or imaginary Britonism. Neither of these reliances boded much good for an embracing Canadianism, but the United States was potentially so overpowering a neighbor that Canadians had to seek reënforcement where they could. The angry Canadian patriots who castigated their fellow countrymen for being "colonially-minded" were themselves often dodging the admission that in an unfriendly world Canada was not strong enough in herself to disdain reënforcement.

Trade unionism provides a good example of this medley of forces.

Speaking generally the Canadian movement, though comparatively weak, was part of the international American Federation of Labor. Yet anyone familiar with its workings could not fail to notice that many of its leaders had either been brought up in the tradition of nineteenth-century British trade unionism or had become indoctrinated with its orthodoxies, with the result that Canadian activities lagged behind both British and American developments. A further complication arose from the existence in Quebec, Canada's largest store of industrial workers, of the quite distinct Catholic trade unions, which were modeled on Continental European workers' associations, and which the Church endeavored to keep close to the principles of the Papal Encyclical *Rerum Novarum* of 1891 until *Quadragesimo Anno* necessitated a shifting after 1931.

The emergence of the American Committee for Industrial Organization in 1936–1937, and its exciting successes in unionizing the steel, rubber, textile, and automotive industries, meant that it speedily came to represent more than half of "international" Canadian unionism. Both industry and public authority quite quickly came to terms with the C.I.O. in Michigan, but in Ontario the Prime Minister, M. F. Hepburn, took a different attitude, with the backing of those who feared that the movement would spread to the mining industry and upset the stock market. The details of the struggle, while spectacular, were not nearly so significant as Hepburn's chosen stand. "The issue," he said, "is whether foreign agitators . . . were to attain their goal of smashing our export business." This attempt to capitalize anti-Americanism failed to prevent General Motors of Canada from making the same sort of settlement with its workers as General Motors Corporation made in the United States, but it was the kind of appeal that would always win at least some Canadian support.[1]

For four or five years after the earthquakes of 1931 in the world economy, both the United States and Canada were obsessed by domestic concerns, particularly after the election of 1932 had brought Franklin D. Roosevelt to the Presidency. He and his Administration very swiftly embarked on a host of experiments which were designed to galvanize the moribund American economy into life again. Not only did these preclude American coöperation in the World Economic Conference of 1933 and therefore nullify its efforts, but they had such widespread effects in Canada that the Dominion had to delay and otherwise modify its own experiments for recovery until the American whirlwinds had somewhat died

1. It had been used in May, 1919, during and after an almost general strike in Winnipeg, and has been a characteristic weapon against Canadian trade unionism, particularly in the metal-mining industry.

down. One revealing aspect of the Roosevelt Administration's enterprises was that a good many of them were talked over in advance with W. D. Herridge, the Canadian Minister at Washington, in order to obtain the critical responses of an understanding, yet detached, North American. Another important consideration was that countless Canadians made a habit of listening by radio to Roosevelt's campaign speeches and to his Presidential discussions of his nation's and the world's affairs. His brilliant mastery of the new entry to the minds of millions meant that he provoked in Canada as well as in his own country many a dream of a "New Deal" for the "forgotten man."

Roosevelt's policies seemed revolutionary because they were immediate and urgent, but they amounted largely to the attempted creation of an even national plateau of social legislation and economic controls by correcting the lags, and eliminating the discrepancies, which existed among the states. The underlying foundation was to be substantial economic self-sufficiency. After centuries of supposed devotion to "rugged individualism," the United States was now hurrying into substantial conformity with the welfare state as worked out in Germany, Great Britain, and Scandinavia. In particular, the British statute book was raided on a wholesale scale and Americans versed in these matters were called to Washington.[2]

The effects upon Canada of some of Roosevelt's domestic policies were singularly far-reaching. The devaluation of the American dollar by 40 per cent launched an already expanding Canadian gold-mining industry into a tremendous boom, and facilitated the foundation in 1935 of the Bank of Canada as an instrument for regulating the national economy. The great apparatus of industrial codes and labor regulations which was reared upon the National Recovery and Wagner-Connery acts of 1933 and 1935 had immediate consequences in Canada, both by compelling a degree of parallel adjustment and by raising American production costs above Canadian for commodities, like lumber, which entered the world market. The lavish "pump-priming," or program of public works, because of its demand for construction materials, inevitably spilled some of its largesse into Canada. The repeal of prohibition instantly created a gaping market for Canadian brews and distillates. The conservation program and the Civilian Conservation Corps provided models which Canadian politicians could not afford to ignore.

On the other side of the ledger the Tennessee Valley Authority obvi-

2. Secretary of Labor Frances Perkins, Professor Felix Frankfurter, and members of the "Brain Trust," which grew out of an old association between Columbia University and the New York State Government during the governorships of A. E. Smith and F. D. Roosevelt, were conspicuous examples.

ously owed much to the long-established Ontario Hydro-Electric Power Commission. The remarkably successful record of the latter had disturbed the trade association of American private electrical utilities so thoroughly that they had paid a distinguished Canadian professor of economics a large fee to publish a blistering attack upon it. The same interests, in alliance with the protectors of the business created by the Port of New York, formed the core of successful resistance to ratification by Congress of the Treaty of July 18, 1932, with Canada, for the deepening of the St. Lawrence Waterway in order to permit the access of ocean vessels to the Great Lakes and the development of very large amounts of electrical power under public authority.

From 1933 onward it became clear that not only did American economic recovery benefit Canada, but Canadians expected a New Deal of their own. Mr. Bennett tried to secure a new lease on power in 1935 by a bold program of this sort which he worked out in collaboration with Mr. Herridge, his brother-in-law.[3] For reasons of haste, ill-health, and dictatorial temperament, Bennett managed this so badly as to split his own party and to present a perfect target for the more astute gradualist, W. L. Mackenzie King.[4] Frightened Conservatives became Liberals over night, and, in October, 1935, Mr. King came into office again with a large majority. His margin of safety and his new allies seemed to encourage his general inclination to wait and see.

In accordance with an ancient Liberal tradition, however, he made an exception so far as loosening up international trade was concerned, and here the American Reciprocal Trade Treaties Act of 1934 created an opportunity which Mr. Bennett's Government had explored with great thoroughness, but with insufficient willingness to run risks.[5] Meanwhile it was clear to the American Secretary of State, Cordell Hull, that, if his cherished new statute was to amount to anything substantial, it must be applied quickly to relations with the United States' best customers of pre-depression days, Canada and Great Britain. Thanks to this sense of urgency and to the very thorough preparatory work done with Canada, a new trade treaty emerged promptly after the Canadian election of 1935. In it the executive branches of the two governments had made much more systematic and genuinely reciprocal adjustments than the legislatures had achieved during recent years. American tariffs were somewhat scaled down, and Canada abandoned the devices which had been adopted from

3. Whence the charge against Bennett of "drawing a Red Herridge across the trail."
4. Judicial review later demonstrated that most of the program exceeded the powers of the Federal Government.
5. The Act was designed to provide outlets for the influence of American price-raising on world prices.

1930 onward in order to protect dollar exchange by diminishing purchases from the United States. The more important effects of the Treaty
were to make easier American sales to Canada of farm implements, auto-
mobiles, electrical apparatus, gasoline, and machinery; and Canadian
sales to the United States of lumber, cattle, dairy products, fresh and
frozen fish, whisky, and potatoes. Even so, both countries' average rates
were still far above those of the days before the Hawley-Smoot Tariff.

In effect, by means of the treaty of 1935 with Canada, the United
States had begun to break her way into the British imperial edifice which
had been erected at the Ottawa Conference of 1932. This became clear
when Secretary Hull swung his forces toward negotiating a trade treaty
with the United Kingdom. It took three years to achieve this end, partly
because the Ottawa treaties had a term of five years, and partly because
Canada and other Dominions had built up positions in the British market
which they were loath to lose. Not only did Great Britain work out new
"Ottawa" agreements with other members of the Commonwealth during
1937 and 1938, but the United States had to make a new treaty with
Canada and Canada a new one with Great Britain before an American
treaty with the United Kingdom was practicable. The greatest triangular
exchange of commodities in the world had thus been "frozen" in patterns
of reciprocal advantage by three carefully drawn treaties at the end of
1938.

Two statements by the members of the Royal Commission on Dominion-
Provincial Relations, whose *Report* of 1940 is a landmark in the history
of federalism as well as in Canadian history, aptly summarize the economic aspects of the triangular relationship of today.

Canadian trade with both the United Kingdom and the United States is of a
complementary nature, and is a classic example of a basically sound division of
labour. While Canadian cereals feed Britain, British textiles clothe Canadians;
while Canadian products of the forest and mine, processed by hydro-electric
power, feed the industries of the United States, the coal and iron products of
the United States equip Canadian factories.

Canada's position is similar to that of a small man sitting in a big poker
game. He must play for the full stakes, but with only a fraction of the capital
resources of his two substantial opponents; if he wins, his profits in relation to
his capital are very large, and if he loses, he may be cleaned out.

It is now apparent that the obsession with which every nation in the
world was pursuing its individual domestic concerns after 1929 was both
a cause of, and an encouragement to, the defiant challenges to world
order which were uttered very soon afterward by Japan, Italy, and Ger-

many. All three countries were peculiarly vulnerable to the abrupt termination of international lending, the drying-up of world trade, and the efforts to achieve or to impose a high degree of economic self-sufficiency in most of the administrative divisions of the world. The narrow-mindedness and poverty which these policies produced in turn accelerated a deterioration in willingness among the Powers to combine for the protection of the weak and for the processes of peaceful change.

A military group in Japan was the first[6] to sound out the possibilities of the world situation by invading Manchuria in 1931 and by embarking on a campaign of assassination and terrorization against the liberal elements of their own nation whose behavior had been so praiseworthy since 1921. They quickly discovered that they need not worry about domestic resistance or foreign reminders of Japan's League and treaty obligations. Although the Hoover Administration was sufficiently disturbed to enter upon open collaboration with the League, and Secretary of State Stimson gave notice that the United States would not recognize changes effected by means alien to the Pact of Paris, American public opinion could not be rallied behind an effort to check Japanese aggression by force. Stimson's attempts to secure British support by transatlantic telephone conversations with Sir John Simon, invoking the Nine-Power Treaty of 1922, were ineffective because Britons did not think that they could count on American action, and because the National Government of Great Britain was trying to keep Japan in the League by shutting its eyes to the doings of the Manchuria Gang. In 1932 the Japanese militarists exposed the bankruptcy of collective security still further by bombing and burning Shanghai, with a sickening total of civilian casualties, and by setting up the puppet state of Manchukuo.

Canada's behavior in this matter exposed her weaknesses. Public opinion, reënforced by sentiments derived from Canada's large missionary establishments in China, was overwhelmingly anti-Japanese and confident that the League could bring Japan to book. This was clearly reflected by Sir George Perley, the principal Canadian delegate to the special Assembly of the League which was summoned to meet at China's request. Doubts which arose subsequently because of obvious British diffidence were reenforced when C. H. Cahan, Canadian delegate to the following Assembly, made a speech which followed Sir John Simon's line of giving conspicuously full consideration to Japan's case. There was an immediate outcry in Canada, but it dwindled into bewildered impotence when the Bennett Government at Ottawa and at Geneva carefully avoided taking a stand

6. The undeclared war of 1929 between China and Russia in Manchuria was an exception to Russia's unaggressive attitude from 1917 onward and was quickly terminated.

which might involve forceful sanctions against Japan. Canada obviously could not act alone, but she might have been more courageously faithful to the substantial group of smaller Powers in the League who were trying to draw attention to the writing on the wall.

In retrospect the year 1932 seems to have been characterized generally by retreats into isolated quasi neutrality on the part of the Powers which might still have combined to operate orderly machinery for the adjustment of international rivalries. These retreats became a rout during the ensuing six years. While a series of Conservative governments in Great Britain, the Roosevelt administrations in the United States, and both Conservative and Liberal governments in Canada earnestly sought methods of avoiding foreign commitments, the futility of this procedure was ever more confidently exposed by the international brigands who had seized power in Japan, Italy, and Germany.

Much of the success of President Roosevelt's "Good Neighbor" or "Hemisphere" Policy[7] can best be understood in this light, although it was also designed to be a gradual reëducation of an isolationist American public in some of the realities of world politics. Roosevelt would do his best to combine the Americas in a common defense of their neutrality against the storms which were brewing in Asia and Europe, and thereby gain time while the compulsions of power politics upon the United States were revealing themselves.

The same kind of putting off, and yet preparing for, the evil day was apparent within a divided Canada, perhaps most clearly in a small group of French-Canadian political leaders. Their statesmanship was forced to embrace both an understanding of the trend of international affairs and the realization that most of their own people were still so self-centered because of their sense of oppression in Canada that they had made little progress toward becoming citizens of the world. They and English-speaking Canadians were caught in a vicious circle, for the flat contrast between their instinctive attitudes to Great Britain accentuated itself in any crisis, and the majority group was never able to believe that the intense, sincere nationalism of the French Canadians really did extend beyond Quebec and include Canada as a whole. If the imaginations of English-speaking Canadians did extend that far, they were likely to be alienated by the explicit frankness of French-Canadian criticisms of British foreign policy. Such men as Ernest Lapointe, upon whom Lau-

7. "In the field of world policy I would dedicate this Nation to the policy of the good neighbor" (First Inaugural Address, March 4, 1933). This principle had been invoked for relations between the United States and British North America in Jay's Treaty of 1794.

rier's mantle seemed to have descended, had therefore to emphasize continuously the complete freedom of action which Canada possessed, in order to make all possible progress toward unity within Canada before the coming world ordeal. Lapointe described it as an independence which neither accepted nor sought to impose domination, but he avoided the implication that Canada's withdrawal was a luxury which could not last. Prime Minister King's realization of this situation after he came into power in 1935 intensified the cautiousness of his Government in foreign affairs.

An added complication in Canada arose from the French Canadians' recourse to their Roman Catholic tradition as a protection against contamination from English-speaking Canada and the United States, both of whom they believed to be almost completely Protestant or materialistic. During the depression they had been subjected to skilful propaganda from Italian consular officers and others which aimed to give the impression that Italian Fascist corporatism was a sincere attempt to create the organic society which had been advocated by St. Thomas Aquinas, toward which Pope Leo XIII had urged the faithful in a series of encyclicals and letters between 1879 and 1900, and which Pius XI had reaffirmed in *Quadragesimo Anno* in 1931.[8] These Catholic and corporatist leanings, coupled with the general disinclination among Canadians to accept commitments abroad which might engender war, played a considerable part in the King Government's disavowal of Dr. W. A. Riddell, the Canadian representative at Geneva who late in 1935 proposed that the League add oil, coal, and iron to the embargo list imposed on Italy for her defiant attack on Abyssinia.[9] They also help to explain why French Canadians overwhelmingly favored Franco and the rebels in the Spanish Civil War, even after it became clear that Italy and Germany had subordinated his cause to their own.

In neither case could Canadian boldness in behalf of collective security derive any encouragement from the behavior of France, Great Britain, or the United States. In the Abyssinian affair the League had its last chance, and it lost it largely because of the cowardice of the British Government.[10] The American Congress responded to the Abyssinian crisis by hastily passing a neutrality act. Hitler sized up the situation accurately

8. The letter *Graves de communi,* which seriously modified the policy of *Rerum Novarum* of 1891, was of January, 1902.

9. He and the King Government had been in a sense committed to the imposition of sanctions by the stand taken earlier by G. H. Ferguson in behalf of the Bennett Government.

10. This view assumes that the Baldwin Government in the United Kingdom chose to misinterpret or misdirect the amazing popular unanimity in favor of vigorous League action which was expressed in the so-called Peace Poll of 1935.

in what would otherwise have been his suicidal military reoccupation of the Rhineland. While he and Mussolini went on to assure Franco's success, France, Great Britain, and the United States met the appeals of the lawful Spanish Government by abandoning their rights to assist it. Mr. King frankly told Parliament on June 18, 1936, what he thought of Canada's position. "There are obvious limitations," he said, "to the amount of pressure a small and distant country, not primarily responsible for what may be the outcome of the League decisions, can apply."

At that time, there was little light or leading for Canada to be had from the United States, for 1936 was an election year and the American State Department was still busy laying the foundations of the Hemisphere Policy. Largely because of the transcendent importance of the Panama Canal in the American outlook, this policy had as yet seemed to ignore Canada except for some gestures of courtesy by both Hoover and Roosevelt which were designed to eradicate the unhappy memories of President Coolidge's unimaginative refusals to take Canada seriously.[11] Ever since Ambassador Morrow's mission to Mexico of 1927–1928 the United States had been building up a record of having abandoned imperialistic aggression in favor of multilateral negotiations under inter-American auspices. Hoover's goodwill tour of Latin America during the winter of 1928–1929 had been followed by a series of withdrawals and readjustments, and Roosevelt carried on the process.

At the Inter-American Conference of 1933 at Montevideo, the United States assisted greatly in securing the unanimous adoption of a resolution affirming that no state had the right to intervene in the internal or external affairs of another. In 1934 the Platt Amendment authorizing American intervention in Cuba was dropped, the Marine Corps withdrew from Haiti, and a more equitable treaty with Panama was signed.[12] A natural climax was reached when, after his victory at the polls in November, 1936, President Roosevelt journeyed all the way to an Inter-American Conference at Buenos Aires and there proposed the Pan-Americanization of the Monroe Doctrine. Although this was too big a meal for immediate digestion, it was characteristic of a defensive policy for the United States and Latin America.

Canada had never responded to a variety of suggestions that she enroll herself in the Pan-American organization. An occasional French Cana-

11. The incidents, which brought about the resignation of the first American Minister to Canada, were related to Coolidge's refusal to establish an appropriate Legation at Ottawa or return ceremonial visits.

12. By an Act of March, 1934, accepted by the Philippine legislature in May, the United States initiated what was to be the complete independence of the Philippines at the end of ten years.

dian had explored the possible reënforcement to be had from collaboration with Latin and Catholic countries, but most Canadians were either
unacquainted with what had been going on or felt that their associations
in the League and the British Commonwealth were sufficient. Habitually
alert to American aggression, Canadians had been receptive to old Latin
American charges that the Pan-American policies of the United States
had been a cloak for imperialism and for plans of hegemony. The ghosts
of Blaine and Theodore Roosevelt still walked. At any rate a trial balloon
sent up by Franklin Roosevelt in the course of a speech at Chautauqua on
August 14, 1936, was almost completely ignored except by French-Canadian isolationists. The President had said there that the United States
could and would, if necessary, defend itself and defend its neighborhood.

In plain fact Japan, Italy, and Germany had thrown the rest of the
world on the defensive by the end of 1936 and were rapidly achieving an
interdependence among themselves which made the alleged believers in
collective security seem very inept indeed. The policy of the Axis Powers
became one of accentuating the isolationism of other nations either by
lavish cultivation of dissension and mistrust, or by picking their outright
victims from among the weaker nations whose individual fates, they calculated, would not evoke decisive responses from France, Great Britain,
Russia, or the United States. China, Abyssinia, Spain, Austria, Czechoslovakia—this was the calendar of their successes by the end of 1938.
France, torn by internal dissension, was already becoming a negligible
obstacle, except in so far as she could be stiffened by Great Britain. Great
Britain had descended to unimagined humiliation in Neville Chamberlain's search for "a general scheme of appeasement" (February 21,
1938) and in his huckstering abandonment of Czechoslovakia. Russia
was enigmatic and was being repaid for her past record of exciting mistrust by being largely ignored in negotiations among the greater European Powers. The United States was an incalculable factor lurking behind several neutrality laws,[13] the doctrine of nonrecognition, and the
Atlantic and Pacific oceans.

While it is difficult to find any substantial justification for the foreign
policy of Baldwin, Simon, and Hoare between 1931 and 1937, it can be
argued that from the spring of 1937 onward Prime Minister Chamberlain
was playing for time while a feverish rearmament program sought to
regain a little of the enormous ground which had been lost since systematic disarmament began in 1921. After the Munich dismemberment of
Czechoslovakia in September, 1938, however, British public opinion

13. Notably those of August, 1935; February, 1936; and May, 1937. The Johnson Act
against loans to defaulting debtors was of 1934.

would tolerate no further retreat. When Hitler broke his bargain by forcibly incorporating Czechoslovakia in March, 1939, and Mussolini pocketed Albania, the British Prime Minister was forced to set up some boundary to German territorial expansion and to declare unequivocally that transgression of it would mean war. Among other limits he chose the frontiers of Poland. Hitler, having on August 22 isolated Poland by a nonaggression pact with Russia, chose to defy him on September 1, 1939. Great Britain and France declared war on September 3. Canada followed suit seven days later. President Roosevelt proclaimed the neutrality of the United States on September 5, fulfilled his obligations under the neutrality acts, and told his people: "I hope the United States will keep out of this war. I believe that it will. And I give you assurances that every effort of your government will be directed toward that end."

During the Czechoslovakian crisis of 1938 President Roosevelt had opened an international bridge in the Thousand Islands and had received an honorary degree from Queen's University, near by in Kingston, Ontario. He seized upon this occasion to make more precise his earlier declaration at Chautauqua. "The Dominion of Canada," he said on August 18, "is part of the sisterhood of the British Empire. I give to you assurance that the people of the United States will not stand idly by if domination of Canadian soil is threatened by any other Empire."[14] The question arises, therefore, why the Parliament of Canada, free to choose its own course, with American protection assured, and with about 30 per cent of the population traditionally opposed to "foreign" war, should have ratified a declaration of war without a division after less than two days of debate.

There had been little certain forewarning of this result in the record of any Canadian political party or large organized group during the past nine years.[15] Mr. Bennett (and his successor, Dr. R. J. Manion) had been no more decisive than Mr. Baldwin, or Mr. King than Mr. Chamberlain, and the Canadian Socialists of the Coöperative Commonwealth Federation had revealed the same confusions as the British Labor party. Canada was doing her utmost not to make any move while other nations, big and small, waited, awe-struck, for a voice that would call "Halt!" to naked aggression on the march.[16] Mr. King, intent on preserving national

14. American opinion polls showed a more than 70 per cent approval of such protection.

15. There had, of course, been separate voices, like Senator Arthur Meighen's unqualified appeals (after 1935) to rally to Great Britain.

16. E.g., King concerning his Government's policy in 1936: "To do nothing itself and if possible to prevent anything occurring which will precipitate one additional factor into all the important discussions which are taking place in Europe." It took the same attitude toward Asia after Japan's outright war on China in 1937.

unity, repeatedly refused to make commitments and declared that Parliament would decide Canada's course when it had to be charted anew. As late as August 8, 1939, he told a Toronto audience: "One thing I will not do, and cannot be persuaded to do, is to say what Canada will do in regard to a situation that may arise at some future time and under circumstances of which we now know nothing." His noncommittal policies continued to win the support of the Canadian electorate from 1935 onward, although such a policy did, of course, lead Canada unprepared into uncalculated commitments. E. J. Tarr of Winnipeg compared the Prime Minister to a juggler who could keep Isolationism, North Americanism, Imperialism, and Collectivism in the air at the same time or mask them in the folds of his magician's handkerchief, "the polished phrases of platitudinous peroration."

At heart the majority of Canadians had wanted to be neutral and had hoped that it might be possible. They did not realize how contradictory were the elements which made up their desire to wash their hands of Europe. There were sharp qualitative and quantitative differences between their repugnance to Axis ruthlessness and their distaste for anti-Axis appeasement which were bound to confuse their behavior. Not only tradition, but matter-of-fact gratitude as well, commanded Canadian support for Great Britain in a crisis of her existence. The explicit demand for neutrality was voiced in Parliament by many French Canadians, by the completely pacifistic leader of the Coöperative Commonwealth Federation, J. S. Woodsworth, and by a majority of his followers. It had been intensified by the shock of the Hoare-Laval agreement for the partition of Abyssinia and by Chamberlain's remarks before and after Munich. While Mr. King and the French-Canadian members of his Cabinet made it quite clear that the Government would not rigidly commit Canada to such a policy, yet statutes had been passed authorizing controls over enlistment and shipments of munitions in order to preserve neutrality.

Mr. King, in his speech on the Address in January, 1939, warned the House of Commons in an oblique and inconspicuous manner that events were driving him toward the regretful apprehension that Great Britain was likely soon to be involved in war and that, if that happened, Canada must follow suit. In March the onrush of events, as represented by Hitler's entry into Prague and Chamberlain's ultimatum of war if territorial aggression continued, carried the Canadian Prime Minister still farther. Although he was now bowing to the inevitable, he could not give up Canada's twenty-year effort to remain aloof without a lamentation which echoed in the hearts of millions of Canadians. On March 30, he said:

The idea that every twenty years this country should automatically and as a matter of course take part in a war overseas for democracy or self-determination of other small nations, that a country which has all it can do to run itself should feel called upon to save, periodically, a continent that cannot run itself, and to these ends risk the lives of its people, risk bankruptcy and political disunion, seems to many a nightmare and sheer madness.

Unfortunately nightmare and madness were imminent.

On the same day Ernest Lapointe, Minister of Justice, took his stand in the face of impending war by making a detailed attack on the shortsightedness of the supporters of neutrality in Quebec and elsewhere in Canada. National unity could not be preserved, he argued, if Canada remained neutral when Great Britain was attacked. "The right itself is meaningless. There is only the policy of neutrality, which would be rather a hazardous policy, hardly compatible with the national situation of Canada. . . . If any dictator in the world has made up his mind that the British Commonwealth is going to be disrupted he is basing his future projects on utter fallacy." Canada was again ready to admit with Laurier: "If England is at war we are at war and liable to attack."

The open question, then as in Laurier's day, was whether Canada's belligerency would be active or passive, and, if active, of what kind. It was agreed by the leaders of all parties that conscription must be avoided, and it was supposed, largely on the basis of British representations, that Canada's principal contributions would be material rather than human. The new unity which was achieved in these discussions during the Spring Session soon afterward received emotional reënforcement from the personal conquests which were made by King George and Queen Elizabeth during their month's visit in the early summer. They and their Canadian peoples seemed to bring to life Governor General Lord Tweedsmuir's skilful pronouncement of October 12, 1937, in Montreal: "A Canadian's first loyalty is not to the British Commonwealth of Nations, but to Canada and to Canada's King."[17]

After the announcement of the German-Russian Pact on August 22,

17. French Canadians commonly terminate this quotation four words short of its ending. In strict fact "Canada's King" can act affecting Canada only upon the advice of the Canadian Cabinet, yet loyalty to him would involve loyalty to the myth and symbol of unity in the British Commonwealth and Empire. George VI personally performed a number of royal duties in Canada, ordinarily the duty of his viceroy, the Governor General, among them reception of a new American Minister to Ottawa and signature of the new Canadian-American trade agreement.

and Hitler's ignoring of Canadian and other appeals to submit the Polish question to negotiation, Canada moved rapidly under the War Measures Act of 1914 to mobilize the products of her past four years of rearmament "in defense of neutrality." Hitler invaded Poland on September 1. True to his promise Mr. King summoned Parliament for September 7 to discuss a declaration of war, with very curious results in terms of international law, including the postponement of President Roosevelt's invoking, against Canada, the American arms embargo under the Neutrality Act, a delay which permitted some highly useful purchases of airplanes and equipment. Thus Canada was at war and not at war between King George's declaration in behalf of the United Kingdom on September 3 and in behalf of Canada on September 10. The only great issue of the debate in the Commons was the Quebec isolationists' case for a declaration of neutrality, as it was ably and vigorously presented by Maxime Raymond.[18] This was answered in the one great speech of the short session, Ernest Lapointe's rejection of Raymond's argument in terms of law, logic, and expediency. Except for a reservation against conscription he pledged his own and his French Cabinet colleagues' full support to the common cause. His peroration, a frank appeal to emotion which he built up around Queen Elizabeth's farewell—*"Que Dieu bénisse le Canada,"* stirred the House to an outburst of enthusiasm unparalleled in members' memories.

The world's mounting fever had made the leaders of English-speaking Canada and some of the leaders of French Canada realize that the Dominion could not stand alone. Faced by a choice of partners, they turned to the belligerent Mother Country rather than to the neutral United States. Disillusion and distress over many recent aspects of British policy were canceled out by instinctive loyalties and by grateful recognition that Great Britain had at last chosen to be the core of resistance to an intolerable deterioration of the ultimate values which Canadians cherished.

In the deepest sense Canadians needed Great Britain psychologically as well as materially. Few of them, except among the French Canadians, could conceive of how they could get along without their principal source of differentiation from Americans, that is, of a sense of a nationality separate from the United States. The great body of French Canadians concurred, with substantial reservations, because they were convinced

18. A Quebec Nationalist amendment against participation in a war outside of Canada withered under criticism by a French-Canadian member. Woodsworth, leader of the Coöperative Commonwealth Federation, bravely and considerately reaffirmed his individual pacifism. His party's policy was to limit participation to economic aid and to defense of Canadian territory.

by their leaders' warnings that they could not do otherwise without inviting civil war. Their leaders, whenever they let their thoughts turn outward from Quebec and Canada, knew that they must choose France and Great Britain rather than the United States. Condemn the Old World as they might and did with deep bitterness, they were well aware that it had not for a century threatened their culture as they felt that it was daily, hourly, threatened by the powerful emanations from their neighbor to the south which were attracting the masses and part of the younger *élite*.

Although most of French Canada was still shackled by an almost incurable isolationism and by a compulsive need to assert its separatism in many kinds of dissidence, it had been forced by external and domestic circumstances to look outward and to take some painful steps toward the acceptance of world citizenship. A cautious, sympathetic Government was prepared to shield it in the hope that it might shed enough of its defensive intransigeance to learn the satisfactions which could be derived from voluntary contribution to an all-Canadian cause. Canadian national unity after 1939 was largely a formal unity, for it involved the difficult task of persuading the English-speaking majority to exercise their imaginations and their tolerance instead of their prejudices in thought, word, and action where French Canada was concerned. No one on either side expected miracles, but the thoughtful knew that every minute gain in conscious collaboration was worth far more than years of lip service toward making Canada more of a nation.

September, 1939, may have revealed Canada's dependences, but for the moment at least it hardened the determination of the immensely more powerful United States to stand aloof. The people and Congress of the United States had spent five years on every kind of legislation calculated to prevent a repetition of the embroilment of 1914–1918. Like Britons and Canadians they wanted to avoid war, and, unlike them, they still believed they could succeed. They had laws against foreign enlistment, foreign loans, and foreign voyages for their ships and their citizens. They had embargoes against the export of munitions to belligerents, even if customers came to collect the goods.[19] In brief the United States had reverted to her oldest national policy, the pursuit and perfection of neutrality which Washington had initiated at the time of the Nootka Sound controversy of 1789. To that cause she was willing to sacrifice her foreign trade and finance, her mercantile marine, the traditional rights of her citizens, and even the concepts of neutral rights and freedom of the seas for which her diplomats had contested for a hundred and fifty years.

19. Congress had refused to renew the "Cash and Carry" provisions of the 1937 Act which had expired on May 1, 1939.

While tempests raged in Asia and Europe the Americas would be converted into a storm cellar for peace-loving peoples.

It was not in human nature, reënforced in this case by consciousness of wealth and power, easily to relinquish that American dream. Many of the best brains in the country had labored, and would continue to labor, for the cause, with the utmost care and ingenuity, knowing that millions of their fellow citizens would applaud them. Yet, all the while, optimism was being corroded by the suspicion that it was too good to be true, and every expansion of the Axis Powers, every revelation of their contempt for any scruple which blocked their paths, deepened the suspicion into conviction. In the autumn of 1939 there was no doubt but that at least Germany aimed at world domination, but it still seemed worth almost anything to hold off in order to see what her chances were of threatening really to attain it.

There was, of course, no question of where most American sympathies lay. It was significant that Roosevelt, in his echo of an appeal for neutrality made by Wilson twenty-five years before, did not, like his predecessor, ask for neutrality in thought. He could not get it, particularly after the unparalleled Nazi persecutions of the Jews and of all real or potential opponents within reach, or after the confident contempt which the Japanese showed for American lives, property, flag, and protests during their war against China. But the President and his Administration, certainly the best informed in history about the proportions of American opinion, had to proceed with the utmost caution lest they outrun the public in translating attitudes into overt actions. Roosevelt's calculated outburst of October 5, 1937, against international lawlessness and his suggestion of a "quarantine" against such anarchy had not evoked enough popular approval to justify the President in pledging concrete support to an international conference at Brussels which aimed to vitalize the Nine-Power Pact of 1922. Even the bombing and sinking by the Japanese of an American gunboat and three tankers in December of that year did not break the people's preference for withdrawing from risks of involvement. In 1938 a Congressional resolution requiring a popular referendum before declaration of war was defeated only by means of some adroit distribution of patronage.

Yet, every day, people and President moved farther toward taking up the positions which they could not in nature avoid, but which predicated participation in a world war. No matter how phrased, American appeals that negotiation be substituted for naked force could not be disregarded forever without aligning the United States against the aggressors, whose every action derided American democratic faiths. Americans could not condemn Great Britain and France for their surrender at Munich without admitting a moral obligation later when they took their stand in behalf of Poland and other intended victims of the Axis. The vicious circle of prestige in the Pacific, which drove the Japanese to find satisfaction for three generations of humiliation by Westerners in openly cruel treatment of helpless white persons, and which made Americans refuse to admit any analogy between the Monroe Doctrine for the Americas and the quite similar Amau Doctrine of 1934 for an unwelcome New Order in East Asia, was breeding explosive energies which could not long be pent up.[20] The loans to China from December, 1938, onward were open to only one interpretation.

The first deep breach in the Great Wall of Neutrality was the Pittman Act of November 4, 1939, by which, after furious debate and the narrowest of majorities, "Cash and Carry" sales of munitions were again permitted. Thus within two months of the outbreak of war, France and Great Britain and their allies were enabled to supply themselves in the United States as long as they could pay for and transport their purchases. Meanwhile, however, American isolationists were passionately propounding their case. A cartoon in the Hartford *Courant* for Columbus Day, 1939, aptly summarized one half of their argument for a nation which had been founded upon the abandonment of Europe and a determination to set up a new kind of society and protect it from European contamination. "Where I made my mistake," Columbus was made to say, "was in going back to Europe after I got away from there." The other half of the argument was easily and persuasively compounded from the disillusionments arising out of participation in the War of 1914 and from comments upon Anglo-French desertions of China, Abyssinia, Spain, Austria, and Czechoslovakia.

Yet, before the end of 1939, the isolationists were steadily losing ground. Their cause suffered substantially from the easily demonstrated unevenness in the knowledge and judgment of Colonel C. A. Lindbergh, their most conspicuous spokesman. For instance, when he asked, referring to Canada, "Can we rightfully permit any country in America to give bases to foreign warships, or to send its army abroad to fight while it remains secure in our protection at home?" he did not know that Canadians had gone to great lengths and expense in order to avoid being

20. An inherent consequence of American popular feelings about the Japanese was that for at least two years after July 26, 1939, when the United States gave six months' notice of abrogation of the commercial treaty of 1911, relatively few Americans realized that the progressive embargo on the supply of munitions and other materials made war with Japan more imminent than war with Germany. Somehow an American blockade seemed different from an Anglo-French one.

indebted for protection to the United States and had been careful to respond politely to Roosevelt's Chautauqua and Kingston offers, but without in any way soliciting aid. In the United States, moreover, Lindbergh's rhetorical question was abruptly deflated the next day, when Senator Key Pittman icily repudiated it as an instance of the kind of assumption of overlordship best illustrated by the Axis Powers.

It was fear, however, which finally made isolationism impossible—the fear which mounted in a great crescendo accompanying the crescendo of German conquest during the spring and early summer of 1940—Denmark, Norway, Luxembourg, the Netherlands, Belgium, France (and Italy's entry into the war). And then fear became colored by grateful admiration of the spectacle of Great Britain, after all seemed lost at Dunkirk, precariously holding off disaster by the spirit of her blasted cities, the high strategy and courage of her airmen, and the weakening armor girt round her by the Navy. When France fell Great Britain's only remaining strong ally and arsenal became Canada, a Canada which was galvanized by the catastrophe into stripping herself of every item of armament and supply that could be sent across the Atlantic and subordinating everything to the production of armed men and munitions on a scale unthinkable during the weird lull of the preceding winter.

The United States, suddenly aware of her future in case the British forlorn hope failed, also moved swiftly to help. We know very little of the network of negotiations between Great Britain and the Americas during the summer of 1940, but thanks to the recent revelations of E. R. Stettinius, Jr., American Under-Secretary of State, we know something of what the United States did, even before France gave up, to remedy Britain's disastrous loss of equipment at Dunkirk by generous sales of American munitions. Six days after the fall of France the *S.S. Eastern Prince* arrived in England from the United States carrying forty-eight cases of field guns, 15,000 machine guns, and 12,000 rifles. By the end of August, the United States Steel Export Company had been enabled to acquire from storage in American arsenals, and had dispatched to Great Britain, 900 75-mm. field guns with 1,000,000 rounds of ammunition, 80,000 machine guns, 500,000 rifles, and 130,000,000 rounds of small-arms ammunition. It was this aid which did most to equip the Canadian as well as the British forces which were awaiting the ever-victorious German armies across the Channel. Until the American munitions arrived the defiant defenders of the British Isles had almost no guns that could stop a tank and little infantry equipment. They knew what Winston Churchill meant when he said on June 4, after Dunkirk:

We shall fight on the beaches, we shall fight on the landing grounds, we shall fight in the fields and in the streets, we shall fight in the hills; and even if, which I do not for a moment believe, this Island or a large part of it were subjugated and starving, then our Empire beyond the seas, armed and guarded by the British Fleet, would carry on the struggle, until, in God's good time, the New World, with all its power and might, steps forth to the rescue and the liberation of the old.

Or again, two weeks later:

Let us therefore brace ourselves to our duty and so bear ourselves that, if the British Commonwealth and Empire lasts for a thousand years, men will still say, "This was their finest hour."

The American rearmament of the British defense forces was little publicized, but it was a recognizable segment of a pattern of forces, shaped by the Roosevelt Administration, which swiftly emerged in the summer of 1940, clear for all to see. The inter-American system, which had limped sadly at Lima in 1938 because of Argentinian reluctance to accept the leadership of the United States, and which had set up at Panama in the fall of 1939 an ambitious but unrealizable neutrality belt hundreds of miles broad round the Western Hemisphere (except Newfoundland and Canada), suddenly came to life for the first time since the Buenos Aires Conference of 1936. At Havana, from July 21 to July 30, the American republics took more positive action than ever before in their consultative history.[21] They "Pan Americanized," or made multilateral, the Monroe Doctrine and the prohibition of transfer of the American possessions of overseas powers. They made substantial progress toward resistance by all the republics to aggression from outside the Americas. They breathed life into the inter-American financial and economic structures which had been little more than envisaged at Panama. And they agreed to set about the active combating of Italian, German, and Japanese attempts to undermine American institutions.

The conspicuous gap in this system was even more solidly filled three weeks later, on August 18, the second anniversary of Roosevelt's Kingston Declaration. At Ogdensburg, New York, on the St. Lawrence boundary, President Roosevelt and Prime Minister King announced the immediate creation of a *Permanent* Joint Defense Board to "consider in the broad sense the defense of *the north half of the Western Hemisphere.*"[22]

21. Canada was unofficially represented by P. E. Corbett, a member of the Canadian Institute of International Affairs, which also engaged J. P. Humphrey to prepare a book for the instruction of Canadians.
22. Italics added.

Two days later Mr. Churchill told the House of Commons that his Government had decided to inform Washington that it was prepared to lease bases to the United States for defense of the Western Hemisphere. On September 3 President Roosevelt announced that the United States was leasing for ninety-nine years a string of six air and naval bases from British Guiana to the Bahamas and had acquired outright similar bases in Bermuda and Newfoundland in exchange "for fifty of our over-age destroyers." Meanwhile surveyors were at work in British Columbia planning an American military road to Alaska, and an earlier reciprocal agreement permitting American and Canadian military aircraft to cross certain portions of each other's country was in active operation.[23]

The general satisfaction and relief in Great Britain, Canada, and the United States over this pell-mell accompaniment to the crucial and dubious Battle of Britain pretty well eclipsed explicit criticism of some of its aspects. British doubts about "giving away the Empire" were silenced by the indubitable evidence that the United States, if only for self-security, would abandon neutrality in order to prevent a British collapse.[24] American cries of "dictatorship" were quieted by the common knowledge that the position of the United States had been made much more secure. In Canada, which had been garrisoning Bermuda and parts of the Caribbean, and had, previous to the new arrangements, taken over the defense of Newfoundland at her front door, there were a few persistent, rueful reflections over the fashion in which the United States had come to overshadow Canada at Britain's side. On August 20, 1940, Mr. Churchill said to the House of Commons:

These two great organizations of the English-speaking democracies, the British Empire and the United States, will have to be somewhat mixed up together in some of their affairs for mutual and general advantage. For my own part, looking out upon the future, I do not view the process with any misgivings. I could not stop it if I wished; no one can stop it. Like the Mississippi, it just keeps rolling along. Let it roll. Let it roll on full flood, inexorable, irresistible, benignant, to broader lands and better days.

To this eloquent enunciation of the central tenet of their own foreign policy, Canadians uttered a deep "Amen." It would have been comforting, nevertheless, if the appropriate river had happened to be the St. Lawrence.

23. The American National Guard was called out on September 1, 1940, and registration under the new Conscription Act began on October 16.

24. Great Britain in return sent formal assurances that she would never surrender or scuttle her navy in the event of her home waters becoming untenable, thus elevating Canada's importance as a potential destination.

Actually an alliance had been struck between the United States and the British Commonwealth and Empire. The wildly confused Presidential election of that autumn may have been rendered electrical by the novelty of a third term for Roosevelt, but most of the voters neither sought nor could find any difference between the foreign policies of the candidates. In the circumstances they decided not to swap horses in the middle of the stream. "There can be no appeasement with ruthlessness," the victorious President reported to the people on December 29, 1940, "we must be the great arsenal of democracy." That soon involved financing the opponents of the Axis, "freezing" Axis and Axis-controlled assets in the United States, and even reaching out alongside Canadian garrisons and naval and air patrols to Newfoundland, Greenland, and Iceland in order to protect deliveries halfway across the Atlantic.

No one was very certain about the workings and future consequences of "Lend-Lease."[25] It promised to be remarkably like a British discovery of the eighteenth century which Canada had recently rediscovered, that is, that it is better to give outright to one's allies than to lend and hold them strictly to account. The Dominion, which had been "lend-leasing" for months, was about to write off a cool billion dollars of British indebtedness. In April, 1941, when Canada could not assemble the American dollars needed for her purchases in the United States and could find no welcome there for her immense sterling credits, the President and the Canadian Prime Minister met this situation by arranging at Hyde Park, New York, for increased American purchases of war materials from Canada and for the administration of Lend-Lease to Great Britain through Canada when the Dominion was working up materials for the British account. Canada declined Lend-Lease aid for herself.

By the time Hitler—fatally delayed by Yugoslavia, Greece, and the British Commonwealth in his multiple drives to reach Suez and the Near East, and to nullify Turkey—opened his assault on Russia in June, 1941, Great Britain and her offspring in America had become welded into one coöperative war machine, except that the Americans had not joined actual battle. Canada was still well ahead of the United States in such things as total war production and in the astounding output of air personnel from her Empire Air Training schools, and she was to remain so for some time. But such primacies, while heartening to the smaller nation, had quickly to be subordinated to the close integration of the three coun-

25. For the precedents of 1798–1799, see pp. 72–73, above. An Act of March 11, 1941, authorized government agencies to turn over "defense articles" to Great Britain and other countries, payment to be "in kind or property, or any other direct or indirect benefit which the President deems satisfactory," with Congress controlling the total by its votes of funds.

tries. So close was it, and so freely did airplane and telephone deliver men and messages from one capital to another, that finished goods, raw materials, and research findings formed a common pool. In addition to the Joint Defense Board the United States and Canada now operated a Joint Material Coördinating Committee and Joint Economic committees, in order to adjust their resources and capacities and money to the maximum advantage. Frequently it was impossible to define the boundaries between American, British, and Canadian enterprise. Indeed Washington had become the operating center for the economic organization of every available part of the world into one weapon for the destruction of tyranny.

When Hitler attacked Russia there was an easing of the intolerable tension under which the British nations and the United States had been living for about a year. The Atlantic Charter, drawn up by Churchill and Roosevelt in August, 1941, was almost indistinguishable from a joint declaration by belligerents, and was accompanied by pledges of aid to Russia and a blunt warning to Japan. Thanks to almost a year of the most comprehensive activity in defense of her cause at home and abroad, the United States was relatively far better prepared for war than in 1917.

The time was ripe, therefore, for the United States and Japan to measure each other's intentions and to make the decision as to war or peace. Washington had given abundant warning of her aims by her two agreements with Russia, her loans to China, and her studied preparations for an attempt to halt Japan by cutting off the supplies which she needed in order to establish a dominant position in Asia and the Pacific. But Japan had been piercing the thin façade of the white man's tenure in the Far East, and her victimization of the French colonies in the Southeast had brought her to the margins of weakly defended territories which contained all the oil, iron, tin, rubber, and other strategic materials which she could ever need. Having decided that Washington was firm in the determination to stop the flow of munitions and war materials which Japan was using to build up an impregnable mastery of the Far East. Tokyo decided on war, and struck massively and without warning on December 7, 1941. American, British, and Canadian[26] forces in the Pacific were thrown on the defensive. Germany and Italy promptly declared war. Only Russia and Japan agreed to leave each other alone. All the great nations of the world were now committed to a fight to a finish and the secondary Powers were either victims of conquest, willing or unwilling allies of the contestants, or well aware of the limitations which the war imposed on their freedom of action.

26. At Hong Kong.

Thus for the second time in twenty-five years Washington was transformed into the operating capital of the English-speaking world. On the first occasion, after 1917, both the economic and the political primacies which had for a century and a half belonged to Great Britain crossed the Atlantic westward, but the people of the United States had not yet acquired the experience and skill which were needed in order to exercise these new powers either for their own benefit or for the world's. The United States almost fatally weakened the League at its beginning, and later made it clear that she could not be depended upon for active aid in efforts to check the rot which destroyed collective security. She soon showed that she lacked the technical knowledge and apparatus needed in order to succeed London as the great broker in international finance, and instead of using her advantageous position to loosen up world trade, she did more than any other nation to strangle it. She did not try systematically to understand Canada, her most important economic partner, or to conduct her foreign policy in terms of the fact that Canada spoke in North American accents in the councils of the British Commonwealth of Nations.

Although the first test of her inescapable leadership among the nations could be fumbled without disaster to the United States, the years since 1929 have demonstrated that another such combination of power and responsibility cannot. The sheer weight of the United States in the world has burdened her people with dreadful responsibilities. They know that, unless they take an active part with other nations in extending the enjoyment of the values which they cherish, some other Power, or group of Powers, will try to impose its pattern of order upon the world. Americans have done most to meet this challenge by coöperating closely with Great Britain and Canada, the two countries in the world whose destinies they have never been able to disentangle from their own. In the crises of a war for survival each of the three has eagerly given and sought aid, so that for its duration, at least, their amalgamation is close and fruitful. In turn all three have given all possible aid to Russia, China, and their other allies.

The crux of the situation, however, will come when the problem of survival has been settled in their favor. Many of the leaders of 1917–1919 realized that, but failed to carry their peoples with them in translating their vision of a better future into corresponding action. Can the statesmen and the peoples of the 'forties profit by the world's experience between two world wars? Apparently they will aim at global organization for order and peace, and in doing so they should be aware of the fatal error of thinking that the mere creation of a world structure absolves

them from endowing it with enough active support from the constituent
nations to assure effective action in carrying out the decisions of the
world community. It may be that the next step toward collective security
will be tentative, or partial, or have to operate in terms of regional associations of nations, but, whatever the shape of things to come, the peoples
of the world can get no farther toward peaceful association by policies of
passivity and negation.

In the nature of things it is mere common sense to build upon past
experience of international association. Just as municipal institutions
are the best education for the operation of larger political entities, so the
experience of naturally interlocked nations can school peoples and their
statesmen for larger international responsibilities. No such group of
nations is more experienced or more capable of contributing to collective
security than Great Britain, the United States, and Canada, although
admittedly they, like all other nations, have much to learn. Their largest
and most difficult task is the discovery of the positive principles by which
to govern their postwar coöperation with their other great allies, with
the smaller nations, and with their present enemies. Yet they also still
have a great deal to learn about the more immediate problem of getting
along together. It may be all right in time of war to echo Mr. Churchill's
"Let it roll" and to trust that peril will splice and hold taut the affairs
of the United States and the British Commonwealth and Empire which
war has "mixed up together." But the inhabitants of the United States
can tell the British Prime Minister that they have learned to their cost
that they dare not let their Mississippi roll. They are forced to maintain
gigantic control works, a corps of skilled engineers, great batteries of
machines, and regiments of laborers in order to detect its vagaries and to
curb it lest it burst its banks and spread destruction. Americans, Britons,
and Canadians may heartily share in the aspiration which was voiced in
"Let it roll on full flood, inexorable, irresistible," but they also know
from the record of the past that they must share in hard work if they are
to make real the rest of Mr. Churchill's sentence—"benignant, to broader
lands and better days."

APPENDIX

BIBLIOGRAPHICAL NOTES

THERE is no comprehensive study of the triangular relationship involving Canada, the United States, and Great Britain, although several monographs covering special periods or episodes proceed from that point of view. The following notes, therefore, will include a varied selection of books and articles, most of which have been directly drawn upon for this volume and whose character will be briefly indicated where desirable. The arrangement of titles is by chapters, and in order to reduce repetition the scope of a work which affects more than one chapter will be specified at the time of its citation. Since such studies almost invariably contain specific descriptions of their documentation, the manuscript and printed source materials available to students will not be described here.

It is perhaps of interest to cite the paper and the discussion out of which grew the series, "The Relations of Canada and the United States," under J. T. Shotwell's direction. It is "Canadian and North American History," *Report* of the Canadian Historical Association for 1931 (Ottawa). A list of the volumes in the series appears on p. 386, below.

There are three notable histories of Canadian-American relations: H. L. Keenleyside, *Canada and the United States* (New York, 1929); J. M. Callahan, *American Foreign Policy in Canadian Relations* (New York, 1937); and E. W. McInnis, *The Unguarded Frontier* (New York, 1942). The first is documented and brings general considerations to bear upon the principal diplomatic relations; the second is almost exclusively diplomatic; and the third is an undocumented account for the general reader which draws substantially on the Carnegie Endowment's series, "The Relations of Canada and the United States."

S. F. Bemis, *A Diplomatic History of the United States* (New York, 1936, 1942); T. A. Bailey, *A Diplomatic History of the American People* (New York, 1940, 1942); and R. A. MacKay and E. B. Rogers, *Canada Looks Abroad* (Toronto, 1938), are standard one-volume reference works on international relations which contain ample guidance to underlying special scholarship. P. E. Corbett, *The Settlement of Canadian-American Disputes* (New Haven, 1937), is a brief, pointed discussion in terms of international law. R. W. Van Alstyne, *American Diplomacy in Action* (Stanford University, 1944), gives close attention to relations with Great Britain and Canada.

Chapter I. The Patterns of the Continent

Probably the best-balanced and most useful modern study of North America as a whole, as well as in its parts, is Henri Baulig, "Amérique Septentrionale," I, *Généralités—Canada*, II, *Etats-Unis* (Paris, 1935). J. R. Smith and M. O. Phillips, *North America* (New York, 1942), reaches up to the Arctic and down to Panama, but breaks up its subject into forty-seven regional studies.

Chapter II. The Peoples and Their Rivalries, 1492–1763

Diamond Jenness, *The Indians of Canada* (Ottawa, 1932); Clark Wissler, *Indians of the United States* (New York, 1940); and J. B. Brebner, *The Explorers of North America, 1492–1806* (New York, 1933). H. A. Innis, *The Fur Trade in Canada* (New Haven, 1930) and *The Cod Fisheries* (New Haven, 1940), are complete histories. G. L. Nute, *Caesars of the Wilderness* (New York, 1943), is an excellent resolution of the problems involved in the careers of Groseilliers and Radisson.

A remarkably effective work, now in progress of publication, which portrays the eighteenth-century British Empire at home and abroad is L. H. Gipson's *The British Empire before the American Revolution* (5 vols., New York, 1936–1942). Volume I discusses the British background, Volumes II and III describe the North American colonies, and Volumes IV and V deal skilfully with North American rivalries as they took shape between 1748 and 1754. For Acadia before 1760, J. B. Brebner, *New England's Outpost* (New York, 1927); for Canada, M. H. Long, *A History of the Canadian People*, I, *New France* (Toronto, 1943); Guy Frégault, *La civilisation de la Nouvelle-France* (Montreal, 1944). Gustave Lanctot (ed.), *Les canadiens français et leurs voisins du sud* (Montreal, 1941), is a comprehensive history coming down to recent times, as do two excellent historical analyses: Georges Vattier, *Essai sur la mentalité canadienne-française* (Paris, 1927), and Mason Wade, *The French-Canadian Mind* (Toronto, 1946). M. L. Hansen and J. B. Brebner, *The Mingling of the Canadian and American Peoples* (New Haven, 1940), begins with what Hansen calls "the establishment of an Atlantic base" and carries the story down to 1938. Max Savelle, *The Diplomatic History of the Canadian Boundary, 1749–1763* (New Haven, 1940).

Chapter III. Diversities under One Flag, 1763

While Gipson's volumes provide the best single treatment of Great Britain and her empire at this time, they may be usefully supplemented by L. B. Namier's two studies: *The Structure of Politics at the Accession of George III* (2 vols., London, 1929) and *England in the Age of the American Revolution* (London, 1930). See also J. H. Rose *et al.*, "The Cambridge History of the British Empire," I, *The Old Empire, from the Beginnings to 1783* (Cambridge, 1929). The British contributors to this large collaborative work frequently reveal an unfortunate ignorance of American and Dominion scholarship. J. C. Miller's *Origins of the American Revolution* (Boston, 1943) is a convenient one-volume reëxamination, although it pays insufficient attention to economic pressures and democratic ambitions and is inadequate as a guide to the enormous literature on its subject. F. J. Turner's sweeping ideas on frontier democracy as expressed in *The Frontier in American History* (New York, 1920) might be balanced by J. F. Jameson's *The American Revolution Considered as a Social Movement* (Princeton, 1926). For the constitutional aspects of Anglo-American differences, consult C. H. McIlwain, *The Ameri-*

can Revolution (Cambridge, 1923) and R. L. Schuyler's rejoinder, *Parliament and the British Empire* (New York, 1929).

For Nova Scotia, 1760–1783, J. B. Brebner, *The Neutral Yankees of Nova Scotia* (New York, 1937), attempts to be comprehensive; a contrasted interpretation will be found in W. B. Kerr, *The Maritime Provinces of British North America and the American Revolution* (Sackville, 1941). A. L. Burt's picture of French Canada, 1760–1791, in *The Old Province of Quebec* (Minneapolis, 1933) may be usefully supplemented by the relevant section of S. D. Clark's *The Social Development of Canada* (Toronto, 1942). D. G. Creighton, in *The Commercial Empire of the St. Lawrence, 1760–1850* (Toronto, 1937), deals in masterly fashion with the economy of the region, its relations to Great Britain and the United States, and the political expressions of the changing situation. H. A. Innis, in "Decentralization and Democracy," *Canadian Journal of Economics and Political Science,* IX (Toronto, 1943), propounds some thought-provoking interpretations of the interplay of politics and economics in North America during the Anglo-French contest, and before and after the American Revolution. Ernest Martin, *Les exilés acadiens en France au XVIIIe siècle et leur établissement en Poitou* (Paris, 1936).

Chapter IV. The Grand Partition, 1763–1791

A. L. Burt's *The United States, Great Britain, and British North America from the Revolution to the Establishment of Peace after the War of 1812* (New Haven, 1940) is an authoritative treatment, particularly of the diplomatic history. It should be supplemented on the economic side by Innis's histories of the fur trade and fisheries, by Creighton, *op. cit.*, and by G. S. Graham's *British Policy and Canada, 1774–1791* (London, 1930). Preliminary studies by Chilton Williamson lead to the expectation of a thorough treatment of the interaction of Vermont and northern New York with the St. Lawrence region along the lines of W. A. Mackintosh's suggestive paper, "Canada and Vermont: A study in historical geography," *Canadian Historical Review,* VIII (Toronto, 1927). Patrick Campbell, *Travels in the Interior Inhabited Parts of North America in the Years 1791 and 1792* (Edinburgh, 1793; Toronto, 1937). For British post-revolutionary policies, see "Cambridge History of the British Empire," II, *The Growth of the New Empire, 1783–1870* (Cambridge, 1940), especially Vincent Harlow's demonstration in Chapter IV of the effects of the Irish situation. Volume VI of this series, *Canada and Newfoundland* (Cambridge, 1930), is a useful reference volume, particularly for the history after 1760.

Chapter V. Oceanic and Continental Conflicts, 1783–1814

In addition to the relevant books previously cited, G. S. Graham's *Sea Power and British North America, 1783–1820* (Cambridge, Mass., 1941) discusses the politico-economic aspects of British policies toward the U.S.A. and B.N.A. in an original and fruitful way. See also L. A. Harper, *The English Navigation*

Laws (New York, 1939). The principal records of lend-lease in 1798–1799
will be found in Vol. I of W. R. Manning (ed.), *Diplomatic Correspondence of
the United States: Canadian relations 1784–1860* (3 vols., Washington, 1940–
1943), and some supplementary material in Appendix IV of the *Report of the
Public Archives of Canada for 1940* (Ottawa, 1941). Hansen and Brebner,
op. cit., and F. Landon, *Western Ontario and the American Frontier* (Toronto,
1941), treat of the population movements. Michael Smith's brochures, e.g., *A
Geographical View of the Province of Upper Canada* (New York, 1813) and
A Geographical View of the British Possessions in North America (Baltimore,
1814), provide an intimate view by an American migrant whose enthusiasm
was little dulled by his sufferings during the War of 1812. E. F. Heckscher's
The Continental System (New York, 1922) is the standard account of the
Anglo-French politico-economic contest. J. W. Pratt, in *The Expansionists of
1812* (New York, 1925), advances (*inter alia*) the argument that "without
the peculiar grievances and ambitions of the West there would have been no
war," which is flatly rejected by A. L. Burt in the work cited under Chapter
IV, above (see his p. 305, note 87). For Burt's treatment of continental factors as contributory causes of the war, see particularly his pp. 302–310.

Chapter VI. A New Alignment of Forces, 1815–1823

In addition to the relevant works previously cited, K. W. Porter's *John
Jacob Astor, Business Man* (2 vols., Cambridge, Mass., 1931), in its text
and notes, is a mine of information, but is somewhat diffident about interpre-
tation. J. P. Pritchett, *The Red River Valley, 1811–1849: A regional study*
(New Haven, 1942), is a detailed reëxamination of the history of the Selkirk
Settlement. The standard account of the birth of the Monroe Doctrine is Dexter
Perkins' *The Monroe Doctrine, 1823–1826* (Cambridge, Mass., 1927), which
should be supplemented by A. P. Whitaker's *The United States and the Independence of Latin America, 1800–1830* (Baltimore, 1941). P. A. Rollins, *The
Discovery of the Oregon Trail* (New York, 1935), is an extraordinarily thor-
ough reëxamination of the whole Astoria adventure which may profitably be
combined with W. J. Ghent, *The Early Far West* (New York, 1931). F. W.
Howay, W. N. Sage, and H. F. Angus, *British Columbia and the United States:
The North Pacific slope from fur trade to aviation* (Toronto, 1942).

R. L. Schuyler, *The Fall of the Old Colonial System: A study in British free
trade, 1770–1870* (New York, 1945), is an admirably lucid and sustained
analysis of its subject.

Chapter VII. Sea, Forests, Waterways, 1815–1850

J. H. Clapham, *An Economic History of Modern Britain* (3 vols., Cambridge, 1926–1938), especially Volume I. L. H. Jenks, *The Migration of
British Capital to 1875* (New York, 1927), is an attractively presented and
effective pioneering work. S. A. Saunders, *Studies in the Economy of the Mari-*

time Provinces (Toronto, 1939), is of uneven value and should be supplemented by the information and insights of Innis's *The Cod Fisheries*.

The literature of the wooden ship is enormous and many of its authors do not rise much above antiquarianism. Some of the outstandingly valuable works are: R. G. Albion, *Forests and Sea Power: The timber problem of the Royal Navy, 1652–1862* (Cambridge, Mass., 1926), and two parts of his history (in progress) of the Port of New York, *The Rise of New York Port, 1815–1860* (New York, 1939), and *Squareriggers on Schedule* (Princeton, 1938); S. E. Morison's classic *The Maritime History of Massachusetts, 1783–1860* (Boston, 1921); F. W. Wallace's remarkable works, *Wooden Ships and Iron Men* (London, 1924), *In the Wake of the Wind Ships* (Toronto, 1927), and *Record of Canadian Shipping: A list of square-rigged vessels, etc., built in the eastern provinces of British North America, 1786–1920* (Toronto, 1929); O. T. Howe and F. C. Matthews, *American Clipper Ships, 1833–1858* (2 vols., Salem, 1926–1927); A. H. Clark, *The Clipper Ship Era* (New York, 1910); and R. C. McKay, *Some Famous Sailing Ships and Their Builder Donald McKay* (New York, 1928).

On North American lumbering, J. E. Defebaugh, *History of the Lumber Industry of America* (2 vols., Chicago, 1906–1907); the picturesque, yet generally reliable *Holy Old Mackinaw* (New York, 1938) of S. H. Holbrook; and A. R. M. Lower *et al., The North American Assault on the Canadian Forest: A history of the lumber trade between Canada and the United States* (Toronto, 1938). Two illuminating sets of reminiscences by New Brunswickers who followed the forests to the western Great Lakes are Isaac Stephenson, *Recollections of a Long Life* (Chicago, 1915), and J. E. Nelligan, "The Life of a Lumberman," *Wisconsin Magazine of History*, XIII (Madison, 1929–1930). James Stevens has collected the printable parts of a great folk myth in *Paul Bunyan* (New York, 1925).

A. B. Corey's *The Crisis of 1830–1842 in Canadian-American Relations* (New Haven, 1941) provides the North American background of border strife and anxious statecraft for the Webster-Ashburton settlements of 1842, and O. P. Chitwood's *John Tyler: Champion of the Old South* (New York, 1939) is also useful. J. R. Baldwin, "The Ashburton-Webster Boundary Settlement," in the *Report* of the Canadian Historical Association for 1938 (Toronto) adds some interesting details.

N. E. Whitford's *History of the Canal System of the State of New York together with Brief Histories of the Canals of the United States and Canada* (2 vols., Albany, 1906) is a remarkable compendium of often inaccessible information, but for the Canadian canals consult also G. P. de T. Glazebrook, *A History of Transportation in Canada* (Toronto, 1938). There is as yet no thorough history of Great Lakes shipping, but G. A. Cuthbertson's *Freshwater* (Toronto, 1931) and Walter Havighurst's *The Long Ships Passing* (New York, 1942) are lesser efforts of interest and good quality. Max Berger's *The British Traveller in America, 1836–1860* (New York, 1943) is a systematic analysis which contains critical bibliographical notes.

Chapter VIII. Pioneers and Democrats, 1815–1850

In addition to *The Mingling of the Canadian and American Peoples,* M. L. Hansen's *The Atlantic Migration* (Cambridge, Mass., 1940), covering the period down to 1860, is the first section of the illuminating work which he did not live to complete, and *The Immigrant in American History* (Cambridge, Mass., 1940) is a collection of his preliminary essays which, while sometimes rashly provocative, are full of fruitful suggestions for students of migration. S. D. Clark, *op. cit.,* provides a comprehensive picture of the frontier in Canada. A. R. M. Lower, *Settlement and the Forest Frontier in Eastern Canada* (Toronto, 1936), is an original, useful work.

A. K. Weinberg's *Manifest Destiny* (Baltimore, 1935), while somewhat overpowering in its elaboration, does not seem likely to be superseded. M. C. Jacobs, *Winning Oregon* (Caldwell, Idaho, 1938), is a systematic analysis of American factors, but should be supplemented by Frederick Merk's articles in the *American Historical Review* (1924, 1932, and 1934) and in *Agricultural History* (1934). See also J. W. Pratt, "James K. Polk and John Bull," *Canadian Historical Review,* XXIV (Toronto, 1943). B. A. De Voto's *The Year of Decision: 1846* (Boston, 1943) is an ingenious synthesis of American expansionism at the expense of Spain and Great Britain.

J. F. Turner's principal ideas are to be found in *The Frontier in American History.* The *Report* of the Canadian Historical Association for 1940 (Toronto, 1940) contains an interesting symposium of papers and discussions on Turner's frontier hypothesis as applied to the histories of New France, Latin America, and the Red River Settlement. For Upper Canada, consult F. Landon, *op. cit.*

J. B. Brebner, "Patronage and Parliamentary Government," in the *Report* of the Canadian Historical Association for 1938 (Toronto, 1938), opens up the subject and furnishes guidance to studies of relevant American, British, and British North American developments. Although it tends to reverse the principle of reading the past into the present, *The Age of Jackson* (New York, 1945), by A. M. Schlesinger, Jr., combines broad scholarship with literary charm in an effective way.

Canadian constitutional history is badly in need of a new and more comprehensive synthesis, for which much of the spade-work in research and politico-economic interpretation has been done, but in the meantime W. P. M. Kennedy, *The Constitution of Canada* (2d edition, Toronto, 1938), and Chester Martin, *Empire and Commonwealth* (Oxford, 1929), tell the story and furnish guidance to supporting materials. H. T. Manning, "The Civil List of Lower Canada," *Canadian Historical Review,* XXIV (Toronto, 1943), reveals the admirable logic by which the French Canadians, unhampered by traditional views of representative government, separated sense from nonsense in the constitutional establishment which they received in 1791.

Merle Curti's *The Growth of American Thought* (New York, 1943) is a general history which pays conspicuous attention to transatlantic interplay and is especially valuable in its text and bibliographical notes concerning the period

1800–1860. There is no analogous work for British North America, although there are many articles of varying worth, most of which are regional and as yet too introspective to establish relationship with Great Britain and the United States. Signs of broader views appear in two recent studies, A. J. M. Smith, *The Book of Canadian Poetry* (Chicago, 1943), and E. K. Brown, *On Canadian Poetry* (Toronto, 1943), but further progress in almost all other fields must await the completion of many kinds of critical studies.

Chapter IX. Free Trade, Reciprocity, Civil War, 1840–1865

Creighton, *op. cit.*, reaches its dramatic climax in the events of 1849 and 1850 in Montreal. L. B. Shippee, *Canadian-American Relations, 1849–1874* (New Haven, 1939), takes up the story at that point and carries it along most effectively. D. C. Masters' terse and authoritative *The Reciprocity Treaty of 1854* (London, 1937) can be profitably supplemented by his "T. C. Keefer and the Development of Canadian Transportation," and Samuel McKee's "Canada's Bid for the Traffic of the Middle West, 1849–1874," both in the *Report* of the Canadian Historical Association for 1940 (Toronto, 1940). G. N. Tucker's *The Canadian Commercial Revolution, 1845–1851* (New Haven, 1936) is thorough and well judged. J. P. Merritt, *Biography of the Hon. W. H. Merritt, M.P.* (St. Catharines, 1875), is interesting, but uncritical. Laurence Oliphant's racy account of the Elgin mission to Washington in *Episodes in a Life of Adventure* (Edinburgh, various dates) is more picturesque and self-revealing than dependable. R. L. Schuyler, *The Fall of the Old Colonial System,* cited above, for this and the following chapter.

Landon, *op. cit.*, provides the most convenient account of the Negro migration to Canada and guidance to works of greater detail. H. G. MacDonald, *Canadian Public Opinion on the American Civil War* (New York, 1926), is more broadly useful than its title suggests, and C. P. Stacey's misleadingly-named *Canada and the British Army, 1846–1871: A study in the practice of responsible government* (London, 1936) contains an excellent account of border relations. E. D. Adams, *Great Britain and the American Civil War* (2 vols., London, 1925), is a scholarly, objective account which is more dependable than the better-known, introspective interpretation which is provided by the famous son of C. F. Adams, the American Minister in London, in *The Education of Henry Adams* (New York, 1907).

Chapter X. Transcontinental Canada, 1865–1871

The best account of American annexationism toward Canada at this time is the unpublished doctoral essay of J. P. Smith (Chicago, 1933) which is summarized and amended in the *Report* of the Canadian Historical Association for 1935. Shippee, *op. cit.*, and Allan Nevins, *Hamilton Fish: The inner history of the Grant Administration* (New York, 1937), are invaluable complementary studies. Howay, Sage, Angus, *op. cit.*, covers the British Columbian developments, and V. J. Farrar, *The Annexation of Russian America to the*

United States (Washington, 1937), deals with the Alaska Purchase in great detail. E. S. Osgood, *The Day of the Cattleman* (Minneapolis, 1929), is an attractive as well as scholarly work. Stacey, *op. cit.*, furnishes the best account of the Fenians and of British efforts to make Canada take over her own defense. Charles Murphy's *D'Arcy McGee* (Toronto, 1937) is largely an edition of his speeches.

D. G. Creighton's *British North America at Confederation* (Ottawa, 1939), an original and illuminating work, is an Appendix to the "Report of the Royal Commission on Dominion-Provincial Relations" (3 vols., Ottawa, 1940), whose first volume, *Canada, 1867–1939,* is the most acute brief politico-economic evaluation of the Dominion's history at present available. W. M. Whitelaw, *The Maritimes and Canada before Confederation* (Toronto, 1934), effectively builds up the background for the Charlottetown and Quebec Conferences. E. W. Watkin's *Canada and the States: Recollections, 1851–1886* (London, 1887) reveals few secrets but exposes the man. Jenks, *op. cit.*, re-creates the financial background of the "new" imperialism in a more reasonable fashion than the quite arbitrary thesis of J. A. Hobson's *Imperialism* (3d ed., London, 1938).

R. G. Trotter, *Canadian Federation: Its origins and achievement* (Toronto, 1924), has been the accepted authority and is in process of amplification and revision. Among the many articles which have thrown added light on the subject since 1924, two by A. G. Bailey on New Brunswick in *Canadian Historical Review,* XXI and XXIII (Toronto, 1940 and 1942) give a clearer idea of that Province's behavior than had been available. G. F. G. Stanley's *The Birth of Western Canada* (New York, 1937) is an informed and thoughtful examination of the peculiar problems involved in the creation of the Province of Manitoba. W. S. Wallace, in "The Growth of Canadian National Feeling," *Canadian Historical Review,* I (Toronto, 1920), brings forward the Canada First movement. Edgar McInnis, "Two North American Federations: A comparison," in R. Flenley (ed.), *Essays in Canadian History presented to George Mackinnon Wrong* (Toronto, 1939), agreeably presents the similarities and contrasts of the American and Canadian constitutions in brief compass.

Chapter XI. Cornerstone of Triune Understanding, 1871–1878

Goldwin Smith, *The Treaty of Washington, 1871* (Ithaca, 1941), does not supplant Shippee, *op. cit.*, and Nevins, *op. cit.* Hunter Miller's *San Juan Archipelago: A study of the joint occupation of San Juan Island* has been published separately (Bellows Falls, Vt., 1943) before appearing in his monumental edition of *Treaties and Other International Acts of the United States* (multi-volume, in progress, Washington, since 1931). R. S. Longley, "Peter Mitchell, Guardian of the North Atlantic Fisheries, 1867–1871," *Canadian Historical Review,* XXII (Toronto, 1941).

A thorough critical study of J. H. Rose is greatly needed, for he was deeply involved in the affairs and the interrelations of Canada, the United States, and

Great Britain throughout his active life, and yet histories of the period reveal little more than tantalizing traces. For his relation to early Canadian representation in London see the essay by M. H. Long in *Canadian Historical Review*, XII (Toronto, 1931).

Chapter XII. Westward the Course of Empire, 1850–1900

W. P. Webb's original and influential *The Great Plains* (Boston, 1931) does not extend into Canada, but A. S. Morton's *History of Prairie Settlement* (Toronto, 1938) can be made to serve quite well in illuminating the Canadian similarities and contrasts. A. R. M. Lower's *Settlement and the Forest Frontier* covers Canadian attempts at agricultural settlement near and within the Canadian Shield. S. H. Holbrook's *Iron Brew* (New York, 1939) provides a lively account of the beginnings of the Great Lakes nexus in iron and steel. A. H. Moehlman, "The Red River of the North," and its map of the advancing frontier, *Geographical Review*, XXV (New York, 1935), are especially valuable (the map is reproduced on page 202 of this book).

The best and most specific book on its subject is *The Railway Interrelations of the United States and Canada* (New Haven, 1937) by W. J. Wilgus, an eminent engineer who was active in the construction and operation of some of the network which he describes and maps. J. B. Hedges, *Henry Villard and the Railways of the Northwest* (New Haven, 1930), and G. J. Pyle, *Life of James J. Hill* (2 vols., New York, 1917), find their complement in H. A. Innis, *A History of the Canadian Pacific Railway* (Toronto, 1923), and in the biographical works which it cites. See also G. P. de T. Glazebrook, *op. cit.,* and R. L. Savage, "American Concern over Canadian Railway Competition in the North-West, 1885–1890," in the *Report* of the Canadian Historical Association (Toronto, 1942).

F. G. Roe's article, "The Extermination of the Buffalo in Western Canada," and A. S. Morton's commentary will be found in *Canadian Historical Review*, XV (Toronto, 1934). Frederick Merk (ed.), *Fur Trade and Empire: George Simpson's Journal, 1824–1825* (Cambridge, Mass., 1931). Osgood, *op. cit.,* is partially complemented for Alberta, at least, by C. M. MacInnes, *In the Shadow of the Rockies* (London, 1930), but a good history of Canada's share in the Cattle Kingdom is lacking.

W. P. Morrell, *The Gold Rushes* (New York, 1941), is valuable because its world-wide scope imparts pattern to the North American enterprises. W. J. Trimble, *The Mining Advance into the Inland Empire* (Madison, Wis., 1914), is a valuable pioneer work whose theme is developed for the whole of Canada by H. A. Innis, *Settlement and the Mining Frontier* (Toronto, 1936), and E. S. Moore, *American Influence in Canadian Mining* (Toronto, 1941).

O. E. Rolvaag's half-dozen fictional works, especially *Giants in the Earth* (New York, 1927), portray movingly the trials of plains agriculture. Two remarkable statistical works provide factual foundations for Hansen's *The Mingling of the Canadian and American Peoples*, particularly after 1850.

They are: R. H. Coats and M. C. MacLean, *The American Born in Canada* (Toronto, 1943), and L. E. Truesdell, *The Canadian Born in the United States* (New Haven, 1943). MacLean was also largely responsible for a searching essay on "The Growth of Population in Canada," in *Seventh Census of Canada, 1931,* I (Ottawa, 1936), Part II, Chapter 1.

Chapter XIII. The Materials of a Triangle, 1896–1940

Two books by J. B. Hedges, *The Federal Railway Land Subsidy Policy of Canada* (Cambridge, Mass., 1934) and *Building the Canadian West: The land and colonization policies of the Canadian Pacific Railway* (New York, 1939), together with Chester Martin, *History of "Dominion Lands" Policy* (Toronto, 1938), and J. W. Dafoe, *Clifford Sifton in Relation to His Times* (Toronto, 1931), explain the apparatus of the occupation of the Canadian west.

Wilgus, *op. cit.*, furnishes the picture of railway transportation, but Cuthbertson, *op. cit.*, and Havighurst, *op. cit.*, require reënforcement, *e.g.*, H. H. Hatcher, *The Great Lakes* (New York, 1944). C. W. Wright, *Economic History of the United States* (New York, 1941), is excellent, but the only Canadian parallel, M. Q. Innis, *An Economic History of Canada* (Toronto, 1935), cannot be equivalent because great gaps still exist in the necessary preliminary research, as, for instance, in hydroelectric power and the pulp and paper industry. On mining, E. S. Moore, *op. cit.*, and Innis, *Settlement and the Mining Frontier.* V. R. Kilduff, "Economic Factors in the Development of Canadian-American Trade," *Southern Economic Journal,* VIII (Chapel Hill, 1941), is succinct and illuminating. On investment, Herbert Marshall, F. A. Southard, and K. W. Taylor, *Canadian-American Industry* (New Haven, 1936), and Dominion Bureau of Statistics, *The Canadian Balance of International Payments* (Ottawa, 1939). H. A. Innis, "Canada and the Panama Canal," Appendix V of Innis and A. F. W. Plumptre (eds.), *The Canadian Economy and Its Problems* (Toronto, 1934). Richard Finnie, *Canada Moves North* (Toronto, 1942).

Canada, Great Britain, and the United States each publish annually admirable contemporary and retrospective statistical summaries of national development. This compact technique answers nearly every imaginable question of measurement. The annuals are: *The Canada Year Book* (Ottawa), *Statistical Abstract of the United Kingdom* (London), and *Statistical Abstract of the United States* (Washington).

Chapter XIV. A Triangle Takes Form, 1880–1917

The literature of American foreign relations has become so large that reference must be made to the general diplomatic histories of T. A. Bailey and S. F. Bemis, and to S. F. Bemis and G. G. Griffin, *Guide to the Diplomatic History of the United States, 1775–1921* (Washington, 1935). Among the principal works which bear upon the triangular relations during this period are: M. W. Williams, *Anglo-American Isthmian Diplomacy, 1815–1915* (Washington,

1916); Dexter Perkins, *The Monroe Doctrine, 1826–1867* (Baltimore, 1933), and *The Monroe Doctrine, 1867–1907* (Baltimore, 1937); C. C. Tansill, *The Foreign Policy of Thomas F. Bayard, 1885–1887* (New York, 1940) and *Canadian-American Relations, 1875–1911* (New Haven, 1943), the second of which provides close documentary studies of the fisheries question, the Alaska boundary dispute, the fur-seals disputes, and reciprocity; Allan Nevins, *Grover Cleveland* (New York, 1934); J. W. Pratt, *The Expansionists of 1898* (New York, 1936); J. B. Bishop's "official" *Theodore Roosevelt and His Time* (2 vols., New York, 1920) and H. F. Pringle's disrespectful *Theodore Roosevelt* (New York, 1931); D. C. Miner, *The Fight for the Panama Route* (New York, 1940); R. H. Heindel, *The American Impact on Great Britain, 1898–1914* (Philadelphia, 1940); L. M. Gelber, *The Rise of Anglo-American Friendship, 1898–1906* (London, 1938); P. C. Jessup, *Elihu Root* (2 vols., New York, 1938); and L. E. Ellis, *Reciprocity: 1911* (New Haven, 1939). P. E. Corbett, *op. cit.,* pp. 19–23, contains a terse and detached account of the Alaska Boundary Award. The sayings of Mr. Dooley (Finley Peter Dunne) appeared in a series of volumes from 1898 to 1919.

Works which give special attention to Canada in these affairs are as yet either somewhat tentative or confined to narrow topics. In general, and furnishing guidance to supporting material, MacKay and Rogers, *op. cit.;* G. P. de T. Glazebrook, *Canadian External Relations: to 1914* (Toronto, 1942); J. W. Dafoe, *Canada: an American Nation* (New York, 1935); R. M. Dawson, *The Development of Dominion Status, 1900–1936* (Oxford, 1937); O. D. Skelton, *Life and Letters of Sir Wilfrid Laurier* (2 vols., Toronto, 1921); C. J. Chacko, *The International Joint Commission between the United States of America and the Dominion of Canada* (New York, 1932); and A. G. Dewey, *The Dominions and Diplomacy: The Canadian contribution* (2 vols., London, 1929).

B. H. Brown, *The Tariff Reform Movement in Great Britain, 1881–1895* (New York, 1943), contains interesting accounts of the almost forgotten parts played in this matter by Galt, Tupper, Macdonald, and G. T. Denison, and of the futile Colonial Conference at Ottawa in 1894 which foreshadowed the effective one there in 1932. F. H. Underhill, "Edward Blake, the Liberal Party, and Unrestricted Reciprocity," in the *Report* of the Canadian Historical Association for 1939 (Toronto), is one of a series of studies of Blake preliminary to a biography. See also J. M. V. Foster, "Reciprocity and the Joint High Commission, 1898–1899," in the same *Report,* and J. B. Brebner, "Canada's Choice in Foreign Affairs," *Quarterly Journal of Inter-American Relations,* I (Washington, 1939).

Chapter XV. North American Withdrawal, 1918–1932

W. B. Kerr has listed and criticized the writings on Canada in the War of 1914 in *Canadian Historical Review,* XIV and XV (Toronto, 1933 and 1934). There is as yet no satisfactory general account either of the Canadian or of the American share in the War. David Carnegie, *The History of Munitions Sup-*

ply in Canada, 1914–1919 (London, 1925), reveals one section of Canada's extraordinary expansion of production. See also J. J. Deutsch, "War Finance and the Canadian Economy, 1914–1921," *Canadian Journal of Economics and Political Science*, VI (Toronto, 1940). In addition to the works on Canadian status previously cited, see G. P. de T. Glazebrook, *Canada at the Paris Peace Conference* (Toronto, 1942), which contains the Paris memorandum on Article X of the League Covenant by C. J. Dougherty; and R. L. Borden, *Canadian Constitutional Studies* (Toronto, 1922).

Paul Birdsall, *Versailles Twenty Years After* (New York, 1941), presents new materials, but is chiefly valuable for its critical examination of the published accounts of the Peace Conference. D. F. Fleming, *The United States and the League of Nations, 1918–1920* (New York, 1932), is scholarly and favorable to Wilson; H. C. Lodge, *The Senate and the League of Nations* (New York, 1925), is neither.

E. H. Armstrong, *The Crisis of Quebec, 1914–1918* (New York, 1937), is a dispassionate, scholarly account, as is G. M. Weir, *The Separate School Question in Canada* (Toronto, 1934).

W. E. Armstrong, *Canada and the League of Nations* (Geneva, 1930), is specific; C. A. W. Manning, *The Policies of the British Dominions in the League of Nations* (London, 1932), is critical; and G. M. Carter, "Some Aspects of Canadian Foreign Policy after Versailles," *Report* of the Canadian Historical Association for 1943 (Toronto), is a retrospective view of the three principal topics with which Canadians were particularly concerned: the relation of the Assembly to the Council; international regulation of raw materials; and Article X.

J. B. Brebner, "Canada, the Anglo-Japanese Alliance, and the Washington Conference," *Political Science Quarterly*, L (New York, 1935), is the accepted account of the Canadian share in negotiations which are admirably handled on the much broader American side in A. W. Griswold, *The Far Eastern Policy of the United States* (New York, 1938). See also A. R. M. Lower, *Canada and the Far East* (New York, 1940).

The following books cover, or provide guidance to, Canadian foreign policy between 1918 and 1939: MacKay and Rogers, *op. cit.;* C. Martin (ed.), *Canada in Peace and War* (Toronto, 1941); F. H. Soward *et al., Canada in World Affairs: The pre-war years* (Toronto, 1941); C. P. Stacey, *The Military Problems of Canada* (Toronto, 1940); and J. P. Humphrey, *The Inter-American System: A Canadian view* (Toronto, 1942). Meighen's Hamilton speech of November 16, 1925, may be found in the Canadian press or, in part, in *The Canadian Annual Review, 1925* (Toronto, 1926).

J. M. Jones, *Tariff Retaliation: Repercussions of the Hawley-Smoot Tariff* (Philadelphia, 1934), necessarily gives great attention to Canada. Probably the most satisfactory account of the Ottawa Conference and subsequent policies is in W. K. Hancock, *Survey of British Commonwealth Affairs*, II, *Problems of Economic Policy, 1918–1939* (London, 1940). C. W. Wright's *Economic History of the United States* is the best thing of its kind, a scholarly revival of political economy. E. C. Hughes, *French Canada in Transition* (Chicago, 1943), is the best study of the effects of industrialization.

In addition to Corbett, *op. cit.*, those interested in the application of international law to Canadian-American relations should consult N. A. M. MacKenzie and L. H. Laing, *Canada and the Law of Nations* (Toronto, 1938), which follows the case-book method.

Statistical underpinning for Hansen's *Mingling of the Canadian and American Peoples* is provided by R. H. Coats and M. C. MacLean, *The American Born in Canada,* and L. E. Truesdell, *The Canadian Born in the United States.*

Chapter XVI. Maelstrom, 1932–1942

In addition to the treatments of recent times which have already been cited (particularly McInnis, *The Unguarded Frontier*), H. F. Angus (ed.), *Canada and Her Great Neighbor* (Toronto, 1938), is a remarkable collection of Canadian opinion, to which it is advisable to apply at least some historical interpretation; J. B. Brebner, "Canadianism," *Report* of the Canadian Historical Association for 1940 (Toronto), is an attempted historical analysis; N. J. Ware and H. A. Logan, *Labor in Canadian-American Relations* (Toronto, 1937), contains the only published attempt to deal with the implications of comparative standards of living; and F. R. Scott's pamphlet, *Canada and the United States* (Boston, 1941), is an effective supplement to his *Canada Today* (2d revised edition, Toronto, 1939).

Since much of the literature concerning recent events is clearly subject to extensive revision, mention need only be made of R. M. Dawson (ed.), *Canada in World Affairs: Two years of war, 1939–1941* (Toronto, 1943), which carries events almost up to the entry of the United States; and E. R. Stettinius, Jr., *Lend Lease: Weapon for Victory* (New York, 1944), which is valuable for its revelation of the aid extended before the United States formally entered the War.

INDEX

225, 238; price rise *1896–1914,* 225, 226, 238; recovery of *1878,* 229; production *1922–1929,* 238, 242, 298; Pacific Coast boom following opening of the Panama Canal *1914,* 241; Canadian gold-mining, following the devaluation of the American dollar, 307; *see also* Depressions

Borah, William E., 276

Borden, Sir Robert L.: fight for complete Canadian autonomy, 245; naval defense, 265; commercial reciprocity, 268; Canadian participation in policy making, 269, 270; offer of help to Great Britain at outbreak of war *1914,* 271; ratification of treaties, 274; a coalition government, and conscription, 278; memorandum on *Article X* of the Covenant, 279; Anglo-American coöperation versus European alliances, 281; Canadian National Railways, 287

Border raids *1837–1842,* 143–144; *see also* Fenian raids; Confederacy

Boston, 5, 111; West Indian trade, 26, 42; tyranny of "bills on London," 43; risks in French-Canadian trade, 44; Montreal traders, 49; fur trade, 95; clipper runs to Liverpool, 112; shipbuilding, 112, 113; wooden buildings, 117; railroads, 123, 205; first train to Montreal *1851,* map, *op.* 174; Canadian-born population, 228, 302

Boston & Lowell R.R., granite rails, 122

Boundary, Canadian-American, 224; climate, 3; forty-ninth parallel, 5, 95, 132, 166; forty-second parallel, 5, 90, 95; local influences on population, 7; British Columbia and Washington, 7; Atlantic end, map, 58; forty-fifth parallel, 57, 59, 144, 146, maps, 58, 147; St. Croix valley, 80, 115; Northwest, map, 91; Pacific area, 95; Aroostook "War" *1839,* 114–115; Isle Royal to the Lake of the Woods, map, 146; frontier guards during Fenian raids, 169; Haro Archipelago, Vancouver Island, San Juan, 183; railroads, 205, 206, 229; customs and border officials, 229; Alaska and British Columbia, 257, map, 258, 259, 261, 262, 272; commission for the adjustment of boundary difficulties, 267; Boundary Waters Treaty, 267; interrelated interests in border areas, 293; "border commuters," 293, 298; border crossings, 295, 301; illegal entry, 298, 301

Bourassa, Henri, isolationist nationalism, Quebec, 265, 269, 278

Brazil: cotton and sugar, 111; reciprocal trade, 180

Brega, G. W., 187

Briand, Aristide, proposal for the outlawry of war, 282

Bright, John, 161, 172, 182; Anglo-American crisis *1861,* 161; "Little Englander," 172, 182

Bristol, England, 16, 240

Britain, Battle of, 324

British Columbia: wheat, 6; Washington boundary, 7; mining, 11, 176, 219, 221, 234; agriculture, 12; from Hudson's Bay Company rule to British colonial government, 166; union with Vancouver Island, 167; opinions on annexation, 168, 178, 182; federation member *1871,* 178, 182; pro-Americanism, 178; railways, 193, 207, map, 218, 219; mountains, 201; railroads in the south and adjacent American territory, map, 218; forests, 220; effect of tariff protection, 221; oil, 233; coal and power, 234; Alaska boundary, 257, map, 258, 259, 272; gold, 259; Alaska highway, 324

British Commonwealth of Nations: Balfour Declaration *1926,* 263, 285; Imperial Conference *1926,* 285; Statute of Westminster, 285; preferential tariff rates, 290; Canadian participation, 314, 317, 327; Alliance with the United States, World War II, 325

British Guiana: Venezuelan affair *1895,* 249–251; lease to United States of air and naval bases, 324

British North America Act *1867,* 173, 174

British Trade Acts (Statutes *1822*), 93

Brock, Sir Isaac, attack on Detroit *1812,* 84, 85

Brown, George, Editor, Toronto *Globe:* Canadian anxieties *1865,* 169; federation, 171, 179; Treaty of Washington, 194, 195

Brown, General Jacob, Niagara *1812,* 84, 86

Brown, John, Abolitionist, 160

Brulé, Étienne, exploration of the Susquehanna, 19

Brussels International Conference, aim to vitalize the Nine Power Pact, 320

Bryan, William Jennings, 220

Bryce, Viscount James: *The American Commonwealth,* American frontier, 133;

29, 35, 37, 38, 59, 60, 97; Royal Proclamation *1763* reserving trans-Appalachian lands to the Indians, 37, 59

Pope, William Henry, 171

Population: proportion of Americans to Canadians, 1, 231, 286; British North America and the United States *1846–1890,* map, *follows* 181; comparative chart, Canada and the United States *1850–1930,* 296; ban on interchange of population *1930,* 302

Canada: American-born in southern Ontario *1783–1850,* 9; Canadian plains *1895,* 9; Canadian population drawn off by expanding American economy, 151, 224, 298, 302; negroes *1871, 1931,* 160; slow down, 224; American-born in Prairie Provinces *1911,* map, 226; gain *1901–1913,* 226; disproportion between population and consumption, 290; loss to the United States *1921–1930,* 296, 298; American-born, *1925–1930,* 298; parentage of American-born, chart, *op.* 298; American-born by countries or census distribution, map, *op.* 298; Americanborn by provinces *1931,* chart, 300; loss to Great Britain, 301; American-born, largest single non-British immigrant group, 302

United States: Canadian-born, middle west *1840–1900,* 9; Canadian-born *1860,* 162; French Canadians in New York and New England, map, 222; Canadians in industrial northeast, 226; Canadian-born, north central states *1890,* 223; Census Bureau study of Canadian-born, *1910,* 228; Canadian-born, distribution *1930,* map, 297; Canadian-born, percentage by States *1930,* chart, 299; French-and English-Canadian-born by selected states *1930,* 299; Canadian-born *1850–1930,* chart, 300; *1930,* percentage of Canadian-born to Canadian population, 301

Porcupine River, 193

Porter, Commissioner, *1826,* 146

Portland, Maine, Canadian railway link, 153, 175, 229

Portland Channel, Alaska boundary dispute, 259, 261

Port Royal, New England warehouses, 26

Portuguese: navigation, 15; Anglo-Portuguese dealings, 16; Northwest Passage, 16; Newfoundland fisheries, 17, 112

Postlethwayt, Malachy, 93

Potash, the pioneer's first cash crop, 36, 126, 127

Power production, 232; *hydroelectric,* 309; Canadian Shield, 2, 233; Central Region, 9; British Columbia, 234; chemicals and fertilizers, 242; treaty for equitable use, 267; border regions, 293; *water and steam,* 65, 217, 233, 235; invention of the turbine and dynamo, 233; electric motor, 235

Power, C. G., Canadian policy with regard to *Article X,* 280

Pownal, Governor Thomas, rights and privileges of colonists as Englishmen, 44

Prague, Hitler's entry, 316

Prairie du Chien, fur trade, 39, 85, 95

Prairie Provinces, 301; American-born population, chart, 226; *see also* Manitoba; Saskatchewan; Alberta

Prairies, Canadian, *see* Plains

Pratt, J. W., 83

Presbyterian Church: Indian missions, 132; religious and educational monopoly, 140

Press gangs, *see* Impressment

Prevost, Commissioner J. C., San Juan boundary, 184

Prévost, Sir George, 85, 86

Pribilof Islands seal herd, 247

Prince Edward Island: Maritime Province, 65; foodstuffs, 70; lumbering, 115; agriculture, smuggling and American trade, 156, 186; attitude toward federation, 171, 172, 177, 186; joins federation *1873,* 178; fisheries difficulties, 186, 194; incident of the potatoes and the American seamen, 248

Proclamation, Queen's, *May 13, 1861,* British neutrality in the American Civil War, 161

Proclamation, Royal, *October 7, 1763,* forbidding colonization west of the Appalachian water shed: licensed traders allowed west, 29, 43; trans-Appalachian lands reserved as Indian hunting ground, 37, 43; hope for a diversion of migration to Quebec, 48; establishes English Province of Quebec, 49, 59; southern boundary of old Province of Quebec, map, 58

Prohibition: United States, 293; "border commuters" to Canada, 293; Canada, 293–294; American bootlegging, and rumrunning, 294

Ulster immigrants in Pennsylvania, 37; in Canada, 245

Uncle Tom's Cabin, 160

Underground Railway for fugitive slaves, 140

Unemployment: Europe, 18; Canada, 290; United States, 300

Union Pacific–Central Pacific, 201, 205, 208; chartered during the Civil War, 168; map, 200

United States: authority of the states, 61, 63; Constitution of *1787,* 63, 64, 68, 75; Bill of Rights, 63; expanding mercantilism and contest with Great Britain, 70, 73, 93, 104, 106, 148; threat of war with France *1798,* 72; regulation of western territorial settlement, 74, 76; new states beyond the Appalachians, 75, 76; early threat of secession and civil war from *1812,* 78, 84, 87, 88, 106; opening up of the West, 78, 133; North and South bargain as to slavery, 78; Manifest Destiny, 83, 88, 131, 133, 144, 182, 196, 246; reentry into British mercantile empire, 93, 106; interests distinct from those of Europe, 108; repudiation of debts, 110, 144; origin and background of American democracy, 135; friendship of Russia, 156; a world power, after the Civil War, 165, 196, 244, 253; fear of the United States, the cause of Canadian federation, 169, 178; New Imperialism, 245, 246, 254, 259; elevation of the citizen above the state, 251; irresistible compulsion to war *1917,* 271; by *1922* a creditor nation, 275; American investment in Latin America, 284; Hemisphere Policy, 284, 311, 313, 314; devaluation of the dollar, 307; inter-American multilateral negotiations, 313; attempt at a popular referendum for a declaration of war, 320; "arsenal of democracy," 325; world responsibility, 327

United States v. *Karnuth,* 298

United States Steel Export Company, 322

Utopian communities, 137, 140

Van Buren, President Martin, 144

Vancouver, George: Anglo-Spanish conference on west coast boundary, 96; explorations and maps, 97

Vancouver, British Columbia, 220; railroads, 207

Vancouver Island: fur trade, 96; Indian massacre, 100; Oregon boundary, 132, 183; gold strike, 166

Van Horne, Sir William: builder of the Canadian Pacific, 206; conquest of the Canadian Shield and the Canadian Rockies, 207; annexation, 268

Venezuelan affair *1895:* Olney amplification of the Monroe Doctrine, 247, 250; Cleveland's suggestion of a boundary Commission, 250; survival of Anglo-American understanding, 252; Anglo-German blockade, 257

Vergennes, Count de, 57

Vermont: Continental Congress, 48; attitude toward the Revolution, 52; Green Mountain Boys, 38, 55, 62; equivocal behavior, 62; relinquishment of claims by New York State, 63; enters Union, 63, 75; Richelieu River outlet, 79; principle of good neighborhood, 80; Canadian trade, 81; canals, 121; popular vote, 135; Confederate border raids, 169

Vetch, Samuel, plan to reach Acadia and New France by sea, 26, 35

Victoria, Queen: neutrality Proclamation, American Civil War, 161; Jubilee, 264

Victoria, British Columbia, 5

Virginia, 18, 21, 35, 37, 40, 43; Indian traders, 24; exploration, 24; slavery, 36; migration, 38; land grants, 43; severe British colonial policy, 48; threat of secession *1798,* 78; British attempt to cut Virginia off from New England in the Revolution, 55; universities, 137

Voltaire, his opinion of French Canada, 33

Voyageurs, 38; fur trade, 98, 100; aids to exploration, 99

Wabash Railway, 229

Wabash River and Valley: Western Post on the route to the Wabash, 76; Tecumseh's headquarters, 83; settlement, 128

Wagner-Connery Act *1935,* 307

Wake Island, United States acquisition of, 253

Walker, Robert J., 170

Walpole, Sir Robert, management of a corrupt Parliament, 40, 45, 50, 67

War of *1812,* 80, 105, 106, 142, 162, 257; mission to England *1794* to clear up threatening conflicts, 71, 72; sensitive area of naval power and national prestige, 73; no deterrent to smuggling, 82; British arrogance to American rights of life and property, from *1807,* 82; Ameri-

THE RELATIONS OF
CANADA AND THE UNITED STATES

A series of studies prepared under the direction of the Carnegie Endowment for International Peace, Division of Economics and History. James T. Shotwell, Director.

ANGUS, H. F. (Editor), Canada and Her Great Neighbor: Sociological Surveys of Opinions and Attitudes in Canada Concerning the United States.

BREBNER, J. B., North Atlantic Triangle: The Interplay of Canada, the United States, and Great Britain.

BURT, A. L., The United States, Great Britain, and British North America: From the Revolution to the Establishment of Peace after the War of 1812.

COATS, R. H., and MACLEAN, M. C., The American Born in Canada: A Statistical Interpretation.

CORBETT, P. E., The Settlement of Canadian–American Disputes: A Critical Study of Methods and Results.

COREY, A. B., The Crisis of 1830–1842 in Canadian–American Relations.

CREIGHTON, D. G., The Commercial Empire of the St. Lawrence, 1760–1850.

ELLIS, L. E., Reciprocity, 1911: A Study in Canadian–American Relations.

GLAZEBROOK, G. P. DET., A History of Transportation in Canada.

HANSEN, M. L., and BREBNER, J. B., The Mingling of the Canadian and American Peoples: Historical.

HOWAY, F. W., ANGUS, H. F., and SAGE, W. N., British Columbia and the United States: The North Pacific Slope from Fur Trade to Aviation.

INNIS, H. A., The Cod Fisheries: The History of an International Economy.

LANCTOT, G., and others, Les Canadiens Français et leurs Voisins du Sud.

LANDON, F., Western Ontario and the American Frontier.

LOWER, A. R. M., and others, The North American Assault on the Canadian Forest: A History of the Lumber Trade between Canada and the United States.

MACKENZIE, N., and LAING, L. H., Canada and the Law of Nations: A Selection of Cases in International Law, affecting Canada or Canadians, decided by Canadian Courts, by certain of the Higher Courts in the United States and Great Britain and by International Tribunals.

MARSHALL, H., SOUTHARD, F. A., and TAYLOR, K. W., Canadian–American Industry: A Study in International Investment.

PRITCHETT, J. P., The Red River Valley, 1811–1849: A Regional Study.

RUDDICK, J. A., and others, The Dairy Industry in Canada. Edited by H. A. INNIS.

SAVELLE, M., The Diplomatic History of the Canadian Boundary, 1749–1763.

SHIPPEE, L. B., Canadian–American Relations, 1849–1874.

TANSILL, C. C., Canadian–American Relations, 1875–1911.

TRUESDELL, L. E., The Canadian Born in the United States: An Analysis of the Statistics of the Canadian Element in the Population of the United States, 1850–1930.

WARE, N. J., and LOGAN, H. A., Labor in Canadian–American Relations: A History of Labor Interaction, and Labor Costs and Labor Standards.

WILGUS, W. J., The Railway Interrelations of the United States and Canada.